# Feature Papers in Computational Chemistry

# Feature Papers in Computational Chemistry

Guest Editors

**Alexander S. Novikov**
**Felipe Fantuzzi**

MDPI

Basel • Beijing • Wuhan • Barcelona • Belgrade • Novi Sad • Cluj • Manchester

*Guest Editors*
Alexander S. Novikov
Institute of Chemistry
Saint Petersburg State
University
St. Petersburg
Russia

Felipe Fantuzzi
School of Natural Sciences
University of Kent
Canterbury
UK

*Editorial Office*
MDPI AG
Grosspeteranlage 5
4052 Basel, Switzerland

This is a reprint of the Special Issue, published open access by the journal *Computation* (ISSN 2079-3197), freely accessible at: https://www.mdpi.com/journal/computation/special_issues/641000370Z.

For citation purposes, cite each article independently as indicated on the article page online and as indicated below:

| Lastname, A.A.; Lastname, B.B. Article Title. *Journal Name* **Year**, *Volume Number*, Page Range. |
|---|

**ISBN 978-3-7258-7905-2 (Hbk)**
**ISBN 978-3-7258-7906-9 (PDF)**
**https://doi.org/10.3390/books978-3-7258-7906-9**

# Contents

# About the Editors

**Alexander S. Novikov**

Alexander S. Novikov is a computational and quantum chemist based at Saint Petersburg State University, Russia. His main research interests include quantum and computational chemistry, supramolecular chemistry, inorganic and coordination chemistry, organometallic chemistry, catalysis, non-covalent interactions, big data in chemistry, and machine learning. His work focuses on theoretical studies of catalytic reactions and organic transformations assisted by metal complexes, including hydrocarbon oxidation, nucleophilic addition, and cycloaddition processes, with emphasis on reaction mechanisms, driving forces, kinetics, and thermodynamics. He also investigates the properties of coordination and organometallic compounds, including conformational isomerism, rotational barriers, chemical bonding, orbital effects, and charge factors. His current research is particularly focused on unusual non-covalent interactions, including hydrogen, halogen and chalcogen bonding, stacking, anagostic and metallophilic interactions. His studies are interdisciplinary, connecting computational modelling with chemistry, physics, crystallography, biology, medicine, materials science, and nanotechnology. He serves as an Editorial Board member of the Computational Chemistry Section of *Computation* and has acted as Guest Editor for Special Issues in *Computation, Crystals,* and *Symmetry.*

**Felipe Fantuzzi**

Felipe Fantuzzi is a Lecturer in Chemistry at the School of Natural Sciences, University of Kent, Canterbury, United Kingdom, where he serves as Director of the Supramolecular, Interfacial and Synthetic Chemistry (SISC) group and Co-Director of the Kent Astrochemistry, Irradiation, Origins and Space (KAIROS) initiative. His main research interests include computational and theoretical chemistry, electronic structure, density functional theory, chemical bond theory, molecular reactivity, main-group and organometallic chemistry, and astrochemistry. His work focuses on the development and application of quantum chemical methods to understand unusual bonding patterns, reactive molecular systems, irradiation-driven processes, and molecules and ices relevant to interstellar, circumstellar, and planetary environments. He is also involved in the computational design and characterisation of functional molecules and materials, with applications in energy, sensing, forensic chemistry, and health-related molecular systems. He leads and contributes to international collaborations across Europe, Latin America, Africa, and India. He has published over 140 scientific articles, and his work has been featured in outlets such as Chemistry World, ChemistryViews, and Scilight.

# Preface

This Reprint brings together contributions published in the Special Issue Feature Papers in Computational Chemistry. The collection reflects the breadth of current computational chemistry, ranging from quantum chemical and density functional theory studies to molecular modelling, machine learning, data analysis, and computational tools for chemical research.

The articles included in this Reprint address a diverse set of chemical problems, including ionic liquid property prediction, molecular docking and covalent binding, quantitative structure-activity relationships, catalytic copolymerisation, battery-related nanostructures, doped oxide materials, crystallographic data preparation for solid-state calculations, and mathematical optimisation in machine learning. These contributions illustrate how computational methods can clarify mechanistic features, support the interpretation of experimental observations, guide molecular and materials design, and accelerate the exploration of complex chemical systems.

This Reprint is intended for researchers, students, and practitioners interested in the development and application of computational methods across chemistry, materials science, molecular modelling, and related disciplines. We hope that this collection will serve as a useful reference and stimulate further work at the interface between theoretical concepts, computational methodology, and practical chemical applications.

**Alexander S. Novikov and Felipe Fantuzzi**
*Guest Editors*

computation

MDPI

Article

# Sequential $H_2$ Adsorption on the Aromatic $Li_6$ Superatom: Field-Activated Physisorption and Thermodynamic Limits

Karen Ochoa Lara [1], Jancarlo Gomez-Vega [2], Rafael Pacheco-Contreras [3] and Octavio Juárez-Sánchez [4,*]

1 Departamento de Investigación en Polímeros y Materiales, Universidad de Sonora, Rosales y Encinas s/n, Col. Centro, Hermosillo CP 83000, Sonora, Mexico; karen.ochoa@unison.mx
2 Departamento de Ciencias Químico-Biológicas, Universidad de Sonora, Rosales y Encinas s/n, Col. Centro, Hermosillo CP 83000, Sonora, Mexico; pedro.gomez@unison.mx
3 Departamento de Física, Matemáticas e Ingeniería, Universidad de Sonora, Campus Navojoa, Lázaro Cárdenas del Río No. 100, Navojoa CP 85880, Sonora, Mexico; rafael.pachecocontreras@unison.mx
4 Departamento de Investigación en Física, Universidad de Sonora, Blvd. Luis Encinas y Rosales, Col. Centro, Hermosillo CP 83000, Sonora, Mexico
* Correspondence: octavio.juarez@unison.com

**Abstract**

Understanding the intrinsic Li–$H_2$ interaction, decoupled from substrate effects, is essential to rationalize the performance of lithium-decorated hydrogen storage materials. To address the current lack of a clean theoretical baseline, we characterized the sequential $H_2$ adsorption on the gas-phase $Li_6$ superatomic cluster using high-level density functional theory (DFT), complemented by Energy Decomposition Analysis (EDA), QTAIM, and NICS(0) calculations. $Li_6$ acts as a structurally rigid platform (RMSD < 0.032 Å) where ligand-induced polarization progressively strengthens its σ-aromaticity (NICS(0) from −2.917 to −13.98 ppm) and increases the HOMO–LUMO gap up to 5.05 eV. EDA identifies the binding as field-activated physisorption, electrostatically dominated (65–67%) and mechanistically distinct from Kubas coordination, as confirmed by QTAIM closed-shell interaction parameters. Negative cooperativity governs an effective loading capacity of $n = 2$ molecules under cryogenic conditions ($T_{eq}$ = 143.76 and 114.64 K), while an entropic bottleneck renders higher loading non-spontaneous at all temperatures. These results establish $Li_6(H_2)_n$ as a foundational gas-phase reference, providing a systematic, contamination-free descriptor set for the intrinsic Li–$H_2$ interaction. This framework is essential for isolating the electronic role of the lithium superatom and unambiguously identifying substrate-induced modulations in supported hydrogen storage materials.

**Keywords:** lithium clusters; superatoms; hydrogen storage; density functional theory; σ-aromaticity; QTAIM; Energy Decomposition Analysis; Non-nuclear attractors; entropic bottleneck; field-activated physisorption

## 1. Introduction

Hydrogen storage in lithium-decorated nanostructured materials is a promising strategy for the sustainable energy economy [1–3]. The Li–$H_2$ interaction governs the thermodynamic performance of these systems. Lithium has been widely used as a dopant in substrates such as graphene, borophene, $B_2S$ monolayers, and corannulene [4–7]. However, existing computational studies analyze lithium clusters on complex surfaces or decorated molecular frameworks [8–10], which introduce substrate effects (electronic charge transfer to/from the support), morphological changes (symmetry breaking and coordination geometry changes), and confinement-related effects that prevent unambiguous attribution of the

Li–$H_2$ interaction descriptors to the cluster itself. In supported systems, it is impossible to determine a priori whether the adsorption enthalpy or the charge distribution reflects intrinsic Li–$H_2$ chemistry or artifacts of the substrate environment. A clean gas-phase theoretical reference on an isolated, electronically well-characterized cluster is therefore not merely convenient, but methodologically necessary [4,5,11], to decouple these contributions and establish transferable descriptors. Any deviation observed in supported systems can then be unambiguously attributed to substrate-specific modulation rather than to the intrinsic superatom chemistry. The $Li_6$ cluster is the ideal candidate for this purpose. It possesses a closed electronic shell, octahedral symmetry, and aromatic superatom character. Furthermore, $Li_6$ units have been shown to retain stabilizing aromatic motifs in assembled hydrogen storage materials [9,11–15].

While hydrogen adsorption on alkali-decorated systems has been extensively reported, existing studies often conflate the intrinsic chemistry of the lithium cluster with artifacts arising from the support, such as substrate-to-cluster charge transfer or confinement-induced distortions [16]. A systematic, gas-phase study at a high level of theory is therefore a methodological necessity to establish the clean limits of Li–$H_2$ coordination. By decoupling these effects, this work provides the intrinsic descriptors required to rationalize the performance of complex decorated materials. This work addresses that gap using density functional theory (DFT) at the ωB97X-D4rev/def2-TZVPPD level with ωB97X-2 single-point refinement. We evaluated sequential adsorption in the gas-phase $Li_6(H_2)_n$ system ($n$ = 1–4) through a multivariate characterization aimed at answering four fundamental questions: structural stability, electronic identity, interaction mechanism, and thermodynamic limits. This approach separates intrinsic electronic effects from thermodynamic constraints and establishes a clean theoretical reference for isolating Li–$H_2$ chemistry from substrate effects in the design of lithium-decorated hydrogen storage materials.

## 2. Materials and Methods

### 2.1. Software

We performed all electronic structure calculations using the ORCA 6.1 package (Max Planck Institute for Chemical Energy Conversion, Mülheim an der Ruhr, Germany) [17–21] with tight convergence criteria (TightOpt and TightSCF) and a high-density integration grid (DefGrid3), including the NICS(0) indices and the Energy Decomposition Analysis (EDA) within the Ziegler–Rauk scheme. We carried out all wavefunction analyses with Multiwfn 3.8 (Beijing Tamaoqian Technology Co., Ltd., Beijing, China) [22], including the Molecular Electrostatic Potential (MESP) and the Quantum Theory of Atoms in Molecules (QTAIM) topological analysis with bond critical point (BCP) parameters. We developed in-house Python 3.12 (Python Software Foundation, Wilmington, DE, USA) [23] scripts for the systematic placement of $H_2$ molecules on the $Li_6$ cluster and for RMSD calculation using the Kabsch algorithm with atomic permutation [24]. We visualized molecular structures, isomers, MESP maps, and molecular orbitals with Jmol 14.32.83 (Jmol Development Team, Northfield, MN, USA) [25], and generated thermodynamic plots with Gnuplot 6.0 (Gnuplot Development Team, online resource) [26].

### 2.2. Level of Theory

We performed geometry optimizations and vibrational frequency analyses using the range-separated hybrid functional ωB97X-D4rev [27,28]. This functional belongs to the fourth rung of Jacob's Ladder and incorporates long-range corrections and fourth-generation dispersion (D4), both critical for describing physisorption in lithium clusters. We combined it with the triple-zeta basis set def2-TZVPPD [29,30], whose diffuse functions (PD suffix) are required to capture the polarizability of $H_2$ molecules under the superatom

 https://doi.org/10.3390/computation14040094

electric field and to describe the interstitial electron density at Non-Nuclear Attractors (NNAs). This level of theory overcomes the known limitations of pure GGA functionals such as PBE, which inadequately describe van der Waals forces and suffer from self-interaction errors. The single-reference character of the systems was verified via CCSD(T) calculations, yielding $T_1$ diagnostic values below 0.011 for both the bare cluster and the representative $Li_6(H_2)_1$ complex.

To achieve chemical accuracy, we refined electronic energies via single-point calculations using the double-hybrid functional ωB97X-2-D3BJ [31–33], which belongs to the fifth rung of Jacob's Ladder and incorporates an MP2 correlation contribution. Its performance on the GMTKN55 benchmark database [34] yields a mean absolute error of ~0.5 kcal/mol for non-covalent interactions, surpassing canonical MP2 and approaching CCSD(T) quality at a fraction of the computational cost. This level of theory has been specifically validated for weakly bound complexes involving light metals and $H_2$, where double-hybrid functionals with dispersion corrections consistently reproduce CCSD(T) interaction energies within ~0.3 kcal/mol [31,34]. This combination is therefore appropriate for the sequential adsorption energies in the −2 kcal/mol regime studied here, where basis set truncation errors are further controlled by the Counterpoise correction. We note that all reported vibrational frequencies are harmonic; the known overestimation of H–H stretching frequencies at this level (~6–7% relative to the experimental fundamental of 4161 $cm^{-1}$) does not affect the relative trends in redshift across the series, which constitute the physically relevant quantity for mechanistic assignment. Raw energies and correction components are provided in Tables S3–S5.

### 2.3. Potential Energy Surface (PES) Sampling

We based the initial geometry of the $Li_6$ cluster (neutral, singlet state) on literature-reported parameters [35]: $D_4h$ symmetry (compressed octahedral geometry, with four equatorial and two axial lithium atoms), with interatomic distances r(Li–Li)eq ≈ 2.98 Å and r(Li–Li)ax–eq ≈ 3.04 Å. To locate the low-lying isomers of the $Li_6(H_2)_n$ complexes (n = 1–4), we implemented an exhaustive search protocol using in-house Python scripts, generating over 200 initial structures through three complementary strategies: symmetry-adapted combinatorial sampling, stochastic sampling, and redundancy filtering.

Symmetry-adapted combinatorial sampling: We systematically placed $H_2$ molecules at high-symmetry sites of the compressed octahedral ($D_4h$) core: vertex (atop), edge-center (bridge), and face-center (hollow) positions. We generated all possible occupancy combinations for each coverage n.

Stochastic sampling: We randomly distributed $H_2$ molecules at varying orientations and distances (2.0 to 5.0 Å) around the cluster to locate non-intuitive local minima.

Redundancy filtering: We screened all optimized structures through an RMSD analysis based on the Kabsch algorithm to discard redundant isomers.

We performed vibrational frequency calculations within the harmonic approximation to confirm the nature of the local minima and to derive thermodynamic corrections. Although we acknowledge that the harmonic approximation systematically overestimates H–H stretching frequencies by approximately 6–7% relative to experimental values, we found that the resulting redshifts (Δν) are consistent across the series and serve as a reliable descriptor for assigning the physisorption mechanism.

### 2.4. Energy Analysis

We construct the total adsorption energy ($\Delta E_{ads,Total}$) additively from four contributions, each designed to isolate a distinct physical phenomenon. First, we obtain the

 https://doi.org/10.3390/computation14040094

zero-point energy correction as the difference between the ZPE of the complex and those of the isolated fragments:

$$\Delta ZPE = ZPE_{complex} - \sum ZPE_{isolated}, \tag{1}$$

while we correct the basis set superposition error (BSSE) using the Counterpoise method:

$$\delta_{CP} = \sum (E_{frag,dist} - E_{frag,ghost}). \tag{2}$$

The interaction energy ($E_{int}$) quantifies the pure electronic attraction between fragments at the distorted geometry they adopt within the complex, excluding the cost of such distortion:

$$E_{int} = E_{complex} - (E_{Li6,dist} + E_{nH2,dist}). \tag{3}$$

We capture this geometric cost through the deformation energy ($E_{def}$), which represents the energetic penalty required to bring each fragment from its isolated equilibrium geometry to the geometry it adopts in the complex:

$$E_{def} = (E_{Li6,dist} - E_{Li6,isolated}) + (E_{nH2,dist} - E_{nH2,isolated}). \tag{4}$$

Finally, we integrate all four contributions into the total adsorption energy:

$$\Delta E_{ads,Total} = E_{int} + E_{def} + \delta_{CP} + \Delta ZPE. \tag{5}$$

### 2.5. Thermodynamic Analysis

We computed standard thermochemical properties within the Rigid Rotor-Harmonic Oscillator (RRHO) approximation at 298.15 K and 1 atm. We construct the internal energy of adsorption (ΔU) from four contributions:

$$\Delta U = E_{int} + E_{def} + \delta_{CP} + \Delta ZPE, \tag{6}$$

where $E_{int}$ is the interaction energy between the cluster and the ligands, $E_{def}$ is the geometric deformation energy of the fragments upon complexation, $\delta_{CP}$ is the Counterpoise BSSE correction, and ΔZPE is the zero-point energy difference. The internal energy of adsorption (ΔU) is numerically equivalent to $\Delta_{Eads,Total}$ defined in Equation (5), but is recast here within the thermodynamic state function formalism as the foundation for deriving ΔH, TΔS, and ΔG:

$$\Delta H = \Delta U + \Delta nRT, \tag{7}$$

$$T\Delta S = T(Scomplex - \sum SisolatedFragments), \tag{8}$$

$$\Delta G = \Delta H - T\Delta S, \tag{9}$$

where Δn is the change in the number of gas-phase molecules (negative for adsorption), R is the universal gas constant, and T = 298.15 K. The TΔS term quantifies the loss of translational and rotational degrees of freedom of the $H_2$ molecules upon binding, and ΔG determines the spontaneity of the process: positive values indicate non-spontaneous adsorption under the reference conditions.

To compare isomers and identify the global minimum (GM), we calculated the relative free energy and the corresponding Boltzmann population:

$$\Delta\Delta G = \Delta G_{isomer} - \Delta G_{GM}, \tag{10}$$

$$P_i = (\exp(-\Delta G_i/(RT))/\sum_j \exp(-\Delta G_j/(RT)))100. \tag{11}$$

To decouple the contribution of each individual ligand and determine the saturation limits, we extended the analysis to sequential thermodynamic parameters ($\Delta X_{seq}$), where X represents any thermodynamic property. We calculated the sequential change upon adsorption of the n-th molecule as

$$\Delta X_{seq}(n) = \Delta X_{cum}(n) - \Delta X_{cum}(n-1), \tag{12}$$

where $\Delta X_{cum}$ denotes the cumulative value for the complex with n ligands. We modeled the temperature dependence of spontaneity using the Gibbs–Helmholtz equation, assuming $\Delta H$ and $\Delta S$ remain constant over the temperature range studied:

$$\Delta G(T) = \Delta H_{seq} - T\Delta S_{seq}. \tag{13}$$

From this relation, we defined the equilibrium (crossover) temperature $T_{eq}$ as the threshold at which the process transitions from endergonic to exergonic ($\Delta G = 0$):

$$T_{eq} = \Delta H_{seq}/\Delta S_{seq}. \tag{14}$$

This protocol allows us not only to identify the structural saturation ceiling of the system, but also to define the thermodynamic operational window (temperature and pressure) required for spontaneous loading of the superatom.

### 2.6. Topological, Magnetic, and Electronic Characterization

We quantified the geometric distortion of the $Li_6$ cluster upon complexation through the RMSD of interatomic distances, computed using the Kabsch algorithm. We evaluated magnetic aromaticity via NICS(0) indices calculated at the geometric center of the cluster. In lithium superatoms, NICS(0) probes the magnetic response of the collective interstitial electron density generated by four Non-Nuclear Attractors (NNAs) located at the centers of four of the eight lateral triangular faces of the compressed octahedral $D_4h$ core (one NNA per unique symmetry-equivalent set of faces under $D_4h$, positioned at the four faces sharing the equatorial plane). The geometric center of the cluster lies at the centroid of these four NNAs and constitutes a direct descriptor of the superatom shell stability, in contrast to planar organic systems where its interpretation differs substantially.

We performed all wavefunction analyses with Multiwfn using the electron density obtained at the ωB97X-D4rev/def2-TZVPPD level. We carried out three analyses. First, we performed QTAIM topological analysis, from which we extracted the bond critical points (BCPs) of the Li$\cdots$H interactions, together with the electron density $\rho(r)$ and its Laplacian $\nabla^2\rho(r)$ at each BCP. Second, we performed Bader charge partitioning to obtain atomic charges and volumes. Third, we derived global reactivity descriptors (conceptual DFT, c–DFT) from the HOMO and LUMO orbital energies. We also computed Pearson correlation coefficients using an in-house Python script to quantify the linear relationships between energy components and structural descriptors of the system.

## 3. Results

### 3.1. Structural Stability and Superatom Identity

We identified the global minima (GM) through an exhaustive potential energy surface (PES) sampling of over 200 structures. As shown in Table S6, the Boltzmann populations for these GMs exceed 71% in all cases, reaching nearly 100% for the most stable complexes.

 https://doi.org/10.3390/computation14040094

Detailed energetic comparisons and geometries for all 20+ competitive isomers are available in Tables S1–S6 and Figure S1 of the Supplementary Material.

Across all complexes, the $Li_6$ cluster (Figure 1) preserves $D_4h$ symmetry with minimal variations in Li–Li interatomic distances, reflected in RMSD values below 0.032 Å (Tables 1 and S7). In contrast, higher-energy isomers exhibit more severe structural distortions (Table S7). We analyzed the redshift of the vibrational frequencies of the adsorbed $H_2$ molecules (Table S9) and found that activated molecules reduce their stretching frequency to 4219 $cm^{-1}$, compared to 4439.86 $cm^{-1}$ for free $H_2$ calculated at the same level of theory, corresponding to a shift of $\Delta\nu \approx -221$ $cm^{-1}$ for the most activated complex; the full series spans $\Delta\nu = -183$ to $-221$ $cm^{-1}$ (Table 2).

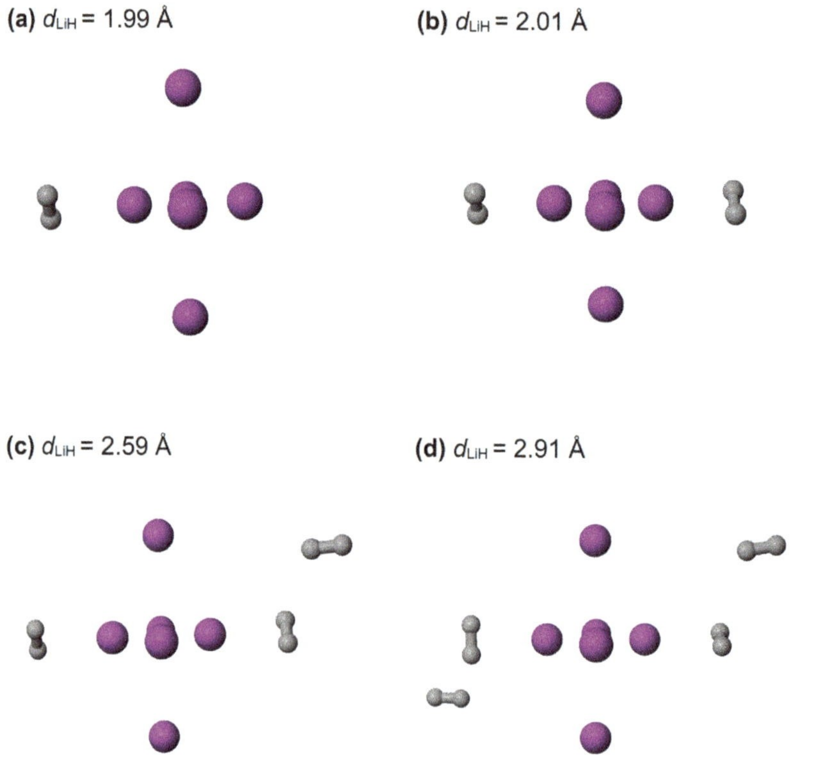


**Figure 1.** Optimized geometries of the $Li_6(H_2)_n$ global minima. (**a**) n = 1, (**b**) n = 2, (**c**) n = 3 and (**d**) n = 4. Coordination distances $d_{Li\text{–}H}$ are reported in Å. Purple and gray spheres represent lithium and hydrogen atoms, respectively. Detailed data for competitive isomers are provided in Tables S1–S6 and Figure S1 of the Supplementary Material.

**Table 1.** Electronic, structural, and magnetic descriptors of the $Li_6(H_2)_n$ global minima.

| System (GM) | [1] NICS(0) (ppm) | [2] Gap (eV) | [3] RMSD |
|---|---|---|---|
| $Li_6$ | −2.92 | 4.60 | 0.0000 |
| $Li_6(H_2)_1$ | −10.74 | 4.89 | 0.0315 |
| $Li_6(H_2)_2$ | −13.98 | 5.04 | 0.0178 |
| $Li_6(H_2)_3$ | −13.85 | 5.04 | 0.0179 |
| $Li_6(H_2)_4$ | −13.70 | 5.05 | 0.0232 |

[1] Nucleus-Independent Chemical Shift. [2] HOMO–LUMO Energy Gap. [3] Root-Mean-Square Deviation.


https://doi.org/10.3390/computation14040094

**Table 2.** Adsorption descriptors for $Li_6(H_2)_n$ global minima.

| System (GM) | [1] $\Delta G_{ads}$ (kcal/mol) | [2] $\Delta E_{seq}$ (kcal/mol) | [3] $d_{Li\text{–}H}$ (Å) | [4] $\nu_{H\text{–}H}$ ($cm^{-1}$) | Status |
|---|---|---|---|---|---|
| $Li_6(H_2)_1$ | 3.05 | −2.25 | 1.99 | 4219 | Favorable |
| $Li_6(H_2)_2$ | 6.94 | −1.85 | 2.01 | 4244, 4246 | Favorable |
| $Li_6(H_2)_3$ | 12.02 | +0.32 | 2.59 | 4247, 4250 | Saturated |
| $Li_6(H_2)_4$ | 16.28 | +0.06 | 2.91 | 4252, 4257 | Saturated |

[1] Gibbs free energies of adsorption. [2] Sequential adsorption energies; this represents the sequential adsorption energy including ZPE, BSSE, and deformation corrections, excluding the thermal enthalpy correction ΔnRT. [3] Coordination distance. [4] Vibrational frequencies.

The electronic identity of the superatom remains stable throughout the series, as confirmed by the minimal variation in the Non-Nuclear Attractor (NNA) properties and their correlation with the NICS indices (Table S15). The HOMO–LUMO gap increases from 4.60 eV in the bare cluster to 4.89–5.05 eV across the complexes (Table 1), indicating progressive electronic stabilization upon ligand loading. We confirmed the presence of four NNAs distributed across the lateral triangular faces of the compressed octahedral ($D_4h$) core (Table S12), each carrying a negative charge of approximately −1.07 e and having volumes close to 212 $Bohr^3$, an intrinsic feature of the superatom shell model. The NICS(0) indices range from −10.74 to −13.98 ppm across the global minima (Tables 1 and S9), representing a substantial enhancement relative to the bare $Li_6$ cluster (−2.917 ppm) and confirming that σ-aromaticity is progressively reinforced upon hydrogen coordination.

To quantify the structural determinants of adsorption stability across the series, we performed a Pearson correlation analysis to identify the physical variables governing the stability of the system (Table S14). We found a very strong positive correlation ($r = 0.98$) between the total adsorption energy ($\Delta E_{ads,Total}$, defined in Section 2.4) and the mean Li–Li distance ($r_{Li\text{–}Li}$), indicating that metallic core expansion is a necessary structural response to stabilize ligand loading. The electronic interaction energy ($E_{int}$) also shows a strong dependence on this core expansion ($r = 0.95$). We found a moderate inverse correlation ($r = -0.69$) between $\Delta E_{ads,Total}$ and the H–H bond distance ($r_{H\text{–}H}$), indicating that greater H–H bond weakening corresponds to a stronger interaction with the superatom. The RMSD parameter shows a correlation of 0.48 with the total adsorption energy, confirming that structural distortions, although minimal, are coupled to the energetic stabilization of the system.

### 3.2. Thermodynamics and Saturation Limits

We report the cumulative enthalpy (ΔH), entropy (−TΔS), and Gibbs free energy (ΔG) contributions at 298.15 K for the $Li_6(H_2)_n$ series (n = 1–4) in Figure 2 and Table 2. In all cases, the entropic term outweighs the enthalpic stabilization, yielding positive ΔG values that increase monotonically along the series, ranging from 3.05 to 16.28 kcal/mol.

To decouple the contribution of each individual ligand, we analyzed the sequential thermodynamic parameters ($\Delta H_{seq}$, $\Delta S_{seq}$) and the equilibrium (crossover) temperature ($T_{eq}$), detailed in Table 3. The first two adsorption steps are exothermic: $\Delta H_{seq} = -2.84$ kcal/mol ($0 \rightarrow 1$) and −2.43 kcal/mol ($1 \rightarrow 2$). From the third step onward ($2 \rightarrow 3$), the process becomes endothermic ($\Delta H_{seq} = +0.46$ kcal/mol), marking the onset of saturation driven by electrostatic and steric repulsions.



https://doi.org/10.3390/computation14040094

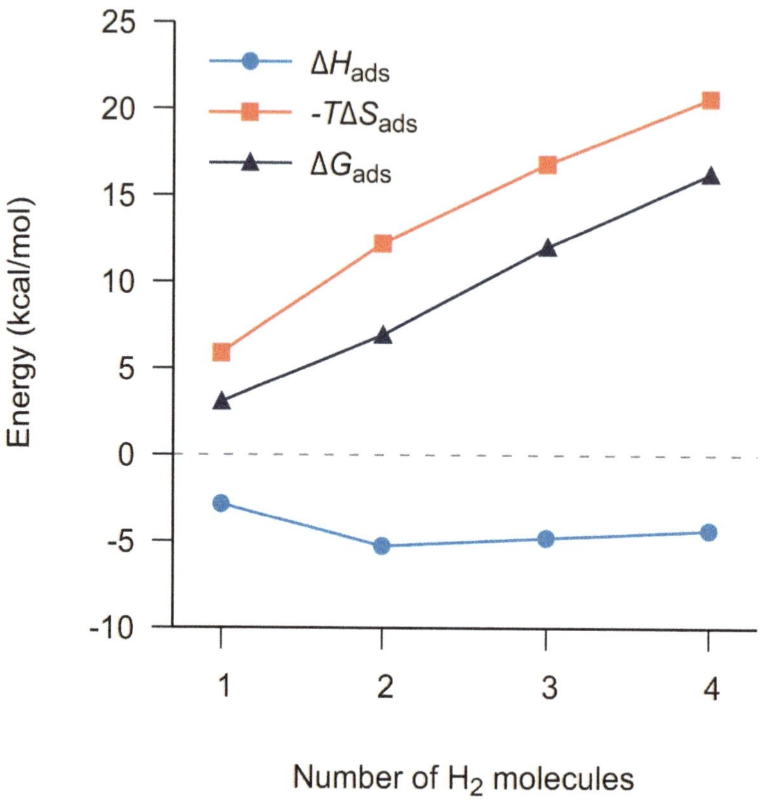


**Figure 2.** Variation of the enthalpic (ΔHads), entropic (−TΔSads), and Gibbs free energy (ΔGads) contributions at 298.15 K and 1 atm as a function of hydrogen loading. The positive $\Delta G_{ads}$ values across the entire range highlight an entropic bottleneck, where the substantial loss of translational and rotational degrees of freedom outweighs the electronic stabilization, preventing spontaneous adsorption at standard temperature.

**Table 3.** Sequential thermodynamics of $H_2$ adsorption on $Li_6$.

| Step | [1] $\Delta H_{seq}$ (kcal/mol) | [2] $\Delta S_{seq}$ (cal/mol·K) | [3] $\Delta G_{298K,seq}$ (kcal/mol) | [4] $T_{eq}$ (K) |
|---|---|---|---|---|
| $0 \rightarrow 1$ | −2.84 | −19.76 | 3.05 | 143.76 |
| $1 \rightarrow 2$ | −2.43 | −21.20 | 3.89 | 114.64 |
| $2 \rightarrow 3$ | 0.46 | −15.50 | 5.08 | N/A |
| $3 \rightarrow 4$ | 0.45 | −12.78 | 4.26 | N/A |

[1] Sequential enthalpy. [2] Sequential entropy. [3] Sequential Gibbs free energy. [4] Equilibrium temperature; this defines the thermodynamic threshold for spontaneity for each adsorption step.

Figure 3 illustrates the temperature dependence of ΔG. Spontaneous adsorption ($\Delta G < 0$) is only achievable under cryogenic conditions. We identified crossover temperatures of $T_{eq}$ = 143.76 K for the first step and $T_{eq}$ = 114.64 K for the second; below these thresholds, the system enters the spontaneous regime, as shown by the zero-crossings in Figure 3. Steps n = 3 and n = 4 exhibit no defined $T_{eq}$ and remain endergonic at all temperatures studied, due to the combination of an unfavorable adsorption enthalpy and a persistent entropic penalty. These results confirm that the effective thermodynamic loading capacity of $Li_6$ is restricted to n = 2 molecules.



https://doi.org/10.3390/computation14040094

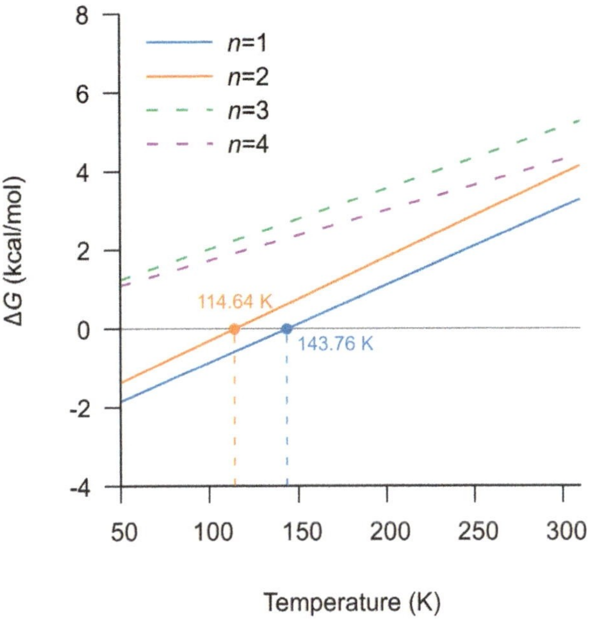


**Figure 3.** Temperature dependence of the sequential Gibbs free energy ($\Delta G_{seq}$) for $H_2$ adsorption on the $Li_6$ cluster. The intersection of each loading step (n = 1–4) with the dashed line ($\Delta G = 0$) defines the equilibrium temperature ($T_{eq}$), marking the transition to spontaneous adsorption. Spontaneity is achieved exclusively in the cryogenic regime for the first ($T < 143.76$ K) and second ($T < 114.64$ K) adsorption steps. For $n \geq 3$, the process remains endergonic ($\Delta G > 0$) across the entire temperature range studied, primarily due to positive enthalpic contributions and the persistent entropic penalty. These results highlight the thermodynamic window required for effective loading and confirm that the structural ceiling of n = 4 is not accessible through spontaneous physisorption under standard or moderate cryogenic conditions.

### 3.3. *Nature of the Interaction: Field-Activated Physisorption*

We analyzed the physical nature of the binding interaction using the Ziegler–Rauk EDA scheme (Table 4; complete data for all isomers in Table S10), in which the exchange–correlation term ($E_{XC}$) is reported separately from the orbital term ($E_{orb}$), rather than being subsumed into it as in the classical formulation. For the n = 1 global minimum, the total interaction energy is $E_{int} = -4.35$ kcal/mol. The dominant attractive contribution is electrostatic ($E_{elstat} = -9.34$ kcal/mol), followed by the orbital term ($E_{orb} = -4.03$ kcal/mol), the exchange–correlation contribution ($E_{XC} = -3.91$ kcal/mol), and dispersion ($E_{disp} = -1.03$ kcal/mol). Pauli repulsion contributes a destabilizing term of +13.96 kcal/mol. Across all complexes, the $E_{elstat}/E_{orb}$ ratio exceeds 2.0, confirming the predominantly electrostatic character of the interaction. The preparation energy ($E_{prep}$) remains minimal throughout the series, ranging from 0.12 to 0.51 kcal/mol (Table 4), representing the minor energetic penalty required to deform the fragments and confirming the structural rigidity of the metallic platform. Note that $\Delta E_{ads,Total}$ (Equation (5)) incorporates thermal and basis set corrections that are not part of the standard $E_{bind}$ reported in EDA schemes. This distinction is crucial to differentiate between purely electronic coordination and effective thermodynamic adsorption.


https://doi.org/10.3390/computation14040094

**Table 4.** Energy Decomposition Analysis (EDA) and binding energy for the $Li_6(H_2)_n$ global minima. All values are reported in kcal/mol. Calculations were performed using the Ziegler–Rauk scheme.

| System (GM) | [1] $E_{int}$ | [2] $E_{prep}$ | [3] $E_{bind}$ | [4] $E_{elstat}$ | [5] $E_{Pauli}$ | [6] $E_{orb}$ | [7] $E_{disp}$ | [8] $E_{XC}$ |
|---|---|---|---|---|---|---|---|---|
| $Li_6(H_2)_1$ | −4.35 | 0.12 | −4.23 | −9.34 | 13.96 | −4.03 | −1.03 | −3.91 |
| $Li_6(H_2)_2$ | −7.95 | 0.31 | −7.65 | −17.06 | 25.25 | −7.24 | −1.72 | −7.19 |
| $Li_6(H_2)_3$ | −8.34 | 0.44 | −7.90 | −18.81 | 27.87 | −7.54 | −1.98 | −7.88 |
| $Li_6(H_2)_4$ | −8.62 | 0.51 | −8.10 | −20.01 | 29.62 | −7.68 | −2.16 | −8.38 |

[1] Total interaction energy ($E_{elstat}$ + $E_{Pauli}$ + $E_{orb}$ + $E_{XC}$ + $E_{disp}$). [2] Preparation (deformation) energy. [3] Binding energy ($E_{int}$ + $E_{prep}$). [4] Electrostatic energy. [5] Pauli repulsion. [6] Orbital energy. [7] Dispersion energy. [8] Exchange–correlation energy.

The QTAIM topological parameters at the bond critical points (BCPs) are presented in Table 5 (extended comparison in Table S11). The electron density ρ(r) at the Li· · · H interactions ranges from 0.0122 to 0.0131 a.u. The Laplacian $\nabla^2\rho(r)$ is positive in all cases, with values between 0.0761 and 0.0827 a.u., characteristic of closed-shell interactions. For n = 3 and n = 4, we detected a slight increase in the electron density at the BCPs associated with $H_2$ molecules in the first coordination sphere.

**Table 5.** Topological properties of the electron density (ρ(r)) and its Laplacian ($\nabla^2\rho(r)$) at the Li· · · H bond critical points (BCPs) for the $Li_6(H_2)_n$ global minima. All parameters are reported in atomic units (a.u.).

| System (GM) | Interaction Type | ρ(r) | $\nabla^2\rho(r)$ | Characterization |
|---|---|---|---|---|
| $Li_6(H_2)_1$ | Li–H (Single) | 0.0130 | 0.0821 | Physisorption |
| $Li_6(H_2)_2$ | Li–H (Symmetric) | 0.0122 | 0.0767 | Physisorption |
| $Li_6(H_2)_3$ | Li–H (Relaxed) | 0.0127 | 0.0765 | Physisorption |
| | Li–H (Compressed) | 0.0131 | 0.0827 | Steric Confinement |
| $Li_6(H_2)_4$ | Li–H (Relaxed) | 0.0125 | 0.0761 | Physisorption |
| | Li–H (Compressed) | 0.0130 | 0.0818 | Steric Confinement |

### 3.4. Electronic Characterization

We calculated Bader charges for all global minima (Table 6). The net charge transfer from the cluster to the $H_2$ molecules is small but differentiated across all complexes. Activated molecules carry negative charges between −0.074 and −0.063 e, while spectator molecules show a significantly smaller charge transfer (−0.015 to −0.014 e).

**Table 6.** QTAIM charge analysis for $Li_6(H_2)_n$ global minima.

| System (GM) | [1] $Q(Li_6)$ (e) | [2] $Q(H_2)_{act}$ (e) | [3] $Q(H_2)_{spec}$ (e) | [4] ΔQ (e) |
|---|---|---|---|---|
| $Li_6(H_2)_1$ | +0.074 | −0.074 | — | +0.074 |
| $Li_6(H_2)_2$ | +0.134 | −0.067 | — | +0.134 |
| $Li_6(H_2)_3$ | +0.145 | −0.065 | −0.015 | +0.145 |
| $Li_6(H_2)_4$ | +0.154 | −0.063 | −0.014 | +0.154 |

[1] Total charge of the lithium core (including NNAs). [2] Average charges of activated. [3] Spectator hydrogen molecules. [4] Net charge transferred from the $Li_6$ core to the adsorbed $H_2$ molecules.

We identified Non-Nuclear Attractors (NNAs) at the center of the octahedral void of $Li_6$ (Tables S12 and S15). These NNAs concentrate a negative charge of approximately −1.07 e for n = 1, which decreases slightly to −1.04 e for n = 4. Their volumes range between 210 and 212 Bohr$^3$ and remain virtually constant throughout the series. This simultaneous stability of the interstitial charge and the NNA volume confirms the closed-shell nature of the cluster and supports the superatom model.



https://doi.org/10.3390/computation14040094

The Molecular Electrostatic Potential (MESP) maps corroborate this charge distribution (Figure 4). The lithium nuclei act as the predominant electrophilic regions of the system. We detected moderate inductive polarization of the H–H bond exclusively at the primary adsorption sites.

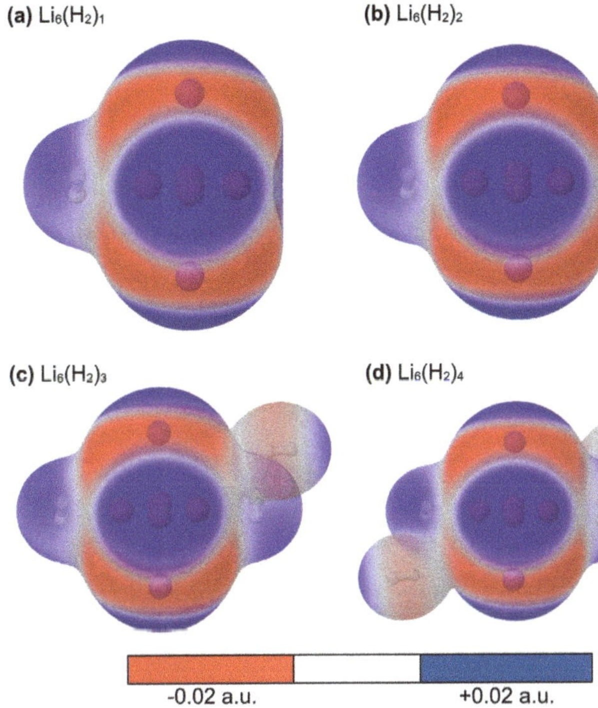


**Figure 4.** Molecular Electrostatic Potential (MESP) maps for the $Li_6(H_2)_n$ complexes. (**a**) n = 1, (**b**) n = 2, (**c**) n = 3 and (**d**) n = 4. The potential is mapped onto the total electron density isosurface (0.001 a.u.). The color scale ranges from −0.02 a.u. (red, nucleophilic) to +0.02 a.u. (blue, electrophilic). These maps identify the Li nuclei as the primary electrophilic sites and visualize the inductive polarization of the $H_2$ molecules. Panels (**c**,**d**) highlight the attenuated interaction of spectator $H_2$ units at larger coordination distances, consistent with the Bader charge transfer values reported in Table 6.

We analyzed the spatial distribution of the frontier molecular orbitals (FMOs) in Figures 5 and 6, as well as their energetic evolution in the orbital energy level diagram in Figure 7. The HOMO is localized exclusively on the metallic core throughout the series. The LUMO incorporates contributions from the σ* antibonding orbitals of the coordinated $H_2$ molecules. From these orbital energies, we derived the global reactivity descriptors (conceptual DFT, c–DFT) (Tables 7 and S13) following the frontier molecular orbital framework for describing chemical reactivity [36]. Although absolute orbital eigenvalues are sensitive to the functional choice, the range-separated ωB97X-D4rev functional ensures a consistent description of the HOMO–LUMO gap and its relative trends across the series. The chemical hardness (η) and electronegativity (χ) show minimal variation relative to the isolated cluster. The chemical potential (μ) and electrophilicity index (ω) converge as ligand loading increases.


https://doi.org/10.3390/computation14040094

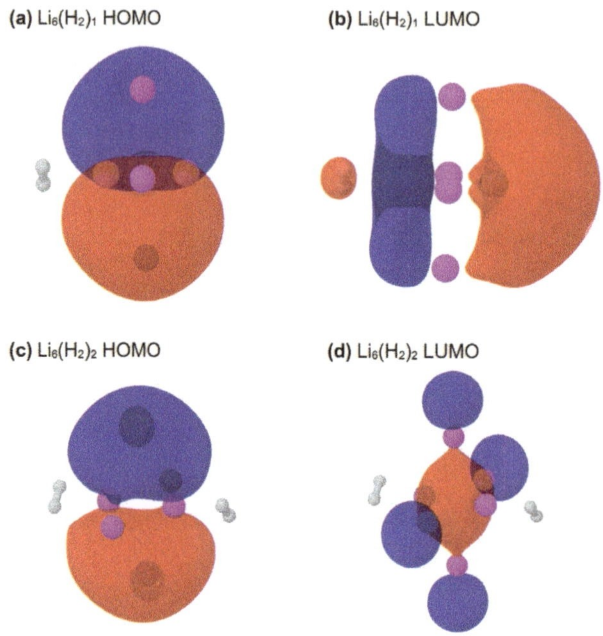


**Figure 5.** Spatial distribution of the frontier molecular orbitals (FMOs) for the $Li_6(H_2)_1$ and $Li_6(H_2)_2$ global minima: (**a**) $Li_6(H_2)_1$ HOMO, (**b**) $Li_6(H_2)_1$ LUMO, (**c**) $Li_6(H_2)_2$ HOMO, and (**d**) $Li_6(H_2)_2$ LUMO. Red and blue lobes represent the positive and negative phases of the wavefunction, respectively, generated at an isovalue of 0.02 e/bohr$^3$. The HOMO remains predominantly localized on the $Li_6$ metallic core, while the LUMO exhibits electronic participation from the $H_2$ antibonding orbitals, facilitating inductive polarization.

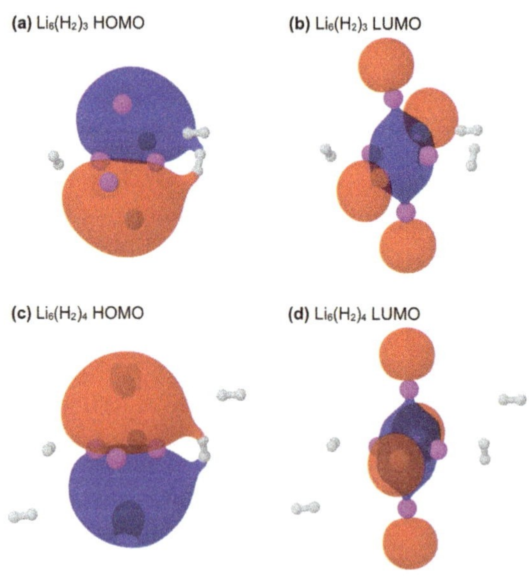


**Figure 6.** Spatial distribution of the FMOs for the $Li_6(H_2)_3$ and $Li_6(H_2)_4$ global minima: (**a**) $Li_6(H_2)_3$ HOMO, (**b**) $Li_6(H_2)_3$ LUMO, (**c**) $Li_6(H_2)_4$ HOMO, and (**d**) $Li_6(H_2)_4$ LUMO. The persistent localization of the HOMO on the lithium core reflects its electronic stability as a superatom even at the saturation limit. The relative stabilization of the HOMO–LUMO gap and chemical hardness (η) reported in Tables 1 and 6 correlates with the inability of the LUMO to effectively coordinate spectator H2 units at larger distances.

 https://doi.org/10.3390/computation14040094

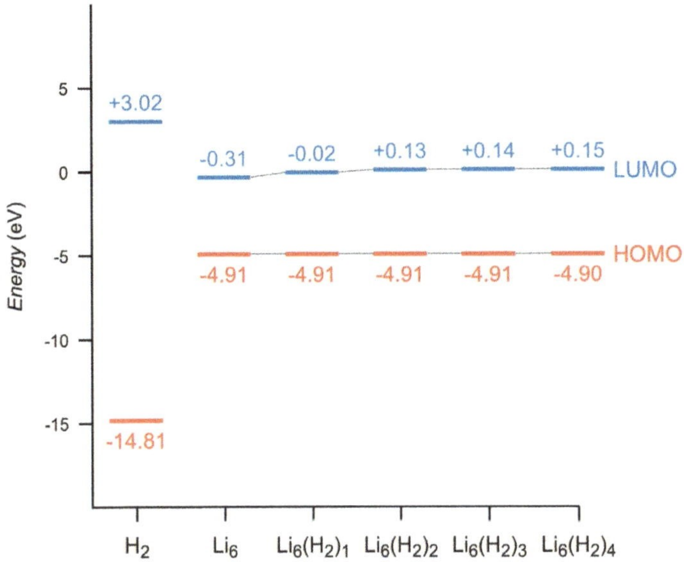


**Figure 7.** Frontier molecular orbital (FMO) energy level diagram for the isolated $H_2$ and $Li_6$ fragments and the $Li_6(H_2)_n$ (n = 1–4) global minima. Energy levels are reported in eV. Red and blue bars represent the Highest Occupied Molecular Orbital (HOMO) and the Lowest Unoccupied Molecular Orbital (LUMO), respectively.

**Table 7.** Global reactivity descriptors for the $Li_6(H_2)_n$ global minima. All parameters are reported in eV.

| System (GM) | [1] $\mu$ | [2] $\eta$ | [3] $\chi$ | [4] $\omega$ |
|---|---|---|---|---|
| $Li_6$ | −2.61 | 2.30 | 2.61 | 1.48 |
| $Li_6(H_2)_1$ | −2.46 | 2.44 | 2.46 | 1.24 |
| $Li_6(H_2)_2$ | −2.39 | 2.52 | 2.39 | 1.13 |
| $Li_6(H_2)_3$ | −2.38 | 2.52 | 2.38 | 1.13 |
| $Li_6(H_2)_4$ | −2.38 | 2.53 | 2.38 | 1.12 |

[1] Electronic chemical potential. [2] Chemical hardness. [3] Electronegativity. [4] Electrophilicity index.

## 4. Discussion

### *4.1. Aromatic Superatom*

Our results demonstrate that the $Li_6$ cluster functions as a structurally rigid platform, whose stability under ligand loading is confirmed by the preservation of $D_4h$ symmetry and RMSD values below 0.032 Å (Table 1). We attribute this robustness to its intrinsic superatom character, whereby the four Non-Nuclear Attractors (NNAs) distributed across the lateral triangular faces of the compressed octahedral ($D_4h$) core act collectively as an electronic anchor that cohesively holds the metallic core against external perturbations, minimizing geometric deformation. A key finding is the near-perfect correlation (r = 0.98) between the adsorption energy and the Li–Li distance; the metallic core undergoes minimal expansion to optimize the interaction without compromising its octahedral topology. This resistance to perturbation is further reflected in the progressive increase in the HOMO–LUMO gap from 4.60 eV in bare $Li_6$ to ≈5.0 eV upon full loading (Table 1), Notably, starting from n = 2, the LUMO energy shifts into the positive regime (unbound), as shown in Table S13. This transition is physically consistent with the cluster's high electronic hardness ($\eta$) and its character as a stable, closed-shell species that does not favor further electronic perturbation,


https://doi.org/10.3390/computation14040094

confirming that hydrogen coordination reinforces rather than compromises the electronic stability of the cluster.

The integrity of the system is ensured by the ligand-induced strengthening of σ-aromaticity from −2.917 ppm in bare $Li_6$ to ≈−13.8 ppm under hydrogen loading, which acts as an "electronic glue" that minimizes deformation under external repulsions. This stability is a direct consequence of the superatom shell model: each NNA carries a substantial negative charge (≈−1.07 e) that remains nearly constant up to n = 4, with associated volumes ranging from 210 to 212 $Bohr^3$ without significant variation despite increasing ligand loading (Tables S12 and S15), reinforcing their collective role as a stabilizing charge anchor.

By residing at the centroid of these four NNAs, the NICS(0) magnetic index probes the collective interstitial electron density and remains free from the local contamination typical of σ covalent bonds. The persistence of strong σ-aromaticity is therefore not a computational artifact but is intrinsically tied to the stability of this collective interstitial density. The parallel evolution of these descriptors (Table S15) confirms that the $Li_6$ core acts as an unaltered electronic anchor even under forced saturation regimes, thus supporting the concept of "NNA-supported aromaticity" that allows $Li_6$ to retain its electronic identity up to n = 4.

The isomeric distribution (Table S6) reveals a coverage-dependent behavior. For n = 1, the global minimum dominates with a Boltzmann population of 97.78%, consistent with a structurally pure species. However, for n = 2, the global minimum population drops to 71.2%, with three isomers competing with significant populations. For n = 3 and n = 4, the distribution broadens further, with global minimum populations of 42.8% and 31.12%, respectively. This progressive isomeric dispersion is consistent with the saturation regime identified in Section 3.2 and provides independent reinforcement of the effective thermodynamic loading limit at n = 2. Despite this broadening distribution, the descriptors obtained (HOMO–LUMO gap, NNA charge, NICS indices, and EDA components) constitute a contamination-free reference set that can be directly employed to assess how a given substrate modulates the adsorption capacity of the $Li_6$ motif in assembled materials. Deviations observed in supported systems can thus be unambiguously attributed to substrate-specific modulation rather than to the intrinsic superatom chemistry.

### 4.2. Nature of the Interaction

We interpret the binding in the $Li_6(H_2)_n$ complexes as field-activated physisorption (consistent with the ion-quadrupole polarization-enhanced mechanism described by Lochan and Head-Gordon [37]) and rule out the formation of Kubas-type complexes. Our multi-physics evidence supports this assignment through three independent criteria: vibrational, energetic, and topological criteria.

We observe a redshift of $\Delta\nu \approx -221$ $cm^{-1}$ and an H–H bond elongation of only 0.014 Å (Table 2). For context, classical Kubas complexes of transition metals such as $W(CO)_3(PR_3)_2(H_2)$ exhibit $\nu_{H\text{-}H}$ frequencies in the range of 2600–3100 $cm^{-1}$, corresponding to redshifts of 1000–1500 $cm^{-1}$ relative to free $H_2$ (~4161 $cm^{-1}$) [38,39]. In contrast, Lochan and Head-Gordon report that $Li^+$-doped light metal systems show typical shifts of only 130–160 $cm^{-1}$ [37,40], a range with which our value of $\Delta\nu \approx -221$ $cm^{-1}$ is fully consistent. This behavior is characteristic of ion-quadrupole polarization-enhanced physisorption, lacking the d → σ back-donation required to form a Kubas-type σ-complex. The molecular integrity of $H_2$ is preserved nearly intact, favoring desorption without significant kinetic barriers.

The Ziegler–Rauk EDA scheme confirms that the stabilization is predominantly electrostatic, contributing between 65% and 67% of the primary attractive interaction ($E_{elstat}$, $E_{orb}$, $E_{disp}$); percentages are computed over these three physically interpretable terms, with


https://doi.org/10.3390/computation14040094

$E_{XC}$ reported separately as it represents the non-classical exchange–correlation correction of the hybrid functional rather than a classical interaction force [41], while the orbital component accounts for a secondary fraction of the stabilization (Table 4). The electric field generated by the superatom polarizes the $H_2$ molecules, but charge transfer is insufficient to establish a strong and stable three-center $Li\cdots H\cdots H$ coordinative bond.

We find a positive Laplacian ($\nabla^2\rho > 0$) and low electron densities ($\rho \approx 0.013$ a.u.) at the $Li\cdots H$ bond critical points (Table 5). These values are diagnostic of closed-shell interactions and exclude the formation of covalent or strongly coordinative bonds. Bader charge analysis (Table 6) further confirms the non-covalent nature of the interaction: charge transfer toward $H_2$ is minimal, preventing the formation of stable hydrides and ensuring full process reversibility. The small dispersion contribution ($E_{disp} = -1.03$ kcal/mol, Table 4) indicates that storage does not rely on long-range van der Waals forces, but on a direct electrostatic response. The MESP maps (Figure 4) support this field-activated physisorption model.

### 4.3. The Entropic Bottleneck

The thermodynamics of the $Li_6(H_2)_n$ system is governed by the competition between electronic stabilization and the loss of translational and rotational degrees of freedom. At 298.15 K, the $-T\Delta S$ term consistently outweighs the enthalpic stabilization, yielding positive $\Delta G$ values that increase along the series (3.05 to 16.28 kcal/mol). Spontaneous adsorption under standard conditions is therefore thermodynamically unfeasible. Nevertheless, the equilibrium (crossover) temperature analysis ($T_{eq}$) allows us to precisely define the operational window of the system.

For the first two adsorption steps, the transition to the spontaneous regime ($\Delta G < 0$) occurs under cryogenic conditions, with $T_{eq}$ = 143.76 K for n = 1 and $T_{eq}$ = 114.64 K for n = 2. While we recognize that the RRHO scheme tends to overestimate the entropic penalty in weakly bound systems by treating hindered translational and rotational modes as harmonic vibrations, we estimate that applying quasi-RRHO corrections would shift these Teq values upward by only 20–40 K. Since this adjustment does not alter our fundamental conclusion that spontaneous loading is restricted to the cryogenic regime (<200 K), we consider the RRHO results to be a robust upper bound that is physically representative of the system's thermodynamic limits. For $n \geq 3$, no defined $T_{eq}$ exists: the endothermic character of the sequential adsorption ($\Delta H_{seq} > 0$), combined with a persistent entropic penalty, keeps $\Delta G$ positive at all temperatures studied.

This effective loading limit at $n = 2$ has a structural origin: saturation of the first coordination sphere and the electrostatic repulsion generated by the high charge density at the central NNAs confine additional $H_2$ molecules to peripheral, energetically unfavorable positions. As a result, the lower symmetry observed for $n = 4$ is a direct consequence of this "forced saturation state," where inter-ligand repulsions prevent the adoption of higher-symmetry configurations. It is important to distinguish that the structural ceiling at n = 4 represents a forced saturation state only, not spontaneously accessible under either standard or moderately cryogenic conditions.

That said, the cryogenic window defined by $T_{eq}$ = 143.76 K and 114.64 K falls within a physically accessible temperature range, providing a quantitative thermodynamic reference rather than a practical storage prescription. In this context, $Li_6$ should not be regarded as a failed adsorbent, but as a well-characterized reversible physisorption platform whose operational window serves as a gas-phase theoretical reference: future $Li_6$-decorated materials in which the substrate favorably modulates the adsorption enthalpy could shift this window toward more practical temperatures.



https://doi.org/10.3390/computation14040094

## 5. Conclusions

Structural Stability: The $Li_6$ cluster acts as a rigid, non-fluxional platform (RMSD < 0.032 Å) throughout the adsorption series. The superatom shell model maintains geometric integrity, consistent with reversible adsorption–desorption cycles without symmetry breaking for $n \leq 2$.

Electronic Identity: Ligand loading strengthens the metallic $\sigma$-aromaticity, with NICS(0) values shifting from $-2.917$ ppm to a range of $-10.74$ to $-13.98$ ppm. This is accompanied by an increased HOMO–LUMO gap (up to 5.05 eV) and enhanced interstitial electron delocalization.

Interaction Mechanism: Energy Decomposition Analysis (EDA) identifies the binding as field-activated physisorption, dominated by electrostatic contributions (65–67%). Kubas-type coordination is excluded based on moderate vibrational redshifts ($\Delta v \approx -183$ to $-221$ cm$^{-1}$) and QTAIM parameters diagnostic of closed-shell interactions ($\nabla^2\rho > 0$, $\rho < 0.013$ a.u.).

Thermodynamic Limits: The system exhibits negative cooperativity, establishing an effective loading capacity of $n = 2$ molecules under cryogenic conditions. An entropic bottleneck renders adsorption non-spontaneous at standard conditions, restricting the operational window to the cryogenic regime ($T_{eq}$ = 143.76 K and 114.64 K). These values are subject to the intrinsic uncertainty of the double-hybrid functional (~0.5 kcal/mol). While we acknowledge these RRHO values as upper-bound estimates, the estimated 20–40 K increase from quasi-RRHO corrections does not alter the robust conclusion that spontaneous loading requires cryogenic conditions.

Gas-phase Theoretical Reference Utility: The substrate-free characterization of $Li_6$ yields a self-consistent set of contamination-free descriptors (Bader charges, NNA charge and volume, NICS(0) indices, EDA contributions, and crossover temperatures) that represent the intrinsic Li–$H_2$ interaction. While these conclusions are derived from high-level theoretical modeling, the consistency between the electronic descriptors (EDA, QTAIM) and the thermodynamic limits provides a robust physical picture. Consequently, the reported $T_{eq}$ values should be interpreted as theoretical thresholds that define the operational window of the $Li_6$ superatom. This constitutes a theoretical baseline against which the performance of $Li_6$-decorated materials can be directly evaluated: deviations observed in supported systems can now be unambiguously attributed to substrate-specific modulation rather than to the superatom chemistry itself, enabling the rational, descriptor-guided design of lithium-decorated hydrogen storage materials.

**Supplementary Materials:** The following supporting information can be downloaded at https://www.mdpi.com/article/10.3390/computation14040094/s1. Figure S1 Optimized geometries for all studied $Li_6(H_2)_n$ (n = 1–4) isomers at the wB97X-D4rev/def2-TZVPPD level of theory. Structural labels correspond to the Cartesian coordinates provided in Table S1. Table S1 Cartesian coordinates (in Å) for the optimized structures of isolated species and $Li_6(H_2)_n$ complexes at the wB97X-D4rev/def2-TZVPPD level of theory; Table S2 Total electronic energies and counterpoise components (CP) at the wB97X-D4rev/def2-TZVPPD level of theory. All values are reported in atomic units (a.u.); Table S3. Total electronic energies and counterpoise components at the wB97X-2-D3BJ/def2-TZVPPD level of theory. All values are reported in atomic units (a.u.); Table S4. Zero-point energies (ZPE), thermal enthalpy corrections (Hcorr), and entropy terms (TS) at the wB97X-D4rev/def2-TZVPPD level. All values reported in atomic units (a.u.) at 298.15 K and 1 atm; Table S5. Energetic components and relative stabilities (kcal/mol) for $Li_6(H_2)_n$ complexes at the wB97X-D4rev/def2-TZVPPD level of theory. Values are derived from electronic energies and ZPE corrections. $\Delta E_{ads,Total}$ represents the final corrected adsorption energy; Table S6. Thermodynamic adsorption properties and Boltzmann population distribution for $Li_6(H_2)_n$ complexes. All energy values are reported in kcal/mol at 298.15 K and 1 atm. $\Delta\Delta G$ represents the relative stability compared to the Global Minimum (GM)

 https://doi.org/10.3390/computation14040094

of each group; Table S7. Geometric descriptors for isolated species and $Li_6(H_2)_n$ complexes at the wB97X-D4rev/def2-TZVPPD level of theory. Distances are reported in Angstroms (Å). Isomers are ordered according to their tThermodynamic stability (ΔΔG) at 298.15 K. RMSD is calculated for the $Li_6$ core relative to the isolated cluster; Table S8. Magnetic aromaticity indices (NICS) for $Li_6(H_2)_n$ complexes at the wB97X-D4rev/def2-TZVPPD level of theory. Isotropic shielding ($\sigma_{iso}$) and NICS(0) values are reported in ppm. Isomers are ordered according to their thermodynamic stability (ΔΔG) at 298.15 K; Table S9. Harmonic stretching frequencies (ν) and classification of adsorbed $H_2$ molecules. All frequencies are reported in $cm^{-1}$. Isomers are ordered according to their thermodynamic stability (ΔΔG) at 298.15 K. Reference isolated $H_2$ (gas) frequency: 4401 $cm^{-1}$; Table S10. Energy Decomposition Analysis (EDA) components for $Li_6(H_2)_n$ complexes, according to the Ziegler–Rauk scheme. All values are reported in kcal/mol. Isomers are ordered according to their thermodynamic stability (ΔΔG) at 298.15 K; Table S11. Topological parameters of the electron density at the Bond Critical Points (BCP) for Li–H interactions in Global Minima. All values are reported in atomic units (a.u.) at the wB97X-D4rev/def2-TZVPPD level of theory. Only the most stable isomers according to Gibbs free energy (ΔG) are reported; Table S12. Atomic Charges and Volumes from Bader Population Analysis (QTAIM) at the wB97X-D4/def2-TZVPPD level of theory. Only the most stable isomers according to Gibbs free energy (ΔG) are reported; Table S13. Frontier molecular orbital indices (NO), energies, and HOMO-LUMO gaps for all $Li_6(H_2)_n$ isomers; Table S14. Pearson correlation coefficients (r) between energy components ($E_{int}$, $E_{def}$ and $\Delta E_{adsTotal}$) and the structural/electronic descriptors for the $Li_6(H_2)_n$ global minima; Table S15. Correlation Table: Superatom Stability vs. Aromaticity.

**Author Contributions:** Conceptualization, O.J.-S. and R.P.-C.; methodology, R.P.-C. and O.J.-S.; software, O.J.-S.; validation, K.O.L., J.G.-V. and R.P.-C.; formal analysis, K.O.L., J.G.-V. and R.P.-C.; investigation, K.O.L., J.G.-V. and R.P.-C.; data curation, R.P.-C. and O.J.-S.; writing—original draft preparation, O.J.-S.; writing—review and editing, K.O.L., J.G.-V., R.P.-C. and O.J.-S.; visualization, O.J.-S.; supervision, O.J.-S.; project administration, O.J.-S. All authors have read and agreed to the published version of the manuscript.

**Funding:** This research received no external funding.

**Data Availability Statement:** The data supporting the findings of this study are available in the Supplementary Material of this article.

**Acknowledgments:** During the preparation of this manuscript, the authors used Gemini 3 Thinking (Google, 2026) for the purposes of translating the original draft from Spanish to English and refining linguistic clarity. The authors have reviewed and edited the output and take full responsibility for the content of this publication.

**Conflicts of Interest:** The authors declare no conflicts of interest.

## Abbreviations

The following abbreviations are used in this manuscript:

| | |
|---|---|
| BCP | Bond Critical Point |
| BSSE | Basis Set Superposition Error |
| CCSD | Coupled Cluster with Singles and Doubles |
| DFT | Density Functional Theory |
| EDA | Energy Decomposition Analysis |
| FMOs | Frontier Molecular Orbitals |
| GAP | HOMO–LUMO Energy Gap |
| GM | Global Minimum |
| HOMO | Highest Occupied Molecular Orbital |
| LUMO | Lowest Unoccupied Molecular Orbital |
| MESP | Molecular Electrostatic Potential |
| NICS | Nucleus-Independent Chemical Shift |


https://doi.org/10.3390/computation14040094

| | |
|---|---|
| NNA | Non-Nuclear Attractor |
| PES | Potential Energy Surface |
| QTAIM | Quantum Theory of Atoms in Molecules |
| RMSD | Root-Mean-Square Deviation |
| RRHO | Rigid Rotor-Harmonic Oscillator |
| ZPE | Zero-Point Energy |

## References

1. Li, Q.; Zhang, Q.; Zhang, L.; Lang, J.; Yuan, W.; An, G.; Lei, T. A comprehensive review of advances and challenges of hydrogen production, purification, compression, transportation, storage and utilization technology. *Renew. Sustain. Energy Rev.* **2026**, *226*, 116196. [CrossRef]
2. Züttel, A. Hydrogen storage methods. *Naturwissenschaften* **2004**, *91*, 157–172. [CrossRef]
3. Jain, I.P.; Lal, C.; Jain, A. Hydrogen storage in Mg: A most promising material. *Int. J. Hydrogen Energy* **2010**, *35*, 5133–5144. [CrossRef]
4. Yuan, L.; Gong, J.; Wang, D.; Su, J.; Zhang, M.; Yang, J. A first principles study of hydrogen storage capacity for Li-decorated porous BNC monolayer. *Comput. Theor. Chem.* **2022**, *1208*, 113578. [CrossRef]
5. Liu, Z.; Zhao, W.; Chai, M. Li-decorated bilayer borophene as a potential hydrogen storage material: A DFT study. *Int. J. Hydrogen Energy* **2024**, *51*, 229–235. [CrossRef]
6. Bi, L.; Yin, J.; Huang, X.; Wang, Y.; Yang, Z. A DFT study of $H_2$ adsorption on lithium decorated 3D hybrid Boron-Nitride-Carbon frameworks. *Int. J. Hydrogen Energy* **2019**, *44*, 15183–15192. [CrossRef]
7. Guardado, A.; Marisol, I.-R.; Mayén-Mondragón, R.; Sánchez, M. Hydrogen adsorption on lithium clusters coordinated to a gC3N4 cavity. *J. Mol. Graph. Model.* **2023**, *122*, 108491. [CrossRef]
8. Srivastava, H.; Srivastava, A.K. Superalkalis for the Activation of Carbon Dioxide: A Review. *Front. Phys.* **2022**, *10*, 870205. [CrossRef]
9. de Heer, W.A. The physics of simple metal clusters: Experimental aspects and simple models. *Rev. Mod. Phys.* **1993**, *65*, 611–676. [CrossRef]
10. Kreibig, U.; Vollmer, M. *Optical Properties of Metal Clusters*; Springer: Berlin/Heidelberg, Germany, 1995. [CrossRef]
11. García-Argote, W.; Medel, E.; Inostroza, D.; Vásquez-Espinal, A.; Solar-Encinas, J.; Leyva-Parra, L.; Ruiz, L.M.; Yañez, O.; Tiznado, W. From Aromatic Motifs to Cluster-Assembled Materials: Silicon–Lithium Nanoclusters for Hydrogen Storage Applications. *Molecules* **2025**, *30*, 2163. [CrossRef] [PubMed]
12. Kaviani, S.; Piyanzina, I.; Nedopekin, O.V.; Tayurskii, D.A. A DFT-D3 investigation on Li, Na, and K decorated C6O6Li6 cluster as a new promising hydrogen storage system. *Int. J. Hydrogen Energy* **2023**, *48*, 30069–30084. [CrossRef]
13. Liu, Z.; Liu, S.; Er, S. Hydrogen storage properties of Li-decorated B2S monolayers: A DFT study. *Int. J. Hydrogen Energy* **2019**, *44*, 16803–16810. [CrossRef]
14. Zhang, Y.; Scanlon, L.G.; Rottmayer, M.A.; Balbuena, P.B. Computational Investigation of Adsorption of Molecular Hydrogen on Lithium-Doped Corannulene. *J. Phys. Chem. B* **2006**, *110*, 22532–22541. [CrossRef] [PubMed]
15. Blanc, J.; Bonačić-Koutecký, V.; Broyer, M.; Chevaleyre, J.; Dugourd, P.; Koutecký, J.; Scheuch, C.; Wolf, J.P.; Wöste, L. Evolution of the electronic structure of lithium clusters between four and eight atoms. *J. Chem. Phys.* **1992**, *96*, 1793–1809. [CrossRef]
16. Qi, H.; Wang, X.; Chen, H. Superalkali NLi4 decorated graphene: A promising hydrogen storage material with high reversible capacity at ambient temperature. *Int. J. Hydrogen Energy* **2021**, *46*, 23254–23262. [CrossRef]
17. Neese, F. Software update: The ORCA program system, version 6.0. *Wiley Interdiscip. Rev. Comput. Mol. Sci.* **2025**, *15*, e70019. [CrossRef]
18. Neese, F. The SHARK Integral Generation and Digestion System. *J. Comput. Chem.* **2023**, *44*, 381–396. [CrossRef]
19. Neese, F. An improvement of the resolution of the identity approximation for the formation of the Coulomb matrix. *J. Comput. Chem.* **2003**, *24*, 1740–1747. [CrossRef]
20. Neese, F.; Wennmohs, F.; Hansen, A.; Becker, U. Efficient, approximate and parallel Hartree-Fock and hybrid DFT calculations. *Chem. Phys.* **2009**, *356*, 98–109. [CrossRef]
21. Helmich-Paris, B.; de Souza, B.; Neese, F.; Izsák, R. An improved chain of spheres for exchange algorithm. *J. Chem. Phys.* **2021**, *155*, 104109. [CrossRef]
22. Lu, T.; Chen, F. Multiwfn: A multifunctional wavefunction analyzer. *J. Comput. Chem.* **2012**, *33*, 580–592. [CrossRef]
23. Van Rossum, G.; Drake, F.L. *Python 3 Reference Manual*; CreateSpace: Scotts Valley, CA, USA, 2009.
24. Kabsch, W. A solution for the best rotation to relate two sets of vectors. *Acta Crystallogr. Sect. A* **1976**, *32*, 922–923. [CrossRef]
25. Jmol: An Open-Source Java Viewer for Chemical Structures in 3D. Available online: https://sourceforge.net/projects/jmol/ (accessed on 1 January 2026).

 https://doi.org/10.3390/computation14040094

26. Williams, T.; Kelley, C. Gnuplot 6.0: An Interactive Plotting Program. Available online: http://www.gnuplot.info/ (accessed on 1 January 2026).
27. Mardirossian, N.; Head-Gordon, M. ωB97X-V: A 10-parameter, range-separated hybrid, generalized gradient approximation density functional with nonlocal correlation, designed by a survival-of-the-fittest strategy. *Phys. Chem. Chem. Phys.* **2014**, *16*, 9904–9924. [CrossRef]
28. Najibi, A.; Goerigk, L. DFT-D4 counterparts of leading meta-generalized-gradient approximation and hybrid density functionals for energetics and geometries. *J. Comput. Chem.* **2020**, *41*, 2562–2572. [CrossRef] [PubMed]
29. Weigend, F.; Ahlrichs, R. Balanced basis sets of split valence, triple zeta valence and quadruple zeta valence quality for H to Rn: Design and assessment of accuracy. *Phys. Chem. Chem. Phys.* **2005**, *7*, 3297–3305. [CrossRef]
30. Rappoport, D.; Furche, F. Property-optimized Gaussian basis sets for molecular response calculations. *J. Chem. Phys.* **2010**, *133*, 134105. [CrossRef] [PubMed]
31. Lin, Y.-S.; Li, G.-D.; Mao, S.-P.; Chai, J.-D. Long-Range Corrected Hybrid Density Functionals with Improved Dispersion Corrections. *J. Chem. Theory Comput.* **2013**, *9*, 263–272.
32. Grimme, S.; Antony, J.; Ehrlich, S.; Krieg, H. A consistent and accurate ab initio parametrization of density functional dispersion correction (DFT-D). *J. Chem. Phys.* **2010**, *132*, 154104. [CrossRef] [PubMed]
33. Grimme, S.; Ehrlich, S.; Goerigk, L. Effect of the damping function in dispersion corrected density functional theory. *J. Comput. Chem.* **2011**, *32*, 1456–1465. [CrossRef]
34. Goerigk, L.; Hansen, A.; Bauer, C.; Ehrlich, S.; Najibi, A.; Grimme, S. A look at the density functional theory zoo with the advanced GMTKN55 database. *Phys. Chem. Chem. Phys.* **2017**, *19*, 32184–32215. [CrossRef]
35. Temelso, B.; Sherrill, C.D. High accuracy ab initio studies of Li6+, Li6−, and three isomers of Li6. *J. Chem. Phys.* **2005**, *122*, 064315. [CrossRef] [PubMed]
36. Yu, J.; Su, N.Q.; Yang, W. Describing chemical reactivity with frontier molecular orbitalets. *JACS Au* **2022**, *2*, 1383–1394. [CrossRef]
37. Lochan, R.C.; Head-Gordon, M. Computational studies of molecular hydrogen binding affinities: The role of dispersion forces, electrostatics, and orbital interactions. *Phys. Chem. Chem. Phys.* **2006**, *8*, 1357–1370. [CrossRef] [PubMed]
38. Grimme, S. Supramolecular Binding Thermodynamics by Dispersion-Corrected Density Functional Theory. *Chem. Eur. J.* **2012**, *18*, 9955–9964. [CrossRef]
39. Kubas, G.J. Metal–dihydrogen and σ-bond coordination: The consummate extension of the Dewar–Chatt–Duncanson model for metal–olefin π bonding. *J. Organomet. Chem.* **2001**, *635*, 37–68. [CrossRef]
40. Morris, R.H. Dihydrogen, dihydride and in between: NMR and structural properties of iron group complexes. *Coord. Chem. Rev.* **2008**, *252*, 2381–2394. [CrossRef]
41. Zhao, L.; von Hopffgarten, M.; Andrada, D.M.; Frenking, G. Energy Decomposition Analysis. *Wiley Interdiscip. Rev. Comput. Mol. Sci.* **2018**, *8*, e1345. [CrossRef]






https://doi.org/10.3390/computation14040094

computation

MDPI

*Article*

# Ab Initio Computational Investigations of Low-Lying Electronic States of Yttrium Lithide and Scandium Lithide

**Jean Tabet [1], Nancy Zgheib [2,*], Sylvie Magnier [3] and Fadia Taher [4]**

1 Laboratory of Experiments and Computation of Materials and Molecules (EC2M), Faculty of Sciences II, Lebanese University, Campus Fanar, Jdeideh P.O. Box 90656, Lebanon; j.tabet@ul.edu.lb
2 Department of Chemical and Petroleum Engineering, Holy Spirit University of Kaslik (USEK), Jounieh P.O. Box 446, Lebanon
3 PhLAM Laboratory, Physique des Lasers Atomes et Molécules, CNRS, Lille University, F-59000 Lille, France; sylvie.magnier@univ-lille.fr
4 Laboratory of Molecular Quantum Mechanics and Modeling (MQMM), Faculty of Engineering III, Lebanese University, Hadath Campus, Beirut P.O. Box 6573/14, Lebanon; ftaher@ul.edu.lb
* Correspondence: nancyzgheib@usek.edu.lb

**Abstract**

Ab initio studies using CASSCF/MRCI calculations have been performed to investigate the spectroscopic properties of YLi and ScLi molecules. Our calculations have computed 25 singlet and triplet states for YLi and 37 electronic states for ScLi. The lowest lying states, including the ground state $^1\Sigma^+$ of YLi, have been investigated for the first time. The spin–orbit coupling in YLi has also been assessed from the splitting between $\Omega$ components generated from the lowest triplet lying $\Lambda$–S states. Regarding ScLi, the ground state is found to be the $(1)^3\Delta$ state. Spectroscopic constants, energy levels at equilibrium, permanent dipole moments, and transition dipole moments have also been calculated. The potential energy curves for all calculated states have been displayed to large bond internuclear distances. In both ScLi and YLi, the potential energy curves have shown a small dissociation energy for the lowest states (1) $^{1,3}\Delta$, (1) $^{1,3}\Pi$ and (1) $^{1,3}\Sigma^+$.

**Keywords:** ab initio calculations; CASSCF/MRCI; YLi; ScLi; diatomic molecules; spectroscopic parameters

## 1. Introduction

In recent years, our research has been focused on the theoretical investigation of diatomic molecules composed of a transition-metal atom combined with either hydrogen or an alkali metal atom [1]. In such molecular systems, the open d shell of transition-metal atoms, particularly scandium and yttrium, plays a crucial role in the electron degeneracy and the angular momentum coupling, generating a complex manifold of closely spaced electronic states and in governing the nature of the chemical bonding [2]. Moreover, the bonding behavior of one valence electron atoms, such as hydrogen and lithium, at different configurations with a transition-metal element provide valuable insight into orbital hybridization effects and the balance between ionic, covalent, and dispersion interaction character of the lowest-lying states.

Furthermore, these molecules of open shells relating to the ground states and of sizable dipole moments are considered promising candidates for ultracold and quantum fields [3]. In addition, in astrophysics, transition-metal lithides contribute to the molecular opacity in cool stars and brown dwarfs [4]. Precisely, lithium bearing molecules are important in stellar and substellar atmosphere models as they can influence radiative transfer and emergent spectra in low temperature as well as the infrared opacity of the cool brown dwarf atmosphere [5].

Despite the increasing number of spectroscopic and theoretical studies conducted over recent decades, several transition-metal alkali diatomic molecules, including ScLi and YLi, remain partially or entirely unexplored, both experimentally and theoretically. A detailed theoretical characterization of the electronic structure and spectroscopic properties of these molecules is therefore expected to contribute to providing a better understanding of the catalytic processes, chemical reaction dynamics, and astrophysical spectroscopy [6,7].

In the present work, we report a systematic ab initio investigation of diatomic molecules formed by scandium and yttrium atoms interacting with the lithium atom, with the aim of characterizing their lowest-lying electronic structure. For the YLi molecule, a comprehensive theoretical description of the singlet and triplet electronic states lying below 11,622 $cm^{-1}$ has been obtained using the multireference configuration interaction method, including single and double excitations (MRCI-SD) [8,9]. For the first time, a total of 25 electronic states of YLi are calculated, and their potential energy curves (PECs), spectroscopic constants, and relative energies at equilibrium with respect to the ground state $X^1\Sigma^+$ are reported. In addition, spin–orbit coupling (SOC) calculations have been applied for the lowest electronic states of YLi to assess their effects on the electronic structure. A major challenge in the theoretical investigation of YLi lies in the absence of any experimental spectroscopic data, as this molecule has not yet been observed. Consequently, an additional objective of this study is to provide reliable estimation of the most intense electronic transition bands in the visible and near-infrared spectral regions. These computations are expected to serve as a guide for future experimental efforts aimed at the detection and identification of YLi electronic states.

For the ScLi molecule, only a limited number of theoretical studies are available, which provide spectroscopic information mainly for the ground state $a^3\Delta$ and for a few low-lying excited states below 10,309 $cm^{-1}$ [10–14]. In the present work, we extend these previous investigations by performing MRCI-SD calculations to explore a larger set of electronic states of ScLi up to 15,515 $cm^{-1}$. The potential energy curves of all computed states are reported, along with the permanent dipole moment (PDM) functions for the lowest electronic states over an internuclear distance range of 2.0–6.3 Å. Energies at equilibrium $T_e$, spectroscopic constants, and transition dipole moments (TDMs) between interacting electronic states are also determined, providing a comprehensive description of the electronic and spectroscopic properties of ScLi.

## 2. Computational Approach

For ScLi and YLi, the optimization of theoretical energies of the electronic states at different bond lengths has been obtained by performing ab initio calculations using the quantum chemistry software MOLPRO (Version 2015.1) [15,16]. The methods of the state-average-complete active space self-consistent field (SA-CASSCF) followed by MRCI including Davidson correction (MRCI + Q) have been employed for these calculations with reference configurations of single and double excitations. For Sc atom, we decided to employ the same basis set used in the calculations of ScH molecule [1], the correlation consistent polarized Valence Triple-ζ aug-cc-PVTZ basis set of (21s,17p, 9d, 3f, 2g) contracted to (8s,7p, 5d, 3f, 2g) [17]. For the Li atom, the correlation consistent polarized Valence Triple-ζ aug-cc-PVTZ basis set of (12s, 6p, 3d, 2f) contracted to (5s, 4p, 3d, 2f) has been chosen [18]. Consequently, in the ScLi computational work, a total of 24 electrons have been considered in the valence space. First, 12 electrons of the inner doubly occupied orbitals $1s^2$ $2s^2$ $2p^6$ of Sc and $1s^2$ of Li have been frozen in the core configuration at the MRCI calculations

 https://doi.org/10.3390/computation14010014

level. Then, the twelve remaining electrons in $3s^2$ $3p^6$ $4s^2$ $3d^1$ of Sc and $2s^1$ of Li have been placed as free electrons in the core–valence correlations through single and double excitations. At the CASSCF level, we included 15 outermost orbitals. The active space in the irreducible representation [a1, b1, b2, a2] consisted of 4σ [Sc: 3d0, 4s, 4pz, Li: 2s], 2π [Sc: 4p±1, 3d±1], and 1δ [Sc: 3d±2]. For the Y atom, the pseudopotential-based correlation consistent polarized Valence Triple-ζ basis set cc-pVTZ-PP of (10s, 9p, 8d, 2f, 1g) contracted to (5s, 5p, 4d, 2f, 1g) has been selected for the calculations [19]. Twenty-eight electrons have been frozen in this effective core potential (ECP28MDF) and the remaining eleven valence electrons of yttrium on the outer $4s^2$, $4p^6$, $4d^1$, $5s^2$ shells have been utilized in the calculations. To obtain accurate spectroscopic constants and spin–orbit coupling (SOC) values, it is essential to employ an appropriate treatment of both core–valence correlation and relativistic effects. Accordingly, the ECP28 effective core potential was adopted, which inherently accounts for scalar relativistic effects through its pseudopotential formulation. In addition, the explicit treatment of the $4s^2$ and $4p^6$ orbitals as semicore states, together with the valence 4d and 5s electrons, provides an improved description of the correlation space and a more reliable representation of core–valence interactions. Consequently, a total of 14 electrons have been considered in the valence space of the YLi molecule. Also, 2 electrons of the inner doubly occupied orbitals $1s^2$ of Li have been frozen in the core configuration in the MRCI calculations and 15 outermost orbitals have been included in the CASSCF step. The 12 remaining electrons in $4s^2$ $4p^6$ $5s^2 4d^1$ of Y and $2s^1$ of Li have been considered for the core–valence correlations through single and double excitations. In both ScF and CI approaches, the definition of state symmetries in the point group $C_{2v}$, due to the limitation of Molpro, is shaped with the four irreducible representations: a1, b1, b2, and a2. The active space in the irreducible representation [a1, b1, b2, a2] consists of 4σ [Y: 4d0, 5s, 5pz, Li: 2s], 2π [Y: 5p±1, 4d±1] and 1δ [Y: 4d±2]. Also, the relativistic effects have been considered in the Y atom through the ECP28MDF. This effect is included to calculate the spin–orbit eigenstates in YLi molecule by using the Breit–Pauli operator, when diagonalizing the total matrix of electronic Hamiltonian with the Hamiltonian of the spin–orbit coupling.

Finally, in the calculations of both ScLi and YLi, the ground state has been taken as the origin reference state. Potential energy curves for these molecules have been constructed as a function of the internuclear distance R following the Dunham analysis [20]. Spectroscopic constants and values of energies at equilibrium have been deduced from the polynomial fitting of order six of the PECs.

## 3. Results and Discussion

Throughout the MRCI calculations for both ScLi and YLi, the energy at equilibrium and spectroscopic constants ($R_e$, $\omega_e$ and $\omega_e\chi_e$) have been obtained from a Morse potential fit taking a few points in the vicinity of the minima of the potential energy. The potential energies for all the obtained singlet and triplet electronic states have been displayed over internuclear distances around the equilibrium and up to the dissociation with a spacing interval of 0.01 Å.

A- ScLi electronic states

37 singlet and triplet states of ScLi correlating to the lowest dissociation channels which are presented in Table 1, have been calculated. Spectroscopic constants and internuclear distances of all triplet and singlet states situated below 15,515 $cm^{-1}$ have been calculated and listed in Table 2 and Table 3, respectively, which also include a comparison with other available theoretical values. As seen in these tables, the internuclear distance and the vibrational harmonic frequency $\omega_e$ are likely similar in MRCI and in MRCI + Q calculations, while the energy varies widely between the two methods, especially for the first lowest

 https://doi.org/10.3390/computation14010014

electronic states. In this study, the ground state is found to be $a^3\Delta$ which agrees with several previous investigations [10–13], except for the work of Wang and Wu, who found $(1)^3\Sigma^-$ as the ground state by performing DFT B3LYP calculations [14]. In our work, the first excited state $(1)^3\Pi$ is located very close to the ground state at $T_e$ = 273 $cm^{-1}$ (MRCI). In ScLi, the spin–orbit constant is expected to be small and less than 90 $cm^{-1}$. This keeps the assumption that the ground state is one of the components $\Omega$ = 1, 2 or 3 of $(1)^3\Delta$ and not any of the $(1)^3\Pi$ components.

**Table 1.** The dissociation limits and the corresponding molecular states of ScLi.

| Atomic States of Sc and Li | Molecular States of ScLi |
|---|---|
| $Sc(^2D) + Li(^2S)$ | $(1)^{3,1}\Delta, (1)^{3,1}\Pi, (1)^{3,1}\Sigma^+$ |
| $Sc(^2D) + Li(^2P)$ | $(1)^{3,1}\Phi, (2)^{3,1}\Delta, (3)^{3,1}\Pi, (2)^{3,1}\Sigma^+, (1)^{3,1}\Sigma^-$ |
| $Sc^+(^3D) + Li^-(^1S)$ | $(1)^{3,1}\Delta, (1)^{3,1}\Pi, (1)^{3,1}\Sigma^+$ |
| $Sc^+(^1D) + Li^-(^1S)$ | $(1)^1\Delta, (1)^1\Pi, (1)^1\Sigma^+$ |
| $Sc(^4F) + Li(^2S)$ | $(1)^{5,3}\Phi, (1)^{5,3}\Delta, (1)^{5,3}\Pi, (1)^{5,3}\Sigma^+, (1)^{5,3}\Sigma^-$ |
| $Sc(^2F) + Li(^2S)$ | $(1)^{3,1}\Phi, (1)^{3,1}\Delta, (1)^{3,1}\Pi, (1)^{3,1}\Sigma^+, (1)^{3,1}\Sigma^-$ |

**Table 2.** Spectroscopic constants for triplet states of ScLi. (a) Our MRCI calculated values; ($a^+$) Our MRCI + Q calculated values; * perturbed values due to avoided crossing; (b) MRCI values from reference [2], (c) MRCI/pseudopotential values from reference [10], (d) and (e) MRCI and ACPF values from [12], (f) values from [13], (g) values from [14].

| State | Ref. | $R_e$ (Å) | $T_e$ ($cm^{-1}$) | $\omega_e$ ($cm^{-1}$) | $\omega_e\chi_e$ ($cm^{-1}$) | $D_e$ ($cm^{-1}$) | $\mu_e$ (D) |
|---|---|---|---|---|---|---|---|
| $(1)^3\Delta$ | a | 3.231 | 0 | 238 | 3.2 | 2267 | 2.41 |
| | $a^+$ | 3.224 | 0 | 230 | 3.1 | | |
| | b | 3.282 | 0 | --- | --- | | |
| | c | 3.493 | 0 | --- | --- | | |
| | d | 3.305 | 0 | 210 | --- | | |
| | e | 3.282 | 0 | 216 | --- | 2460 | |
| | f | 3.238 | 0 | 223 | --- | 3153 | 1.83 |
| $(1)^3\Pi$ | a | 3.162 | 273 | 242 | 3.3 | 2031 | 2.36 |
| | $a^+$ | 3.153 | 219 | 234 | 3.3 | | |
| | f | 3.179 | 83 | 231 | --- | 3099 | 2.31 |
| $(1)^3\Sigma^+$ | a | 3.190 | 636 | 228 | 3.2 | 1654 | 2.39 |
| | $a^+$ | 3.184 | 517 | 218 | 3.4 | | |
| | f | 3.203 | 525 | 197 | --- | 2662 | 2.11 |
| $(1)^3\Sigma^-$ | a | 2.646 | 4048 | 334 | 1.6 | 13,080 | 1.12 |
| | $a^+$ | 2.634 | 2600 | 334 | 1.4 | | |
| | f | 2.668 | 2637 | 330 | --- | 15,352 | 1.25 |
| | g | 2.622 | 0 | 326 | --- | | |
| $(2)^3\Pi$ | a | 2.784 | 5023 | 351 | 2.3 | 12,073 | 0.53 |
| | $a^+$ | 2.791 | 4046 | 371 | 2.2 | | |
| | f | 2.792 | 4033 | 368 | --- | 13,638 | 1.88 |
| $(1)^3\Phi$ | a | 2.806 | 5593 | 327 | 3.0 | 11,524 | 0.30 |
| | $a^+$ | 2.803 | 4871 | 325 | 2.0 | | |
| | f | 2.861 | 4931 | 318 | --- | 12,804 | 1.70 |
| $(2)^3\Delta$ | a | 2.867 | 6642 | 324 | 1.8 | 10,521 | 2.26 |
| | $a^+$ | 2.861 | 6282 | 322 | 1.7 | | |
| | f | 2.883 | 5733 | 304 | --- | 12,030 | 3.05 |
| $(3)^3\Pi$ | a | 2.835 | 6829 | 321 | 2.4 | 10,306 | 0.05 |
| | $a^+$ | 2.824 | 5970 | 325 | 2.0 | | |
| $(2)^3\Sigma^+$ | a | 2.889 | 7659 | 317 | 2.0 | 9465 | 1.65 |
| | $a^+$ | 2.883 | 7216 | 315 | 1.9 | | |
| | f | 2.924 | 8423 | 296 | --- | 9533 | 2.26 |


https://doi.org/10.3390/computation14010014

**Table 2.** *Cont.*

| State | Ref. | $R_e$ (Å) | $T_e$ ($cm^{-1}$) | $\omega_e$ ($cm^{-1}$) | $\omega_e\chi_e$ ($cm^{-1}$) | $D_e$ ($cm^{-1}$) | $\mu_e$ (D) |
|---|---|---|---|---|---|---|---|
| $(3)^3\Delta$ | a | 2.924 | 8611 | 315 | 1.5 | 8476 | 5.59 |
| | $a^+$ | 2.920 | 7451 | 314 | 1.4 | | |
| | f | 2.910 | 6792 | 310 | --- | 11,047 | 2.49 |
| $(4)^3\Pi$ | a | 2.944 | 9691 | 314 | 2.6 | 7461 | 6.40 |
| | $a^+$ | 2.956 | 8535 | 330 | 2.0 | | |
| $(2)^3\Phi$ | a | 2.978 | 9861 | 348 | 2.4 | 22,779 | 6.86 |
| | $a^+$ | 2.992 | 8637 | 317 | 2.2 | | |
| $(2)^3\Sigma^-$ | a | 2.953 | 10,005 | 334 | 1.8 | 22,423 | 7.62 |
| | $a^+$ | 2.956 | 8881 | 309 | 2.0 | | |
| $(3)^3\Sigma^+$ | a | 3.294 | 11,877 | 288 | 1.4 | 17,121 | 3.89 |
| | $a^+$ | 3.315 | 10,726 | 230 | 1.4 | | |
| $(5)^3\Pi$ | a * | 3.284 | 12,123 | 214 | --- | 16,958 | 5.31 |
| | $a^+$ * | 3.281 | 10,968 | 210 | --- | | |
| $(4)^3\Delta$ | a | 3.245 | 12,128 | 210 | 2.3 | 5047 | 0.99 |
| | $a^+$ | 3.242 | 10,851 | 204 | 2.2 | | |
| $(6)^3\Pi$ | a | 3.039 | 13,282 | 364 | 2.4 | 19,463 | 4.45 |
| | $a^+$ | 3.034 | 12,149 | 349 | 2.5 | | |
| $(3)^3\Sigma^-$ | a | 2.967 | 14,333 | 331 | 2.0 | 18,389 | 4.42 |
| | $a^+$ | 2.954 | 13,245 | 307 | 2.1 | | |

**Table 3.** Spectroscopic constants for singlet states of ScLi. (a) Our MRCI calculated values; ($a^+$) Our MRCI + Q calculated values; * Perturbed values due to avoided crossing; (f) values from reference [13].

| State | Ref. | $R_e$ (Å) | $T_e$ ($cm^{-1}$) | $\omega_e$ ($cm^{-1}$) | $\omega_e\chi_e$ ($cm^{-1}$) | $D_e$ ($cm^{-1}$) | $\mu_e$ (D) |
|---|---|---|---|---|---|---|---|
| $(1)^1\Delta$ | a | 3.220 | 524 | 233 | 3.4 | 1736 | 3.48 |
| | $a^+$ | 3.214 | 154 | 228 | 3.1 | | |
| | f | 3.201 | 417 | 213 | --- | 2815 | 0.61 |
| $(1)^1\Sigma^+$ | a | 3.168 | 621 | 242 | 1.7 | 1652 | 0.76 |
| | $a^+$ | 3.162 | 111 | 227 | 2.2 | | |
| | f | 3.226 | 361 | 238 | --- | 2878 | 3.46 |
| $(1)^1\Pi$ | a | 3.276 | 1645 | 224 | 4.2 | 617 | 1.04 |
| | $a^+$ | 3.264 | 1455 | 197 | 4.3 | | |
| | f | 3.309 | 1269 | 178 | --- | 1969 | 0.81 |
| $(2)^1\Pi$ | a | 2.820 | 4976 | 352 | 3.1 | 12,072 | 0.14 |
| | $a^+$ | 2.813 | 3904 | 368 | 3.5 | | |
| | f | 2.853 | 3957 | 326 | --- | 13,964 | 1.52 |
| $(1)^1\Sigma^-$ | a | 2.846 | 5170 | 326 | 1.8 | 11,900 | 2.44 |
| | $a^+$ | 2.834 | 4324 | 331 | 1.7 | | |
| | f | 2.868 | 3947 | 317 | --- | 13,909 | 3.63 |
| $(2)^1\Delta$ | a | 2.788 | 6675 | 324 | 2.0 | 10,401 | 2.03 |
| | $a^+$ | 2.782 | 5527 | 343 | 2.2 | | |
| | f | 2.842 | 5607 | 317 | --- | 12,251 | 0.38 |
| $(2)^1\Sigma^+$ | a | 2.755 | 8270 | 309 | 1.9 | 8847 | 1.70 |
| | $a^+$ | 2.742 | 7090 | 322 | 1.8 | | |
| | f | --- | --- | --- | --- | | |
| $(1)^1\Phi$ | a | 2.885 | 8740 | 305 | 1.8 | 8384 | 0.89 |
| | $a^+$ | 2.864 | 7894 | 303 | 1.4 | | |
| | f | 2.880 | 7874 | 310 | --- | 10,196 | 0.03 |
| $(3)^1\Pi$ | a | 2.857 | 8995 | 322 | 2.5 | 8109 | 1.42 |
| | $a^+$ | 2.844 | 8040 | 326 | 2.5 | | |
| | f | 2.926 | 7567 | 302 | --- | 10,468 | 0.64 |
| $(3)^1\Delta$ | a | 2.924 | 11,239 | 319 | 3.7 | 5914 | 5.74 |
| | $a^+$ | 2.929 | 9876 | 306 | 3.0 | | |



https://doi.org/10.3390/computation14010014

Table 3. *Cont.*

| State | Ref. | $R_e$ (Å) | $T_e$ ($cm^{-1}$) | $\omega_e$ ($cm^{-1}$) | $\omega_e\chi_e$ ($cm^{-1}$) | $D_e$ ($cm^{-1}$) | $\mu_e$ (D) |
|---|---|---|---|---|---|---|---|
| **$(4)^1\Pi$** | a | 2.938 | 12,030 | 297 | 3.8 | 5125 | 3.81 |
| | $a^+$ | 2.932 | 10,725 | 304 | 3.2 | | |
| **$(3)^1\Sigma^+$** | a * | 2.776 | 12,335 | --- | --- | 5177 | 4.14 |
| | $a^+$ * | 2.864 | 10,536 | --- | --- | | |
| | f | 3.282 | 10,309 | 247 | --- | 7756 | 2.62 |
| **$(4)^1\Sigma^+$** | a * | 3.044 | 12,416 | 371 | 3.7 | 16,761 | 4.98 |
| | $a^+$ * | 3.048 | 10,777 | 382 | 4.3 | | |
| **$(4)^1\Delta$** | a | 3.166 | 12,511 | 279 | 0.9 | 20,264 | 6.28 |
| | $a^+$ | 3.154 | 10,981 | 265 | 1.8 | | |
| **$(5)^1\Pi$** | a | 3.134 | 13,653 | 306 | 1.6 | 15,494 | 0.71 |
| | $a^+$ | 3.165 | 12,616 | 277 | 2.0 | | |
| **$(5)^1\Sigma^+$** | a | 3.014 | 14,985 | 325 | 1.1 | 14,155 | 7.04 |
| | $a^+$ | 3.013 | 13,827 | 323 | 1.4 | | |
| **$(5)^1\Delta$** | a | 3.026 | 15,123 | 352 | 2.1 | 17,292 | 6.68 |
| | $a^+$ | 3.014 | 14,337 | 328 | 2.4 | | |
| **$(6)^1\Pi$** | a | 3.014 | 15,222 | 338 | 2.2 | 17,457 | 7.14 |
| | $a^+$ | 3.012 | 14,261 | 332 | 3.1 | | |
| **$(2)^1\Phi$** | a | 2.979 | 15,515 | 332 | 2.1 | 17,272 | 7.12 |
| | $a^+$ | 2.978 | 14,530 | 325 | 1.9 | | |

The PECs of all the calculated electronic states are displayed in Figure 1 and Figure 2, respectively. As seen, the lowest excited states $(1)^{1,3}\Delta$, $(1)^{1,3}\Pi$, $(1)\ ^{1,3}\Sigma^+$ of the first limit of dissociation Sc($^2$D) + Li($^2$S) are found to be less bounded compared to the other excited states. Moreover, these lowest electronic states have longer bond lengths $R_e$ and the lowest vibration harmonic frequency $\omega_e$. Again, due to the small dissociation energy, the well of these lowest states are not deep, which limits them to a few vibrational levels. In these PECs, due to the states interaction, several avoided crossings have been obtained between states of the same symmetry and multiplicity of spin at different internuclear distances (Figures 3–9). Most of these avoided crossings did not affect our theoretical calculations of the spectroscopic parameters except the crossing between $(3)^1\Sigma^+$ and $(4)^1\Sigma^+$ for which the deformation is in the vicinity of the equilibrium position at $R_e$ = 3.04 Å. For the $(3)^1\Sigma^+$, the obtained hump as a double well is not due to a metastable state but due to the avoided crossing. The crossing between $(3)^1\Delta$ and $(4)^1\Delta$ at $R_e$ = 3.38 Å also slightly affected the calculated constants for $(4)^1\Delta$, (Figure 6).

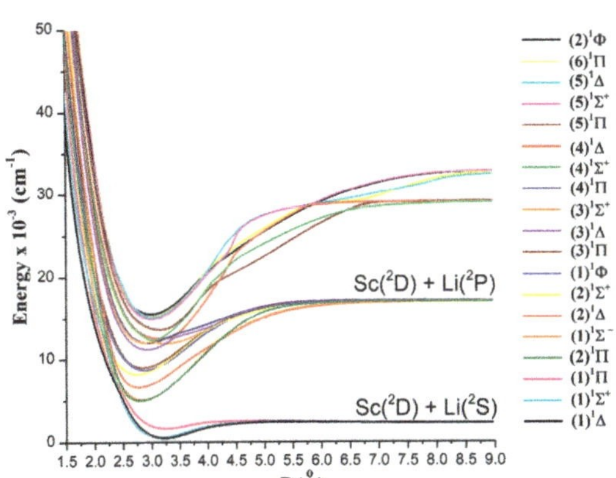


**Figure 1.** Potential energy curves (MRCI) for the low-lying singlet electronic states of ScLi.


https://doi.org/10.3390/computation14010014

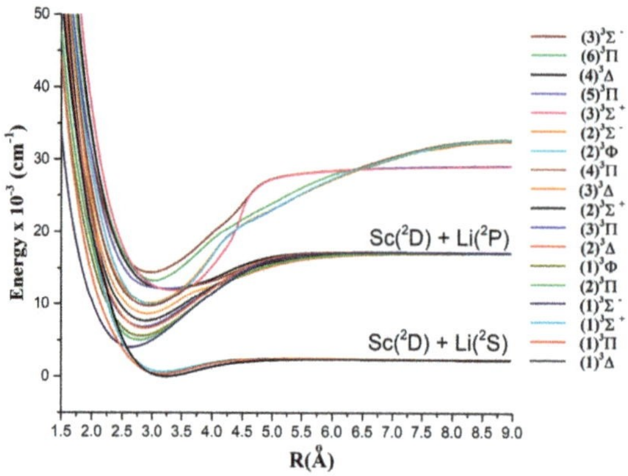


**Figure 2.** Potential energy curves (MRCI) for the low-lying triplet electronic states of ScLi.

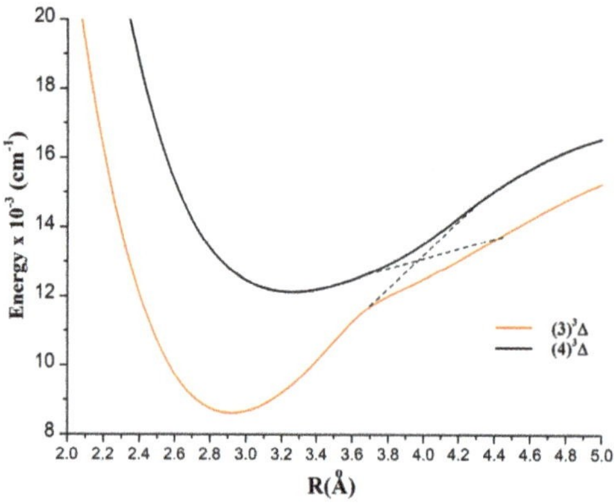


**Figure 3.** Avoided crossing between the (3)$^3\Delta$ and (4)$^3\Delta$ states of ScLi.

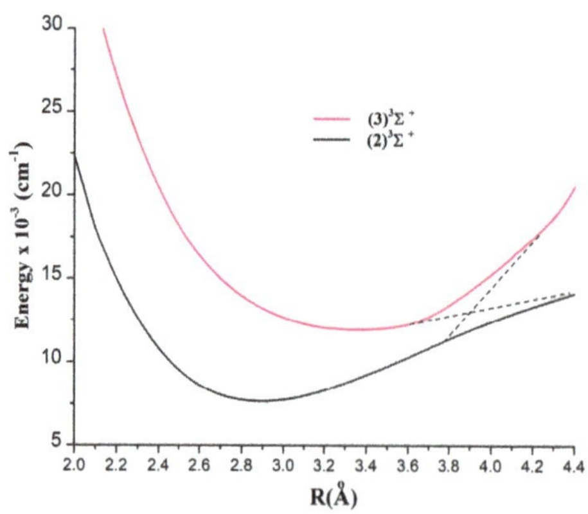


**Figure 4.** Avoided crossing between the (2)$^3\Sigma^+$ and (3)$^3\Sigma^+$ states of ScLi.

Additionally, the permanent dipole moments of the lowest states as a function of the bond length have been plotted in Figure 10. As seen, the ionic behavior is almost present in these states at lower bond distances near the equilibrium. However, these states encountered a monotonically decrease in their ionicity to approach zero at bond lengths around 5.5 Å to reach a separation into two neutral elements. Some negative values for several states have been obtained around 2.0 Å due to the molecular polarity of $Sc^+Li^-$.


https://doi.org/10.3390/computation14010014

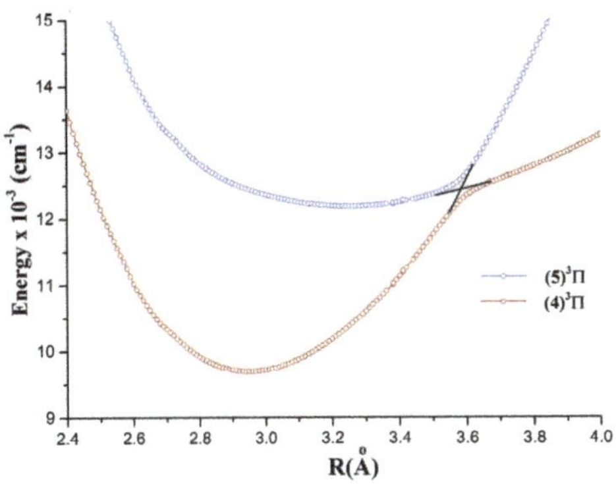


Figure 5. Avoided crossing (MRCI) between the $(4)^3\Pi$ and $(5)^3\Pi$ states of ScLi.

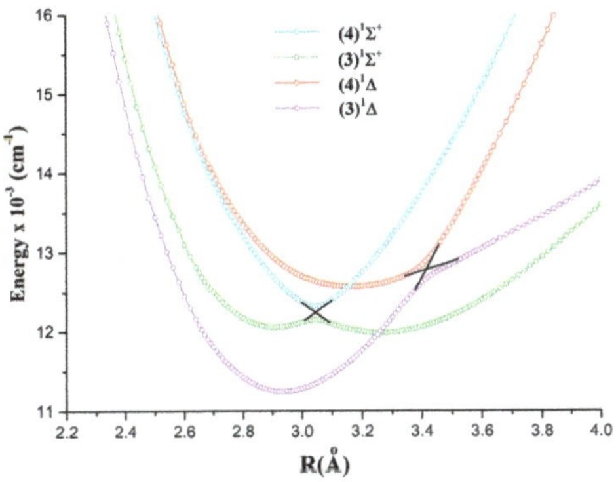


Figure 6. Avoided crossing (MRCI) between the $(3)^1\Delta$ and $(4)^1\Delta$ states and between the $(3)^1\Sigma^+$ and $(4)^1\Sigma^+$ states of ScLi.

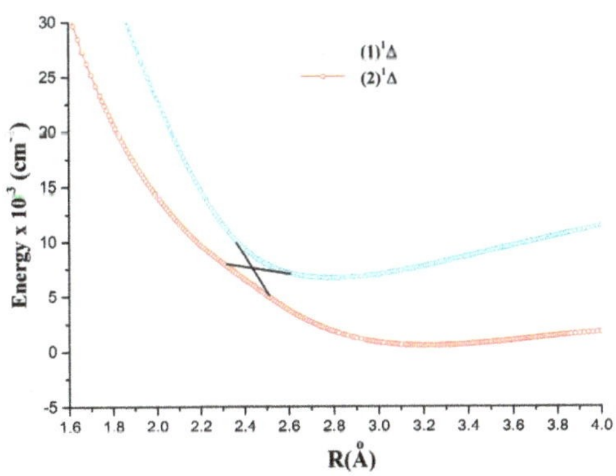


Figure 7. Avoided crossing (MRCI) between the $(1)^1\Delta$ and $(2)^1\Delta$ states of ScLi.

Also, in order to inquire about the possible observed transition bands in ScLi, the allowed dipole transition moments TDMs between triplet states are shown in Figures 11–14 and between singlet states are illustrated in Figures 15–18. Some electronic transitions exhibited remarkable hump of higher values of TDMs due to the perturbation effect in their related electronic states and the avoided crossing during interchanges of configurations.



https://doi.org/10.3390/computation14010014

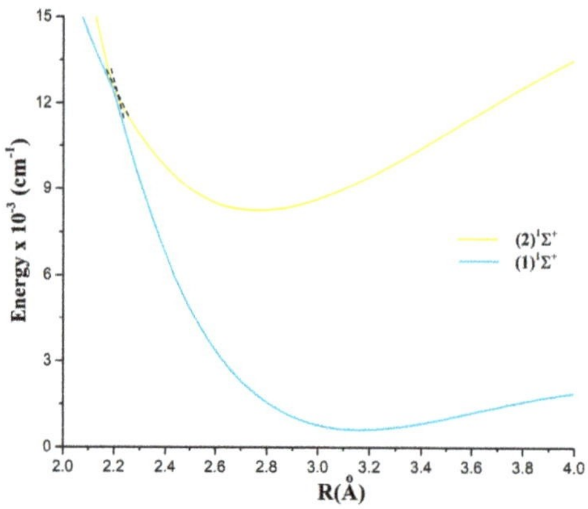


**Figure 8.** Avoided crossing (MRCI) between the $(1)^1\Sigma^+$ and $(2)^1\Sigma^+$ states of ScLi.

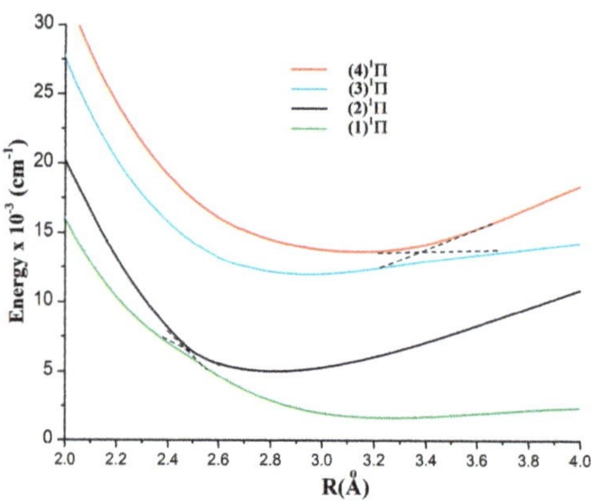


**Figure 9.** Avoided crossing (MRCI) between the $(1)^1\Pi$ and $(2)^1\Pi$ and between $(3)^1\Pi$ and $(4)^1\Pi$ states of ScLi.

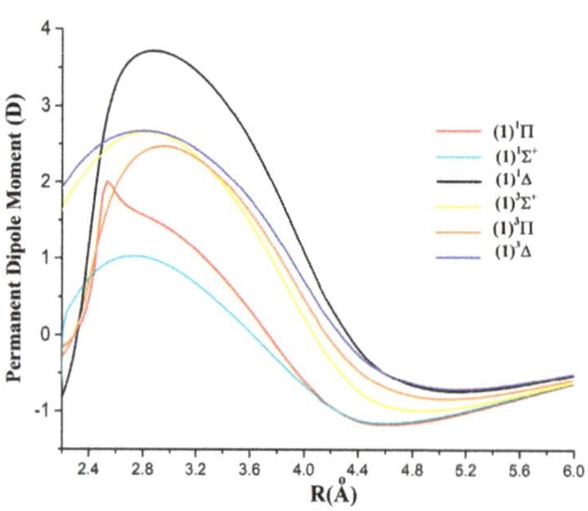


**Figure 10.** Permanent dipole moments (Debye) of the six lowest states of ScLi.

B- YLi electronic states

Our present computational work on YLi focuses on the set of low-lying singlet and triplet states that correlate with the first three lowest dissociation limits of the YLi molecule. The lowest correlation of molecular electronic states of YLi with their corresponding atoms

 https://doi.org/10.3390/computation14010014

is represented in Table 4. A total of 25 electronic states have been computed in this work. These states, which are ionic in the vicinity of the minimum equilibrium position, correlated with the neutral asymptotes of Y($^2$D) + Li($^2$S), Y($^2$D) + Li($^2$P), and Y($^2$P) + Li($^2$S). However, some of the other remaining states related to these dissociation channels are not reported in this study as they are higher in energy or have a multiplicity higher than a triplet.

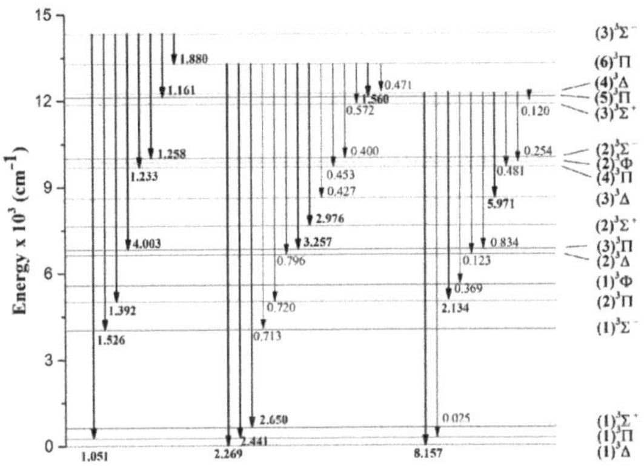


**Figure 11.** The transition dipole moments (Debye) for ScLi triplet states at $R_e$ = 3.231 Å.

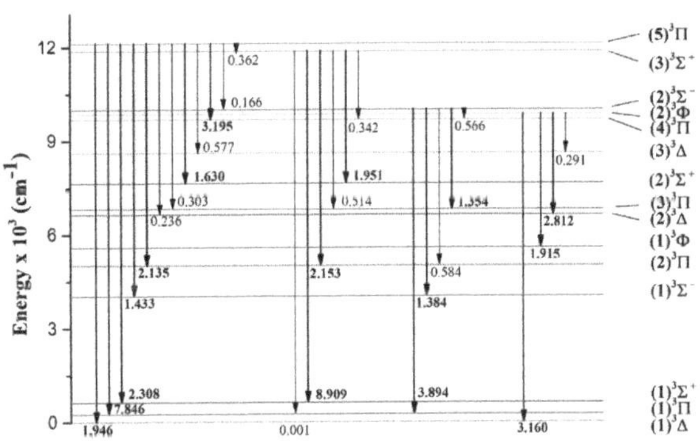


**Figure 12.** The transition dipole moments (Debye) for ScLi triplet states at $R_e$ = 3.231 Å. (cont.).

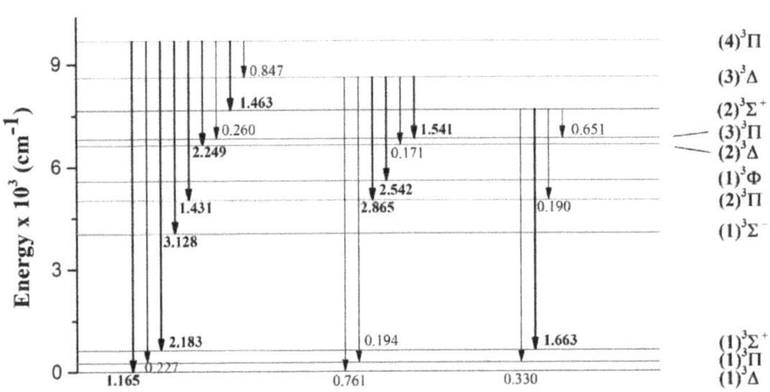


**Figure 13.** The transition dipole moments (Debye) for ScLi triplet states at $R_e$ = 3.231 Å. (cont.).

 https://doi.org/10.3390/computation14010014

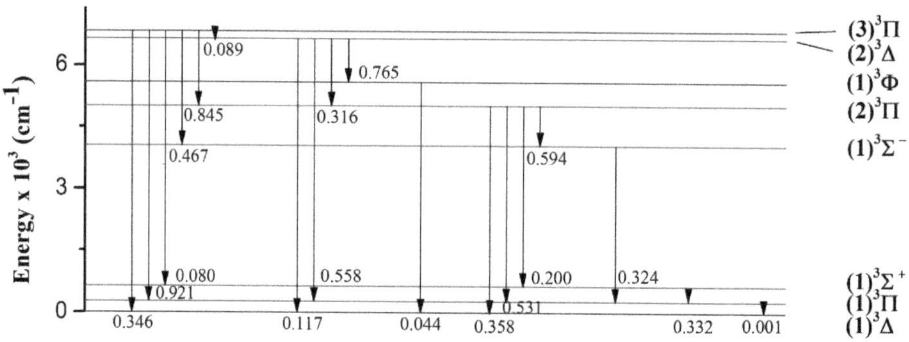


**Figure 14.** The transition dipole moments (Debye) for ScLi triplet states at $R_e$ = 3.231 Å. (cont.).

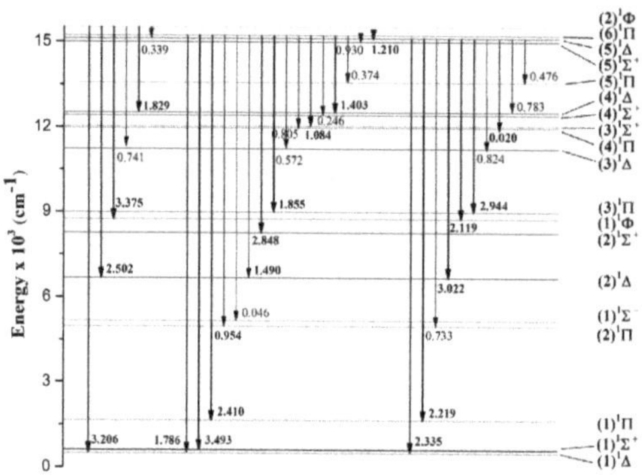

**Figure 15.** The transition dipole moments (Debye) for ScLi singlet states at $R_e$ = 3.231 Å.

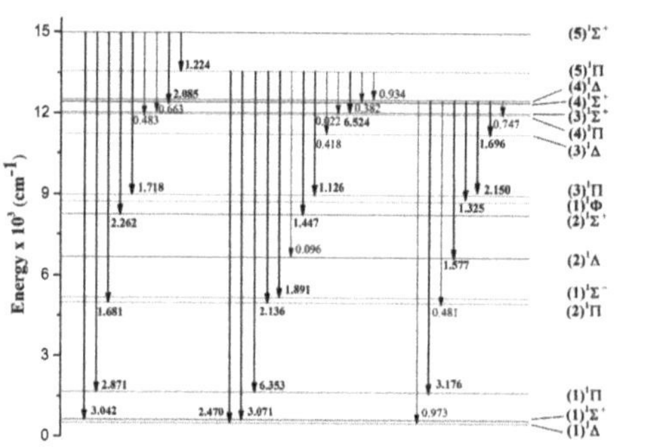

**Figure 16.** The transition dipole moments (Debye) for ScLi singlet states at $R_e$ = 3.231 Å. (cont.).

**Table 4.** The dissociation Limits and the corresponding molecular states of YLi.

| Atomic States of Y and Li | Molecular States of YLi |
|---|---|
| $Y(^2D) + Li(^2S)$ | $(1)^{3,1}\Delta$, $(1)^{3,1}\Pi$, $(1)^{3,1}\Sigma^+$ |
| $Y(^2P) + Li(^2S)$ | $(3)^{3,1}\Pi$, $(1)^{3,1}\Sigma^+$, |
| $Y(^2D) + Li(^2P)$ | $(1)^{3,1}\Phi$, $(2)^{3,1}\Delta$, $(3)^{3,1}\Pi$, $(2)^{3,1}\Sigma^+$, $(1)^{3,1}\Sigma^-$ |
| $Y(^4F) + Li(^2S)$ | $(1)^{5,3}\Phi$, $(1)^{5,3}\Delta$, $(1)^{5,3}\Pi$, $(1)^{5,3}\Sigma^+$, $(1)^{5,3}\Sigma^-$ |
| $Y^+(^1S) + Li^-(^1S)$ | $(1)^1\Sigma^+$ |
| $Y^+(^3D) + Li^-(^1S)$ | $(1)^{3,1}\Delta$, $(1)^{3,1}\Pi$, $(1)^{3,1}\Sigma^+$ |


https://doi.org/10.3390/computation14010014

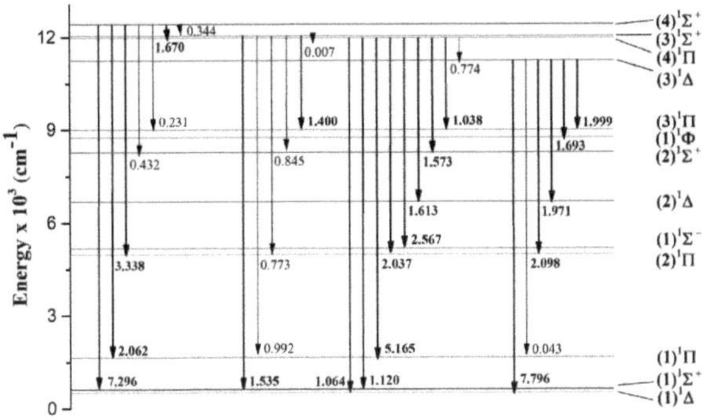

**Figure 17.** The transition dipole moments (Debye) for ScLi singlet states at $R_e$ = 3.231 Å. (cont.).

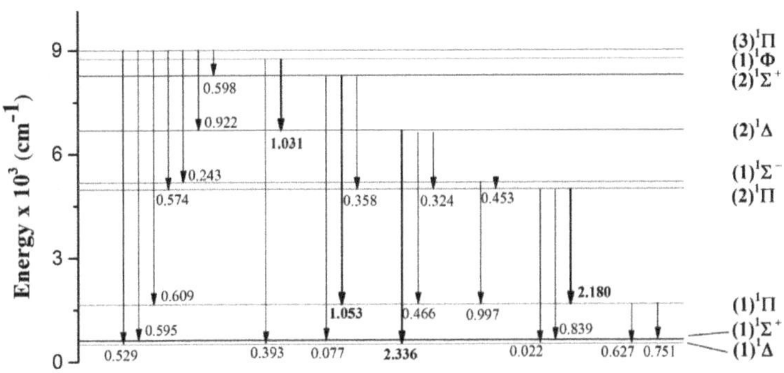

**Figure 18.** The transition dipole moments (Debye) for ScLi singlet states at $R_e$ = 3.231 Å. (cont.).

The results obtained from MRCI and those with Davidson correction (MRCI +Q), which encompass the spectroscopic constants, internuclear distances and the energy at equilibrium $T_e$ referred to zero energy level for the ground state are summarized in Table 5 for singlet states and Table 6 for triplet states. The ground state is found to be $X^1\Sigma^+$ and it dissociates into the lowest asymptote $Y(^2D) + Li(^2S)$. As seen in these tables, the results obtained from MRCI and those with (MRCI + Q) [21,22] are likely homogenous.

Additionally, the first six electronic states, which correlated to the first dissociation channel, all have vibrational harmonic frequencies lower than those of the other higher states and their bond length are shifted to the right. Also, these states are found to be of the same bonding character, as they are all less bonded (Figure 19). These lowest states have similar bonding behavior to those corresponding states described in ScLi (Figure 10) and in lithium dimer molecules [23]. As seen, the $(1)^3\Pi$ is found to be the first excited state lying at 1524 $cm^{-1}$ from the ground state and the $(1)^3\Delta$ is lying at 1843 $cm^{-1}$, close to $(1)^3\Pi$. To our knowledge, for YLi, there are no previous calculations or experiments available to be able to assess the molecular properties and the assignment of the electronic states. That is why, to examine the accuracy of our obtained results, we made a comparison with the electronic structure of YH by analogy. In other words, based on similarity, it is expected to obtain the analogous lower electronic structure with a compassing in the energy when going from hydrogen to the alkali metal Li. The assignment of the ground state $(1)^1\Sigma^+$, the first lowest states $(1)^3\Pi$, $(1)^3\Delta$, $(1)^1\Pi$, states $(1)^1\Delta$, states $(1)^3\Pi$ and $(1)^3\Sigma^+$, are all supported by the same electronic picture in YH [24–26]. The potential energy curves (PECs) for the singlet and triplet electronic states of YLi are displayed in Figure 20 and Figure 21, respectively. Also, state interactions have led to several avoided crossings between states of the same symmetry and multiplicity of spin at different internuclear



https://doi.org/10.3390/computation14010014

distances (Figures 22–25). Globally, these crossings did not significantly affect the calculated spectroscopic constants.

**Table 5.** Spectroscopic constants for singlet states of YLi (first entry: MRCI; second entry MRCI + Q). (*): Fictive values due to avoided crossing.

| State | $R_e$ (Å) | $T_e$ ($cm^{-1}$) | $\omega_e$ ($cm^{-1}$) | $\omega_e\chi_e$ ($cm^{-1}$) | $D_e$ ($cm^{-1}$) | $\mu_e$ (D) |
|---|---|---|---|---|---|---|
| **$(1)^1\Sigma^+$** | 3.234 | 0 | 278 | 2.3 | | 0.59 |
| | 3.232 | 0 | 271 | 2.8 | 5541 | |
| **$(1)^1\Delta$** | 3.358 | 2687 | 219 | 2.7 | | 3.53 |
| | 3.353 | 2766 | 210 | 2.8 | 2897 | |
| **$(1)^1\Pi$** | 3.323 | 3454 | 202 | 2.6 | | 0.36 |
| | 3.327 | 3690 | 192 | 2.9 | 2103 | |
| **$(2)^1\Pi$** | 2.946 | 6181 | 330 * | 2.2 | | 1.14 |
| | 2.934 | 5672 * | 326 * | 2.0 | 10,149 | |
| **$(1)^1\Sigma^-$** | 2.965 | 6685 | 316 | 1.7 | | 2.99 |
| | 2.952 | 6358 | 317 | 1.7 | 13,344 | |
| **$(2)^1\Delta$** | 3.248 | 7325 * | 223 * | 2.1 | | 1.32 |
| | 3.233 | 6925 * | 193 * | 1.8 | 12,626 | |
| **$(2)^1\Sigma^+$** | 2.914 | 7532 * | 348 * | 2.9 | | 2.87 |
| | 2.919 | 6918 * | 360 * | 3.2 | 7871 | |
| **$(3)^1\Pi$** | 3.007 | 9529 | 302 | 1.4 | | 1.98 |
| | 3.002 | 8791 | 298 | 1.7 | 11,324 | |
| **$(3)^1\Sigma^+$** | 2.994 | 10,138 | 350 | 2.8 | | 0.07 |
| | 2.998 | 9655 | 353 | 2.9 | 10,241 | |
| **$(1)^1\Phi$** | 2.975 | 10,722 | 306 | 1.8 | | 1.29 |
| | 2.962 | 10,184 | 307 | 1.7 | 10,275 | |
| **$(3)^1\Delta$** | 3.006 | 11,759 | 309 | 2.2 | | 3.66 |
| | 2.993 | 10,815 | 309 | 2.0 | 9555 | |
| **$(4)^1\Pi$** | 3.054 | 11,622 | 311 | 2.6 | | 2.11 |
| | 3.059 | 11,143 | 302 | 2.4 | 9075 | |

**Table 6.** Spectroscopic constants for triplet states of YLi (first entry: MRCI; second entry MRCI + Q).

| State | $R_e$ (Å) | $T_e$ ($cm^{-1}$) | $\omega_e$ ($cm^{-1}$) | $\omega_e\chi_e$ ($cm^{-1}$) | $D_e$ ($cm^{-1}$) | $\mu_e$ (D) |
|---|---|---|---|---|---|---|
| **$(1)^3\Pi$** | 3.18 | 1524 | 232 | 2.2 | | 1.98 |
| | 3.16 | 1800 | 233 | 2.0 | 3940 | |
| **$(1)^3\Delta$** | 3.36 | 1843 | 229 | 2.2 | | 1.90 |
| | 3.35 | 2399 | 216 | 2.1 | 3260 | |
| **$(1)^3\Sigma^+$** | 3.29 | 2301 | 227 | 2.8 | | 2.61 |
| | 3.28 | 2761 | 222 | 3.2 | 2924 | |
| **$(1)^3\Sigma^-$** | 2.75 | 4410 | 325 | 1.3 | | 1.27 |
| | 2.72 | 3583 | 338 | 1.5 | 16,150 | |
| **$(2)^3\Pi$** | 2.97 | 6103 | 313 | 1.5 | | 1.48 |
| | 2.97 | 5925 | 309 | 1.7 | 9773 | |
| **$(1)^3\Phi$** | 2.93 | 6622 | 319 | 1.6 | | 0.23 |
| | 2.92 | 6647 | 319 | 1.9 | 13,604 | |
| **$(3)^3\Pi$** | 2.97 | 8051 | 305 | 1.5 | | 0.52 |
| | 2.95 | 7701 | 301 | 1.5 | 12,057 | |
| **$(2)^3\Delta$** | 2.99 | 8436 | 313 | 1.8 | | 2.82 |
| | 2.97 | 8653 | 310 | 1.7 | 10,995 | |
| **$(4)^3\Pi$** | 3.04 | 8902 | 343 | 2.4 | | 4.19 |
| | 3.04 | 8871 | 339 | 2.3 | 11,535 | |
| **$(2)^3\Sigma^+$** | 3.02 | 9680 | 297 | 2.1 | | 1.64 |
| | 3.01 | 9708 | 288 | 2.3 | 6037 | |
| **$(3)^3\Delta$** | 3.07 | 9837 | 305 | 1.8 | | 3.14 |
| | 3.07 | 9473 | 300 | 1.9 | 11,015 | |


https://doi.org/10.3390/computation14010014

**Table 6.** *Cont.*

| State | $R_e$ (Å) | $T_e$ ($cm^{-1}$) | $\omega_e$ ($cm^{-1}$) | $\omega_e\chi_e$ ($cm^{-1}$) | $D_e$ ($cm^{-1}$) | $\mu_e$ (D) |
|---|---|---|---|---|---|---|
| **$(2)^3\Phi$** | 3.17 | 11,136 | 297 | 1.1 | | 7.62 |
| | 3.17 | 10,780 | 282 | 1.3 | 9697 | |
| **$(2)^3\Sigma^-$** | 3.02 | 11,442 | 283 | 2.0 | | 6.75 |
| | 3.00 | 10,758 | 288 | 2.4 | --- | |

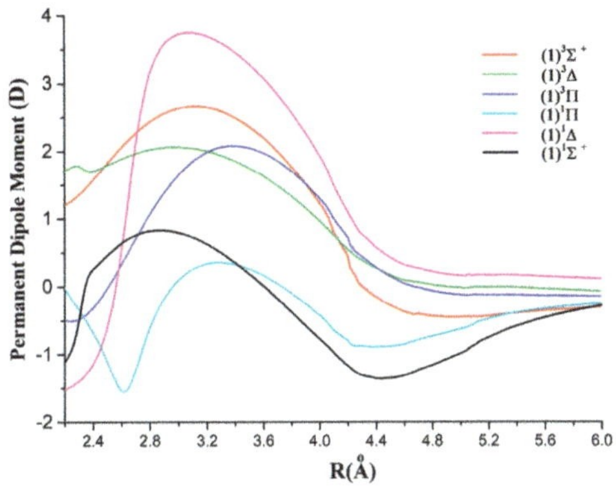


**Figure 19.** Permanent dipole moment (Debye) for the first six low lying states of YLi.

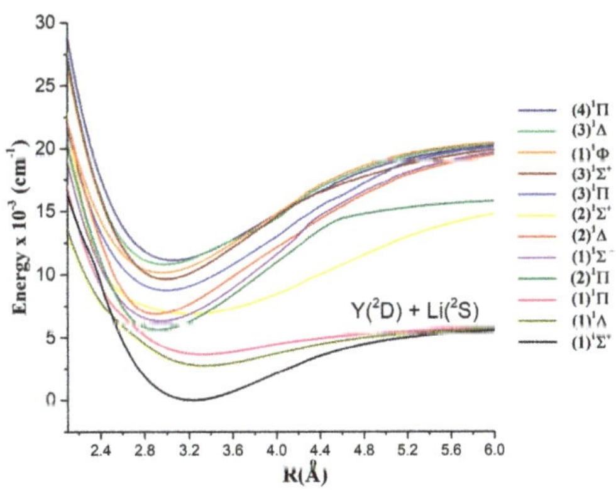


**Figure 20.** Potential energy curves (MRCI + Q) for singlet states of YLi.

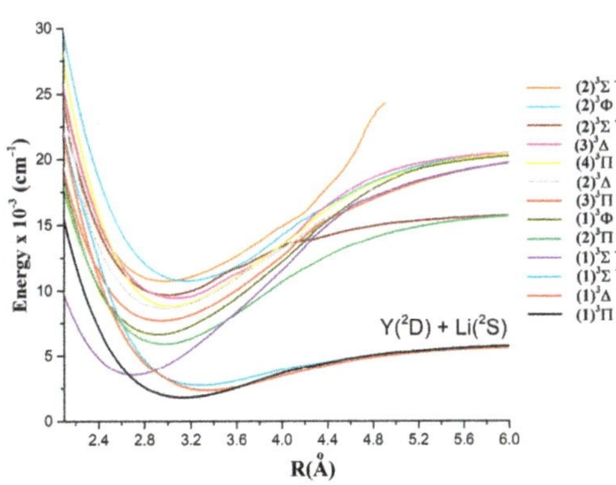


**Figure 21.** Potential energy curves (MRCI + Q) for triplet states of YLi.


https://doi.org/10.3390/computation14010014

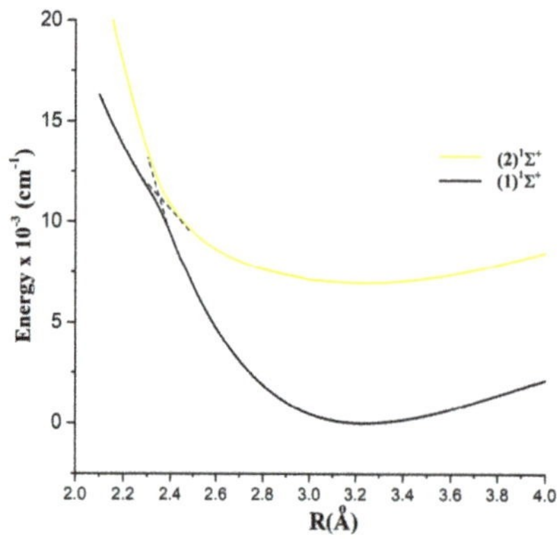


Figure 22. Avoided crossing between the $(1)^1\Sigma^+$ and $(2)^1\Sigma^+$ states of YLi.

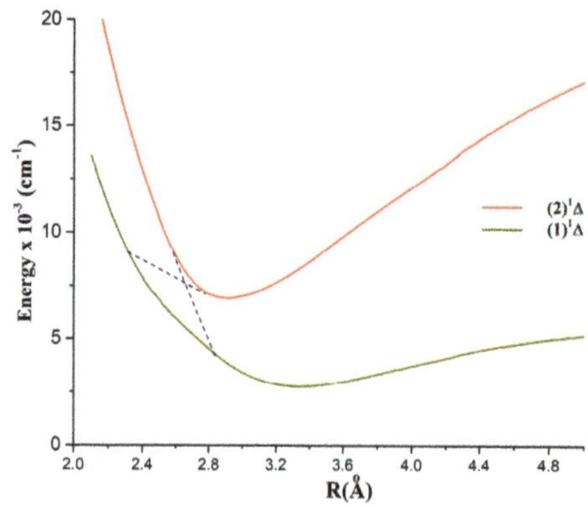


Figure 23. Avoided crossing between the $(1)^1\Delta$ and $(2)^1\Delta$ states of YLi.

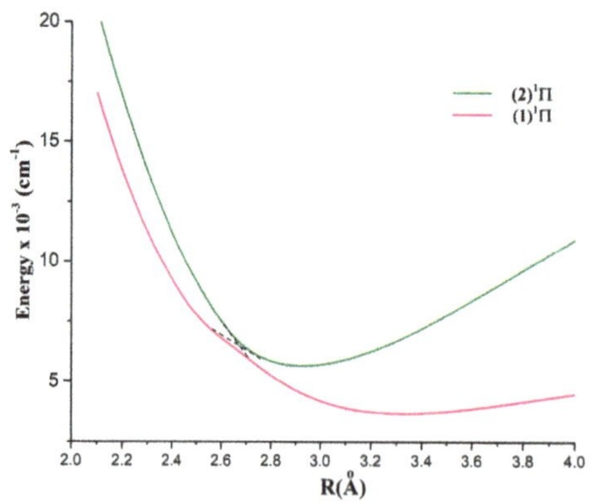


Figure 24. Avoided crossing between the $(1)^1\Pi$ and $(2)^1\Pi$ states of YLi.

From these results, the obtained permanent dipole moments PDMs of all these calculated states at their corresponding internuclear distances are reported in Table 5 and Table 6, respectively. Also, the PDMs of the six lowest states of YLi have been plotted as a function of the bond length and are shown in Figure 19. As discussed in the ScLi section, similar evolutions have been obtained for these PDMs as they are significant at shorter bond lengths below 4.0 Å and then they started to vanish clearly to tend towards zero at around 6.0 Å. Also, to point out the possible intense transition bands, the allowed


https://doi.org/10.3390/computation14010014

TDMs between singlet states are shown in Figures 26 and 27 and between triplet states in Figures 28 and 29. These TDMs could lead to observations of several strong transition bands like: $(3)^1\Pi \rightarrow (1)^1\Sigma^+$, $(2)^1\Sigma^+ \rightarrow (1)^1\Sigma^+$, $(2)^3\Sigma^+ \rightarrow (1)^3\Pi$ and $(2)^3\Phi \rightarrow (1)^3\Delta$.

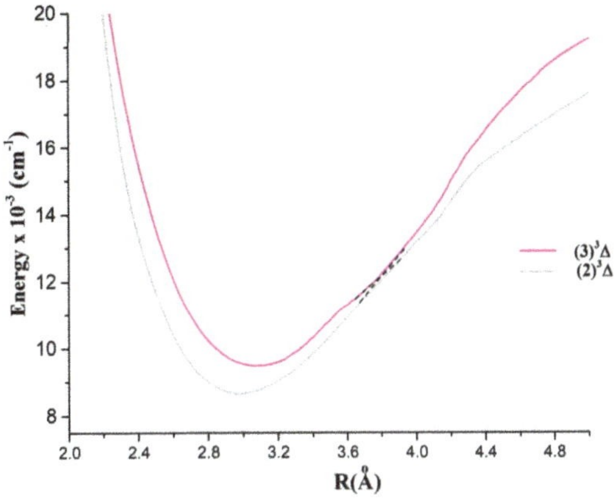


**Figure 25.** Avoided crossing between the $(2)^3\Delta$ and $(3)^3\Delta$ states of YLi.

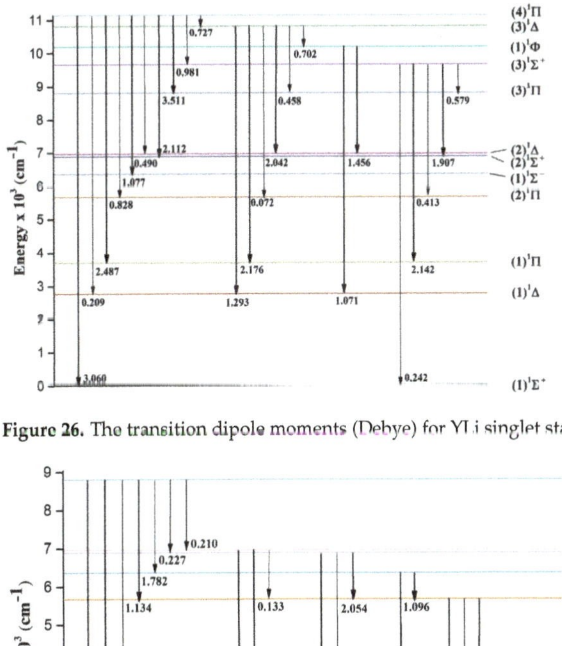


**Figure 26.** The transition dipole moments (Debye) for YLi singlet states at $R_e$ = 3.234 Å.

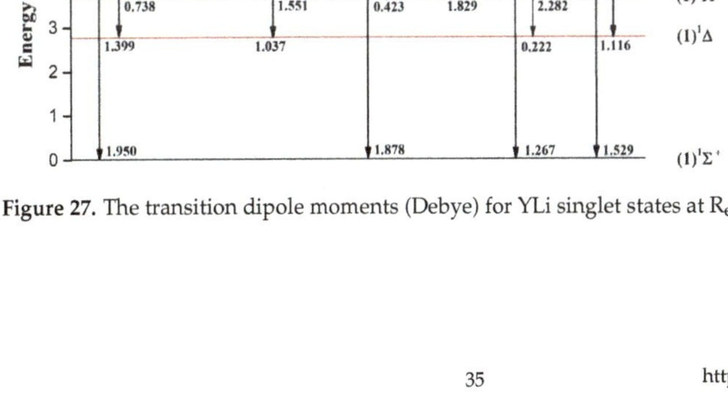


**Figure 27.** The transition dipole moments (Debye) for YLi singlet states at $R_e$ = 3.234 Å. (cont.).



https://doi.org/10.3390/computation14010014

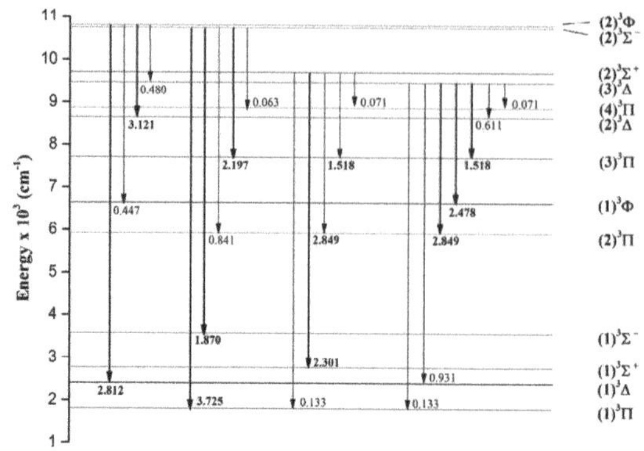


**Figure 28.** The transition dipole moments (Debye) for YLi triplet states at $R_e = 3.234$ Å.

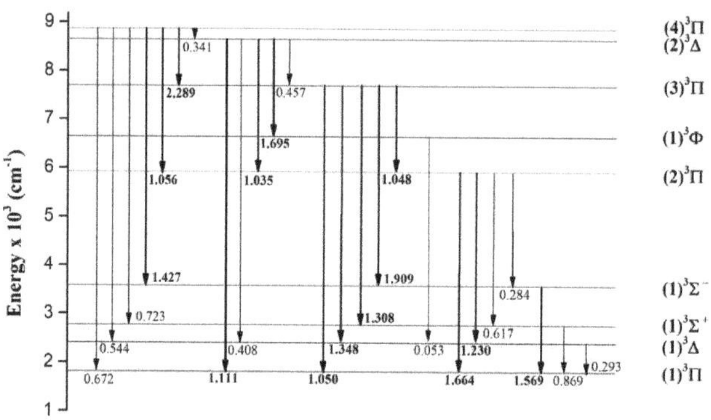


**Figure 29.** The transition dipole moments (Debye) for YLi triplet states at $R_e = 3.234$ Å. (cont.).

Moreover, in this study, spin–orbit couplings SOCs have been undertaken for the first lowest electronic states to estimate the value of the spin–orbit constant A. The Λ-S wave functions in MRCI calculations for the lowest states have been considered for the spin–orbit CI calculations to assess their effects in the lowest lying electronic states. In this study, we assigned 12 lowest electronic components $\Omega^{(\pm)}$ and their different composition percentages of the Λ–S symmetry related to the lowest states $(1)^{1,3}\Delta$, $(1)^{1,3}\Pi$, and $(1)^{1,3}\Sigma^+$, (Table 7). Table 8 reports the spectroscopic constants, internuclear distances, and the energy at equilibrium $T_e$ of these electronic components $\Omega^{(\pm)}$. These obtained parameters are almost identical to those of their corresponding Λ-S parent states. The PECs of these electronic components are illustrated in Figure 30. By focusing on the energy values of the components generated from $(1)^3\Delta$ and $(1)^3\Pi$, we found that the estimated spin–orbit constant A varies between 70 $cm^{-1}$ and 130 $cm^{-1}$. This value is comparable to the spin–orbit effect in Yttrium atom and indicates that the case a of Hund is present here [27]. Moreover, to question the reliability of SOC value, which is unexplored experimentally or theoretically, we enquire about its value in YH for $(1)^3\Delta$ and $(1)^3\Pi$ states [28] and found approximately equivalent values to those in YLi.



https://doi.org/10.3390/computation14010014

**Table 7.** Percentage composition of $\Omega^{(\pm)}$ state wave function (MRCI) in terms of S-$\Lambda$ at $R_e$ = 3.232 Å from the parents $(1)^{1,3}\Sigma^+$, $(1)^{1,3}\Pi$ and $(1)^{1,3}\Delta$ molecular states of YLi.

| Ω<br>Main Parent | $X\ ^1\Sigma^+$ | $(1)^3\Pi$ | $(1)^3\Delta$ | $(1)^3\Sigma^+$ | $(1)^1\Delta$ | $(1)^1\Pi$ |
|---|---|---|---|---|---|---|
| $(1)0^+$ $[(1)^1\Sigma^+]$ | 98 | 2 | | | | |
| $(1)0^-$ $[(1)^3\Pi]$ | | 91 | | 9 | | |
| $(1)1$ $[(1)^3\Pi]$ | | 76 | 19 | 5 | | |
| $(2)0^+$ $[(1)^3\Pi]$ | 2 | 98 | | | | |
| $(1)2$ $[(1)^3\Pi]$ | | 75 | 22 | | 3 | |
| $(2)1$ $[(1)^3\Delta]$ | | 15 | 79 | 4 | | 2 |
| $(2)2$ $[(1)^3\Delta]$ | | 24 | 75 | | 1 | |
| $(1)3$ $[(1)^3\Delta]$ | | | 100 | | | |
| $(3)1$ $[(1)^3\Sigma^+]$ | | 9 | 1 | 89 | 1 | |
| $(2)0^-$ $[(1)^3\Sigma^+]$ | | 9 | | 91 | | |
| $(3)2$ $[(1)^1\Delta]$ | | 1 | 4 | | 95 | |
| $(4)1$ $[(1)^1\Pi]$ | | | | 3 | | 97 |

**Table 8.** MRCI Spectroscopic constants including the spin–orbit splitting of the lowest components $\Omega^{(\pm)}$ of YLi.

| States | $R_e$ (Å) | $T_e$ (cm$^{-1}$) | $\omega_e$ (cm$^{-1}$) | $\omega_e x_e$ (cm$^{-1}$) | $A\Lambda\Sigma$ [cm$^{-1}$] |
|---|---|---|---|---|---|
| $(1)0^+$ $[(X)^1\Sigma^+]$ | 3.236 | 0 | 276 | 2.1 | |
| $(1)0^-$ $[(1)^3\Pi]$ | 3.203 | 1341 | 235 | 2.6 | −70 |
| $(1)1$ $[(1)^3\Pi]$ | 3.203 | 1411 | 230 | 2.5 | 0 |
| $(2)0^+$ $[(1)^3\Pi]$ | 3.203 | 1479 | 234 | 2.5 | 68 |
| $(1)2$ $[(1)^3\Pi]$ | 3.206 | 1542 | 231 | 2.5 | 131 |
| $(2)1$ $[(1)^3\Delta]$ | 3.354 | 1796 | 234 | 2.3 | −228 |
| $(2)2$ $[(1)^3\Delta]$ | 3.354 | 2024 | 233 | 2.4 | 0 |
| $(1)3$ $[(1)^3\Delta]$ | 3.357 | 2174 | 236 | 2.3 | 150 |
| $(3)1$ $[(1)^3\Sigma^+]$ | 3.287 | 2377 | 241 | 3.3 | −51 |
| $(2)0^-$ $[(1)^3\Sigma^+]$ | 3.287 | 2428 | 242 | 3.4 | |
| $(3)2$ $[(1)^1\Delta]$ | 3.359 | 2801 | 223 | 2.6 | |
| $(4)1$ $[(1)^1\Pi]$ | 3.324 | 3538 | 207 | 2.6 | |

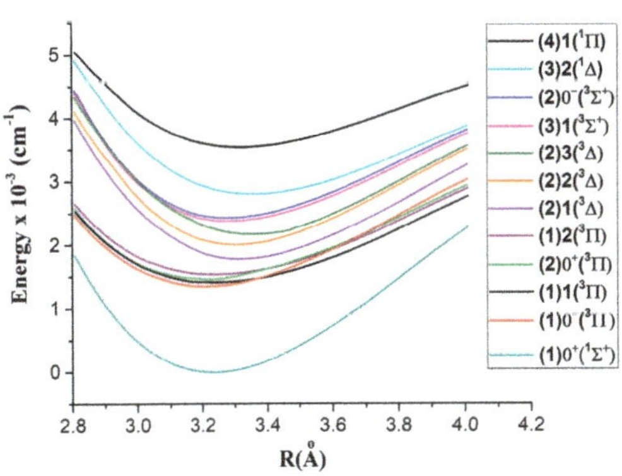


**Figure 30.** The potential energy curves (MRCI) for the lowest lying components $\Omega^{(\pm)}$ of YLi.

## 4. Conclusions

The ab initio CASSCF/MRCI calculations on ScLi and YLi molecules have computed the ground state and the lowest singlet and triplet electronic states, their spectroscopic constants, and the equilibrium bond lengths. The ground state and the first lying electronic

 https://doi.org/10.3390/computation14010014

states of ScLi have been validated through comparison to other previous theoretical calculations. In this study, the obtained ground state of ScLi of symmetry $^3\Delta$ has an internuclear distance $R_e$= 3.231 Å and a dissociation energy value $D_e$ = 2267 $cm^{-1}$, as expected. For YLi, the ground state has been assigned as (1) $^1\Sigma^+$ of $R_e$ = 3.232 Å and of a dissociation energy $D_e$ = 5541 $cm^{-1}$. The obtained lowest lying electronic structure of YLi has been investigated for the first time up to 11,622 $cm^{-1}$. The manifold of the obtained computed states has been validated by comparing its analogy with the lowest low-lying electronic states in YH molecule. The calculated PECs for both ScLi and YLi have shown less bonded states for the first six lying states correlating from the first asymptote. The obtained transition dipole moments are important as they can provide a reliable indication to identify experimentally the strong transitions bands in the visible and near-infrared regions especially for several electronic transitions like $(3)^1\Pi \rightarrow (1)^1\Sigma^+$, $(2)^1\Sigma^+ \rightarrow (1)^1\Sigma^+$, $(2)^3\Sigma^- \rightarrow (1)^3\Pi$, and $(2)^3\Phi \rightarrow (1)^3\Delta$ in both ScLi and YLi.

**Author Contributions:** Conceptualization, S.M.; Methodology, S.M. and F.T.; Software, J.T.; Validation, S.M. and F.T.; Investigation, J.T.; Resources, N.Z.; Writing–original draft, F.T.; Writing–review and editing, F.T.; Visualization, J.T.; Supervision, N.Z. and F.T.; Funding acquisition, N.Z. All authors have read and agreed to the published version of the manuscript.

**Funding:** This research received no external funding.

**Data Availability Statement:** The original contributions presented in this study are included in the article. Further inquiries can be directed to the corresponding author.

**Acknowledgments:** We are thankful to the MESOCENTRE-Lille supported by Lille University for providing computational resources.

**Conflicts of Interest:** The authors declare no conflict of interest.

## References

1. Tabet, J.; Adem, Z.; Taher, F. Ab initio investigation of ground and excited states of ScH molecule. *Spectrochim. Acta Part A Mol. Biomol. Spectrosc.* **2021**, *256*, 119742. [CrossRef]
2. Feldet, M.; Phung, Q.M. Ab Initio Methods in First-Row Transition Metal Chemistry. *Eur. J. Inorg. Chem.* **2022**, *15*, 15–24. [CrossRef]
3. Carr, L.D.; DeMille, D.; Krems, R.V.; Ye, J. Cold and ultracold molecules: Science, technology and applications. *New J. Phys.* **2009**, *11*, 055049. [CrossRef]
4. Tennyson, J.; Harris, G.J.; Barber, R.J.; La Delfa, S.; Voronin, B.A.; Kaminsky, B.M.; Pavlenko, Y.V. Molecular line lists for modelling the opacity of cool stars. *Mol. Phys.* **2007**, *105*, 701–714. [CrossRef]
5. Weck, P.F.; Schweitzer, A.; Kirby, K.; Hauschildt, P.H.; Stancil, P.C. Molecular Line Opacity of LiCl in the Mid-Infrared Spectra of Brown Dwarfs. *Astrophys. J.* **2004**, *613*, 567–571. [CrossRef]
6. Harrison, J. Electronic Structure of Diatomic Molecules Composed of a First-Row Transition Metal and Main-Group Element (H–F). *Chem. Rev.* **2000**, *100*, 679−716. [CrossRef] [PubMed]
7. López, R.; Díaz, N.; Suárez, D. Alkali and Alkaline-Earth Cations in Complexes with Small Bioorganic Ligands: Ab Initio Benchmark Calculations and Bond Energy Decomposition. *Chemphyschem* **2020**, *21*, 99–112. [CrossRef]
8. Werner, H.J.; Knowles, P.J. An efficient internally contracted multiconfiguration–reference configuration interaction method. *J. Chem. Phys.* **1988**, *89*, 5803–5814. [CrossRef]
9. Knowles, P.J.; Werner, H.J. An efficient method for the evaluation of coupling coefficients in configuration interaction calculations. *Chem. Phys. Lett.* **1988**, *145*, 514–522. [CrossRef]
10. Beckmann, H.O.; Pacchioni, G.; Jeung, G.H. Electronic structure and reactivity of the transition-metal lithides ScLi, CuLi and PdLi. *Chem. Phys. Lett.* **1985**, *116*, 423–428. [CrossRef]
11. Harrison, J. Electronic structure of scandium lithide. *J. Phys. Chem.* **1983**, *87*, 1323. [CrossRef]
12. Lawson, D.; Harrison, J. Electronic Structures of ScLi, TiLi, VLi, CrLi, and CuLi and their Positive Ions. *J. Phys. Chem.* **1996**, *100*, 6081. [CrossRef]
13. Kassem, S.; Zeid, I.; Korek, M. Theoretical studies of the excited electronic states of the molecule ScLi and its ions ScLi+ with a feasibility study of laser cooling. *Can. J. Chem.* **2023**, *101*, 33–42. [CrossRef]

 https://doi.org/10.3390/computation14010014

14. Wang, M.Y.; Wu, Z.J. Electronic Structures of 3d-Metal Monolithides. *J. Clust. Sci.* **2005**, *16*, 547–558. [CrossRef]
15. Werner, H.J.; Knowles, J.P.; Knizia, G.; Manby, F.R.; Schutz, M. MOLPRO, Version 2010.1, A Package of Ab Initio Programs. 2010. Available online: http://www.molpro.net (accessed on 15 March 2015).
16. Bergner, A.; Dolg, M.; Kuchle, W.; Stoll, H.; Preuss, H. Ab initio energy-adjusted pseudopotentials for elements of groups 13–17. *Mol. Phys.* **1993**, *80*, 1431–1441. [CrossRef]
17. Balabanov, N.B.; Peterson, K.A. Systematically convergent basis sets for transition metals. I. All-electron correlation consistent basis sets for the 3d elements Sc-Zn. *J. Chem. Phys.* **2005**, *123*, 064107. [CrossRef]
18. Prascher, B.; Woon, D.; Peterson, K.; Dunning, T.; Wilson, A. Gaussian basis sets for use in correlated molecular calculations. VII. Valence, core-valence, and scalar relativistic basis sets for Li, Be, Na, and Mg. *Theor. Chem. Acc.* **2011**, *128*, 69–82. [CrossRef]
19. Peterson, K.; Figgen, D.; Dolg, M.; Stoll, H. Energy-consistent relativistic pseudopotentials and correlation consistent basis sets for the 4 d elements Y–Pd. *J. Chem. Phys.* **2007**, *126*, 124101. [CrossRef]
20. Dunham, J. The energy levels of a rotating vibrator. *Phys. Rev. B* **1932**, *41*, 721. [CrossRef]
21. Langhoff, S.; Davidson, E. Configuration interaction calculations on the nitrogen molecule. *Int. J. Quantum Chem.* **1974**, *8*, 61–72. [CrossRef]
22. Davidson, E.; Silver, D. Size consistency in the dilute helium gas electronic structure. *Chem. Phys. Lett.* **1977**, *52*, 403–406. [CrossRef]
23. Minaev, B. Ab initio study of low-lying triplet states of the lithium dimer. *Spectrochim. Acta Part A Mol. Biomol. Spectrosc.* **2005**, *62*, 790–799. [CrossRef] [PubMed]
24. Balasubramanian, K.; Wang, J.Z. Spectroscopic properties and potential energy curves of 29 electronic states of YH. *J. Mol. Spectrosc.* **1989**, *133*, 82–89. [CrossRef]
25. Ram, R.; Bernath, P. Fourier transform emission spectroscopy of new infrared systems of LaH and LaD. *J. Chem. Phys.* **1996**, *104*, 6444–6451. [CrossRef]
26. Jakubek, Z.; Nakhate, S.G.; Simard, B.; Balfour, W. Laser-Induced Fluorescence Molecular Beam Investigation of New Singlet and Triplet Electronic States of Yttrium Monohydride. *J. Mol. Spectrosc.* **2002**, *211*, 135–146. [CrossRef]
27. Nist, A. *Handbook of Basic Atomic Spectra; NIST Standard Reference Data 108*; Sansonetti, J.E., Martin, W.C., Eds.; Quantum Measurement Division, PML: Gaithersburg, MD, USA, 2013. Available online: https://www.nist.gov/ (accessed on 24 December 2025). [CrossRef]
28. Armentrout, P.B.; Sunderlin, L.S. *Transition Metal Hydrides*; DedreÂu, A., Ed.; VCH Publishers: New York, NY, USA, 1992; pp. 1–64.





https://doi.org/10.3390/computation14010014

computation

MDPI

Article

# Predicting Properties of Imidazolium-Based Ionic Liquids via Atomistica Online: Machine Learning Models and Web Tools

**Stevan Armaković [1] and Sanja J. Armaković [2,*]**

[1] Department of Physics, Faculty of Sciences, University of Novi Sad, 21000 Novi Sad, Serbia; stevan.armakovic@df.uns.ac.rs

[2] Department of Chemistry, Biochemistry and Environmental Protection, Faculty of Sciences, University of Novi Sad, 21000 Novi Sad, Serbia

* Correspondence: sanja.armakovic@dh.uns.ac.rs

**Abstract:** Machine learning models and web-based tools have been developed for predicting key properties of imidazolium-based ionic liquids. Two high-quality datasets containing experimental density and viscosity values at 298 K were curated from the ILThermo database: one containing 434 systems for density and another with 293 systems for viscosity. Molecular structures were optimized using the GOAT procedure at the GFN-FF level to ensure chemically realistic geometries, and a diverse set of molecular descriptors, including electronic, topological, geometric, and thermodynamic properties, was calculated. Three support vector regression models were built: two for density (IonIL-IM-D1 and IonIL-IM-D2) and one for viscosity (IonIL-IM-V). IonIL-IM-D1 uses three simple descriptors, IonIL-IM-D2 improves accuracy with seven, and IonIL-IM-V employs nine descriptors, including DFT-based features. These models, designed to predict the mentioned properties at room temperature (298 K), are implemented as interactive applications on the *atomistica.online* platform, enabling property prediction without coding or retraining. The platform also includes a structure generator and searchable databases of optimized structures and descriptors. All tools and datasets are freely available for academic use via the official web site of the *atomistica.online* platform, supporting open science and data-driven research in molecular design.

**Keywords:** atomistic calculations; structure optimization; force field; machine learning; density; viscosity; ionic liquids; imidazolium

## 1. Introduction

Ionic liquids (ILs) are a class of salts that remain in the liquid state at or near room temperature, typically below 100 °C [1,2]. Unlike conventional salts such as sodium chloride, which form rigid crystalline solids at room temperature, ILs are composed entirely of bulky organic cations and various anions that inhibit lattice formation due to their asymmetry and charge delocalization [3]. This structural nature leads to a low melting point and a liquid state over a wide temperature range. ILs can be broadly classified based on the nature of their cations (e.g., imidazolium, pyridinium, ammonium, phosphonium) and anions (e.g., halides, tetrafluoroborate, hexafluorophosphate, bis(trifluoromethylsulfonyl)imide). Further subclassifications may include protic vs. aprotic ILs, task-specific ILs, and deep eutectic solvents, which share similar behavior under certain conditions.

ILs are widely recognized for their unique physicochemical properties that distinguish them from conventional molecular solvents [4–6]. These properties include very low and almost negligible vapor pressure, high thermal and chemical stability, non-flammability, high ionic conductivity, and a wide electrochemical window. ILs also possess significant structural tenability. Namely, by varying the cation–anion combinations, it is possible to obtain target values of properties such as viscosity, density, hydrophobicity, polarity, and solvation ability [4,7–11]. In particular, imidazolium-based ILs have been extensively studied due to their balanced physical properties and chemical stability. However, even though ILs have promising potential, some of their physical properties can vary dramatically depending on molecular structure and operating conditions, which complicates their design and application.

Due to this unique suite of properties, ILs have attracted widespread attention for various practical applications. They are used as green solvents in synthetic chemistry and catalysis, as electrolytes in batteries and supercapacitors, as lubricants, and in separation processes such as $CO_2$ capture, biomass dissolution, and liquid–liquid extraction [7,12,13]. ILs also show promise in pharmaceutical formulations, electrochemical devices, and the stabilization of nanomaterials [14–16]. Nevertheless, challenges remain. Many ILs are costly to synthesize and purify, their biodegradability and toxicity profiles are still under investigation, and their physical properties are not always predictable a priori. These limitations emphasize the need for predictive models and digital tools that can accelerate IL design and screening, particularly for critical properties such as viscosity and density.

Atomistic modeling has become a crucial step in the development of novel materials [17–22]. By simulating systems at the atomic and electronic levels, quantum mechanical methods such as density functional theory (DFT) or modern wavefunction-based methods, combined with molecular dynamics (MD), enable researchers to investigate electronic configurations, thermodynamic behavior, conformational dynamics, and intermolecular forces with high precision [23–25]. These approaches offer the possibility to predict properties that complement and extend beyond experimental observation, guiding the design of functional materials and molecules across chemistry, physics, and materials science.

Due to their complexity and ability to fine-tune properties, ionic liquids are especially well-suited for atomistic calculations. Methods like DFT are commonly used to explore the electronic structure and chemical behavior of their components. These calculations offer insights into charge distribution, molecular orbitals, hydrogen bonding, and interactions between ions [26–28]. DFT calculations are also helpful for quantifying properties such as dipole moments, polarizability, electrostatic potential maps, and binding energies between cations and anions [29–31]. These electronic-level descriptors are crucial for understanding how subtle variations in ion structures affect macroscopic properties, such as viscosity, conductivity, and thermal stability. In addition, DFT-derived data often serve as the basis for developing machine learning (ML) models, providing a consistent and reproducible way to represent molecular systems numerically.

Aside from atomistic calculations, ML has emerged as a crucial approach in molecular science, providing new strategies for predicting properties, providing insights into structure–property relationships, and informing the design of novel compounds [32–34]. By analyzing data and through learning patterns, ML models can simulate complex quantum or thermodynamic behaviors without the need for computationally intensive simulations for each new system. This is important when it comes to ILs, where small structural changes can lead to significant variations in their properties. ML algorithms such as support vector regression (SVR), random forests, and neural networks can use molecular descriptors, derived from quantum mechanical calculations, cheminformatics, or topology, to construct accurate predictive models for properties like viscosity and density [35–37]. As an addition to atomistic calculations, ML enables high-throughput screening of candidate molecules and accelerates the discovery of new materials.

In the area of ML modeling of ionic liquid properties, density prediction has been the subject of a significant number of studies [38]. One of the earliest examples was reported by Valderrama et al. [39], who combined group-contribution theory with an artificial neural network (ANN). The model achieved excellent accuracy, with average absolute deviations of only 0.15% for the training set and 0.26% for an external prediction set (maximum deviation below 2.5%). Barati-Haroon et al. [40] developed a hybrid adaptive neuro-fuzzy inference system (ANFIS) to predict the densities of neat ionic liquids as well as IL–water mixtures, focusing on various imidazolium-based systems. Using 602 data points covering 146 ILs, their model achieved excellent predictive test-set performance, with overall $R^2 = 0.985$ and an average absolute relative deviation of only 0.66%. Paduszyński [41] compiled an extensive dataset of over 41,000 density values for 2267 ionic liquids and developed a group-contribution QSPR model. The final recommended approach combined multiple linear regression (MLR) for the reference density with a least-squares support vector machine (LSSVM) for temperature–pressure corrections. This model achieved excellent accuracy, with $R^2$ above 0.998 and average errors of about 1%. More recently, Baran and Kloskowski [42] critically evaluated the use of graph neural networks (GNNs) for predicting density, viscosity, and surface tension of ionic liquids. Their study demonstrated that GNNs can effectively process structural information from cations and anions, achieving predictive performance with test-set $R^2$ values up to ~0.95 for density, ~0.69 for viscosity, and ~0.79 for surface tension, while also showing robustness to mislabeled or noisy data. Other interesting studies where deep learning methods were applied for predicting various properties of ionic liquids are by Acar et al. [43], Fan et al. [44], and Abranches et al. [45].

To support the integration of atomistic modeling in molecular research, we developed *atomistica.online* two years ago as a freely accessible, web-based platform tailored for academic use [46,47]. Launched initially as a single-tool website offering an input file generator for the widely used ORCA [48–55] molecular modeling code, the platform quickly evolved to address broader computational needs. It was soon expanded with additional input generators and remote execution interfaces for semiempirical codes such as xTB [56–59], g-xTB [60], and MOPAC [61–69], as well as powerful utilities like Multiwfn [70–73] for wavefunction analysis, Packmol [74,75] for building initial molecular structures, and interfaces for running recently developed ML models for energy prediction and geometry optimization based on Meta's FAIR initiative [76]. *Atomistica.online* provided a unified environment where users can upload molecular structures, perform automated atomistic calculations, and access predictive ML models. Today, all these capabilities, along with over 20 specialized applications, are integrated into a comprehensive online application called Atomistica Online 2025, available at https://atomistica.online.

This work aimed to develop robust ML models capable of accurately predicting two key physicochemical properties of imidazolium-based ILs, density and viscosity at room temperature (298 K), based on molecular descriptors derived from simple molecular and atomistic calculations. In addition to the model development, a central goal was to build accessible, user-friendly online applications incorporated within the Atomistica Online 2025 application, enabling researchers to quickly estimate these properties by inputting descriptors obtained from their calculations. The platform is freely available for academic use and is designed to support research, teaching, and early-stage screening of novel ILs. Another important objective was to curate and publish high-quality, descriptor-rich datasets for both properties, which can not only serve as training resources for further ML efforts but can also be expanded and enriched by platform users. Through this work, it was aimed to accelerate the design, understanding, and application of ILs by bridging advanced atomistic modeling with modern data-driven tools.

## 2. Workflow and Computational Details

The development of ML models for predicting density and viscosity of imidazolium-based ILs followed a structured multi-step computational workflow, integrating data extraction, structure generation, descriptor calculations, model training, and app deployment (Figure 1). All IL structures used in this study were sourced from the ILThermo database [77] maintained by NIST, which provides a comprehensive collection of experimentally measured thermophysical properties of ILs. However, since ILThermo does not offer 3D molecular structures, the ILThermoPy [72] Python (version 3.10.16) library was used to extract molecular information in the form of SMILES strings for both cations and anions.

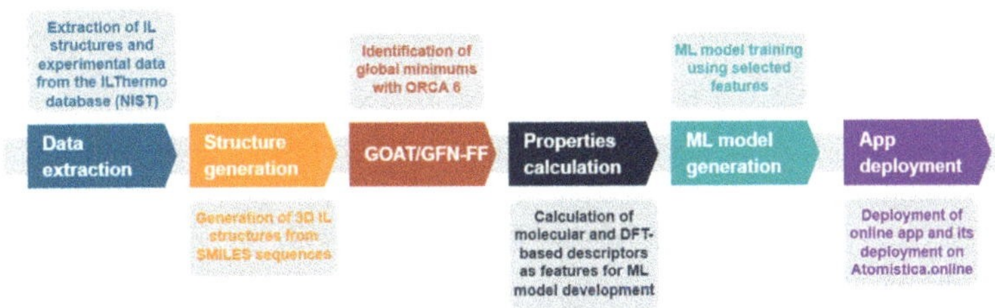


**Figure 1.** Illustration of the workflow adopted in this work.

To reconstruct 3D structures from SMILES representations, a custom Python pipeline based on the RDKit [78] and Open Babel [79] libraries was developed. This script systematically generated initial 3D geometries of ILs by converting SMILES to spatial coordinates and pre-optimizing each ion using the universal force field (UFF). Ionic liquid ion pairs were assembled by placing the cation and anion at an initial separation distance of 5 Å, ensuring a consistent and non overlapping starting configuration. This procedure was carried out independently for two datasets: one corresponding to ILs with experimentally measured density and another for those with viscosity data.

Following initial geometry construction, the GOAT [80–82] workflow was applied to locate low-energy, likely global minimum structures. The GOAT workflow was used as implemented in the ORCA6 molecular modeling code [48–55,83]. This step employed the GFN-FF force field [84], developed by Prof. Stefan Grimme and coworkers as a part of their activities in developing modern semiempirical methods [56–59]. GFN-FF was selected as a practical compromise between computational efficiency and accuracy for high-throughput geometry optimization of ionic liquids. While such systems pose challenges due to strong electrostatic interactions, charge delocalization, and polarization effects, GFN-FF offers a substantial speed advantage compared to semiempirical methods such as GFN2, enabling optimization of hundreds of structures within a reasonable timeframe. Importantly, GFN-FF is derived from the GFN family of methods and has been parameterized and benchmarked on diverse datasets, including GMTKN55, which contains ionic liquid structures. This provided confidence that it could deliver geometries of sufficient quality for descriptor generation, while acknowledging that, as a non-polarizable generic force field, it may be less accurate for highly charged, strongly polarizable systems. Given these considerations, we regard GFN-FF as fully adequate for this initial step, with plans to re-optimize the structures using higher-level methods in our future research efforts.

These optimized geometries were then subjected to calculations of simple molecular descriptors and quantum-mechanically obtained descriptors through single-point energy calculations at the M06-2X/6-31+G(d,p) level using ORCA6 and Maestro. Maestro was used as incorporated in the Schrödinger Materials Science 2024-1 Suite [85–89].

The outcome of this pipeline was two high-quality datasets containing computed descriptors for 434 ILs (density set) and 294 ILs (viscosity set). Each dataset included a comprehensive set of molecular descriptors, including quantum-derived electronic properties, topological indices, geometric features, and thermodynamic quantities such as the heat of formation (calculated using the MOPAC code [61–69]). These datasets were used to train and evaluate several ML regression models using Python and scikit-learn, including random forest, gradient boosting, and SVR. Among these, SVR provided the most accurate and robust predictions for both properties.

The units of targets were $kg/m^3$ for density and Pa·s for viscosity. Targets were modeled on the natural-log scale. Model fitting and cross-validation used the log-transformed targets; test-set predictions were back-transformed to the original units for reporting, and all errors and figure axes are shown on the original scales unless stated otherwise.

For the density models (IonIL-IM-D1 and IonIL-IM-D2), the dataset was split into training and test sets using an 80:20 ratio via the train_test_split function from scikit-learn, with a fixed random_state = 42 to ensure reproducibility. The split was performed after descriptor calculation and dataset assembly, ensuring that both sets were processed identically. For the viscosity model (IonIL-IM-V), a slightly different split ratio of 85:15 was applied, also using a fixed random_state = 42. This choice was made to retain a somewhat larger training set for the more complex viscosity prediction task, where data availability is more limited.

Given these considerations, the repeated 5-fold cross-validation results (50 folds in total) are considered the reliable indicators of generalizability for all models. Cross-validation averages performance across multiple randomized partitions, thereby mitigating the influence of any single favorable train–test split and reducing the risk of overestimating model performance.

Trained models were further evaluated through repeated k-fold cross-validation, and their performance was assessed using metrics such as $R^2$, MAE, and RMSE. To improve interpretability and ensure model transparency, a feature importance analysis was performed. The SHapley Additive exPlanations (SHAP) approach was used to identify the most influential molecular descriptors contributing to each property prediction. The final, validated models, IonIL-IM-D1 and IonIL-IM-D2 for density and IonIL-IM-V for viscosity, were deployed as interactive online tools on the *atomistica.online* platform, enabling users to estimate IL properties based on calculations of descriptors on their ILs.

Feature selection was performed using a structured multi-step procedure designed to reduce redundancy and improve model interpretability. Descriptor importance was first assessed using the random forest algorithm. Their contributions to predictive performance were then evaluated with SHAP. Finally, subsets of descriptors were systematically tested, and those yielding the highest accuracy with the smallest number of features were retained for the final models. This approach resulted in compact descriptor sets.

## 3. Results and Discussion

### 3.1. Machine Learning Models for Density (IonIL-IM-D1 and IonIL-IM-D2)

In designing a predictive model for the density of imidazolium-based ILs, an innovative and practical strategy was adopted. The primary goal was to develop a model with the smallest possible number of features, making it usable in an online application where the user can quickly perform predictions based on calculations for their ionic liquids. At the same time, an alternative model was built with a slightly higher number of features to achieve somewhat improved accuracy, thus balancing simplicity with predictive performance.

All selected descriptors are readily obtainable using free and open-source cheminformatics software, ensuring wide accessibility and ease of use. Under this framework, two SVR models were developed:

- IonIL-IM-D1, a three-feature model designed to maximize simplicity and practical deployability while retaining strong predictive performance.
- IonIL-IM-D2, a seven-feature model incorporating additional physicochemical descriptors to achieve somewhat higher accuracy at the cost of slightly increased complexity.

The details and performance of each model are described in the following subsections.

#### 3.1.1. IonIL-IM-D1

The IonIL-IM-D1 model was designed to predict ionic liquid density using only three informative yet straightforward descriptors: molecular weight, number of atoms, and AlogP. These quantities can be easily obtained using free, open-source software, which supports fast and practical applications, such as online screening tools. Specifically, molecular weight reflects the overall mass of the ionic liquid's ion pair; the number of atoms serves as a proxy for molecular size and complexity; and AlogP estimates the hydrophobic/hydrophilic balance, correlating with molecular packing and cohesive interactions relevant to density. Permutation importance analysis confirmed the strong relevance of these features, while their simplicity guarantees rapid calculation and broad accessibility for users. Despite this minimal feature set, IonIL-IM-D1 demonstrates robust predictive performance, as discussed in the following sections.

The IonIL-IM-D1 model presented excellent predictive performance on the independent test set. Namely, it achieved an $R^2$ of 0.906, a mean absolute error (MAE) of 28.352, and a root mean square error (RMSE) of 49.803. These results demonstrate the ability of this model to estimate IL density from molecular descriptors accurately. Robustness was confirmed through repeated cross-validation (5 folds $\times$ 10 repeats), yielding a mean $R^2$ of 0.835 with a standard deviation of 0.0575 across 50 folds. The final tuned SVR used an RBF kernel with $C = 11.779678304389181$, $\varepsilon = 0.002929232298636805$, and $\gamma =$ "*auto*". Together, these results indicate the model's reliability and suitability for high-throughput screening and rational design of ILs.

The parity plot (Figure 2) shows excellent agreement between the predicted and measured densities, with the majority of data points clustering tightly around the ideal correlation line. This pattern confirms the high predictive accuracy of the IonIL-IM-D1 model, reflected in a test set $R^2$ of 0.906.

While minor deviations are visible at lower density values, these can reasonably be attributed to the greater structural diversity and conformational flexibility of ionic liquid constituents in that range. Remarkably, this level of performance was achieved using only three simple and easily accessible molecular descriptors, underlining the efficiency and practicality of the model. Overall, the model captures the trend and scale of experimental densities with high reliability, strongly supporting its utility for predictive screening, virtual design, and rapid evaluation of new ILs.

Next, a feature importance analysis based on the permutation importance measure has been performed to gain insights into how individual molecular descriptors contribute to the predictive performance of the IonIL-IM-D1 model (Figure 3).

Permutation-based importance results revealed that molecular weight is the dominant feature, having the most significant influence on the density predictions of the model. This is consistent with the fundamental role of molecular mass in determining volumetric packing and density in ILs.

The number of atoms emerged as the second most significant contributor. As a descriptor, it describes important aspects of molecular size and complexity, which in turn affect how ILs organize in the condensed phase. The third feature, AlogP, contributed positively to the model's performance by reflecting the hydrophobic/hydrophilic balance of the ionic liquid components, a property closely linked to cohesive forces and thus to the final density.

Overall, this feature importance profile confirms that even a minimalist descriptor set can provide a robust and physically meaningful basis for predicting ionic liquid densities. This ranking further supports the interpretability of the IonIL-IM-D1 model. It reinforces its suitability for use in accessible, user-friendly online tools aimed at the rapid evaluation and rational design of new ILs.

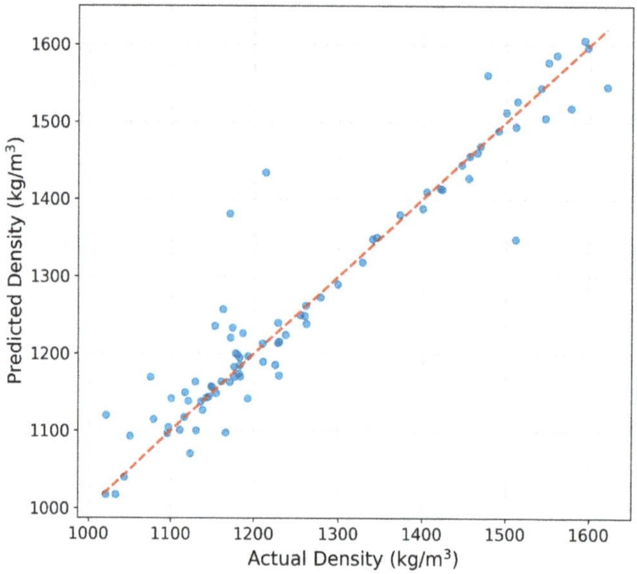


**Figure 2.** Predicted vs. experimental density values for the test set using the IonIL-IM-D1 model.

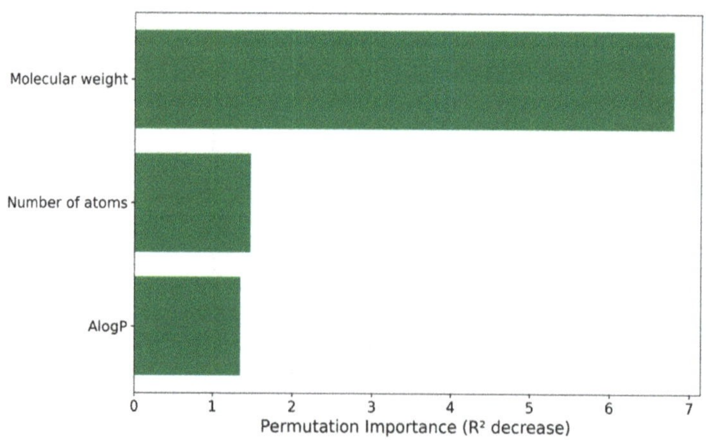


**Figure 3.** Permutation-based feature importance plot for the IonIL-IM-D1 model.

To further explore the IonIL-IM-D1 model, a SHAP analysis was performed. Figure 4 presents the SHAP summary plot, which illustrates the contribution of each descriptor to the model's density predictions across the test set.

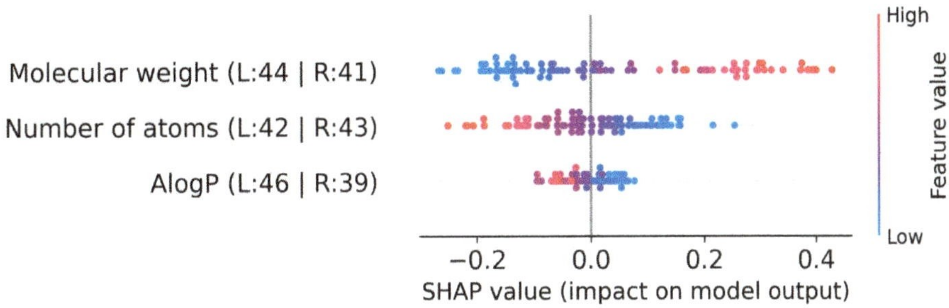


**Figure 4.** SHAP summary plot for the IonIL-IM-D1 model.

Consistent with the permutation importance results, molecular weight was again the most influential feature, with SHAP values demonstrating a predominantly positive contribution to predicted density. This confirms that higher molecular weights generally shift the predicted density upwards, as would be expected from fundamental volumetric considerations.

In contrast, the number of atoms showed a predominantly negative SHAP pattern for higher feature values, with red points concentrated on the negative side of the SHAP scale. This suggests that, after accounting for molecular weight, molecules with a larger number of atoms tend to decrease the predicted density. This trend is logical and can be easily explained. Smaller and simpler molecules typically pack more efficiently in the liquid state, which leaves less free volume and thereby increases density. On the other hand, more complex molecules with a greater number of atoms may exhibit branched structures unable to pack tightly, resulting in reduced density.

Finally, AlogP displayed a distribution of SHAP values centered near zero but with both positive and negative effects depending on the specific compound. This pattern may suggest that, while AlogP is less dominant than molecular weight, it still modulates the predicted density through its impact on polarity and hydrophobic interactions within the ionic liquid.

3.1.2. IonIL-IM-D2

The IonIL-IM-D2 model was developed to check whether a larger set of molecular descriptors could enhance predictive accuracy for ionic liquid density. Similar to IonIL-IM-D1, this model incorporated four additional descriptors alongside molecular weight, number of atoms, and AlogP: molar refractivity, polarizability, number of rotatable bonds, and number of heavy atoms. These features can also be easily calculated using free and open-source cheminformatics tools, maintaining accessibility. By expanding the number of descriptors, IonIL-IM-D2 aims to achieve improved performance while preserving interpretability and practical usability. Its details and results are discussed in the following sections.

The IonIL-IM-D2 model achieved better predictive performance on the independent test set, achieving an $R^2$ of 0.922, a MAE of 27.00 kg/m$^3$, and an RMSE of 45.47 kg/m$^3$. The final tuned SVR in this case used an RBF kernel with $C = 61.42327338216255$, $\varepsilon = 0.005889416322480806$, and $\gamma = 0.075$. Compared to IonIL-IM-D1, these results indicate a modest but meaningful improvement in predictive accuracy, reflecting the result of incorporating additional molecular descriptors. Robustness was also improved, confirmed by repeated cross-validation (5 folds × 10 repeats), yielding a mean $R^2$ of 0.8846 with a standard deviation of 0.0474 across 50 folds. These values are slightly better and indicate higher stability than the corresponding values for IonIL-IM-D1.

In Figure 5, the differences between measured and predicted values are presented. The results indicate an excellent agreement between predicted and measured densities, with the majority of points clustering closely along the ideal correlation line. Compared to the IonIL-IM-D1 model, the IonIL-IM-D2 model achieves slightly improved alignment across the whole density range, confirming its enhanced predictive accuracy.

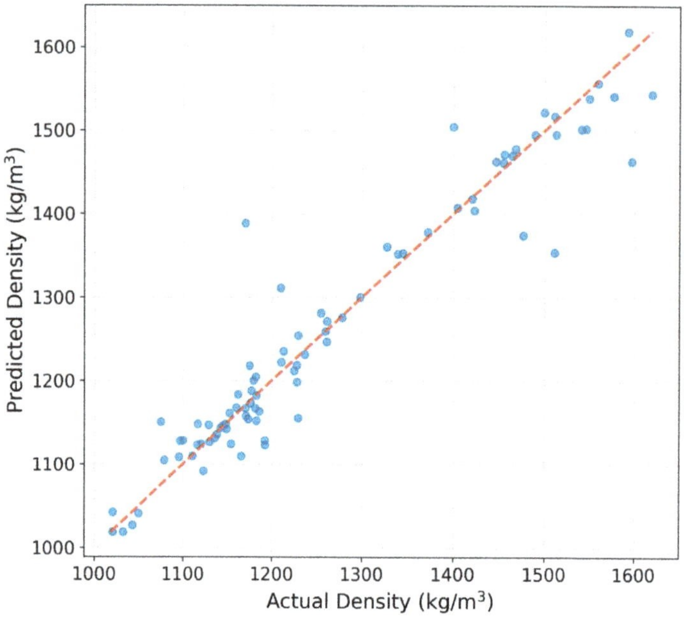


**Figure 5.** Predicted vs. experimental density values for the test set using the IonIL-IM-D2 model.

Minor deviations are still observed at lower densities, likely due to structural variability among the ILs; however, the model captures both trends and absolute values with high accuracy overall. These results further support the IonIL-IM-D2 model's practical applicability for predictive screening and rational design of new ILs.

To better understand how each of the seven input descriptors influenced the IonIL-IM-D2 model, a permutation-based feature importance analysis was again performed, and the results are presented in Figure 6.

Consistent with the IonIL-IM-D1 results, molecular weight was once again recognized as the most significant predictor, indicating its fundamental influence on the density of ILs. The second most important feature was molar refractivity, which captures contributions from electronic polarizability and molecular packing characteristics. The number of heavy atoms contributed meaningfully to the model, showing it is relevant in describing the backbone structure and overall size of the ionic liquid's ion pair. Descriptors such as the number of atoms, polarizability, AlogP, and number of rotatable bonds showed smaller, though still noticeable, contributions to the overall predictive performance. These features likely captured subtler aspects of molecular flexibility, polarity, and cohesive interactions that, while not dominant, help fine-tune the model's predictions.

Last, regarding the models for density, the SHAP analysis for the IonIL-IM-D2 model has been performed (Figure 7).

The molecular weight showed a high positive contribution in SHAP analysis, with higher values contributing to increased predicted densities. Both the number of heavy atoms and the number of atoms showed similar influences, generally reducing predicted density as their values increased. This suggests that larger or more structurally complex ion pairs may hinder tight packing and introduce more free volume, thereby lowering density.

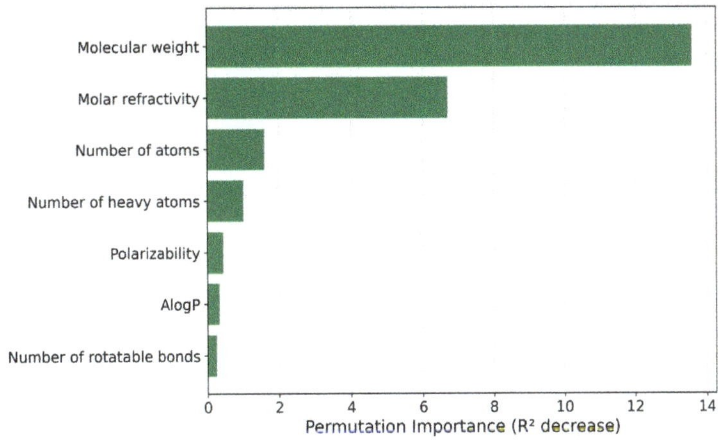


**Figure 6.** Permutation-based feature importance plot for the IonIL-IM-D2 model.

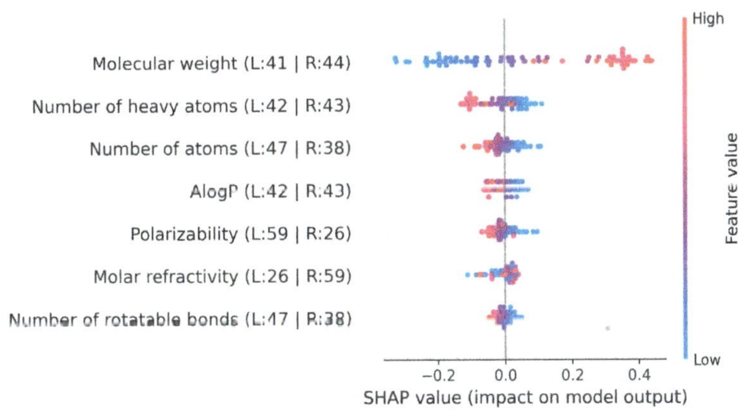


**Figure 7.** SHAP summary plot for the IonIL-IM-D2 model.

AlogP displayed SHAP values centered around zero, with a balanced distribution of positive and negative effects depending on the compound, indicating a subtle and context-dependent contribution related to hydrophobicity and polarity. Polarizability contributed slightly to the decrease in density predictions, suggesting that highly polarizable molecules may have less efficient packing due to their ability to distort and interact. Molar refractivity showed some small positive SHAP values, which indicates that structures with higher refractivity may favor stronger cohesive interactions and enhanced packing, thereby marginally increasing density. The number of rotatable bonds exhibited SHAP values tightly located around zero, which indicates a limited direct role in density prediction. However, it may still interact indirectly with other structural features.

Overall, these SHAP results confirm that, while molecular weight remains the dominant factor, the additional descriptors in IonIL-IM-D2 help capture more subtle effects relevant to ionic liquid density, supporting the model's accuracy and interpretability for practical screening applications.

### 3.2. ML Model for Viscosity (IonIL-IM-V)

In addition to density modeling, the SVR approach was used again to develop an ML model for predicting the viscosity of imidazolium-based ILs, referred to as IonIL-IM-V. Unlike the density models, IonIL-IM-V required a broader and more complex feature set to achieve acceptable performance, ultimately using nine descriptors. Several of these descriptors, such as quantities related to average local ionization energy (ALIE), electrostatic potential, and the energy of the lowest unoccupied molecular orbital (LUMO), were derived from quantum mechanical calculations at the DFT level, reflecting the greater complexity of modeling viscosity compared to density. Minimal value of ESP (ESP min) and mean value of ALIE (ALIE mean) were expressed in kcal/mol, negative variance of ESP (ESP neg variance) was expressed in $(kcal/mol)^2$, while LUMO was expressed in a.u. Although the model did not reach the same level of robustness as IonIL-IM-D1 or IonIL-IM-D2, it still achieved promising predictive results on the test set, suggesting it could serve as a valuable starting point for future adjustments and the development of better prediction models. Details of its structure, performance, and interpretability are presented in the following sections.

The IonIL-IM-V model achieved an $R^2$ of 0.918 on the independent test set, with a mean absolute error (MAE) of 0.175 and a root mean square error (RMSE) of 0.280. Using the final tuned configuration, the model is an RBF-kernel SVR with hyperparameters $C = 10.062206443505287$, $\varepsilon = 0.019437288893351404$, and $\gamma =$ *"auto"*. While these numbers suggest strong predictive accuracy on a single hold-out set, the mean cross-validation $R^2$ was considerably lower at 0.5573, with a relatively high standard deviation of 0.1111 across 50 folds. This large gap between the static test split and the averaged CV performance clearly indicates that the model suffers from limited generalizability and is prone to overfitting. Such a discrepancy is a known phenomenon when a specific train–test split happens to be particularly favorable, and it underlines the importance of using cross-validation as the more reliable indicator of expected performance on new, unseen data.

It is important to mention that viscosity is a significantly more complex property than density, because it depends on numerous factors, including molecular size, shape, intermolecular forces, ion pairing, and dynamic interactions within the liquid phase. Capturing all of these contributions in a single predictive framework is inherently challenging, especially when the dataset is limited in both size and diversity. In this context, IonIL-IM-V should be seen as a proof-of-concept model that demonstrates the feasibility of viscosity prediction for imidazolium-based ILs but also makes clear the need for larger, more balanced datasets and advanced feature engineering to achieve higher generalizability.

The parity plot for IonIL-IM-V (Figure 8) highlights good alignment to a certain extent between predicted and measured viscosities, particularly within the lower viscosity range, where most of the data points are concentrated. However, a clear imbalance in the dataset is evident, with far fewer samples at higher viscosities.

This imbalance, coming from the current limitation of the ILthermo dataset when it comes to the imidazolium-based ionic liquids, has direct implications for the model's performance and generalizability. Because the dense cluster of low-viscosity samples dominates the training process, the model can learn patterns in this region very effectively, while the sparsely represented high-viscosity points are more likely to be treated as noise. This imbalance is therefore a possible contributor to the observed overfitting and the large discrepancy between the optimistic $R^2$ value obtained on the static test set and the considerably lower mean cross-validation score.

The lower number of high-viscosity data likely contributes to the increased scatter and larger errors observed for these points. Such an imbalance is expected to a certain extent because reliable measurements of highly viscous ILs are experimentally more demanding and less frequently reported. Nevertheless, the model showed relatively significant accuracy in the low-viscosity region, which marks it as a promising first step. To improve generalization and reduce overfitting, future work should focus on rebalancing the dataset by incorporating a greater proportion of high-viscosity IL measurements, thereby ensuring that the model learns from a more uniform distribution of the target property.

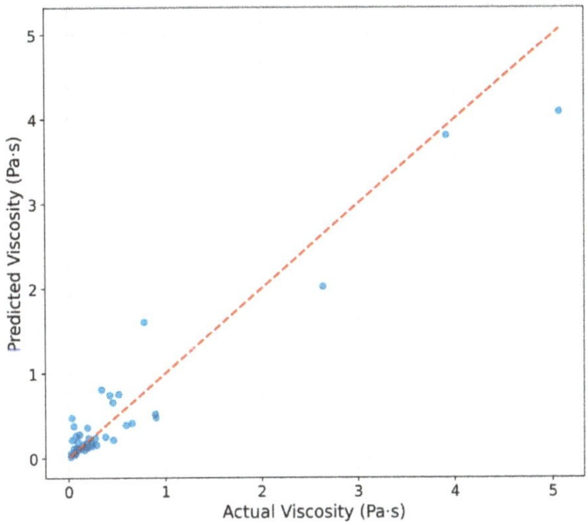


**Figure 8.** Predicted vs. experimental viscosity values for the test set using the IonIL-IM-V model.

Further, a permutation-based feature importance study has been performed to understand better how each of the nine input descriptors influenced the IonIL-IM-V model (Figure 9).

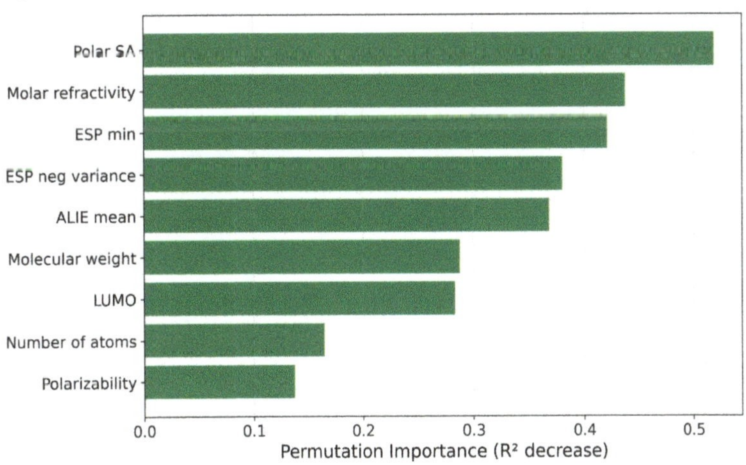


**Figure 9.** Permutation-based feature importance plot for the IonIL-IM-V model.

The permutation importance analysis highlighted molar refractivity and polar surface area (Polar SA) as the most influential features for predicting ionic liquid viscosity, suggesting that molecular volume and accessible surface area play a significant role in flow resistance and ion mobility. ESP min and ESP negative variance also ranked highly. They showed the importance of charge distribution and electrostatic interactions in controlling viscosity. Furthermore, ALIE mean, which reflects local ionization energies, and molecular weight contributed meaningfully, indicating the importance of molecular size and stability. Features describing frontier orbital energy (LUMO), atomic count (number of atoms), and polarizability showed additional relevance, supporting the notion that viscosity arises from a complex interplay of geometric, electronic, and dynamic molecular properties. These insights could inform future feature engineering by emphasizing descriptors linked to molecular packing, intermolecular forces, and ion–ion interactions, thereby further improving the IonIL-IM-V model. Further, the SHAP analysis for the IonIL-IM-V model has been performed (Figure 10).

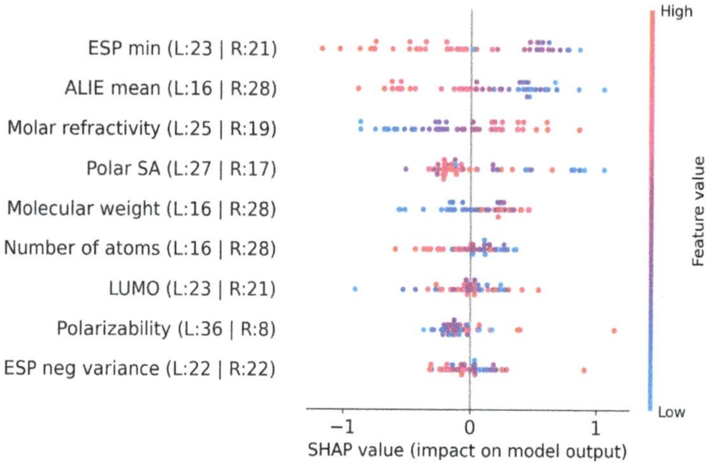


**Figure 10.** SHAP summary plot for the IonIL-IM-V model.

The SHAP analysis presented in Figure 10 was crucial for understanding the importance of individual features in the IonIL-IM-V model. Among the most impactful descriptors, ESP minimum and ALIE mean exhibited clear inverse contributions, with lower ESP minimum values and lower ALIE mean values tending to decrease the predicted viscosity. Molar refractivity showed a direct positive contribution, where higher values increased the model's viscosity estimates. This can be interpreted as the role of molecular volume in reducing ion mobility. Polar SA showed a relatively strong negative influence, meaning that larger surface areas lowered predicted viscosity, potentially due to higher charge delocalization and reduced ion pairing strength. Molecular weight and number of atoms displayed similar importance in terms of magnitude but in opposite directions: higher molecular weight increased the predicted viscosity, while a higher number of atoms tended to decrease it, highlighting subtle differences between mass-driven resistance and structural complexity. Finally, LUMO energy, ESP negative variance, and polarizability showed mixed influences, with both higher and lower values variably shifting the predictions toward increased or decreased viscosity.

It is important to note that these interpretations are derived from an overfit model and, therefore, may not represent true physical structure–property relationships but rather reflect the patterns the model learned to fit the specific training data. As such, while the SHAP results offer insight into how the model processed the input features, they should be interpreted with caution, particularly in the context of the limited generalizability demonstrated by the IonIL-IM-V model.

### 3.3. *Online Applications for Predicting Properties of Ionic Liquids and Datasets*

The IonIL-IM-D1, IonIL-IM-D2, and IonIL-IM-V models are freely available as interactive web applications hosted on the Atomistica Online 2025 application (https://atomistica.online). These applications are designed to make predictive modeling of ILs highly accessible to both experts and non-experts in materials science. By inputting a set of pre-calculated molecular descriptors, users can instantly obtain predicted values for either the density or viscosity of their ionic liquid candidates.

The web interface is streamlined for intuitive use. Users first select the property they wish to predict from the main menu on the left-hand side (via the "IL Density Predictor" and "IL Viscosity Predictor" links). For density prediction, two models are available: IonIL-IM-D1 and IonIL-IM-D2. Interfaces for using these models are presented in Figure 11. Users can enter the descriptor values manually or via copy–paste, and the predicted density is displayed immediately after pressing the "Calculate density" button.

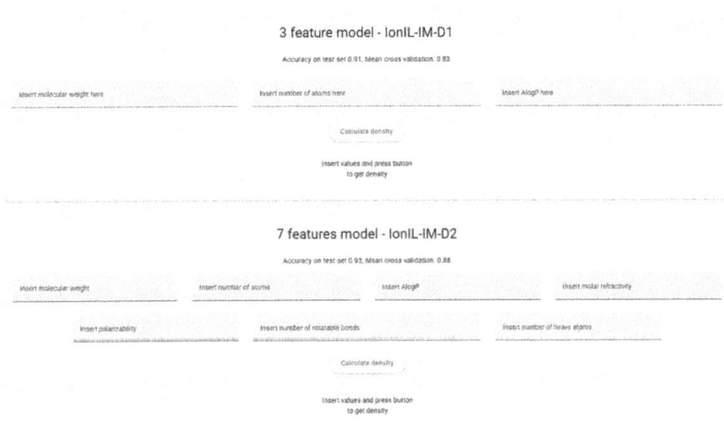


**Figure 11.** The interface for using the IonIL-IM-D1 and IonIL-IM-D2 ML models.

For viscosity, the model requires nine molecular descriptors, including quantum mechanically derived features, which reflect the increased complexity of this property (Figure 12).

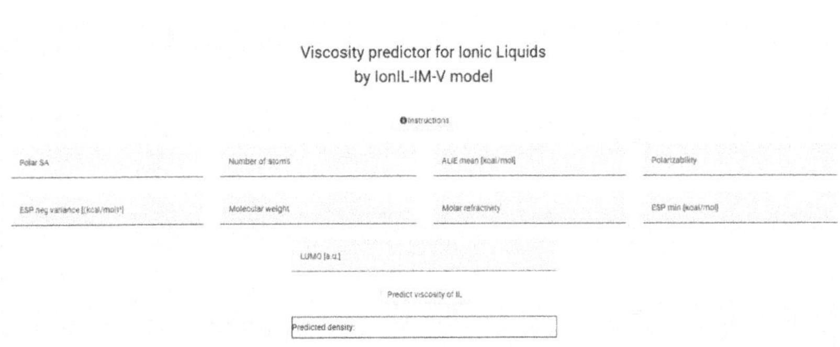


**Figure 12.** The interface for using the IonIL-IM-V model.

These applications are helpful for teaching, research, and exploratory design of ILs by eliminating the need for coding, software installation, or model retraining. They are particularly valuable for early-stage hypothesis testing, enabling researchers to screen candidate ILs before starting time- and resource-intensive synthesis or experimental characterization. The platform is entirely web-based and optimized for both desktop and mobile use, free for academic and teaching purposes.

In addition to the predictive models, each corresponding application includes, at the bottom of the page, curated and searchable databases of the ILs used to train the density and viscosity models (Figure 13).

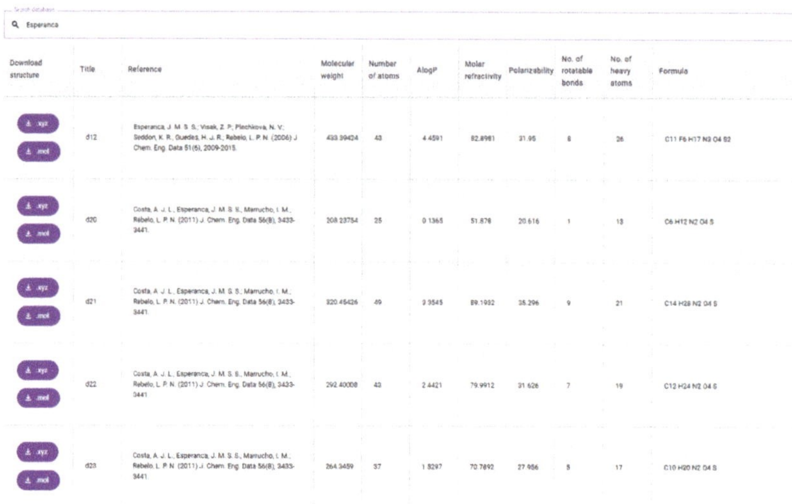
Search database
Esperanca

| Download structure | Title | Reference | Molecular weight | Number of atoms | AlogP | Molar refractivity | Polarizability | No. of rotatable bonds | No. of heavy atoms | Formula |
|---|---|---|---|---|---|---|---|---|---|---|
| .xyz .mol | d12 | Esperanca, J. M. S. S.; Visak, Z. P.; Plechkova, N. V.; Seddon, K. R.; Guedes, H. J. R.; Rebelo, L. P. N. (2006) J. Chem. Eng. Data 51(6), 2009-2015. | 433.39424 | 43 | 4.4591 | 82.8981 | 31.95 | 8 | 26 | C11 F6 H17 N3 O4 S2 |
| .xyz .mol | d20 | Costa, A. J. L.; Esperanca, J. M. S. S.; Marrucho, I. M.; Rebelo, L. P. N. (2011) J. Chem. Eng. Data 56(8), 3433-3441. | 208.23754 | 25 | 0.1365 | 51.878 | 20.616 | 1 | 13 | C6 H12 N2 O4 S |
| .xyz .mol | d21 | Costa, A. J. L.; Esperanca, J. M. S. S.; Marrucho, I. M.; Rebelo, L. P. N. (2011) J. Chem. Eng. Data 56(8), 3433-3441. | 320.45426 | 49 | 3.3545 | 89.1932 | 35.296 | 9 | 21 | C14 H28 N2 O4 S |
| .xyz .mol | d22 | Costa, A. J. L.; Esperanca, J. M. S. S.; Marrucho, I. M.; Rebelo, L. P. N. (2011) J. Chem. Eng. Data 56(8), 3433-3441. | 292.40008 | 43 | 2.4421 | 79.9912 | 31.626 | 7 | 19 | C12 H24 N2 O4 S |
| .xyz .mol | d23 | Costa, A. J. L.; Esperanca, J. M. S. S.; Marrucho, I. M.; Rebelo, L. P. N. (2011) J. Chem. Eng. Data 56(8), 3433-3441. | 264.3459 | 37 | 1.3297 | 70.7892 | 27.956 | 5 | 17 | C10 H20 N2 O4 S |

**Figure 13.** Searchable and interactive dataset for density, used for the generation of IonIL-IM-D models.

These interactive and searchable datasets, developed as part of this study, include 434 imidazolium-based ILs for density and 293 ILs for viscosity. Each entry is annotated with experimentally measured properties and a suite of molecular descriptors. For every ionic liquid in the datasets, users can download optimized global minimum structures, available in both xyz and mol formats. These optimized structures can be used immediately for property calculations or serve as reliable starting points for further re-optimizations at higher levels of theory. Each table entry also includes the molecular formula, SMILES representation, and the full reference citation associated with the IL.

Additionally, all GOAT/GFN-FF-optimized structures are available in bundled archives. The datasets are also provided as downloadable csv files containing all calculated molecular descriptors, making them suitable for direct use in ML workflows and further analysis.

### 3.4. Ionic Liquid Structure Generator

Last but not least, one more outcome of this study is presented: the development of a simple online structure generator for ILs, available through the Atomistica Online 2025 application. This tool was developed using a systematic approach: first, all unique ionic liquid structures were extracted as SMILES strings from the ILThermoPy Python library. From this curated list of ILs, all cations and anions were programmatically separated and stored in two distinct and searchable tables. Each ion is labeled with its IUPAC convention name, allowing users to browse or filter through them easily. Since it is challenging to know the exact names of ions for generating a certain IL, all ions are available in two easily searchable tables with buttons to invoke ions for the generation of IL. In the search field for cations and anions, it is sufficient to type a part of the desired ion's name, and the table will be sorted (Figure 14).

**Figure 14.** Screenshot from the online IL generator.

The platform enables users to select any combination of cation and anion, upon which a 3D structure of the resulting ion pair is generated and pre-optimized using the universal force field (UFF). This process provides immediate access to chemically meaningful starting geometries. The tool addresses a fundamental need in the field of ionic liquid design and modeling. The chemical diversity of ILs is virtually limitless, with millions of theoretically possible combinations of cations and anions. However, generating realistic, pre-optimized 3D structures for these combinations remains a tedious and time-consuming task for most researchers, particularly those without a strong background in programming or computation. By automating this step, the structure generator makes easy access to ready-to-use IL geometries, significantly simplifying the process of exploring new ionic liquid systems, performing quantum mechanical or MD calculations, or integrating structures into ML workflows.

Approximately 1300 cations and 400 anions were extracted from the database, meaning that users can theoretically generate over half a million unique ion pairs. Because the generated structures are UFF pre-optimized and provided in a standardized format, they can be used directly for further optimization (e.g., via GOAT or DFT) or for generating molecular descriptors. Furthermore, a generated intermolecular system consisting of a cation and an anion allows users to generate MD systems through the Online Packmol application of Atomistica Online 2025, which uses the famous Packmol program [74,75] in the background.

## 4. Conclusions

In this work, the development, validation, and deployment of ML models designed to predict the density and viscosity of imidazolium-based ILs at room temperature (298 K) using molecular descriptors derived from simple and atomistic calculations have been presented. By collecting high-quality datasets and applying clear computational workflows, including geometry optimization via the GOAT protocol using the GFN-FF force field, a solid foundation has been established for building interpretable, robust, and accessible predictive models.

For density prediction, two models were developed: IonIL-IM-D1, which utilized only three simple descriptors (molecular weight, number of atoms, and AlogP), and IonIL-IM-

D2, which employed seven descriptors to capture more complex structural and electronic features. IonIL-IM-D1 achieved a test set $R^2$ of 0.91, MAE of 28.35 kg/m$^3$, and RMSE of 49.80 kg/m$^3$, with a mean cross-validation $R^2$ of 0.84. These results indicated that even a minimal descriptor set can yield high predictive accuracy. IonIL-IM-D2 further improved performance, achieving a test set $R^2$ of 0.92, MAE of 27.00 kg/m$^3$, and RMSE of 45.47 kg/m$^3$, with a mean cross-validation $R^2$ of 0.88. These results confirm that density is a property well-suited to ML prediction using readily accessible molecular features.

Viscosity prediction was a greater challenge due to the more complex nature of this property. The IonIL-IM-V model utilized nine descriptors, including several derived from DFT calculations such as ALIE, ESP, and frontier orbital energies. Despite this complexity, the model achieved a respectable test set $R^2$ of 0.92, MAE of 0.175, and RMSE of 0.280. While cross-validation results indicated reduced robustness (mean $R^2$ of 0.56 with higher variance), the model provides a solid foundation for further development and illustrates the feasibility of using ML to tackle even challenging physicochemical properties. However, the limited size of the viscosity dataset and the strong sensitivity of viscosity to experimental conditions introduce additional sources of uncertainty. Furthermore, the reliance on computationally demanding quantum descriptors may reduce the model's general applicability, highlighting the need for future work on larger datasets and simplified descriptor sets.

All three models are deployed as web-based applications within *atomistica.online* platform (https://atomistica.online), which was developed to ensure maximum accessibility for both researchers and students. Users can input pre-calculated descriptors and obtain immediate predictions for density or viscosity without requiring coding expertise, software installation, or model retraining. The platform also includes searchable and interactive databases of all ILs used to train the models, each annotated with descriptors and experimental values. Users can also:

- Download optimized structures obtained via GOAT/GFN-FF in both xyz and mol formats;
- Access and download complete datasets as csv files containing all calculated molecular descriptors;
- Download bundled archives containing all optimized IL structures used in model development.

Additionally, we also developed an ionic liquid structure generator, which theoretically enables users to create over 500,000 cation–anion combinations using a curated library of ~1300 cations and ~400 anions. The resulting structures are automatically built and pre-optimized using the UFF, making them ideal starting points for further quantum mechanical or ML-based investigations.

Altogether, this work delivers a unified framework for data-driven IL modeling by combining simple molecular descriptors, atomistic calculations, ML, and online software engineering.

**Author Contributions:** Conceptualization, S.A. and S.J.A.; methodology, S.A. and S.J.A.; software, S.A.; validation, S.A. and S.J.A.; formal analysis, S.A. and S.J.A.; investigation, S.A. and S.J.A.; resources, S.A.; data curation, S.A. and S.J.A.; writing—original draft preparation, S.A. and S.J.A.; visualization, S.A. and S.J.A.; supervision, S.A.; project administration, S.A. and S.J.A.; funding acquisition, S.A. and S.J.A. All authors have read and agreed to the published version of the manuscript.

**Funding:** The authors gratefully acknowledge the financial support of the Ministry of Science, Technological Development and Innovation of the Republic of Serbia (Grant Nos. 451-03-137/2025-03/200125 and 451-03-136/2025-03/200125).

**Data Availability Statement:** The original contributions presented in the study are included in the article material, further inquiries can be directed to the corresponding author.

**Acknowledgments:** The Association for the International Development of Academic and Scientific Collaboration (https://aidasco.org/ accessed on 1 July 2025.), Centrohem d.o.o. (https://www.centrohem.co.rs/ accessed on 1 July 2025.), and Serbian Natural History Society (https://spd.rs/ accessed on 1 July 2025.), who supported the research by providing part of the computer resources.

**Conflicts of Interest:** The authors declare no conflicts of interest.

## References

1. Kaur, G.; Kumar, H.; Singla, M. Diverse Applications of Ionic Liquids: A Comprehensive Review. *J. Mol. Liq.* **2022**, *351*, 118556. [CrossRef]
2. Welton, T. Ionic Liquids: A Brief History. *Biophys. Rev.* **2018**, *10*, 691–706. [CrossRef]
3. Angell, C.A.; Ansari, Y.; Zhao, Z. Ionic Liquids: Past, Present and Future. *Faraday Discuss.* **2011**, *154*, 9–27. [CrossRef]
4. Lei, Z.; Dai, C.; Hallett, J.; Shiflett, M. Introduction: Ionic Liquids for Diverse Applications. *Chem. Rev.* **2024**, *124*, 7533–7535. [CrossRef] [PubMed]
5. Fabre, E.; Murshed, S.M.S. A Review of the Thermophysical Properties and Potential of Ionic Liquids for Thermal Applications. *J. Mater. Chem. A* **2021**, *9*, 15861–15879. [CrossRef]
6. Shamshina, J.L.; Rogers, R.D. Ionic Liquids: New Forms of Active Pharmaceutical Ingredients with Unique, Tunable Properties. *Chem. Rev.* **2023**, *123*, 11894–11953. [CrossRef]
7. Yalcin, D.; Drummond, C.J.; Greaves, T.L. Solvation Properties of Protic Ionic Liquids and Molecular Solvents. *Phys. Chem. Chem. Phys.* **2019**, *22*, 114–128. [CrossRef] [PubMed]
8. Nordness, O.; Brennecke, J.F. Ion Dissociation in Ionic Liquids and Ionic Liquid Solutions. *Chem. Rev.* **2020**, *120*, 12873–12902. [CrossRef] [PubMed]
9. Eyckens, D.J.; Henderson, L.C. A Review of Solvate Ionic Liquids: Physical Parameters and Synthetic Applications. *Front. Chem.* **2019**, *7*, 263. [CrossRef]
10. Chatterjee, K.; Pathak, A.D.; Lakma, A.; Sharma, C.S.; Sahu, K.K.; Singh, A.K. Synthesis, Characterization and Application of a Non-Flammable Dicationic Ionic Liquid in Lithium-Ion Battery as Electrolyte Additive. *Sci. Rep.* **2020**, *10*, 9606. [CrossRef]
11. Anis, A.; Shi, K.; Hagen, E.; Wang, Y.; Biswas, P.; Zachariah, M.R. Role of Anions in the Electrochemical Modulation of Flammability of Ionic Liquids. *Combust. Flame* **2025**, *275*, 113994. [CrossRef]
12. Pacheco-Fernández, I.; Pino, V. Green Solvents in Analytical Chemistry. *Curr. Opin. Green Sustain. Chem.* **2019**, *18*, 42–50. [CrossRef]
13. Choi, Y.H.; Verpoorte, R. Green Solvents for the Extraction of Bioactive Compounds from Natural Products Using Ionic Liquids and Deep Eutectic Solvents. *Curr. Opin. Food Sci.* **2019**, *26*, 87–93. [CrossRef]
14. Lebedeva, O.; Kultin, D.; Kustov, L. Electrochemical Synthesis of Unique Nanomaterials in Ionic Liquids. *Nanomaterials* **2021**, *11*, 3270. [CrossRef]
15. Torrinha, Á.; Oliveira, T.M.B.F.; Ribeiro, F.W.P.; de Lima-Neto, P.; Correia, A.N.; Morais, S. (Bio)Sensing Strategies Based on Ionic Liquid-Functionalized Carbon Nanocomposites for Pharmaceuticals: Towards Greener Electrochemical Tools. *Nanomaterials* **2022**, *12*, 2368. [CrossRef]
16. de Jesus, S.S.; Maciel Filho, R. Are Ionic Liquids Eco-Friendly? *Renew. Sustain. Energy Rev.* **2022**, *157*, 112039. [CrossRef]
17. Thomas, R.; Mary, Y.S.; Resmi, K.S.; Narayana, B.; Sarojini, S.B.K.; Armaković, S.; Armaković, S.J.; Vijayakumar, G.; Alsenoy, C.V.; Mohan, B.J. Synthesis and Spectroscopic Study of Two New Pyrazole Derivatives with Detailed Computational Evaluation of Their Reactivity and Pharmaceutical Potential. *J. Mol. Struct.* **2019**, *1181*, 599–612. [CrossRef]
18. Mary, Y.S.; Mary, Y.S.; Thomas, R.; Narayana, B.; Samshuddin, S.; Sarojini, B.K.; Armaković, S.; Armaković, S.J.; Pillai, G.G. Theoretical Studies on the Structure and Various Physico-Chemical and Biological Properties of a Terphenyl Derivative with Immense Anti-Protozoan Activity. *Polycycl. Aromat. Compd.* **2021**, *41*, 825–840. [CrossRef]
19. Haruna, K.; Kumar, V.S.; Armaković, S.J.; Armaković, S.; Mary, Y.S.; Thomas, R.; Popoola, S.A.; Almohammedi, A.R.; Roxy, M.S.; Al-Saadi, A.A. Spectral Characterization, Thermochemical Studies, Periodic SAPT Calculations and Detailed Quantum Mechanical Profiling Various Physico-Chemical Properties of 3,4-Dichlorodiuron. *Spectrochim. Acta Part A Mol. Biomol. Spectrosc.* **2020**, *228*, 117580. [CrossRef]
20. Beegum, S.; Mary, Y.S.; Mary, Y.S.; Thomas, R.; Armaković, S.; Armaković, S.J.; Zitko, J.; Dolezal, M.; Van Alsenoy, C. Exploring the Detailed Spectroscopic Characteristics, Chemical and Biological Activity of Two Cyanopyrazine-2-Carboxamide Derivatives Using Experimental and Theoretical Tools. *Spectrochim. Acta Part A Mol. Biomol. Spectrosc.* **2020**, *224*, 117414. [CrossRef] [PubMed]

21. Al-Otaibi, J.S.; Mary, Y.S.; Armaković, S.; Thomas, R. Hybrid and Bioactive Cocrystals of Pyrazinamide with Hydroxybenzoic Acids: Detailed Study of Structure, Spectroscopic Characteristics, Other Potential Applications and Noncovalent Interactions Using SAPT. *J. Mol. Struct.* **2020**, *1202*, 127316. [CrossRef]
22. Bielenica, A.; Beegum, S.; Mary, Y.S.; Mary, Y.S.; Thomas, R.; Armaković, S.; Armaković, S.J.; Madeddu, S.; Struga, M.; Van Alsenoy, C. Experimental and Computational Analysis of 1-(4-Chloro-3-Nitrophenyl)-3-(3,4-Dichlorophenyl)Thiourea. *J. Mol. Struct.* **2020**, *1205*, 127587. [CrossRef]
23. Cortés-Arriagada, D. Intermolecular Driving Forces on the Adsorption of DNA/RNA Nucleobases to Graphene and Phosphorene: An Atomistic Perspective from DFT Calculations. *J. Mol. Liq.* **2021**, *325*, 115229. [CrossRef]
24. Behbahani, A.F.; Rissanou, A.; Kritikos, G.; Doxastakis, M.; Burkhart, C.; Polińska, P.; Harmandaris, V.A. Conformations and Dynamics of Polymer Chains in Cis and Trans Polybutadiene/Silica Nanocomposites through Atomistic Simulations: From the Unentangled to the Entangled Regime. *Macromolecules* **2020**, *53*, 6173–6189. [CrossRef]
25. Sutton, C.; Levchenko, S.V. First-Principles Atomistic Thermodynamics and Configurational Entropy. *Front. Chem.* **2020**, *8*, 757. [CrossRef]
26. Moraes, A.S.; Pinheiro, G.A.; Lourenço, T.C.; Lopes, M.C.; Quiles, M.G.; Dias, L.G.; Da Silva, J.L.F. Screening of the Role of the Chemical Structure in the Electrochemical Stability Window of Ionic Liquids: DFT Calculations Combined with Data Mining. *J. Chem. Inf. Model.* **2022**, *62*, 4702–4712. [CrossRef]
27. Kuusik, I.; Kook, M.; Pärna, R.; Kivimäki, A.; Käämbre, T.; Reisberg, L.; Kikas, A.; Kisand, V. The Electronic Structure of Ionic Liquids Based on the TFSI Anion: A Gas Phase UPS and DFT Study. *J. Mol. Liq.* **2019**, *294*, 111580. [CrossRef]
28. Bardak, C.; Atac, A.; Bardak, F. Effect of the External Electric Field on the Electronic Structure, Spectroscopic Features, NLO Properties, and Interionic Interactions in Ionic Liquids: A DFT Approach. *J. Mol. Liq.* **2019**, *273*, 314–325. [CrossRef]
29. Zheng, D.; Jiang, S.; Zheng, P.; Zhou, D.; Qiu, J.; Gao, L. Molecular Mechanism for the Interaction of Natural Products with Ionic Liquids: Insights from MD and DFT Study. *J. Mol. Liq.* **2024**, *399*, 124440. [CrossRef]
30. Thomas, E.; Vijayalakshmi, K.P.; George, B.K. Kinetic Stability of Imidazolium Cations and Ionic Liquids: A Frontier Molecular Orbital Approach. *J. Mol. Liq.* **2019**, *276*, 721–727. [CrossRef]
31. He, Y.; Guo, Y.; Yan, F.; Yu, T.; Liu, L.; Zhang, X.; Zheng, T. Density Functional Theory Study of Adsorption of Ionic Liquids on Graphene Oxide Surface. *Chem. Eng. Sci.* **2021**, *245*, 116946. [CrossRef]
32. Walters, W.P.; Barzilay, R. Applications of Deep Learning in Molecule Generation and Molecular Property Prediction. *Acc. Chem. Res.* **2021**, *54*, 263–270. [CrossRef]
33. Noé, F.; Tkatchenko, A.; Müller, K.-R.; Clementi, C. Machine Learning for Molecular Simulation. *Annu. Rev. Phys. Chem.* **2020**, *71*, 361–390. [CrossRef]
34. Wigh, D.S.; Goodman, J.M.; Lapkin, A.A. A Review of Molecular Representation in the Age of Machine Learning. *WIREs Comput. Mol. Sci.* **2022**, *12*, e1603. [CrossRef]
35. Nakhaei-Kohani, R.; Ali Madani, S.; Mousavi, S.-P.; Atashrouz, S.; Abedi, A.; Hemmati-Sarapardeh, A.; Mohaddespour, A. Machine Learning Assisted Structure-Based Models for Predicting Electrical Conductivity of Ionic Liquids. *J. Mol. Liq.* **2022**, *362*, 119509. [CrossRef]
36. Bobbitt, N.S.; Allers, J.P.; Harvey, J.A.; Poe, D.; Wemhoner, J.D.; Keth, J.; Greathouse, J.A. Machine Learning Predictions of Diffusion in Bulk and Confined Ionic Liquids Using Simple Descriptors. *Mol. Syst. Des. Eng.* **2023**, *8*, 1257–1274. [CrossRef]
37. Racki, A.; Paduszyński, K. Recent Advances in the Modeling of Ionic Liquids Using Artificial Neural Networks. *J. Chem. Inf. Model.* **2025**, *65*, 3161–3175. [CrossRef]
38. Koutsoukos, S.; Philippi, F.; Malaret, F.; Welton, T. A Review on Machine Learning Algorithms for the Ionic Liquid Chemical Space. *Chem. Sci.* **2021**, *12*, 6820–6843. [CrossRef] [PubMed]
39. Valderrama, J.O.; Reátegui, A.; Rojas, R.E. Density of Ionic Liquids Using Group Contribution and Artificial Neural Networks. *Ind. Eng. Chem. Res.* **2009**, *48*, 3254–3259. [CrossRef]
40. Barati-Harooni, A.; Najafi-Marghmaleki, A.; Mohammadi, A.H. ANFIS Modeling of Ionic Liquids Densities. *J. Mol. Liq.* **2016**, *224*, 965–975. [CrossRef]
41. Paduszyński, K. Extensive Databases and Group Contribution QSPRs of Ionic Liquids Properties. 1. Density. *Ind. Eng. Chem. Res.* **2019**, *58*, 5322–5338. [CrossRef]
42. Baran, K.; Kloskowski, A. Graph Neural Networks and Structural Information on Ionic Liquids: A Cheminformatics Study on Molecular Physicochemical Property Prediction. *J. Phys. Chem. B* **2023**, *127*, 10542–10555. [CrossRef] [PubMed]
43. Acar, Z.; Nguyen, P.; Lau, K.C. Machine-Learning Model Prediction of Ionic Liquids Melting Points. *Appl. Sci.* **2022**, *12*, 2408. [CrossRef]
44. Fan, D.; Xue, K.; Liu, Y.; Zhu, W.; Chen, Y.; Cui, P.; Sun, S.; Qi, J.; Zhu, Z.; Wang, Y. Modeling the Toxicity of Ionic Liquids Based on Deep Learning Method. *Comput. Chem. Eng.* **2023**, *176*, 108293. [CrossRef]
45. Abranches, D.O.; Zhang, Y.; Maginn, E.J.; Colón, Y.J. Sigma Profiles in Deep Learning: Towards a Universal Molecular Descriptor. *Chem. Commun.* **2022**, *58*, 5630–5633. [CrossRef]

46. Armaković, S.; Armaković, S.J. Atomistica.Online—Web Application for Generating Input Files for ORCA Molecular Modelling Package Made with the Anvil Platform. *Mol. Simul.* **2023**, *49*, 117–123. [CrossRef]
47. Armaković, S.; Armaković, S.J. Online and Desktop Graphical User Interfaces for Xtb Programme from Atomistica.Online Platform. *Mol. Simul.* **2024**, *50*, 560–570. [CrossRef]
48. Liakos, D.G.; Guo, Y.; Neese, F. Comprehensive Benchmark Results for the Domain Based Local Pair Natural Orbital Coupled Cluster Method (DLPNO-CCSD(T)) for Closed- and Open-Shell Systems. *J. Phys. Chem. A* **2020**, *124*, 90–100. [CrossRef]
49. Guo, Y.; Riplinger, C.; Liakos, D.G.; Becker, U.; Saitow, M.; Neese, F. Linear Scaling Perturbative Triples Correction Approximations for Open-Shell Domain-Based Local Pair Natural Orbital Coupled Cluster Singles and Doubles Theory [DLPNO-CCSD(T0/T)]. *J. Chem. Phys.* **2020**, *152*, 024116. [CrossRef]
50. Neese, F. The SHARK Integral Generation and Digestion System. *J. Comput. Chem.* **2022**, *44*, 381–396. [CrossRef]
51. Teale, A.M.; Helgaker, T.; Savin, A.; Adamo, C.; Aradi, B.; Arbuznikov, A.V.; Ayers, P.W.; Baerends, E.J.; Barone, V.; Calaminici, P.; et al. DFT Exchange: Sharing Perspectives on the Workhorse of Quantum Chemistry and Materials Science. *Phys. Chem. Chem. Phys.* **2022**, *24*, 28700–28781. [CrossRef] [PubMed]
52. Neese, F.; Wennmohs, F.; Hansen, A.; Becker, U. Efficient, Approximate and Parallel Hartree–Fock and Hybrid DFT Calculations. A 'Chain-of-Spheres' Algorithm for the Hartree–Fock Exchange. *Chem. Phys.* **2009**, *356*, 98–109. [CrossRef]
53. Neese, F. Software Update: The ORCA Program System, Version 4.0. *WIREs Comput. Mol. Sci.* **2018**, *8*, e1327. [CrossRef]
54. Neese, F. The ORCA Program System. *WIREs Comput. Mol. Sci.* **2012**, *2*, 73–78. [CrossRef]
55. Neese, F.; Wennmohs, F.; Becker, U.; Riplinger, C. The ORCA Quantum Chemistry Program Package. *J. Chem. Phys.* **2020**, *152*, 224108. [CrossRef]
56. Bannwarth, C.; Caldeweyher, E.; Ehlert, S.; Hansen, A.; Pracht, P.; Seibert, J.; Spicher, S.; Grimme, S. Extended Tight-Binding Quantum Chemistry Methods. *WIREs Comput. Mol. Sci.* **2021**, *11*, e1493. [CrossRef]
57. Bannwarth, C.; Ehlert, S.; Grimme, S. GFN2-xTB—An Accurate and Broadly Parametrized Self-Consistent Tight-Binding Quantum Chemical Method with Multipole Electrostatics and Density-Dependent Dispersion Contributions. *J. Chem. Theory Comput.* **2019**, *15*, 1652–1671. [CrossRef]
58. Ehlert, S.; Stahn, M.; Spicher, S.; Grimme, S. Robust and Efficient Implicit Solvation Model for Fast Semiempirical Methods. *J. Chem. Theory Comput.* **2021**, *17*, 4250–4261. [CrossRef]
59. Grimme, S.; Bannwarth, C.; Shushkov, P. A Robust and Accurate Tight-Binding Quantum Chemical Method for Structures, Vibrational Frequencies, and Noncovalent Interactions of Large Molecular Systems Parametrized for All Spd-Block Elements (Z = 1–86). *J. Chem. Theory Comput.* **2017**, *13*, 1989–2009. [CrossRef]
60. Froitzheim, T.; Müller, M.; Hansen, A.; Grimme, S. G-xTB: A General-Purpose Extended Tight-Binding Electronic Structure Method For the Elements H to Lr (Z = 1–103). *ChemRxiv* **2025**.
61. Dewar, M.J.S.; Hashmall, J.A.; Venier, C.G. Ground States of Conjugated Molecules. IX. Hydrocarbon Radicals and Radical Ions. *J. Am. Chem. Soc.* **1968**, *90*, 1953–1957. [CrossRef]
62. Dewar, M.J.S.; Zoebisch, E.G.; Healy, E.F.; Stewart, J.J.P. Development and Use of Quantum Mechanical Molecular Models. 76. AM1: A New General Purpose Quantum Mechanical Molecular Model. *J. Am. Chem. Soc.* **1985**, *107*, 3902–3909. [CrossRef]
63. Dewar, M.J.S.; Thiel, W. Ground States of Molecules. 38. The MNDO Method. Approximations and Parameters. *J. Am. Chem. Soc.* **1977**, *99*, 4899–4907. [CrossRef]
64. Rocha, G.B.; Freire, R.O.; Simas, A.M.; Stewart, J.J.P. RM1: A Reparameterization of AM1 for H, C, N, O, P, S, F, Cl, Br, and I. *J. Comput. Chem.* **2006**, *27*, 1101–1111. [CrossRef]
65. Stewart, J.J.P. Optimization of Parameters for Semiempirical Methods I. Method. *J. Comput. Chem.* **1989**, *10*, 209–220. [CrossRef]
66. Stewart, J.J.P. Optimization of Parameters for Semiempirical Methods II. Applications. *J. Comput. Chem.* **1989**, *10*, 221–264. [CrossRef]
67. Stewart, J.J.P. MOPAC: A Semiempirical Molecular Orbital Program. *J. Comput. Mol. Des.* **1990**, *4*, 1–103. [CrossRef] [PubMed]
68. Stewart, J.J.P. Optimization of Parameters for Semiempirical Methods V: Modification of NDDO Approximations and Application to 70 Elements. *J. Mol. Model.* **2007**, *13*, 1173–1213. [CrossRef]
69. Thiel, W.; Voityuk, A.A. Extension of the MNDO Formalism Tod Orbitals: Integral Approximations and Preliminary Numerical Results. *Theoret. Chim. Acta* **1992**, *81*, 391–404. [CrossRef]
70. Lu, T. A Comprehensive Electron Wavefunction Analysis Toolbox for Chemists, Multiwfn. *J. Chem. Phys.* **2024**, *161*, 082503. [CrossRef]
71. Lu, T.; Chen, Q. Van Der Waals Potential: An Important Complement to Molecular Electrostatic Potential in Studying Intermolecular Interactions. *J. Mol. Model.* **2020**, *26*, 315. [CrossRef]
72. Lu, T.; Manzetti, S. Wavefunction and Reactivity Study of Benzo[a]Pyrene Diol Epoxide and Its Enantiomeric Forms. *Struct. Chem.* **2014**, *25*, 1521–1533. [CrossRef]
73. Lu, T.; Chen, F. Multiwfn: A Multifunctional Wavefunction Analyzer. *J. Comput. Chem.* **2012**, *33*, 580–592. [CrossRef] [PubMed]

74. Martínez, J.M.; Martínez, L. Packing Optimization for Automated Generation of Complex System's Initial Configurations for Molecular Dynamics and Docking. *J. Comput. Chem.* **2003**, *24*, 819–825. [CrossRef]
75. Martínez, L.; Andrade, R.; Birgin, E.G.; Martínez, J.M. PACKMOL: A Package for Building Initial Configurations for Molecular Dynamics Simulations. *J. Comput. Chem.* **2009**, *30*, 2157–2164. [CrossRef]
76. Sharing New Breakthroughs and Artifacts Supporting Molecular Property Prediction, Language Processing, and Neuroscience. Available online: https://ai.meta.com/blog/meta-fair-science-new-open-source-releases/ (accessed on 9 July 2025).
77. Ionic Liquids Database—ILThermo. Available online: https://ilthermo.boulder.nist.gov/ (accessed on 9 July 2025).
78. Landrum, G.; Tosco, P.; Kelley, B.; Rodriguez, R.; Cosgrove, D.; Vianello, R.; Sriniker; Gedeck, P.; Jones, G.; Kawashima, E.; et al. Rdkit/Rdkit: 2025_03_6 (Q1 2025) Release 2025. *Zenodo* **2025**. [CrossRef]
79. O'Boyle, N.M.; Banck, M.; James, C.A.; Morley, C.; Vandermeersch, T.; Hutchison, G.R. Open Babel: An Open Chemical Toolbox. *J. Cheminformatics* **2011**, *3*, 33. [CrossRef]
80. de Souza, B. GOAT: A Global Optimization Algorithm for Molecules and Atomic Clusters. *Angew. Chem. Int. Ed.* **2025**, *64*, e202500393. [CrossRef] [PubMed]
81. Goedecker, S. Minima Hopping: An Efficient Search Method for the Global Minimum of the Potential Energy Surface of Complex Molecular Systems. *J. Chem. Phys.* **2004**, *120*, 9911–9917. [CrossRef] [PubMed]
82. Wales, D.J.; Doye, J.P.K. Global Optimization by Basin-Hopping and the Lowest Energy Structures of Lennard-Jones Clusters Containing up to 110 Atoms. *J. Phys. Chem. A* **1997**, *101*, 5111–5116. [CrossRef]
83. Neese, F. Software Update: The ORCA Program System—Version 5.0. *WIREs Comput. Mol. Sci.* **2022**, *12*, e1606. [CrossRef]
84. Spicher, S.; Grimme, S. Robust Atomistic Modeling of Materials, Organometallic, and Biochemical Systems. *Angew. Chem. Int. Ed.* **2020**, *59*, 15665–15673. [CrossRef] [PubMed]
85. Cao, Y.; Balduf, T.; Beachy, M.D.; Bennett, M.C.; Bochevarov, A.D.; Chien, A.; Dub, P.A.; Dyall, K.G.; Furness, J.W.; Halls, M.D.; et al. Quantum Chemical Package Jaguar: A Survey of Recent Developments and Unique Features. *J. Chem. Phys.* **2024**, *161*, 052502. [CrossRef] [PubMed]
86. Cao, Y.; Halls, M.D.; Vadicherla, T.R.; Friesner, R.A. Pseudospectral Implementations of Long-Range Corrected Density Functional Theory. *J. Comput. Chem.* **2021**, *42*, 2089–2102. [CrossRef]
87. Cao, Y.; Hughes, T.; Giesen, D.; Halls, M.D.; Goldberg, A.; Vadicherla, T.R.; Sastry, M.; Patel, B.; Sherman, W.; Weisman, A.L.; et al. Highly Efficient Implementation of Pseudospectral Time-Dependent Density-Functional Theory for the Calculation of Excitation Energies of Large Molecules. *J. Comput. Chem.* **2016**, *37*, 1425–1441. [CrossRef]
88. Jacobson, L.D.; Bochevarov, A.D.; Watson, M.A.; Hughes, T.F.; Rinaldo, D.; Ehrlich, S.; Steinbrecher, T.B.; Vaitheeswaran, S.; Philipp, D.M.; Halls, M.D. Automated Transition State Search and Its Application to Diverse Types of Organic Reactions. *J. Chem. Theory Comput.* **2017**, *13*, 5780–5797. [CrossRef]
89. Bochevarov, A.D.; Harder, E.; Hughes, T.F.; Greenwood, J.R.; Braden, D.A.; Philipp, D.M.; Rinaldo, D.; Halls, M.D.; Zhang, J.; Friesner, R.A. Jaguar: A High-Performance Quantum Chemistry Software Program with Strengths in Life and Materials Sciences. *Int. J. Quantum Chem.* **2013**, *113*, 2110–2142. [CrossRef]

computation

MDPI

Article

# Withangulatin A Identified as a Covalent Binder to Zap70 Kinase by Molecular Docking

**Corentin Bedart [1], Gérard Vergoten [1] and Christian Bailly [2,3,4,*]**

[1] U1286—INFINITE—Institute for Translational Research in Inflammation, CHU Lille, Inserm, University of Lille, 59000 Lille, France; corentin.bedart@univ-lille.fr (C.B.)
[2] Institut de Chimie Pharmaceutique Albert Lespagnol (ICPAL), Faculté de Pharmacie, University of Lille, 59000 Lille, France
[3] UMR9020-U1277—CANTHER—Cancer Heterogeneity Plasticity and Resistance to Therapies, CHU Lille, Inserm, CNRS, University of Lille, 59000 Lille, France
[4] OncoWitan, Scientific Consulting Office, 59290 Lille, France
* Correspondence: christian.bailly@univ-lille.fr

**Abstract:** Inhibitors of the tyrosine kinase Zap70 are actively searched to improve treatments of lymphoid malignancies and autoimmune diseases associated with an abnormal T-cell response. The natural product withaferin A (WFA) has been characterized as a covalent inhibitor of Zap70 capable of blocking the migration of human T-cells. By analogy, we postulated that other withanolides equipped with a thiol-reactive, α,β-unsaturated ketone may form covalent complexes with Zap70. The hypothesis was tested using a molecular modeling approach with a panel of 12 withanolides docked onto the kinase domain of Zap70. Seven natural products revealed a capability to form stable complexes with Zap70 comparable to that of WFA, including withangulatin A, 4β-hydroxywithanolide E, withaperuvin, and ixocarpalactone A. Withangulatin A surpassed all the other withanolides for its ability to engage an interaction with Zap70 kinase and to form covalent complexes via bonding to the Cys346 residue close to the enzyme active site. The physicochemical and ADMET properties of withangulatin A were analyzed via Density Functional Theory calculations and an analysis of its Fukui function descriptors. The C3 position of the enone moiety was identified as the most reactive (nucleophilic) site of the molecule. Withangulatin A revealed a satisfactory ADMET profile with no major toxicity anticipated. It represents a potential hit to guide the design of Zap70 inhibitors.

**Keywords:** cysteine bonding; molecular docking; withaferin A; withangulatin A; withanolides; Zap70 kinase

## 1. Introduction

The protein Zap70 (zeta-chain-associated protein kinase 70 kDa) is a non-receptor tyrosine kinase which plays an essential role in T-cell receptor (TCR) signaling in thymocytes and peripheral T-cells. The kinase is recruited to the intracellular ζ-chains of the T-cell receptor to phosphorylate the TCR/CD3 multimeric protein complex, thus contributing to the diversification and amplification of TCR signaling. The correct functioning of the kinase is necessary to complete the development of thymocytes and T-cells in the thymus [1,2]. The protein is also expressed in NK cells and a subset of B cells. Aberrant expression of Zap70 has been reported in several inflammatory pathologies and its contribution to tumor immunity has been highlighted. Zap70 plays a role in several malignancies, notably in chronic lymphocytic leukemia (CLL) [3]. The protein is considered as a strong prognostic biomarker for patients with CLL [4]. Activated Zap70 represents a drug target to combat certain solid tumors due to its role as a driver of proliferation and tumor transformation and its implication in resistance to PI3K inhibitors in cancer cells [5]. Zap70 is viewed as an immunotherapeutic target to treat laryngeal cancer [6], lymphoid malignancies, and various autoimmune diseases associated with an abnormal T-cell response, including psoriasis and lupus [7,8].

These considerations have stimulated the search for different types of inhibitors of Zap70, acting either as direct blockers of the kinase domain or as disruptors of the interaction with the T-cell antigen receptor [8,9]. Zap70 inhibitors include natural and semi-synthetic products and diverse, rationally designed small molecules with a heterocyclic scaffold. In recent years, several types of inhibitors have been reported including arglabin derivatives, pyridopyrimidinones, and imidazopyrimidine-carboxamide derivatives to mention a few potent compounds [10–12]. Drug design approaches can benefit from a solid structural basis for the inhibition of the enzyme, with the crystallographic structure of the tyrosine kinase domain [13,14] and the identification of a druggable pocket close to the activation loop of the kinase [15].

Recently, the drug discovery strategy has been oriented toward the design and development of covalent inhibitors targeting cysteine residues that are essential for the correct functioning of the kinase. Thiol-reactive small molecules interfering with protein activity have been discovered [16]. There are several important cysteine residues in the kinase domain and the surrounding areas. In particular, C564 residue located in the kinase domain of Zap70 corresponds to a palmitoylation site, and its acylation contributes to the regulation of T-cell-mediated immunity [17,18]. The imidazopyrimidine-carboxamide derivative RDN009, bearing a chloroacetamide reactive group ($IC_{50}$ = 44.8 nM), is one of the most potent covalent inhibitors of Zap70 targeting C346, which also represents a critical site (Figure 1) [10]. Recently, this compound has been optimized to enhance its activity, leading to the derivative RDN2150 potently active against the kinase ($IC_{50}$ = 14 nM) and showing promising inhibitory effects on T-cell activation and inflammatory cytokine production [19]. The cysteine reactivity of RDN2150 is due to an acrylamide moiety, which is a mildly reactive warhead commonly found in approved covalent kinase drugs, such as afatinib and dacomitinib [20]. The α,β-unsaturated amide moiety of these compounds serves as a warhead to react with cysteine thiols. A similar reactive group with an α,β-unsaturated keto structure is found in the natural product β-epoxyarglabin and related sesquiterpene lactones such as grosheimin, which have been shown to react covalently with the C39 of Zap70 [12].

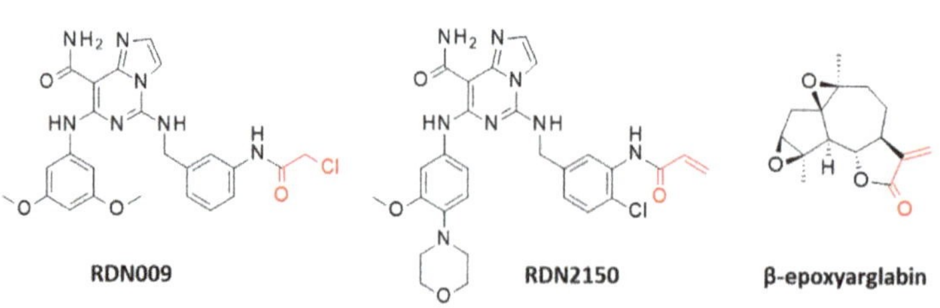


**Figure 1.** Structures of three covalent inhibitors of Zap70. The thiol-reactive moiety is shown in red.

Covalent binding to Zap70 has also been demonstrated with the withanolide-type steroid called withaferin A (WFA), which is essentially found in the medicinal plant *Withania somnifera* (L.) Dunal [21]. This compound presents a C-28 steroidal lactone based on an ergostane skeleton (Figure 2). WFA shows marked antitumor and anti-inflammatory effects [22]. The compound belongs to a large family of more than 1200 withanolides, which includes many antitumor compounds such as withanolide A, withangulatin A, withanone, physapruin A, and others [23]. WFA stands as a leading compound in the family, owing to its multiple pharmacological properties and, in particular, its potent antitumor efficacy [24–26]. It is a reactive molecule capable of covalently binding to the exposed cysteine residues of certain proteins, such as vimentin, Hsp90, Ikkβ, Nrf2, annexin II, and a few others [27].

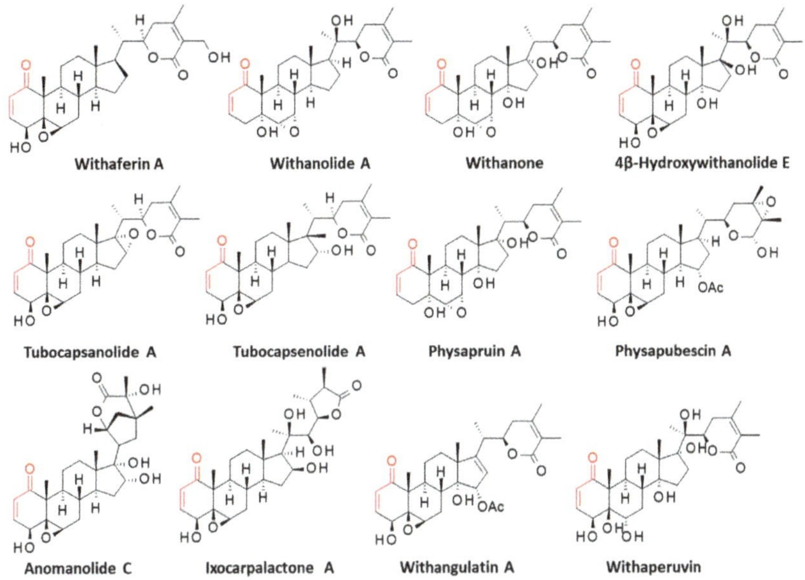


**Figure 2.** Structures of selected withanolides bearing a thiol-reactive enone moiety (in red).

WFA has been shown to inhibit Zap70 by forming covalent complexes with cysteine residues. Covalent binding of the product to the kinase has been demonstrated experimentally, and a molecular modeling analysis has predicted that two cysteines C560 and/or C564 could serve as potential thiol donors for the covalent drug attachment [28]. But at present, the exact cysteine site in Zap70 has not been evidenced experimentally. WFA reacts with cysteine thiol via its α,β-unsaturated ketone (enone) moiety which functions as a Michael acceptor (electrophile) susceptible to covalently modifying cysteine residues in proteins or thiol-containing compounds such as glutathione (GSH) and homocysteine [29,30]. Occasionally, an adduct can form from the thiol addition to the epoxide at the C-6 position, as observed upon the bioconversion of an extract of *Withania somnifera* by the fungus *Beauveria bassiana* in the presence of glutathione [31]. But in most cases, it is the α,β-unsaturated ketone moiety that reacts with thiols to form conjugates and cysteine adducts.

In the present study, we have analyzed the protein binding and compared the reactivity of a series of withanolides towards Zap70. The three-dimensional structure of the active kinase domain of Zap70 non-covalently bound to staurosporine was used as a structural model (PDB: 1U59) [14]. Twelve withanolides, all bearing a reactive α,β-unsaturated ketone moiety, were selected (Figure 2). Some of them are known to react covalently with cysteines in certain proteins. This is the case for WFA and tubocapsenolide A, which can form cysteine adducts with the chaperone protein Hsp90 [32,33], and for 4β-hydroxywithanolide E (4β-HWNE), which can bind to a cysteine residue of the transcription factor Keap1, so as to interrupt its interaction with Nrf2 [34]. Withangulatin A has been shown to form cysteine-bound covalent complexes with PHGDH (3-phosphoglycerate dehydrogenase), Prdx-6 (peroxiredoxin 6), and SERCA-2 (sarco/endoplasmic reticulum calcium-ATPase 2) [35–37]. The other withanolides have not been shown to form covalent complexes, but they carry the same reactive enone moiety. Some of them show prominent anticancer properties, such as physapruin A (from *Physalis peruviana*), which induces oxidative stress and DNA damages in cancer cells [38–41], and anomanolide C (from *Tubocapsicum anomalum*), which can suppress the progression of triple-negative breast tumors in mice [42]. By analogy to WFA, we hypothesized that some of these reactive compounds could also covalently bind to Zap70 and form covalent cysteine adducts. The results of our molecular docking study are presented here.

## 2. Materials and Methods

### 2.1. Molecular Structures and Software

The three-dimensional structure Zap70 non-covalently bound with staurosporine was retrieved from the protein data bank (PDB: 1U59) and used as a model for the docking analysis. It is a high-resolution structure (2.30 Å) obtained by X-ray diffraction [14]. The molecular docking analysis was performed with the GOLD software (version 5.3, Cambridge Crystallographic Data Centre, Cambridge, UK). Prior to the docking operations, the structure of each ligand was optimized using a classical Monte Carlo conformational searching procedure via the BOSS software v4.9 [43]. Molecular graphics and analysis were performed using Discovery Studio Visualizer, Biovia 2020 (Dassault Systèmes BIOVIA Discovery Studio Visualizer 2020, San Diego, Dassault Systèmes, 2020). The web server Computed Atlas of Surface Topography of proteins (CASTp) 3.0 was used to identify potential ligand-binding sites on the tubulin dimer. The molecular modeling software Chimera 1.15 was used for visualization [44].

### 2.2. In Silico Molecular Docking Procedure

The staurosporine binding area within the kinase domain of Zap70 was considered as the potential binding site for the studied withanolides. During the process, the side chains of the following amino acids within the binding site were rendered fully flexible: Leu344, Cys346, Phe349, Val352, Lys369, Glu386, Met390, Lys424, Asp479, and Phe480. A docking grid, centered in the volume defined by the central amino acid, has been defined based on shape complementarity and geometry considerations. In general, up to 100 poses considered as energetically reasonable are selected during the search for the correct binding mode of the ligand. The decision to select a trial pose is based on ranked poses, using the fitness scoring function (PLP score incorporated in GOLD v5.3) [45]. The same procedure was used to establish molecular models for all studied natural products.

In general, 6 poses are selected per analysis. The ranking leads to the evaluation of the empirical potential energy of the interaction ($\Delta E$), defined using the expression $\Delta E(\text{interaction}) = E(\text{complex}) - [E(\text{protein}) + E(\text{ligand})]$. The SPASIBA spectroscopic force field is used to calculate the final energy. The required parameters are derived from vibrational wavenumbers obtained in the infrared and Raman spectra of a large series of compounds of diverse chemical nature (organic molecules, amino acids, saccharides, nucleic acids, and lipids). The last step corresponds to validation using the SPASIBA force field, an essential step to determine the best protein–ligand structure. This force field has been specifically developed to provide refined empirical MM force field parameters [46]. SPASIBA (integrated into CHARMM) empirical energies of interaction are calculated. It is an excellent system for reproducing crystal-phase infrared data. SPASIBA has been specifically developed to provide refined empirical molecular mechanics force field parameters [47]. The Boss program and the Molecular Mechanics/Generalized Born Surface Area (MM/GBSA) procedure were used to evaluate the free energies of hydration ($\Delta G$) in relation to aqueous solubility [48].

The docking analysis was performed with the different withanolides interacting with the kinase domain of Zap70 in a non-covalent process. The potential formation of a covalent C-S linkage between the α,β-unsaturated ketone unit of the natural products and the C346 thiol group was inferred from the calculated distance between the reactive groups, as described previously for other covalent drug–protein complexes [49,50].

### 2.3. *DFT Calculations and Predicted Physicochemical and ADMET Properties*

All Density Functional Theory (DFT) calculations were performed with the ORCA v5.0.4 software package, using the B3LYP-D3/def2-SVP computational level and the water implicit solvation CPCM [51], from the 3D coordinates of ligands previously generated using Auto3D [52]. The DFT calculations provided a better understanding of the reactivity and stability of our compounds, in particular, by obtaining the energies of the HOMO (Highest Occupied Molecular Orbital, serving as an electron donor) and the LUMO (Lowest Unoccupied Molecular Orbital, acting as an electron acceptor) orbitals, for the calculation of the HOMO-LUMO gaps. The reactivity of the molecules was further analyzed using Fukui functions and dual descriptors to determine the nucleophilicity (f−), electrophilicity (f+), and radical attack susceptibility (Δf(r)) of the heavy atoms.

Several machine learning-based approaches were used to predict a wide range of critical parameters, starting from the SMILES string of the studied compounds. SolTranNet [53] was used to predict the aqueous solubility with the calculation of logS values, PredPS [54] to predict the stability of compounds in human plasma using an attention-based graph neural network, and PredMS [55] to estimate the metabolic stability of the compounds in human liver microsomes from a random forest model. FP-ADMET [56], a toolbox of prediction models using mostly random forest models, allowed for the prediction of a wide range of physicochemical, ADMET, and ADMET related parameters.

## 3. Results

### 3.1. *Protein Structure and Binding Site Analysis*

The structure of the active kinase domain of Zap70 bound to staurosporine (1U59) was used to locate the position of the different cysteine residues. The kinase domain comprises seven cysteine residues at C346, C405, C510, C560, C564, C575, and C596, but only one, C346, is positioned at the entrance of the ATP binding site where the crystallographic ligand (staurosporine) is bound, as represented in Figure 3. The other residues, notably C560-C564, are located on the external surface of the protein. A binding site analysis was performed using the web server CASTp 3.0, which is a convenient tool to analyze the topography of proteins and to locate potential drug-binding sites [57]. The analysis revealed the position of only one large binding area, corresponding to the ATP and staurosporine binding pocket (Figure 4). The cavity is quite large, sufficient to accommodate a polycyclic molecule such as WFA. Six other small cavities were identified with CAST, but they are very narrow (<50 Å$^3$), probably too small to serve as potential binding sites. The estimated volume of the central cavity is 774.7 Å$^3$ according to the method of static accessibility [58] and 2134.5 Å$^3$ when measuring the solvent-accessible surface [57]. The same calculation method applied to WFA gave a value of 1374.5 Å$^3$. It is thus clear that the molecule can fit only in the large cavity, not the small hollows around the protein. For this reason, we focused our analysis on the main kinase activity site and performed a docking analysis to compare the binding of WFA and its analogs to this site, and the possible formation of a covalent interaction with cysteine 346 located at the gate of the active site.

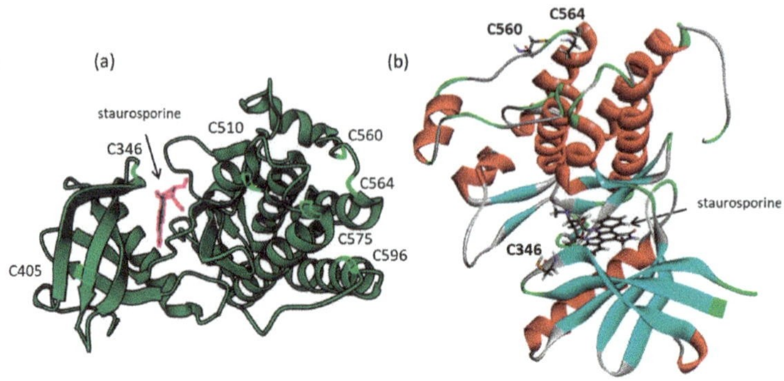


**Figure 3.** Structure of the active kinase domain of Zap70 bound to staurosporine (from Lys328 to His612, from PDB 1U59) [14]. (**a**) A global view of the active kinase domain with the different cysteine residues. (**b**) A view of the staurosporine-bound protein with the α-helices (in red) and β-sheets (in cyan). The position of three cysteine residues is indicated, including C346 in the kinase active site and C560-C564 exposed on the protein surface.

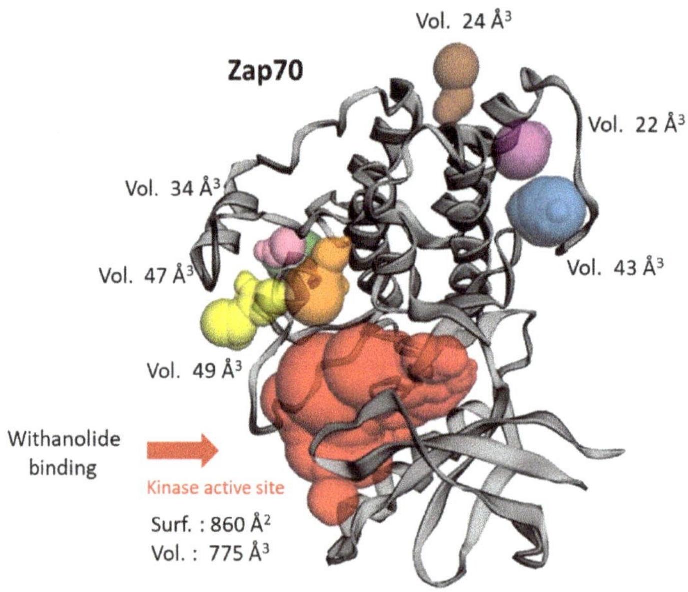


**Figure 4.** The binding site analysis of Zap70 (using web server CASTp 3.0) primarily reveals the position of the ATP-binding site in the center of the protein (in red) and a few minor areas around the protein, with the indicated volumes.

### *3.2. Covalent Binding of WFA to Zap70*

WFA was docked into the active kinase domain of Zap70, and the empirical energy of interaction (ΔE) and the free energy of hydration (ΔG) of the interaction were calculated (Table 1). WFA can fit easily into the binding cavity, as represented in Figure 5. The compound remains significantly exposed, because the cavity is large, with an extended solvent-accessible area. However, the extended molecule bridges the two lips of the cavity and anchors itself relatively deeply into the protein site. The fit is satisfactory (ΔE = −69.30 kcal/mol), controlled by the diversity of molecular contacts between the ligand and the protein. Notably, four hydrogen bonds contribute to the stability of the complex, between the withanolide and residues Asn348, Phe349, Arg460, and Lys484, in addition to various van der Waals contacts (Figure 6). Interestingly, the small molecule sits at a short distance from Cys346 to position the enone moiety close to the thiol group of the cysteine residue. Under these conditions, covalent binding can be easily established, as represented in Figure 7. The molecule adopts a configuration which places its enone moiety close to the SH group of C346, thus favoring the subsequent formation of the thioether linkage, while the opposite lactone part of the molecule is interacting with the protein via residues Arg460 and Lys484. The covalent binding of the natural product to the C346 residue of Zap70 deserves further study using a more appropriate methodology (e.g., quantum mechanical) for describing the covalent bond formation with greater precision.

**Table 1.** Calculated potential energy of interaction (ΔE) and free energy of hydration (ΔG) for the interaction of withanolides with Zap70 (1U59).

| Compounds | CID [1] | ΔE (kcal/mol) | ΔG (kcal/mol) |
|---|---|---|---|
| Anomanolide C | 44423050 | −61.40 | −21.50 |
| 4β-Hydroxywithanolide E | 73621 | −75.50 | −24.30 |
| Ixocarpalactone A | 327287 | −75.50 | −24.85 |
| Physapruin A | 21607598 | −56.35 | −19.70 |
| Physapubescin | 78077011 | −72.00 | −22.40 |
| Tubocapsanolide A | 16680369 | −63.40 | −20.00 |
| Tubocapsenolide A | 16679812 | −70.20 | −23.90 |
| Withaferin A | 265237 | −69.30 | −19.10 |
| Withangulatin A | 147647 | −93.55 | −21.90 |
| Withanolide A | 11294368 | −60.15 | −19.90 |
| Withanone | 21679027 | −55.30 | −21.00 |
| Withaperuvin | 333470 | −75.35 | −20.10 |

[1] Compound identity number, as defined in PubChem (https://pubchem.ncbi.nlm.nih.gov (accessed on 6 June 2024)).

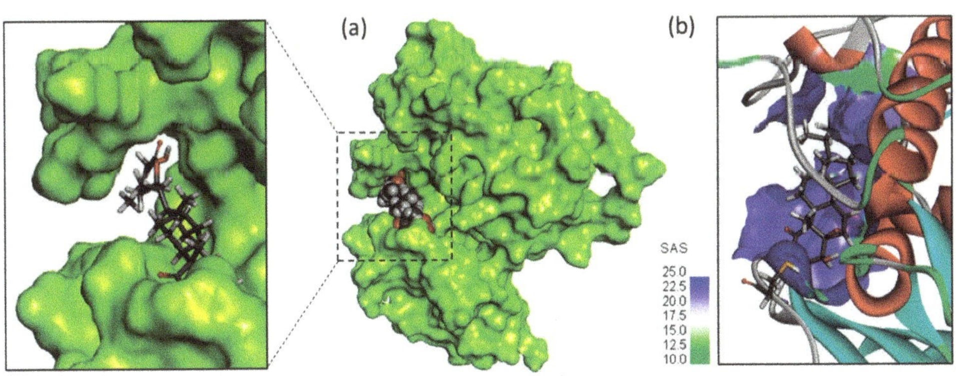


**Figure 5.** Molecular model of compound WFA bound to Zap70. (**a**) A surface model of the protein with the compound bound to the kinase site and a close-up view of the binding area. (**b**) A ribbon model of Zap70 with the WFA bound to the active site. The α-helices (in red) are shown together with the solvent-accessible surface (SAS) area surrounding the drug-binding zone (color code indicated).

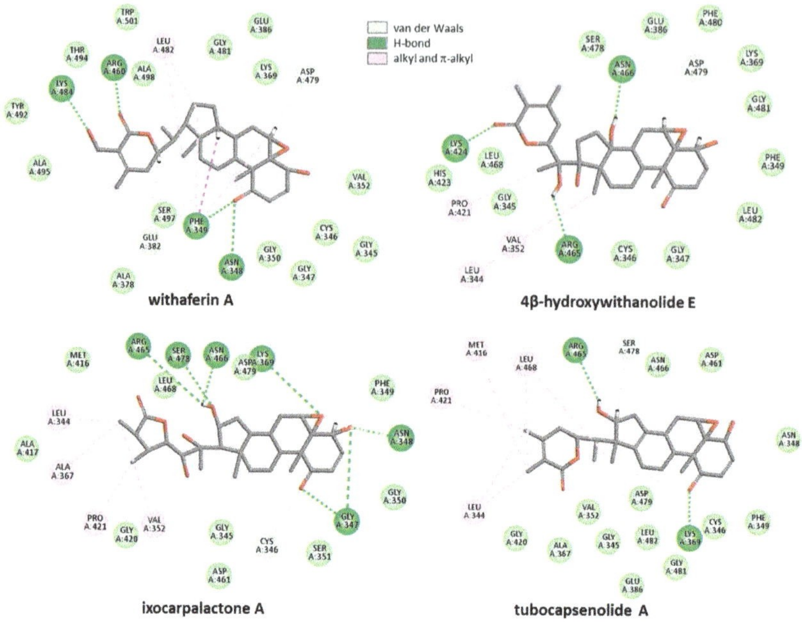


**Figure 6.** Binding map contacts for four withanolides bound to Zap70 (color code indicated). The compounds rank in order in terms of potential binding to Zap70: 4β-hydroxywithanolide E = ixocarpalactone A > withaferin A > tubocapsenolide A (Table 1).

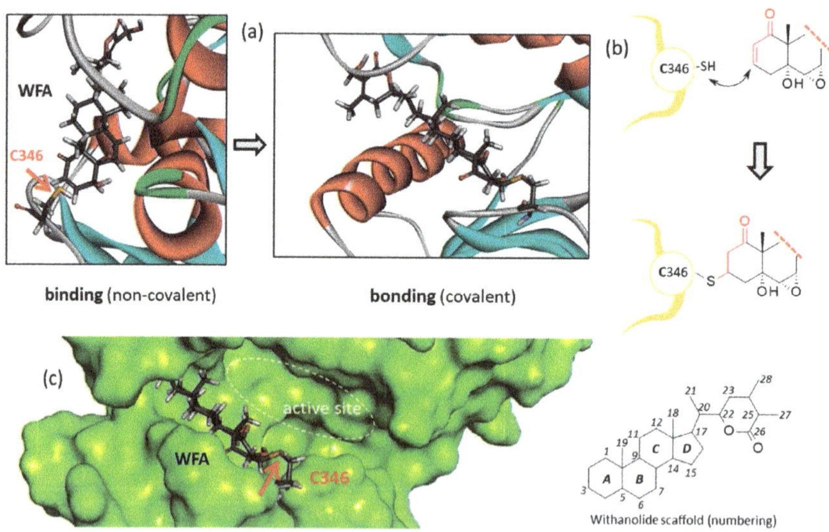


**Figure 7.** Covalent binding of WFA to Zap70 via Cys346. (**a**) The binding to bonding process permitted by the close proximity between the enone moiety of WFA and thiol group of C346. (**b**) The reaction scheme and (**c**) a detailed view of WFA covalently bound to C346 at the gate of the kinase active site.

### *3.3. Comparative Molecular Docking of Withanolides to Zap70*

The docking analysis was repeated with each of the 12 selected withanolides to calculate the corresponding binding energies (Table 1). Although all molecules present the same framework, with a common ergostane scaffold and the key reactive enone group, significant variations were observed between the molecules in terms of binding to Zap70. As expected, the free energy of hydration (ΔG) is relatively similar, whereas the potential energy of interaction (ΔE) varies importantly from one molecule to the other. Arbitrarily, we can separate the compounds in three groups: (1) the weak binder including withanone, withanolide A, physapruin A, anomanolide C, and tubocapsanolide A (−55.3 kcal/mol < ΔE < −63.4 kcal/mol); (2) the good binder including 4β-hydroxywithanolide E, ixocarpalactone A, physapubescin, tubocapsenolide A, WFA, and withaperuvin (−69.3 kcal/mol < ΔE < −75.5 kcal/mol); and (3) a single compound with a very favorable binding energy, withangulatin A (Table 1).

The compounds of the second group showed a behavior more or less comparable to that of WFA. They all can fit into the protein active site at a relative proximity to the C346 residue. The binding configuration varies slightly from one compound to another, leading to variable molecular contacts. Typical examples are represented in Figure 6. The case of ixocarpalactone A is interesting to note because its C16-OH group contributes importantly to the protein interaction with an implication in up to three H-bonds with residues Arg465, Asn466, and Ser478. But the molecular arrangement moves away the C346-SH group, which then becomes less accessible for bonding. The same observation was made with the weakest ligand, withanone. In this case, the compound is positioned close to the upper lip of the protein, with a short H-bond distance between Arg465 and the C1-carbonyl and C5-OH (2.6 Å), thus placing the C3 position away from the C346-SH group. On the opposite side, the same H-bond distances are longer with withangulatin A (3.0–3.3 Å), positioning the ligand closer to the C346-SH group, and thus favoring the realization of the covalent link. The spatial distance between the C346-SH group and the C3 position of the different withanolides tested here varied from 3.0 Å to >5.0 Å. The shortest distance was observed with withangulatin A (Figure 8).

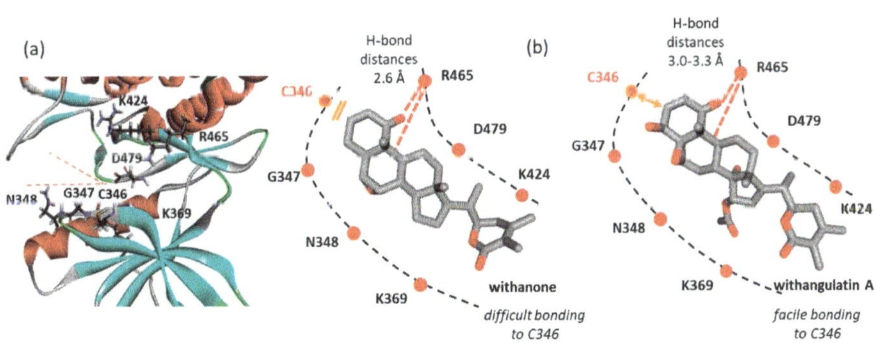


**Figure 8.** Withangulatin A binding to the kinase site. (**a**) A view of the binding area with the two lips of the site. A hinge region separates two zones with residues K369, C346, G347, and N348 on one side and K424, R465, and D479 on the other side. (**b**) Withanone becomes close to R465 but distant from C346, whereas withangulatin A remains close to C346, at a distance suitable for covalent binding to C346.

Withangulatin A was found to be the best ligand in the series, with a strong capability to form stable complexes with the kinase. It surpassed all the other withanolide derivatives with a free energy of interaction largely more negative (about 35%) compared to WFA and the other compounds (Table 1). The compound is ideally shaped to interact with the enzyme. The binding (non-covalent) step places the ligand in the kinase domain through the H-bond interaction with two key lysine residues, Lys369 and Lys424. The formation of the covalent linkage slightly modifies the positioning of the drug in its site, but the H-bond between the lactone unit and Lys424 is maintained (Figure 9).

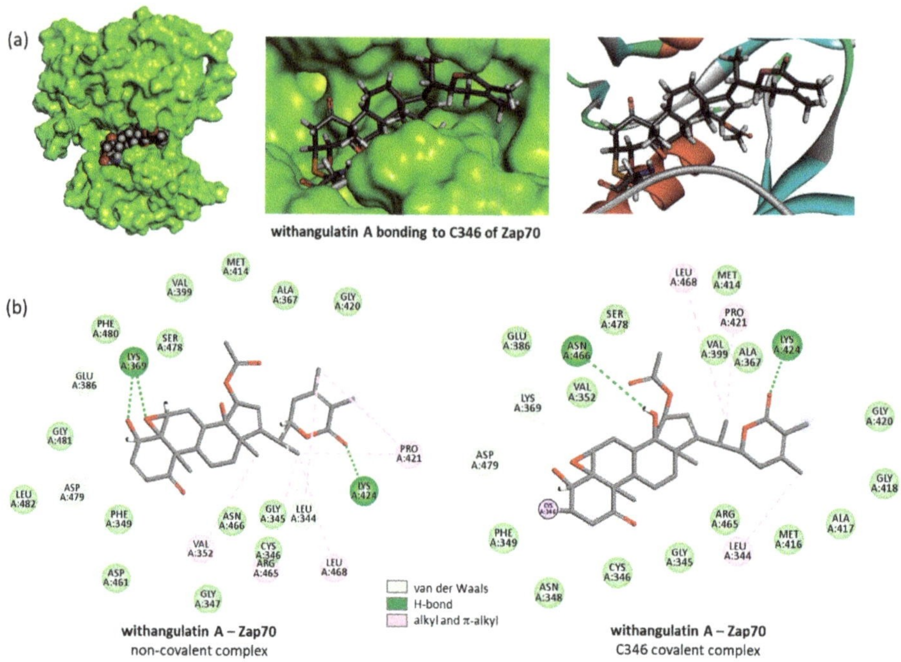


**Figure 9.** Binding and bonding of withangulatin A to Zap70-active kinase domain. (**a**) Molecular model of the drug–protein complex, with a close-up view of the ligand covalently bound to C346. (**b**) Binding map contacts for withangulatin A non-covalently and covalently bound to Zap70 (color code indicated).

To sum it up, the docking analysis suggested that WFA can form covalent complexes with the Cys346 of Zap70 kinase, and similar stable complexes can form with a few other withanolides including ixocarpalactone A, physapubescin, tubocapsenolide A, and withaperuvin. But one product stands out with its high capability for binding to Zap70 kinase: withangulatin A. This antitumor natural product exhibits a remarkable ability for bonding to the Cys346 thiol residue of Zap70, surpassing all other withanolides in terms of protein-binding capability.

### 3.4. Comparative Reactivity and Druggability of Withangulatin A and WFA

The discovery of withangulatin A as a potential top binder to Zap70 prompted us to further analyze this natural product as a drug candidate. We used additional in silico methods, notably the Density Functional Theory (DFT) and machine learning approaches, to evaluate the relative chemical stability and reactivity of this compound compared to WFA. The DFT analysis, performed at the B3LYP-D3/def2-SVP computational level of theory, allowed us to compare their electronic behavior. The calculation showed that the two compounds exhibit similar HOMO and LUMO energies. The HOMO-LUMO gap energy (about 3 eV) is comparable for the two compounds, thus suggesting an identical chemical stability (Figure 10). However, the two compounds have different charge density locations in the HOMO and LUMO. For instance, the LUMO and HOMO in WFA are mainly located on the A-ring around the enone moiety, whereas in withangulatin A, the LUMO has the charge density on the enone part of the ring A, but the HOMO has electron density on the D-ring (Figure 10b). For WFA, both the HOMO and LUMO are located on the same side of the molecular plane near the reactive position (C23/C31). For withangulatin A, the orbital interactions are different, with more distance between the HOMO and LUMO sites. It seems that the presence of the acetyl group (at C5) of withangulatin A can affect the rate at which an electronic transition can occur between orbitals. The DFT analysis predicts that the two natural products are equally stable, but the enone moiety of WFA may be slightly more reactive than that of withangulatin A.

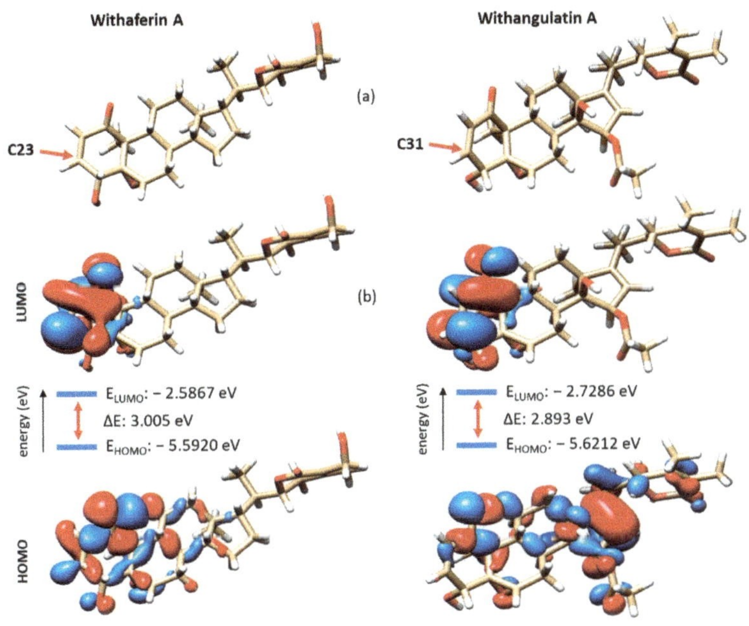


**Figure 10.** (**a**) Optimized structures of withaferin A and withangulatin A. The arrow points to the most nucleophilic site, as detailed in Figure S1. (**b**) Electron density distribution of HOMO and LUMO. The energy band gap is indicated with the respective frontier molecular orbital energies ($E = E_{LUMO} - E_{HOMO}$).

In parallel, we used Fukui functions and the dual descriptor to obtain quantitative measures of the nucleophilicity and electrophilicity of all atoms in the two compounds. Data for the carbon and oxygen atoms are shown in Figure S1 (H atoms are not shown for clarity, but all atomic positions were analyzed). The analysis clearly shows that the most reactive C-site of the molecule is the expected C3 enone position (labeled C23 and C31 for WFA and withangulatin A, respectively, in Figure S1). This C3 position is significantly more reactive than the two carbons of the epoxide and also corresponds to the most sterically accessible position, as shown out in Figure 10a. It is also interesting to note that the nucleophilicity index measured for WFA at position C5 (position C23 in Figure S1: nucleophilicity 0.07713) is lower than that measured for withangulatin A at the same position (position C31 in Figure S1: nucleophilicity 0.08533). Therefore, this specific position in withangulatin A may be more reactive than initially expected based on the DFT calculations mentioned above.

The expression of Fukui functions (interpreted as a variation in nucleophilicity or electrophilicity) points out to a locus in the chemical reactivity of the withanolides. To our knowledge, such an analysis has never been performed before. The only related work refers to a quantum mechanical study, also based on DFT calculations, with two different withanolides: withacoagulin J and withanolide H isolated from W. coagulans [59]. The band gap was a little larger with these two compounds (4.8 eV). Withanolide H, which has a reactive enone in the A-ring unlike withacoagulin J, showed a HOMO/LUMO pattern comparable to that of WFA. This type of analysis is useful to predict the chemical reactivity of the molecules.

Next, we used machine learning models to predict the physicochemical and metabolic properties of the two compounds. As expected, the machine learning model SolTranNet predicted a very low aqueous solubility for the two compounds, with logS values of −4.87 and −5.26 for WFA and withangulatin A, respectively (a soluble compound is defined as a compound with logS > −4 [53]). Such compounds require the development of a solvent-based formulation or liposomal drug delivery system, as proposed for WFA [60,61]. The attention-based graph neural network PredPS [52] predicted that the two molecules are relatively unstable in human plasma (with probability scores of 0.83 and 0.98 for WFA and withangulatin A, respectively). We also tested the random forest model PredMS [62] to predict their metabolic stability, but in this case, the calculated probability scores were considered unreliable (0.47 and 0.54 for WFA and withangulatin A, respectively). Nevertheless, WFA was predicted to be more stable than withangulatin A.

The predictive models of FP-ADMET [63] were used to compare the ADMET (absorption, distribution, metabolism, excretion, and toxicity) properties of the two compounds. The system is based on a repository of molecular fingerprints, which essentially correspond to drug-like molecules. In our case, the predictions have a relatively low confidence and credibility because this type of complex molecule is underrepresented in the training set. Nevertheless, the machine learning model pointed out three noteworthy aspects: (i) The two compounds seem to be phototoxic in vitro (parameter credibility 0.62–0.75) but not phototoxic to humans; (ii) the predicted hERG cardiotoxicity was negative for the two compounds, and, similarly, they do not present myotoxicity; and (iii) the predicted urinary toxicity was negative for WFA but positive for withangulatin A. However, these machine learning results should be treated with caution, as the training sets contain few examples of such complex compounds. A larger training set would be required to refine the predictions of their ADMET properties in addition to experimental measurements.

## 4. Discussion

The medicinal use of the plant *Withania somnifera* (L.) Dunal is well recognized, notably in the traditional Indian medical system to treat inflammatory diseases, microbial infections, hepatic dysfunctions, and other ailments. The plant is also used to treat cancer and in the prevention of neurodegenerative diseases [64–66]. *W. somnifera* is a rich source of bioactive molecules, in particular withanolides endowed with anticancer properties [21,23]. The lead compound is withaferin A (WFA), which has revealed a large panel of pharmacological activities useful to combat inflammation, cancer, and neuropathological disorders [25]. It is a highly potent withanolide capable of binding to many proteins and triggering covalent reactions with cysteine residues of various proteins including NFκB, SERCA-2, β-tubulin, vimentin, and a few enzymes such as Pin1 and Zap70 [27]. Up to now, WFA is the only withanolide known to bind to Zap70, which is a key tyrosine kinase implicated in T-cell immunity. The covalent binding of WFA to the exposed cysteines of Zap70 has been evidenced recently [28]. This study paved the way for the discovery of additional binders with a withanolide scaffold similar to WFA. In this frame, we selected 12 withanolides equipped with a reactive α,β-unsaturated ketone moiety to compare their ability to form covalent complexes with the kinase. The selected withanolides include compounds previously characterized as potent anticancer agents, such as physapruin A, 4β-hydroxywithanolide E, and withanone [41,67,68]. Our molecular docking approach is comparable to that used recently to study other anticancer agents [69,70].

The molecular docking analysis points to seven compounds susceptible to form stable complexes with Zap70: 4β-hydroxywithanolide E, ixocarpalactone A, physapubescin, tubocapsenolide A, WFA, withaperuvin, and withangulatin A. The first six compounds exhibit a roughly equal capability to engage molecular interactions in the active site of Zap70. In particular, 4β-hydroxywithanolide E, withaperuvin, and ixocarpalactone A display the same high ability to form stable complexes with Zap70. The analysis of the structure-binding relationships in the series is difficult due to the complexity of the molecules. However, the following four criteria can be underlined: (i) The C5-C6 epoxide moiety of WFA is not absolutely required for kinase interaction (not present in whitaperuvin A), (ii) a hydroxyl group at C16 contributes favorably to the kinase interaction (as observed with ixocarpalactone A and tubocapsenolide A), (iii) the presence of a hydroxyl group at C20 reinforces the protein interaction, and (iv) in all cases, the lactone E-ring plays an important role in the protein interaction. Thus, the docking analysis suggests clearly that WFA is not the only withanolide susceptible to forming covalent complexes with Zap70.

One compound emerges from the study as a promising Zap70 binder: withangulatin A, which is a well-known anti-inflammatory, immuno-suppressive, and antifibrotic agent [71–73]. This withanolide, essentially isolated from *Physalis angulata* L. [55,56], has been characterized previously as a covalent protein binder. Withangulatin A has been shown to form cysteine-mediated covalent complexes with the enzymes 3-phosphoglycerate dehydrogenase (PHGDH) [35], peroxiredoxin 6 (Prdx-6) [36], and sarco/endoplasmic reticulum calcium-ATPase 2 (SERCA-2) [37]. It is also an inhibitor of glutaminase 1 ($IC_{50}$ = 18.2 μM) [74] and a regulator of the expression of cyclooxygenase 2 [75] and ADP-ribosylation factor 6 (ARF6) [76]. This multitargeted reactive molecule can interfere with different processes in cells. Here, we provide in silico evidence that it is also a potential strong binder to the kinase Zap70.

Withangulatin A surpassed all the other tested withanolides in terms of complex formation and reactivity with the Cys346 position of Zap70. This cysteine residue located at the entrance of the active site represents a more attractive site than those located on the external surface of the protein, such as C560-C564. The product fits well into the active site of the kinase, placing its reactive enone moiety close to the thiol group of Cys346. The model suggests that a covalent reaction can occur easily to generate a stable protein–drug adduct, as described experimentally with WFA. A detailed analysis of the reactivity of the molecule, using DFT calculations, indicates that the enone moiety of withangulatin A exhibits a high reactivity, with the C3 position (labeled C31 in Figure 10) as the main reactive site. The docking analysis was performed with a catalytic subunit of Zap70 corresponding to the active kinase domain of the protein (open conformation). It would be useful to determine if the covalent binding of WFA can also occur when the protein is in a closed, autoinhibited conformation, so as to prevent the opening of its conformation [77].

The ADMET profile of withangulatin A suggests that it is a druggable molecule. The only point to watch out for is potential urinary toxicity, but apart from that, the molecule does not present major toxic aspects or unacceptable properties. This natural product exhibits a low oral bioavailability, and it can easily hydrolyze in human plasma [78]. Withangulatin A has already been exploited in drug design strategies. Recently, Zhou and coworkers have synthesized two large series of withangulatin derivatives and identified potent antiproliferative agents, including a C-4 ester derivative 70 times more potent than the parent compound, withangulatin A [74,79]. In the same vein, semisynthetic analogs of withangulatin A targeting thioredoxin reductase have been designed, and potent cysteine-reactive analogs bearing an α,β-unsaturated ketone have been identified [80]. Other derivatives targeting the allosteric site of glutaminase C have been proposed recently [81]. According to our calculations, withangulatin A is a potential hit compound, which can be used to guide the design of drug candidates. Zap70 shall be considered as a potential target for these compounds.

## 5. Conclusions

The computational study has identified withangulatin A as a potential inhibitor of the kinase Zap70 via covalent binding to the Cys346 residue in the enzyme active site. This compound emerged as the best ligand among a series of 12 withanolides equipped with a thiol-reactive, α,β-unsaturated ketone. The study paves the way for the design of novel Zap70 inhibitors, which are needed to improve the treatment of lymphoid malignancies and autoimmune diseases associated with an abnormal T-cell response.

**Supplementary Materials:** The following supporting information can be downloaded at: https://www.mdpi.com/article/10.3390/computation13090207/s1, Figure S1: Condensed Fukui functions and dual descriptors for the heavy atoms of withaferin A and withangulatin A.

**Author Contributions:** C.B. (Corentin Bedart), Methodology, Formal analysis, Software, Writing—original draft, and Writing—review and editing; G.V., Methodology, Software; C.B. (Christian Bailly), Conceptualization, Investigation, Supervision, Writing—original draft, and Writing—review and editing; All authors have read and agreed to the published version of the manuscript.

**Funding:** This research received no external funding.

**Data Availability Statement:** Data is contained within the article and Supplementary Material.

**Conflicts of Interest:** Author Christian Bailly was employed by the company OncoWitan. The remaining authors declare that the research was conducted in the absence of any commercial or financial relationships that could be construed as a potential conflict of interest.

## Abbreviations

The following abbreviations are used in this manuscript:

| | |
|---|---|
| CLL | Chronic lymphocytic leukemia |
| DFT | Density functional theory |
| 4β-HWNE | 4β-hydroxywithanolide E |
| WFA | Withaferin A |
| Zap70 | Zeta-chain associated protein kinase 70 kDa |

## References

1. Ashouri, J.F.; Lo, W.L.; Nguyen, T.T.T.; Shen, L.; Weiss, A. ZAP70, too little, too much can lead to autoimmunity. *Immunol. Rev.* **2022**, *307*, 145–160. [CrossRef] [PubMed]
2. Au-Yeung, B.B.; Shah, N.H.; Shen, L.; Weiss, A. ZAP-70 in Signaling, Biology, and Disease. *Annu. Rev. Immunol.* **2018**, *36*, 127–156. [CrossRef] [PubMed]
3. Chen, J.; Moore, A.; Ringshausen, I. ZAP-70 Shapes the Immune Microenvironment in B Cell Malignancies. *Front. Oncol.* **2020**, *10*, 595832. [CrossRef] [PubMed]
4. Liu, Y.; Wang, Y.; Yang, J.; Bi, Y.; Wang, H. ZAP-70 in chronic lymphocytic leukemia: A meta-analysis. *Clin. Chim. Acta* **2018**, *483*, 82–88. [CrossRef]
5. Demir, M.; Cizmecioglu, O. ZAP70 Activation Compensates for Loss of Class IA PI3K Isoforms Through Activation of the JAK-STAT3 Pathway. *Cancer Diagn. Progn.* **2022**, *2*, 391–404. [CrossRef]
6. Ren, L.; Li, P.; Li, Z.; Chen, Q. AQP9 and ZAP70 as immune-related prognostic biomarkers suppress proliferation, migration and invasion of laryngeal cancer cells. *BMC Cancer* **2022**, *22*, 465. [CrossRef]
7. Yang, M.L.; Lam, T.T.; Kanyo, J.; Kang, I.; Zhou, Z.S.; Clarke, S.G.; Mamula, M.J. Natural isoaspartyl protein modification of ZAP70 alters T cell responses in lupus. *Autoimmunity* **2023**, *56*, 2282945. [CrossRef]
8. Kaur, M.; Singh, M.; Silakari, O. Insight into the therapeutic aspects of 'Zeta-Chain Associated Protein Kinase 70 kDa' inhibitors: A review. *Cell Signal.* **2014**, *26*, 2481–2492. [CrossRef]

9. Visperas, P.R.; Wilson, C.G.; Winger, J.A.; Yan, Q.; Lin, K.; Arkin, M.R.; Weiss, A.; Kuriyan, J. Identification of Inhibitors of the Association of ZAP-70 with the T Cell Receptor by High-Throughput Screen. *SLAS Discov.* **2017**, *22*, 324–331. [CrossRef]
10. Rao, D.; Li, H.; Ren, X.; Sun, Y.; Wen, C.; Zheng, M.; Huang, H.; Tang, W.; Xu, S. Discovery of a potent, selective, and covalent ZAP-70 kinase inhibitor. *Eur. J. Med. Chem.* **2021**, *219*, 113393. [CrossRef]
11. Masip, V.; Lirio, Á.; Sánchez-López, A.; Cuenca, A.B.; Puig de la Bellacasa, R.; Abrisqueta, P.; Teixidó, J.; Borrell, J.I.; Gibert, A.; Estrada-Tejedor, R. Expanding the Diversity at the C-4 Position of Pyrido[2,3-d]pyrimidin-7(8H)-ones to Achieve Biological Activity against ZAP-70. *Pharmaceuticals* **2021**, *14*, 1311. [CrossRef]
12. Khlebnikov, A.I.; Schepetkin, I.A.; Kishkentaeva, A.S.; Shaimerdenova, Z.R.; Atazhanova, G.A.; Adekenov, S.M.; Kirpotina, L.N.; Quinn, M.T. Inhibition of T Cell Receptor Activation by Semi-Synthetic Sesquiterpene Lactone Derivatives and Molecular Modeling of Their Interaction with Glutathione and Tyrosine Kinase ZAP-70. *Molecules* **2019**, *24*, 350. [CrossRef] [PubMed]
13. Deindl, S.; Kadlecek, T.A.; Brdicka, T.; Cao, X.; Weiss, A.; Kuriyan, J. Structural basis for the inhibition of tyrosine kinase activity of ZAP-70. *Cell* **2007**, *129*, 735–746. [CrossRef]
14. Jin, L.; Pluskey, S.; Petrella, E.C.; Cantin, S.M.; Gorga, J.C.; Rynkiewicz, M.J.; Pandey, P.; Strickler, J.E.; Babine, R.E.; Weaver, D.T.; et al. The three-dimensional structure of the ZAP-70 kinase domain in complex with staurosporine: Implications for the design of selective inhibitors. *J. Biol. Chem.* **2004**, *279*, 42818–42825. [CrossRef]
15. Huber, R.G.; Fan, H.; Bond, P.J. The Structural Basis for Activation and Inhibition of ZAP-70 Kinase Domain. *PLoS Comput. Biol.* **2015**, *11*, e1004560. [CrossRef]
16. Visperas, P.R.; Winger, J.A.; Horton, T.M.; Shah, N.H.; Aum, D.J.; Tao, A.; Barros, T.; Yan, Q.; Wilson, C.G.; Arkin, M.R.; et al. Modification by covalent reaction or oxidation of cysteine residues in the tandem-SH2 domains of ZAP-70 and Syk can block phosphopeptide binding. *Biochem. J.* **2015**, *465*, 149–161. [CrossRef] [PubMed]
17. Schultz, A.; Schnurra, M.; El-Bizri, A.; Woessner, N.M.; Hartmann, S.; Hartig, R.; Minguet, S.; Schraven, B.; Simeoni, L. A Cysteine Residue within the Kinase Domain of Zap70 Regulates Lck Activity and Proximal TCR Signaling. *Cells* **2022**, *11*, 2723. [CrossRef] [PubMed]
18. Tewari, R.; Shayahati, B.; Fan, Y.; Akimzhanov, A.M. T cell receptor-dependent S-acylation of ZAP-70 controls activation of T cells. *J. Biol. Chem.* **2021**, *296*, 100311. [CrossRef]
19. Rao, D.; Yang, T.; Feng, H.; An, Q.; Zhang, S.; Yu, J.; Ren, X.; Diao, X.; Huang, H.; Tang, W.; et al. Discovery and Structural Optimization of Covalent ZAP-70 Kinase Inhibitors against Psoriasis. *J. Med. Chem.* **2023**, *66*, 12018–12032. [CrossRef]
20. Boike, L.; Henning, N.J.; Nomura, D.K. Advances in covalent drug discovery. *Nat. Rev. Drug Discov.* **2022**, *21*, 881–898. [CrossRef]
21. Yadav, N.; Tripathi, S.; Sangwan, N.S. Phyto-therapeutic potential of *Withania somnifera*: Molecular mechanism and health implications. *Phytother. Res.* **2024**, *38*, 1695–1714. [CrossRef]
22. Xing, Z.; Su, A.; Mi, L.; Zhang, Y.; He, T.; Qiu, Y.; Wei, T.; Li, Z.; Zhu, J.; Wu, W. Withaferin A: A Dietary Supplement with Promising Potential as an Anti-Tumor Therapeutic for Cancer Treatment—Pharmacology and Mechanisms. *Drug Des. Devel. Ther.* **2023**, *17*, 2909–2929. [CrossRef]
23. Zhang, Q.; Yuan, Y.; Cao, S.; Kang, N.; Qiu, F. Withanolides: Promising candidates for cancer therapy. *Phytother. Res.* **2024**, *38*, 1104–1158. [CrossRef]
24. Kumar, S.; Mathew, S.O.; Aharwal, R.P.; Tulli, H.S.; Mohan, C.D.; Sethi, G.; Ahn, K.S.; Webber, K.; Sandhu, S.S.; Bishayee, A. Withaferin A: A Pleiotropic Anticancer Agent from the Indian Medicinal Plant *Withania somnifera* (L.) Dunal. *Pharmaceuticals* **2023**, *16*, 160. [CrossRef] [PubMed]
25. Kumar, P.; Banik, S.P.; Goel, A.; Chakraborty, S.; Bagchi, M.; Bagchi, D. Revisiting the Multifaceted Therapeutic Potential of Withaferin A (WA), a Novel Steroidal Lactone, W-ferinAmax Ashwagandha, from *Withania somnifera* (L) Dunal. *J. Am. Nutr. Assoc.* **2024**, *43*, 115–130. [CrossRef] [PubMed]
26. Abeesh, P.; Guruvayoorappan, C. The Therapeutic Effects of Withaferin A against Cancer: Overview and Updates. *Curr. Mol. Med.* **2024**, *24*, 404–418. [CrossRef] [PubMed]
27. Bailly, C. Covalent binding of withanolides to cysteines of protein targets. *Biochem. Pharmacol.* **2024**, *226*, 116405. [CrossRef]
28. Fazil, M.H.U.T.; Chirumamilla, C.S.; Perez-Novo, C.; Wong, B.H.S.; Kumar, S.; Sze, S.K.; Vanden Berghe, W.; Verma, N.K. The steroidal lactone withaferin A impedes T-cell motility by inhibiting the kinase ZAP70 and subsequent kinome signaling. *J. Biol. Chem.* **2021**, *297*, 101377. [CrossRef]
29. Fuska, J.; Fusková, A.; Rosazza, J.P.; Nicholas, A.W. Novel cytotoxic and antitumor agents. IV. Withaferin A: Relation of its structure to the in vitro cytotoxic effects on P388 cells. *Neoplasma* **1984**, *31*, 31–36.
30. Nicholas, A.W.; Rosazza, J.P. Reactions of withaferin-A with model biological nucleophiles. *Bioorg Chem.* **1976**, *5*, 367–372. [CrossRef]
31. Rabhi, C.; Arcile, G.; Le Goff, G.; Da Costa Noble, C.; Ouazzani, J. Neuroprotective Effect of CR-777, a Glutathione Derivative of Withaferin A, Obtained through the Bioconversion of *Withania somnifera* (L.) Dunal Extract by the Fungus *Beauveria bassiana*. *Molecules* **2019**, *24*, 4599. [CrossRef]

32. Goode, K.M.; Petrov, D.P.; Vickman, R.E.; Crist, S.A.; Pascuzzi, P.E.; Ratliff, T.L.; Davisson, V.J.; Hazbun, T.R. Targeting the Hsp90 C-terminal domain to induce allosteric inhibition and selective client downregulation. *Biochim. Biophys. Acta Gen. Subj.* **2017**, *1861*, 1992–2006. [CrossRef] [PubMed]
33. Chen, W.Y.; Chang, F.R.; Huang, Z.Y.; Chen, J.H.; Wu, Y.C.; Wu, C.C. Tubocapsenolide A, a novel withanolide, inhibits proliferation and induces apoptosis in MDA-MB-231 cells by thiol oxidation of heat shock proteins. *J. Biol. Chem.* **2008**, *283*, 17184–17193. [CrossRef]
34. Yang, W.J.; Chen, X.M.; Wang, S.Q.; Hu, H.X.; Cheng, X.P.; Xu, L.T.; Ren, D.M.; Wang, X.N.; Zhao, B.B.; Lou, H.X.; et al. 4β-Hydroxywithanolide E from Goldenberry (Whole Fruits of *Physalis peruviana* L.) as a Promising Agent against Chronic Obstructive Pulmonary Disease. *J. Nat. Prod.* **2020**, *83*, 1217–1228. [CrossRef]
35. Chen, C.; Zhu, T.; Liu, X.; Zhu, D.; Zhang, Y.; Wu, S.; Han, C.; Zhang, H.; Luo, J.; Kong, L. Identification of a novel PHGDH covalent inhibitor by chemical proteomics and phenotypic profiling. *Acta Pharm. Sin. B* **2022**, *12*, 246–261. [CrossRef]
36. Chen, C.; Gong, L.; Liu, X.; Zhu, T.; Zhou, W.; Kong, L.; Luo, J. Identification of peroxiredoxin 6 as a direct target of withangulatin A by quantitative chemical proteomics in non-small cell lung cancer. *Redox Biol.* **2021**, *46*, 102130. [CrossRef]
37. Zhu, T.; Chen, C.; Wang, S.; Zhang, Y.; Zhu, D.; Li, L.; Luo, J.; Kong, L. Cellular target identification of Withangulatin A using fluorescent analogues and subsequent chemical proteomics. *Chem. Commun.* **2019**, *55*, 8231–8234. [CrossRef] [PubMed]
38. Yu, T.J.; Cheng, Y.B.; Lin, L.C.; Tsai, Y.H.; Yao, B.Y.; Tang, J.Y.; Chang, F.R.; Yen, C.H.; Ou-Yang, F.; Chang, H.W. Physalis peruviana-Derived Physapruin A (PHA) Inhibits Breast Cancer Cell Proliferation and Induces Oxidative-Stress-Mediated Apoptosis and DNA Damage. *Antioxidants* **2021**, *10*, 393. [CrossRef]
39. Yu, T.J.; Shiau, J.P.; Tang, J.Y.; Yen, C.H.; Hou, M.F.; Cheng, Y.B.; Shu, C.W.; Chang, H.W. Physapruin A Induces Reactive Oxygen Species to Trigger Cytoprotective Autophagy of Breast Cancer Cells. *Antioxidants* **2022**, *11*, 1352. [CrossRef] [PubMed]
40. Yu, T.J.; Yen, C.Y.; Cheng, Y.B.; Yen, C.H.; Jeng, J.H.; Tang, J.Y.; Chang, H.W. Physapruin A Enhances DNA Damage and Inhibits DNA Repair to Suppress Oral Cancer Cell Proliferation. *Int. J. Mol. Sci.* **2022**, *23*, 8839. [CrossRef]
41. Yu, T.J.; Shiau, J.P.; Tang, J.Y.; Farooqi, A.A.; Cheng, Y.B.; Hou, M.F.; Yen, C.H.; Chang, H.W. Physapruin A Exerts Endoplasmic Reticulum Stress to Trigger Breast Cancer Cell Apoptosis via Oxidative Stress. *Int. J. Mol. Sci.* **2023**, *24*, 8853. [CrossRef]
42. Chen, Y.M.; Xu, W.; Liu, Y.; Zhang, J.H.; Yang, Y.Y.; Wang, Z.W.; Sun, D.J.; Li, H.; Liu, B.; Chen, L.X. Anomanolide C suppresses tumor progression and metastasis by ubiquitinating GPX4-driven autophagy-dependent ferroptosis in triple negative breast cancer. *Int. J. Biol. Sci.* **2023**, *19*, 2531–2550. [CrossRef]
43. Jorgensen, W.L.; Tirado-Rives, J. Molecular modeling of organic and biomolecular systems using BOSS and MCPRO. *J. Comput. Chem.* **2005**, *26*, 1689–1700. [CrossRef]
44. Tian, W.; Chen, C.; Lei, X.; Zhao, J.; Liang, J. CASTp 3.0: Computed atlas of surface topography of proteins. *Nucleic Acids Res.* **2018**, *46*, W363–W367. [CrossRef] [PubMed]
45. Jones, G.; Willett, P.; Glen, R.C.; Leach, A.R.; Taylor, R. Development and validation of a genetic algorithm for flexible docking. *J. Mol. Biol.* **1997**, *267*, 727–748. [CrossRef] [PubMed]
46. Meziane-Tani, M.; Lagant, P.; Semmoud, A.; Vergoten, G. The SPASIBA force field for chondroitin sulfate: Vibrational analysis of D-glucuronic and *N*-acetyl-D-galactosamine 4-sulfate sodium salts. *J. Phys. Chem. A* **2006**, *110*, 11359–11370. [CrossRef] [PubMed]
47. Lagant, P.; Nolde, D.; Stote, R.; Vergoten, G.; Karplus, M. Increasing normal modes analysis accuracy: The SPASIBA spectroscopic force field introduced into the CHARMM program. *J. Phys. Chem. A* **2004**, *108*, 4019–4029. [CrossRef]
48. Jorgensen, W.L.; Ulmschneider, J.P.; Tirado-Rives, J. Free energies of hydration from a generalized Born model and an ALL-atom force field. *J. Phys. Chem. B* **2004**, *108*, 16264–16270. [CrossRef]
49. Vergoten, G.; Bailly, C. Molecular docking of cryptoconcatones to α-tubulin and related pironetin analogues. *Plants* **2023**, *12*, 296. [CrossRef]
50. Bailly, C.; Vergoten, G. Interaction of microcolin cyanobacterial lipopeptides with phosphatidylinositol transfer protein (PITP)—Molecular docking analysis. *Future Pharmacol.* **2025**, *5*, 13. [CrossRef]
51. Neese, F.; Wennmohs, F.; Becker, U.; Riplinger, C. The ORCA quantum chemistry program package. *J. Chem. Phys.* **2020**, *152*, 224108. [CrossRef]
52. Liu, Z.; Zubatiuk, T.; Roitberg, A.; Isayev, O. Auto3D: Automatic Generation of the Low-Energy 3D Structures with ANI Neural Network Potentials. *J. Chem. Inf. Model.* **2022**, *62*, 5373–5382. [CrossRef]
53. Francoeur, P.G.; Koes, D.R. SolTranNet-A Machine Learning Tool for Fast Aqueous Solubility Prediction. *J. Chem. Inf. Model.* **2021**, *61*, 2530–2536, Erratum in *J. Chem. Inf. Model.* **2021**, *61*, 4120–4123. [CrossRef]
54. Jang, W.D.; Jang, J.; Song, J.S.; Ahn, S.; Oh, K.S. PredPS: Attention-based graph neural network for predicting stability of compounds in human plasma. *Comput. Struct. Biotechnol. J.* **2023**, *21*, 3532–3539. [CrossRef]
55. Lee, S.W.; Pan, M.H.; Chen, C.M.; Chen, Z.T. Withangulatin I, a new cytotoxic withanolide from Physalis angulata. *Chem. Pharm. Bull.* **2008**, *56*, 234–236. [CrossRef]
56. Chen, C.M.; Chen, Z.T.; Hsieh, C.H.; Li, W.S.; Wen, S.Y. Withangulatin A, a new withanolide from Physalis angulata. *Heterocycles* **1990**, *31*, 1371–1375. [CrossRef]

57. Connolly, M.L. Solvent-accessible surfaces of proteins and nucleic acids. *Science* **1983**, *221*, 709–713. [CrossRef] [PubMed]
58. Lee, B.; Richards, F.M. The interpretation of protein structures: Estimation of static accessibility. *J. Mol. Biol.* **1971**, *55*, 379–400. [CrossRef]
59. Khan, S.A.; Adhikari, A.; Ayub, K.; Farooq, A.; Mahar, S.; Qureshi, M.N.; Rauf, A.; Khan, S.B.; Ludwig, R.; Mahmood, T. Isolation, characterization and DFT studies of epoxy ring containing new withanolides from Withania coagulans Dunal. *Spectrochim. Acta A Mol. Biomol. Spectrosc.* **2019**, *217*, 113–121. [CrossRef] [PubMed]
60. Abeesh, P.; Vishnu, W.K.; Guruvayoorappan, C. Preparation and characterization of withaferin A loaded pegylated nanoliposomal formulation with high loading efficacy: In vitro and in vivo anti-tumour study. *Mater. Sci. Eng. C Mater. Biol. Appl.* **2021**, *128*, 112335. [CrossRef]
61. Abeesh, P.; Guruvayoorappan, C. Withaferin A-Encapsulated PEGylated Nanoliposomes Induce Apoptosis in B16F10 Melanoma Cells by Regulating Bcl2 and Bcl xl Genes and Mitigates Murine Solid Tumor Development. *J. Environ. Pathol. Toxicol. Oncol.* **2024**, *43*, 29–42. [CrossRef]
62. Ryu, J.Y.; Lee, J.H.; Lee, B.H.; Song, J.S.; Ahn, S.; Oh, K.S. PredMS: A random forest model for predicting metabolic stability of drug candidates in human liver microsomes. *Bioinformatics* **2022**, *38*, 364–368. [CrossRef]
63. Venkatraman, V. FP-ADMET: A compendium of fingerprint-based ADMET prediction models. *J. Cheminform.* **2021**, *13*, 75. [CrossRef]
64. Philips, C.A.; Theruvath, A.H. A comprehensive review on the hepatotoxicity of herbs used in the Indian (Ayush) systems of alternative medicine. *Medicine* **2024**, *103*, e37903. [CrossRef]
65. Lerose, V.; Ponticelli, M.; Benedetto, N.; Carlucci, V.; Lela, L.; Tzvetkov, N.T.; Milella, L. *Withania somnifera* (L.) Dunal, a Potential Source of Phytochemicals for Treating Neurodegenerative Diseases: A Systematic Review. *Plants* **2024**, *13*, 771. [CrossRef]
66. Kumar, P.; Banik, S.P.; Goel, A.; Chakraborty, S.; Bagchi, M.; Bagchi, D. A critical assessment of the whole plant-based phytotherapeutics from *Withania somnifera* (L.) Dunal with respect to safety and efficacy vis-a-vis leaf or root extract-based formulation. *Toxicol. Mech. Methods* **2023**, *33*, 698–706. [CrossRef] [PubMed]
67. Stephen, A.; Tune, B.X.J.; Wu, Y.S.; Batumalaie, K.; Sekar, M.; Sarker, M.M.R.; Subramaniyan, V.; Fuloria, N.K.; Fuloria, S.; Gopinath, S.C.B. Withanone as an Emerging Anticancer Agent and Understanding Its Molecular Mechanisms: Experimental and Computational Evidence. *Curr. Cancer Drug Targets* **2025**, *25*, 574–585. [CrossRef]
68. Sun, L.; Zhou, L.; Chen, M.; Zhong, R.; Liu, J. Amelioration of systemic lupus erythematosus by Withangulatin A in MRL/lpr mice. *J. Cell Biochem.* **2011**, *112*, 2376–2382. [CrossRef] [PubMed]
69. Hassan, A.; Mosallam, A.M.; Ibrahim, A.O.A.; Badr, M.; Abdelmonsef, A.H. Novel 3-phenylquinazolin-2,4(1H,3H)-diones as dual VEGFR-2/c-Met-TK inhibitors: Design, synthesis, and biological evaluation. *Sci. Rep.* **2023**, *13*, 18567. [CrossRef]
70. Gomha, S.M.; Abdelhady, H.A.; Hassain, D.Z.H.; Abdelmonsef, A.H.; El-Naggar, M.; Elaasser, M.M.; Mahmoud, H.K. Thiazole-Based Thiosemicarbazones: Synthesis, Cytotoxicity Evaluation and Molecular Docking Study. *Drug Des. Devel. Ther.* **2021**, *15*, 659–677. [CrossRef] [PubMed]
71. Wang, H.C.; Hu, H.H.; Chang, F.R.; Tsai, J.Y.; Kuo, C.Y.; Wu, Y.C.; Wu, C.C. Different effects of 4beta-hydroxywithanolide E and withaferin A, two withanolides from Solanaceae plants, on the Akt signaling pathway in human breast cancer cells. *Phytomedicine* **2019**, *53*, 213–222. [CrossRef]
72. Sun, L.; Liu, J.W.; Liu, P.; Yu, Y.J.; Ma, L.; Hu, L.H. Immunosuppression effect of Withangulatin A from *Physalis angulata* via heme oxygenase 1-dependent pathways. *Process Biochem.* **2011**, *46*, 482–488. [CrossRef]
73. Liu, Q.; Chen, J.; Wang, X.; Yu, L.; Hu, L.H.; Shen, X. Withagulatin A inhibits hepatic stellate cell viability and procollagen I production through Akt and Smad signaling pathways. *Acta Pharmacol. Sin.* **2010**, *31*, 944–952. [CrossRef] [PubMed]
74. Zhou, W.X.; Chen, C.; Liu, X.Q.; Li, Y.; Lin, Y.L.; Wu, X.T.; Kong, L.Y.; Luo, J.G. Discovery and optimization of withangulatin A derivatives as novel glutaminase 1 inhibitors for the treatment of triple-negative breast cancer. *Eur. J. Med. Chem.* **2021**, *210*, 112980. [CrossRef] [PubMed]
75. Sun, L.; Liu, J.; Cui, D.; Li, J.; Yu, Y.; Ma, L.; Hu, L. Anti-inflammatory function of Withangulatin A by targeted inhibiting COX-2 expression via MAPK and NF-kappaB pathways. *J. Cell Biochem.* **2010**, *109*, 532–541. [CrossRef]
76. Sun, D.J.; Yang, Y.Y.; Liu, Y.; Ma, X.X.; Li, H.; Chen, L.X. Identification of ADP-ribosylation factor 6 as the cellular target of withangulatin A against TNBC cells by ferroptosis. *Res. Sq.* **2022**. [CrossRef]
77. Klammt, C.; Novotná, L.; Li, D.T.; Wolf, M.; Blount, A.; Zhang, K.; Fitchett, J.R.; Lillemeier, B.F. T cell receptor dwell times control the kinase activity of Zap70. *Nat. Immunol.* **2015**, *16*, 961–969. [CrossRef]
78. Zhuang, Y.; Wang, Y.; Li, N.; Meng, H.; Li, Z.; Luo, J.; Qiu, Z. Hydrolytic Metabolism of Withangulatin A Mediated by Serum Albumin Instead of Common Esterases in Plasma. *Eur. J. Drug Metab. Pharmacokinet.* **2023**, *48*, 363–376. [CrossRef] [PubMed]
79. Zhou, W.X.; Chen, C.; Liu, X.Q.; Li, Y.; Kong, L.Y.; Luo, J.G. Synthesis and biological evaluation of novel withangulatin A derivatives as potential anticancer agents. *Bioorg. Chem.* **2021**, *108*, 104690. [CrossRef]

80. Wang, C.; Li, S.; Zhao, J.; Yang, H.; Yin, F.; Ding, M.; Luo, J.; Wang, X.; Kong, L. Design and SAR of Withangulatin A Analogues that Act as Covalent TrxR Inhibitors through the Michael Addition Reaction Showing Potential in Cancer Treatment. *J. Med. Chem.* **2020**, *63*, 11195–11214. [CrossRef]
81. Saghiri, K.; Daoud, I.; Melkemi, N.; Mesli, F. Molecular docking/dynamics simulations, MEP analysis, and pharmacokinetics prediction of some withangulatin A derivatives as allosteric glutaminase C inhibitors in breast cancer. *Chem. Data Collect.* **2023**, *46*, 101044. [CrossRef]

*computation*

MDPI

*Article*

# A Quantitative Structure–Activity Relationship Study of the Anabolic Activity of Ecdysteroids

**Durbek Usmanov [1,2,*], Ugiloy Yusupova [2], Vladimir Syrov [2], Gerardo M. Casanola-Martin [1] and Bakhtiyor Rasulev [1,3,*]**

[1] Department of Coatings and Polymeric Materials, North Dakota State University, Fargo, ND 58102-7207, USA; gerardo.casanolamart@ndsu.edu

[2] Institute of the Chemistry of Plant Substances, Academy of Sciences of the Republic of Uzbekistan, Tashkent 100170, Uzbekistan; yusupovauyu@gmail.com (U.Y.); syrov46@mail.ru (V.S.)

[3] Department of Chemistry, National University of Uzbekistan, Tashkent 100174, Uzbekistan

* Correspondence: durbek.usmanov@ndsu.edu (D.U.); bakhtiyor.rasulev@ndsu.edu (B.R.)

**Abstract:** Phytoecdysteroids represent a class of naturally occurring substances known for their diverse biological functions, particularly their strong ability to stimulate protein anabolism. In this study, a computational machine learning-driven quantitative structure–activity relationship (QSAR) approach was applied to analyze the anabolic potential of 23 ecdysteroid compounds. The ML-based QSAR modeling was conducted using a combined approach that integrates Genetic Algorithm-based feature selection with Multiple Linear Regression Analysis (GA-MLRA). Additionally, structure optimization by semi-empirical quantum-chemical method was employed to determine the most stable molecular conformations and to calculate an additional set of structural and electronic descriptors. The most effective QSAR models for describing the anabolic activity of the investigated ecdysteroids were developed and validated. The proposed best model demonstrates both strong statistical relevance and high predictive performance. The predictive performance of the resulting models was confirmed by an external test set based on $R^2_{test}$ values, which were within the range of 0.89 to 0.97.

**Keywords:** ecdysteroid; anabolic activity; structure–activity relationship; QSAR; quantum-chemical calculations

## 1. Introduction

Phytoecdysteroids represent a class of natural bioactive compounds exhibiting multiple pharmacological activities [1–3]. These compounds are well-documented for their strong ability to stimulate protein synthesis and promote anabolic processes [2,3]. Anabolic processes contribute to the formation of organs and tissues by promoting cell growth, differentiation, and overall body enlargement through the synthesis of complex biomolecules. Ecdysteroids are hormones that regulate cell proliferation, growth, and developmental cycles in insects and other invertebrates. Recent studies suggest that the anabolic effect of ecdysterone—a naturally occurring steroid hormone believed to enhance physical performance—is mediated through its interaction with estrogen receptors (ERs) [2,3]. In comparison to banned anabolic agents like metandienone, plant-based ecdysterone demonstrated a notably strong anabolic effect in a recent study conducted on rats [2]. Nevertheless, extensive scientific investigations, particularly those involving human subjects, remain limited and scarcely available [1]. At the same time, ecdysteroids are commonly promoted as dietary supplements among athletes, with effects related to enhancing strength, supporting muscle growth during resistance training, reducing fatigue, and improving recovery. A literature review demonstrates that numerous studies have documented a broad spectrum of pharmacological effects of ecdysteroids in mammals, with the majority of these effects being beneficial to physiological function [3]. A considerable number of studies have investigated the growth-enhancing properties of ecdysterone across diverse animal species, such as rats, mice, Japanese quail, and cattle. As a result, growing concern has emerged regarding its potential misuse by athletes, prompting increased scrutiny from anti-doping authorities [2].

The literature indicates that ecdysteroids have been primarily isolated from plants such as *Silene*, *Lyhnis*, and *Dianthus* [4,5]. Given that some of these plants are endemic and do not grow in Uzbekistan, it was important to identify alternative local sources of phytoecdysteroids. An extensive search of the local flora revealed that plants of the *Silene* family are well-distributed in the region. The distribution of ecdysteroids among plant species remains poorly systematized, with no established rules governing their presence. These compounds are often detected in taxonomically diverse and unrelated plants, which complicates research efforts and suggests that their biological function is not yet clearly understood. To date, no definitive phytohormonal role has been confirmed. Nevertheless, a key observation is that certain plants can accumulate substantial amounts of ecdysteroids in specific parts of plants, such as leaves, roots, or seeds, during particular stages of their growth cycle. Plants containing ecdysteroids have been used in traditional medicine for centuries. One of the richest known sources is *Leuzea carthamoides* Iljin (family Asteraceae), a species native to Central Asia. This plant, which thrives under harsh environmental conditions, contains ecdysteroids in its dried roots and seeds at concentrations of 0.4% and 2%, respectively. Owing to anabolic, tonic, and other physiological effects, the pharmacological product derived from this plant, known as "Ecdisten", has gained popularity among recreational athletes seeking rapid muscle growth and improved physical appearance [6]. In a 1996 study, Slama et al. isolated 96% pure 20-hydroxyecdysone (20E) from Leuzea seeds and tested its anabolic effects on Japanese quail. Administering 100 mg/kg of pure 20E led to a 115% increase in body mass, comparable to the 109.5% gain from seed-derived 20E equivalents. The results confirmed that Leuzea's growth-promoting effects in vertebrates are primarily due to its ecdysteroid content [7].

Although the precise mechanism of action remains uncertain, it is generally believed that the majority of ecdysteroid-induced responses are mediated through intracellular receptor complexes—namely, the ecdysone receptor (EcR) and ultraspiracle protein (USP)—both of which are members of the nuclear receptor superfamily [8], and that influence the transcriptional activity of targeted gene clusters. However, the last research demonstrates that this group of compounds may also present non-genomic activity [9]. Several studies have explored natural ecdysteroids, though typically using limited compound sets. Consequently, structure–activity relationship (SAR) analyses are susceptible to variables such as the selected invertebrate species, its developmental stage, and the configuration of the bioassay. Moreover, common challenges inherent to biological testing—such as the purity of the test compound, its absorption, distribution, and metabolic processing—further complicate interpretation. Despite these limitations, phytoecdysteroids (PEs) have consistently shown notable hormonal activity in a range of insect-based bioassay systems. Data obtained from both in vitro [10] experiments and various in vivo assays, particularly pupariation bioassays in Dipteran species such as *Calliphora* and *Musca* [11], have led to the identification of key structural features associated with high biological activity: (a) a cis fusion between the A and B rings; (b) the presence of a 7-en-6-one moiety; and (c) a fully intact sterol side chain bearing a 22R-oriented oxygen function, occasionally accompanied by additional alkyl substitutions at the 24$\alpha$-position; (d) an oxygen-containing group, typically a 3β-hydroxyl (3β-OH); and (e) hydroxyl groups at C-14α and C-2β, with additional –OH groups often found at C-20 and C-25. A more recent comprehensive investigation of 20-hydroxyecdysone (20E) conjugates—including fatty acid and benzoic acid mono-, di-, and tri-esters, as well as glycosides and glycosidic esters—using standard bioassays in *Sarcophaga* (Diptera) and *Galleria* (Lepidoptera), demonstrated that both the 2-acetyl and 25-benzoate derivatives retained considerable biological activity. In contrast, the di- and tri-ester forms, as well as all glycosidic derivatives of 20E, exhibited significantly reduced or negligible activity compared to the parent compound [12]. PEs containing an 11α-hydroxyl group demonstrate a binding affinity to the ecdysteroid receptor of *Chironomus tentans* (Diptera) that is comparable to that of analogs lacking this group. The capacity of these compounds to elicit a hormonal response shows a strong correlation with their receptor-binding affinity, as indicated by the stimulation of acetylcholinesterase activity involved in cellular differentiation [13]. Nevertheless, studies in living organisms indicate that even slight differences in molecular structure can produce substantially different physiological effects [14].

As an alternative to traditional biological experiments, ML-based quantitative structure–activity relationship (QSAR) analysis has emerged as a powerful tool over the past three decades for exploring the biological activities and physicochemical properties of diverse organic and natural compounds, particularly those that are challenging to isolate in adequate amounts for experimental study [15–22]. Applying this approach, the set of ecdysteroids has been studied [23]. SAR was investigated using Comparative Molecular Field Analysis (CoMFA), resulting in the development of two predictive models with strong performance characteristics [23]. Based on these models, a pharmacophore hypothesis was proposed to describe ligand interaction with the ecdysteroid receptor. According to this hypothesis, receptor binding arises from the combined contributions of several molecular features, including heteroatoms at positions C-2, C-3, C-20, and C-22; a pronounced dipole at C-6; and a moderately bulky hydrophobic group positioned beyond C-22, all arranged at spatial angles and distances similar to those in 20-hydroxyecdysone (20E). While each feature enhances binding affinity, none is individually essential. Compared to earlier SAR models based on empirical observations, it is now evident that elements such as the cis A/B ring fusion, the 7-double bond, the 6-keto group, the complete eight-carbon side chain, and specific hydroxyl substitutions are not strictly required for biological activity. However, the absence of the 7-en-6-one moiety appears to significantly reduce activity. Additionally, the effect of adding or removing specific structural elements is not always additive; for instance, the presence or absence of hydroxyl groups at C-5 or C-25 can have varying impacts depending on the overall molecular context. Although it remains uncertain whether an entirely different molecular scaffold incorporating several or all of the proposed pharmacophore features would retain biological activity, the CoMFA-derived models are already being effectively used to predict the activity of novel ecdysteroid analogs before their synthesis. [24]. Additionally, computational studies of phytoecdysteroids based on ligand–receptor binding models have further advanced understanding of the ecdysteroid receptor [23]. In a separate survey, Ravi et al. employed 4D-QSAR methodologies using the same dataset previously used for CoMFA modeling [25,26].

The current study presents a combined computational and QSAR analysis of 23 ecdysteroids isolated from various plant sources, which were studied in vivo for the activity. The primary objective is to identify the structural descriptors underlying anabolic activity (AA) and to construct a predictive QSAR model that can help in guiding the design of potent and selective anabolic agents based on the new natural ecdysteroids and ecdysteroid scaffold.

# 2. Materials and Methods

## 2.1. Dataset and Biological Data

The dataset employed in this study comprises 23 ecdysteroid compounds (see Figure 1), with anabolic activity (AA) data sourced from our previous work [27]. The anabolic activity values were determined from in vivo experiments conducted on rat models, measuring radioactivity uptake (cpm/g) in target tissues following administration of each ecdysteroid compound at 5 mg/kg. The original activity values, determined at a dosage of 5 mg/kg, were converted into logarithmic molar units (log(AA)) for use as response variables in the QSAR analysis. The molecular structures of the compounds and their corresponding experimental log(AA) values are presented in Figure 1 and Table 1, respectively.

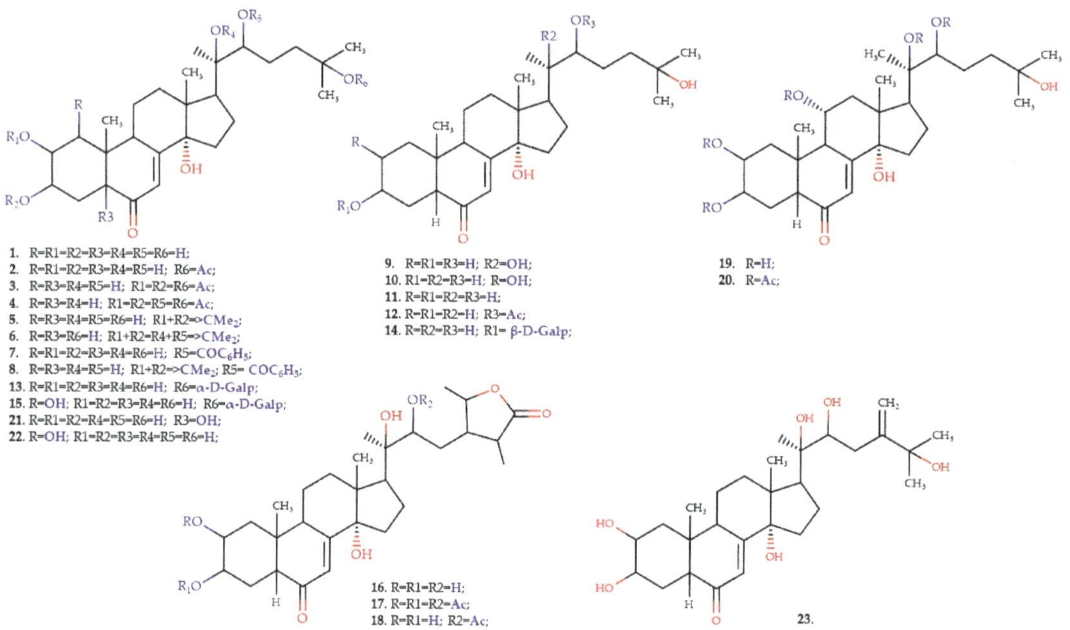


**Figure 1.** The structures of the compounds that were used in the study.

**Table 1.** List of ecdysteroid compounds with experimentally determined anabolic activity values (log scale).

| No. | Ecdysteroids' List | Activity (Radioactivity, cpm/g) | Log[AA] | Log[AA] Calc for 2-Desc. Model | Residual |
|---|---|---|---|---|---|
| 1 | 20-hydroxyecdysone | 228.633 ± 8.683 * | 6.947 | 6.891 | −0.056 |
| 2 | ViticosteroneE | 209.016 ± 1.414 * | 6.879 | 6.926 | 0.047 |
| 3 | 20-hydroxyecdysone 2,3,22-triacetate | 211.172 ± 2.562 * | 6.957 | 6.891 | −0.066 |
| 4 | 20-hydroxyecdysone 2,3,20,22-tetraacetate | 203.142 ± 2.488 * | 6.936 | 6.670 | −0.266 |
| 5 *** | 20-hydroxyecdysone 2,3-monoacetonide | 169.810 ± 2.862 * | 6.539 | 6.486 | −0.053 |
| 6 | 20-hydroxyecdysone 2,3-20,22-diacetonide | 150.520 ± 3.574 ** | 6.193 | 6.251 | 0.058 |
| 7 | 20-hydroxyecdysone 22-benzoate | 188.850 ± 2.890 * | 6.786 | 6.655 | −0.131 |

**Table 1.** *Cont.*

| No. | Ecdysteroids' List | Activity (Radioactivity, cpm/g) | Log[AA] | Log[AA] Calc for 2-Desc. Model | Residual |
|---|---|---|---|---|---|
| 8 | 20-hydroxyecdysone 22-benzoate 2,3-monoacetonide | 163.280 ± 5.280 * | 6.523 | 6.541 | 0.018 |
| 9 | 2-deoxy-20-hydroxyecdysone | 188.533 ± 4.872 * | 6.683 | 6.655 | −0.028 |
| 10 *** | Ecdysone | 158.200 ± 3.629 * | 6.302 | 6.450 | 0.148 |
| 11 | 2-deoxyecdysone | 153.220 ± 4.830 ** | 6.173 | 6.095 | −0.078 |
| 12 | 2-deoxyecdysone 22-acetate | 152.720 ± 4.624 * | 6.199 | 6.367 | 0.168 |
| 13 | SileneosideA | 236.450 ± 7.167 * | 7.108 | 7.046 | −0.062 |
| 14 | SileneosideE | 177.482 ± 4.896 * | 6.698 | 6.810 | 0.112 |
| 15 *** | SileneosideC | 184.120 ± 2.440 | 6.796 | 6.873 | 0.077 |
| 16 | Cyasterone | 241.750 ± 2.522 * | 7.039 | 7.077 | 0.038 |
| 17 | Cyasterone 2,3,22-triacetate | 218.362 ± 5.270 * | 7.024 | 7.113 | 0.089 |
| 18 | Cyasterone 22-acetate | 266.166 ± 2.363 * | 7.164 | 7.111 | −0.053 |
| 19 | Turkesterone | 264.512 ± 6.012 * | 7.104 | 7.093 | −0.011 |
| 20 *** | Turkesteronetetraacetate | 255.250 ± 3.798 * | 7.198 | 7.010 | −0.188 |
| 21 | PolypodineB | 196.890 ± 8.250 * | 6.777 | 6.888 | 0.111 |
| 22 | IntegristeroneA | 175.520 ± 5.018 * | 6.587 | 6.717 | 0.130 |
| 23 | 24(28)-dehydromakisteronA | 219.400 ± 2.758 * | 6.912 | 6.891 | −0.021 |

Note: ***—prediction set of compounds; differences reliable for * $p < 0.001$; ** $p < 0.01$.

## 2.2. Computational Approach

In this work, HyperChem 8 software package is applied to draw chemical structures for further optimization [28]. The RM1 (Recife Model 1) semi-empirical quantum-chemical method is used for optimizing geometries of molecules to obtain minimal energy conformations [29]. To gain deeper insight into the experimental findings, a set of quantum-chemical descriptors was calculated and utilized in the cheminformatics analysis. It includes the energies of the highest occupied molecular orbital (HOMO, indication of nucleophilicity) and the lowest unoccupied molecular orbital (LUMO, indication of electrophilicity), dipole moment (including its X, Y, and Z components), total energy, LogP (lipophilicity index), refractivity, polarizability, and atomic charges. The numerical values of these descriptors are represented in Table 2.

**Table 2.** Numerical values of quantum-chemical descriptors calculated in this work.

| No. | E, kcal/mol | Hyener * | Log P | Refc | Polar | HOMO | LUMO | $\mu$ | $\mu_x$ | $\mu_y$ | $\mu_z$ |
|---|---|---|---|---|---|---|---|---|---|---|---|
| 1 | −7703.24 | −13.36 | 1.79 | 128.87 | 50.94 | −9.99 | 0.16 | 4.31 | −0.14 | −3.58 | −2.39 |
| 2 | −8249.68 | −10.64 | 1.92 | 138.02 | 54.7 | −10.06 | 0.10 | 1.18 | 0.31 | −0.79 | −0.82 |
| 3 | −9343.35 | −4.5 | 2.18 | 156.33 | 62.21 | −10.12 | 0.05 | 2.77 | −2.67 | −0.02 | 0.69 |
| 4 | −9890.02 | −2.41 | 2.31 | 165.48 | 65.96 | −10.02 | 0.14 | 1.79 | −0.39 | −1.59 | 0.70 |
| 5 | −8424.28 | −7.07 | 3.17 | 141.08 | 55.67 | −10.01 | 0.18 | 5.96 | −0.51 | −5.28 | −2.70 |
| 6 | −9148.60 | −4.23 | 4.55 | 153.28 | 60.4 | −10.11 | 0.08 | 3.58 | −0.43 | −2.64 | −2.38 |
| 7 | −9175.95 | −13.39 | 3.07 | 162.33 | 62.52 | −9.82 | −0.15 | 5.16 | 2.30 | −4.44 | −1.24 |
| 8 | −9894.08 | −6.81 | 4.45 | 174.54 | 67.25 | −9.86 | −0.19 | 6.46 | 0.61 | −5.94 | −2.46 |
| 9 | −7597.34 | −8.53 | 2.46 | 127.51 | 50.3 | −9.88 | 0.28 | 5.98 | 0.97 | −4.98 | −3.15 |
| 10 | −7598.16 | −11.72 | 2.81 | 127.42 | 50.3 | −10.01 | 0.15 | 4.31 | 0.79 | −3.55 | −2.32 |
| 11 | −7494.59 | −7.21 | 3.58 | 126.06 | 49.67 | −9.94 | 0.22 | 4.53 | 1.30 | −3.38 | −2.71 |
| 12 | −8043.12 | −5.68 | 3.71 | 135.21 | 53.42 | −10.02 | 0.15 | 3.75 | −0.78 | −3.64 | −0.42 |
| 13 | −9766.51 | −25.89 | 0.57 | 161.29 | 64.36 | -9.99 | 0.15 | 3.61 | 1.27 | −3.23 | −0.98 |
| 14 | −9554.91 | −18.47 | 2.36 | 158.47 | 63.09 | −9.79 | 0.36 | 4.64 | 2.13 | −4.12 | 0.18 |

**Table 2.** *Cont.*

| No. | E, kcal/mol | Hyener * | Log P | Refc | Polar | HOMO | LUMO | μ | $\mu_x$ | $\mu_y$ | $\mu_z$ |
|---|---|---|---|---|---|---|---|---|---|---|---|
| 15 | −9864.45 | −27.44 | -0.05 | 162.49 | 65 | −10.02 | 0.12 | 4.71 | 1.88 | −3.77 | −2.09 |
| 16 | −8134.09 | −12.63 | 2.14 | 136.05 | 53.92 | −10.18 | −0.003 | 3.66 | 3.26 | 1.35 | 0.99 |
| 17 | −9775.19 | −3.98 | 2.52 | 163.51 | 65.19 | −10.16 | 0.01 | 4.81 | 3.71 | 0.74 | 2.96 |
| 18 | −8682.18 | −10.76 | 2.27 | 145.21 | 57.68 | −10.19 | −0.02 | 6.65 | 6.13 | 0.35 | 2.55 |
| 19 | −7798.46 | −14.18 | 0.8 | 130.46 | 51.58 | −9.98 | 0.13 | 7.27 | 0.73 | −5.45 | −4.75 |
| 20 | −9985.27 | −6.43 | 1.32 | 167.07 | 66.6 | −10.25 | −0.08 | 6.96 | 4.01 | −5.27 | −2.15 |
| 21 | −7797.66 | −15.02 | 1.02 | 130.23 | 51.58 | −10.01 | 0.01 | 7.19 | −0.06 | −6.23 | −3.60 |
| 22 | −7804.91 | −16.11 | 1.16 | 130.08 | 51.58 | −10.08 | 0.05 | 4.29 | 1.62 | −3.35 | −2.14 |
| 23 | −7851.29 | −13.45 | 1.87 | 133.04 | 52.58 | −9.42 | 0.05 | 2.81 | 1.98 | −1.78 | −0.92 |

* Hyener = Hyperpolarizability energy estimate; Refc = refractive coefficient (estimated from refractivity data).

### 2.3. Cheminformatics Analysis

The initial selection of predictive models was conducted using the GA-MLRA technique, which combines a genetic algorithm (GA) with multiple linear regression analysis (MLRA) [30,31], as implemented in the QSARINS v2.2.3 software package [32,33]. To convert chemical structures into numerical representations, the optimized structures were used to calculate constitutional, topological, and molecular descriptors using DRAGON 6 software package [34]. The descriptor categories incorporated in the study included: (i) functional group-based descriptors, (ii) descriptors derived from atom-centered fragments, and (iii) topological indices such as molecular walk counts [35]. Following data curation and the removal of non-informative (zero-variance) descriptors, a final set of 384 distinct descriptors was retained to characterize the chemical diversity of the studied compounds and develop a final set of QSAR models. The most effective models were selected based on several performance criteria, including a high coefficient of determination ($R^2$) for both the training and external validation sets, low standard deviation ($s$), and a minimal number of descriptors to ensure model simplicity. Additionally, a high Fisher statistic ($F$) and the absence of multicollinearity among descriptors were considered key factors in the selection process. The final QSAR models were further validated using the leave-one-out (LOO) cross-validation method, with predictive performance assessed by the cross-validated coefficient ($Q^2$), calculated from the predictive residual sum of squares.

To detect redundancy and avoid overrepresentation of specific chemical features, pairwise correlation coefficients were calculated for all descriptors included in the model. Descriptors exhibiting high intercorrelation ($r^2 > 0.9$) or constant values were excluded from further analysis to prevent bias in explaining the dependent variable. Additionally, descriptors with cross-correlation coefficients exceeding 0.6 were deliberately avoided during model construction to ensure descriptor independence and model robustness.

## 3. Results

For model training and validation, the complete set of 23 ecdysteroid compounds was divided in an 80:20 ratio, with 19 compounds allocated to the training set and 4 compounds reserved for external validation. This division was not performed randomly; instead, it was guided by structural diversity to ensure that at least one representative from each structural class present in the training set was also included in the test set. The application of the GA-MLRA method resulted in the identification of four statistically significant models, each incorporating different descriptor subsets, that demonstrated strong predictive capability for the anabolic activity (AA) of ecdysteroids. The statistical metrics for all developed models are summarized in Table 3.

**Table 3.** Statistical characteristics of the one-, two-, three-, and four-variable models.

| Model, No./# of Descriptors | Training Set, $n$ = 19 | | | | Prediction Set, $n$ = 4 | |
|---|---|---|---|---|---|---|
| | $R^2$ | $s$ | $F$ | $Q^2$ | $R^2$ | $s$ |
| - (1 descr-s) | 0.67 | 0.19 | 33.87 | 0.58 | 0.53 | 0.27 |
| 1 (2 descr-s) | 0.89 | 0.11 | 64.66 | 0.84 | 0.89 | 0.13 |
| 2 (3 descr-s) | 0.88 | 0.12 | 37.68 | 0.83 | 0.97 | 0.11 |
| 3 (4 descr-s) | 0.95 | 0.08 | 61.98 | 0.91 | 0.89 | 0.15 |

The equation below represents the two-descriptor QSAR model:

$$\text{Log [AA]} = 0.808\ (\pm 0.175)\ SIC0 - 0.582(\pm 0.193)\ G3p + 6.491\ (\pm 0.142) \quad (1)$$

The model demonstrates strong performance, exhibiting high $R^2$ and $Q^2$ values for both the training and test sets. Graphical illustrations of the model's predictive ability are presented in Figure 2. A comparison of experimental and predicted log(AA) values, based on Equation (1), is provided in Table 1.

Descriptors definitions: SIC0—Structural Information Content index of order 0, representing the neighborhood symmetry of atoms; part of the class of information indices and G3p—Third principal component directional WHIM descriptor, weighted by atomic polarizability; belongs to the WHIM (Weighted Holistic Invariant Molecular) descriptor family. This model highlights the positive contribution of the first descriptor and the negative contribution of the second descriptor to the predicted anabolic activity (log[AA]), with a high level of statistical confidence in the coefficients.

In addition to the two-variable model, two other models with three and four descriptors were also developed.

The model with three descriptors is represented by Equation (2) as follows:

$$\text{Log [AA]} = 0.412\ (\pm 0.217)\ GATS5e - 0.454\ (\pm 0.219)\ G3p - 0.830\ (\pm 0.210)\ ALOGP2 + 6.957(\pm 0.182) \quad (2)$$

This model exhibits excellent fit for both training and test sets. A graphical representation is provided in Figure S1 of the Supplementary Information.

Equation (3) represents a model with four descriptors as follows:

$$\text{Log [AA]} = 0.643\ (\pm 0.367)\ Mp - 0.595\ (\pm 0.923)\ TIE - 0.480\ (\pm 0.169)\ G3p - 1.188\ (\pm 0.629)\ ALOGP + 7.337\ (\pm 0.116) \quad (3)$$

Among all developed models, the four-variable model yields the highest $R^2$ value for the training set and performs well in predicting the external test set. The corresponding plot is shown in Figure S2 of the Supplementary Information.

Overall, all models demonstrate similarly strong statistical performance and predictive accuracy. However, the three-variable model (Equation (2)) provides the highest external predictive ability with $R_{ext}^2$ = 0.97. Nevertheless, it is important to highlight that the two-variable model (Model 1) achieved the best $y$-randomization ($y$-scrambling) validation results, indicating superior robustness. Therefore, Model 1 may be considered the most reliable and generalizable model for predicting the anabolic activity of ecdysteroids.

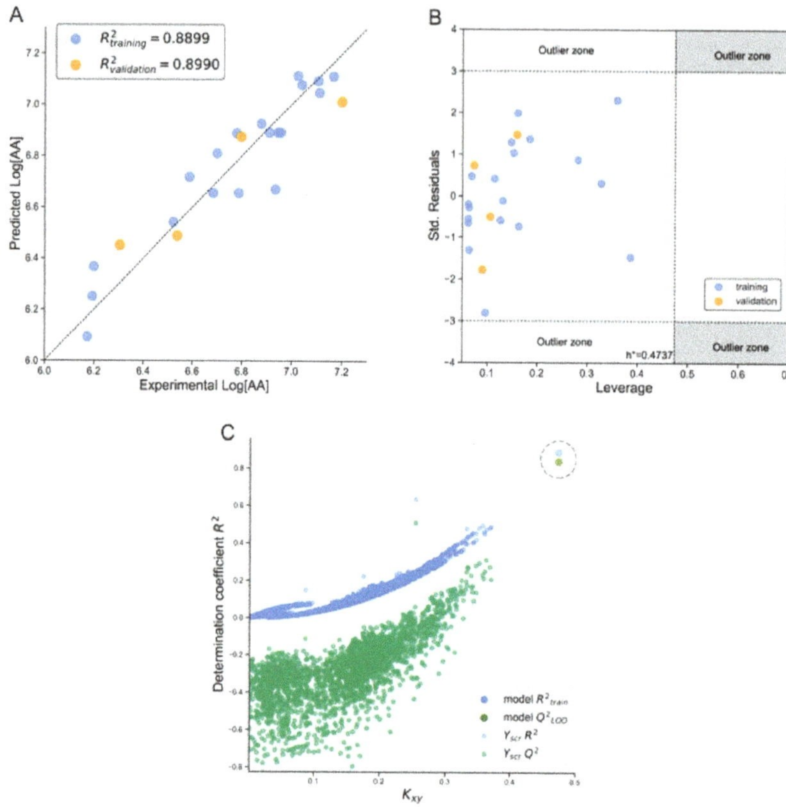


**Figure 2.** Graphical evaluation of the statistical performance of the best two-descriptor QSAR model: (**A**) correlation plot of predicted versus experimental log(AA) values for training (blue) and validation (orange) sets; (**B**) Williams plot showing standardized residuals versus leverage values—all compounds lie within the model's applicability domain ($h^* = 0.474$); (**C**) Y-randomization (Y-scrambling) test confirming robustness of the model.

## 4. Discussion

In the context of the developed QSAR models, a detailed examination of the selected molecular descriptors provides insight into the key structural and physicochemical features that govern anabolic activity in ecdysteroids. As presented in the Results section, the most statistically significant models incorporated the following descriptors: SIC0, a measure of structural information content that reflects zero-order neighborhood symmetry; G3p, a third-order WHIM (Weighted Holistic Invariant Molecular) descriptor associated with molecular symmetry and weighted by atomic polarizability; and Mp, representing the mean atomic polarizability normalized to a carbon atom, falling under the category of constitutional descriptors. Additionally, the TIE descriptor captures E-state topological information, accounting for the electronic environment of atoms in the molecular topology. GATS5e is a 2D autocorrelation descriptor indicating the spatial distribution of Sanderson electronegativity at a lag of 5 bonds. Finally, the lipophilicity of molecules is characterized by ALOGP (Ghose-Crippen logP) and ALOGP2 (its squared form), both of which relate to the molecule's hydrophobic character and are essential for membrane permeability and receptor binding. These descriptors collectively highlight the relevance of electronic distribution, molecular shape, symmetry, and hydrophobicity in modulating the anabolic activity of ecdysteroids.

The first selected descriptor, SIC0, belongs to the class of information content indices. These descriptors are derived from the molecular graph and quantify structural complexity by calculating the distribution of equivalence classes within the molecule [35]. This information-based descriptor incorporates neighborhood symmetry as well as data related to neighbor degree and edge multiplicity within the molecular graph. According to the regression coefficient, an increase in the SIC0 value correlates positively with enhanced anabolic activity (AA) in ecdysteroids. In the selected QSAR model, SIC0 emerges as a key positive contributor to biological activity. Notably, the lead compounds (**19**, **21**, and **22**) exhibit the highest SIC0 values, aligning with their superior anabolic potential. In contrast, compound **6**, which demonstrates the lowest biological activity, is characterized by a significantly smaller SIC0 value.

As observed, the descriptor G3p is included in all three of the discussed models, and its contribution is substantial based on the magnitude of its regression coefficient. G3p refers to the third component, directional WHIM index, weighted by atomic polarizability, and is categorized under the WHIM (Weighted Holistic Invariant Molecular) descriptors. These descriptors capture the three-dimensional molecular geometry and encode information about molecular size, shape, symmetry, and atom-related properties—such as polarizability—which are crucial for understanding interactions with biological targets [36]. WHIM descriptors are molecular descriptors based on statistical indices calculated on the projections of the atoms along principal axes [37]. WHIM descriptors are designed to capture essential three-dimensional (3D) molecular information such as size, shape, symmetry, and atomic distribution relative to fixed reference axes. Specifically, directional WHIM symmetry descriptors $\gamma 1$, $\gamma 2$ and $\gamma 3$, represent the degree of symmetry along each principal axis of the molecule. These are calculated as the mean information content associated with atomic distribution relative to the center of the score values [38]. The symmetry index $\gamma'_m$ for the $m$-th component is calculated using the following formula:

$$\gamma'_m = -\left[\frac{n_s}{n} * \log_2 \frac{n_s}{n} + n_a * \left(\frac{1}{n} * \log_2 \frac{1}{n}\right)\right] \gamma_m = \frac{1}{1+\gamma'_m} \qquad 0 < \gamma_m \leq 1$$

where $n_s$ is the number of atoms symmetrically distributed along the $m$-th component, $n_a$ is the number of asymmetrically distributed atoms, and $n$ is the total number of atoms in the molecule. A higher $\gamma_m$ value implies greater symmetry, and these values are used as part of the WHIM descriptor set to encode structural features relevant to molecular recognition and activity. Thus, according to the model and regression coefficient, the increase in G3p value in ecdysteroids decreases the AA potency.

While descriptors such as SIC0 and G3p are mathematical constructs derived from molecular graphs and 3D geometry, they can be interpreted in a chemically meaningful way. SIC0 is a measure of structural information content, which increases with greater atomic diversity and topological complexity—often associated with branching or asymmetry in the molecule. Thus, analogs with greater substitution patterns or higher degrees of structural variation near active sites may exhibit elevated SIC0 values. Conversely, a lower G3p value implies reduced 3D symmetry or non-uniform polarizability distribution. Therefore, in practical terms, designing analogs with asymmetrical polarizable groups, such as selective acylation, esterification, or hydroxyl substitutions, reduces G3p while increasing SIC0. These structural modifications are feasible via semisynthetic derivatization of natural ecdysteroids. Hence, although abstract in formulation, these descriptors point toward tangible molecular changes that can be implemented and tested in future analog design efforts.

Mp is a mean atomic polarizability descriptor (scaled on carbon atom) is among constitutional indices [39]. The descriptor is synergistic with the G3p descriptor, as G3p is also weighted by polarizability.

The TIE descriptor represents an electrotopological state (E-state), i.e., a topological parameter and belongs to the class of topological indices. It encodes information about the molecule's topology and atomic electronic environment, contributing to the model by capturing features related to molecular connectivity and electronic distribution [40].

Next descriptor, GATS5e, is Geary autocorrelation of lag 5 weighted by the Sanderson electronegativity descriptor, belongs to 2D autocorrelation descriptors [41]. The presence of this descriptor confirms that electronegativity plays an important role in anabolic activity exhibited by ecdysteroid compounds. These results are in accordance with those displayed in the dendrogram in Figure 3. As can be seen in the picture there are three main clusters of compounds in the dendrogram. In the first cluster (left side) most compounds are with the lowest activity and sharing a maximum common substructure (MSC) displayed as MCS1. In the case of the third cluster (right side) the compounds with the highest activity are included, and the MSC3 has the same features as the MSC_ecdysteroids for the whole dataset. In the bottom part are included the two lowest active compounds (**6** and **11**) and the two highest active natural products (**18** and **20**) where the last ones have the main differences with the MSC related to the presence of (O-C=O) groups showing a positive relationship to the activity corroborating that the increase in electronegativity given by the amount of carbonyl groups plays a fundamental role in the activity.

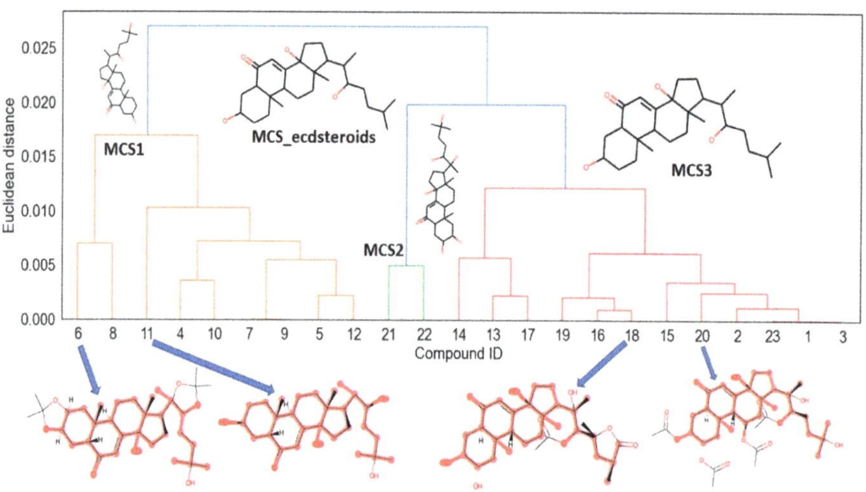


**Figure 3.** Hierarchical cluster analysis of the dataset and maximum common substructure search. MCS1: Maximum common substructure in cluster 1. MCS2: Maximum common substructure in cluster 2. MCS3: Maximum common substructure in cluster 3.

Two other descriptors—ALOGP and ALOGP2 (squared ALOGP)—are octanol-water partition descriptors that encode the lipophilicity property of molecules, which are responsible for the solubility of compounds in water [42,43]. The presence of these types of descriptors confirms the importance of lipophilicity factors or water solubility in the exhibition of anabolic activity by ecdysteroid compounds.

Interestingly, none of the quantum-mechanical (QM) descriptors, such as HOMO, LUMO, dipole moments, or total energy, were retained in any of the final regression models. This outcome suggests that the variability in anabolic activity across the studied ecdysteroids is more effectively captured by topological, structural, and physicochemical descriptors rather than electronic properties or processes. One main explanation is the significant influence of structural factors. Furthermore, many QM descriptors tend to be highly correlated with other types of structural descriptors, such as WHIM or polarizability-based indices, causing them to be excluded by the genetic algorithm during variable selection. Thus, while QM descriptors provide valuable molecular insights, their exclusion from the final models highlights that simpler structural/topological descriptors offer sufficient predictive power for this particular chemical series.

Overall, it can be concluded that the polarizability, electronegativity, and lipophilicity properties of the molecules, together with structural factors, play a significant role in the AA potency exhibition of investigated ecdysteroid compounds. Future efforts will focus on sourcing or synthesizing novel ecdysteroid analogs that optimize key molecular features, such as high polarizability, favorable lipophilicity, and balanced topological symmetry, based on the present QSAR findings. Further in vivo and in vitro validation studies are planned to assess their anabolic potential and explore additional pharmacological properties.

## 5. Conclusions

A comprehensive QSAR study was conducted on a set of 23 ecdysteroid compounds to investigate and predict their anabolic activity (AA). The modeling framework employed genetic algorithms for descriptor selection and multiple linear regression analysis for model construction. Molecular mechanics and quantum-chemical computations were initially employed to optimize molecular structures and generate physicochemical descriptors for further modeling.

Three best predictive models were developed using two, three, and four descriptors, respectively. The two-variable model demonstrated the best balance of transparence, simplicity and predictive power, yielding squared correlation coefficients of $R^2 = 0.89$ for the training set and $R^2 = 0.84$ for the test set. William's plot confirmed that all compounds fall within the model's applicability domain; furthermore, $y$-scrambling validation verified the robustness and reliability of the model. The two key descriptors identified in the optimal model were SIC0, a structural information content index reflecting molecular symmetry, and G3p, a directional WHIM descriptor weighted by polarizability. These descriptors were found to be significant contributors to anabolic potency, offering structural-level insights into the biological activity of the compounds.

Overall, the results of this study indicate that polarizability, electronegativity, lipophilicity, and topological symmetry are critical molecular features influencing anabolic activity. The two-variable model (Model 1) thus represents a robust and interpretable QSAR tool for estimating the anabolic potential of newly synthesized or virtual ecdysteroid derivatives belonging to this functional class.

**Supplementary Materials:** The following supporting information can be downloaded at: https://www.mdpi.com/article/10.3390/computation13080195/s1, Figure S1. Graphical representation of statistical performance of 3-variable model; Figure S2. Graphical representation of statistical performance of the 4-variable model.

**Author Contributions:** Conceptualization, D.U., G.M.C.-M., V.S. and B.R.; methodology, D.U., U.Y., G.M.C.-M. and B.R.; software, D.U., U.Y. and G.M.C.-M.; validation, D.U., U.Y., and G.M.C.-M.; formal analysis, D.U., U.Y., V.S., G.M.C.-M. and B.R.; investigation, D.U., U.Y., G.M.C.-M. and B.R.; resources, D.U., V.S. and B.R.; data curation, D.U., U.Y. and G.M.C.-M.; writing—original draft preparation, D.U. and U.Y.; writing—review and editing, D.U., U.Y., V.S., G.M.C.-M. and B.R.; visualization, D.U., U.Y. and G.M.C.-M.; supervision, V.S. and B.R.; project administration, V.S. and B.R.; funding acquisition, V.S. and B.R. All authors have read and agreed to the published version of the manuscript.

**Funding:** This research was supported in part by National Science Foundation (NSF) [MRI Award number 2019077].

**Data Availability Statement:** The original contributions presented in this study are included in the article. Further inquiries can be directed to the corresponding author(s).

**Acknowledgments:** D.U. thank the Ministry of Innovation Development of the Republic of Uzbekistan and the Fund to Support Innovative Development and Innovative ideas for the travel grant provided. Authors thank Paola Gramatica for generously providing a free license for the QSARINS software. This work used resources of the Center for Computationally Assisted Science and Technology (CCAST) at North Dakota State University, which was made possible in part by the National Science Foundation (NSF) [MRI Award number 2019077]. Supercomputing support provided by the CCAST HPC System at NDSU is gratefully acknowledged. D.U. thanks the Department of Coatings and Polymeric Materials (NDSU) for providing training and computer facilities to perform this project.

**Conflicts of Interest:** The authors declare no conflicts of interest.

## References

1. Isenmann, E.; Ambrosio, G.; Joseph, J.F.; Mazzarino, M.; de la Torre, X.; Zimmer, P.; Kazlauskas, R.; Goebel, C.; Botrè, F.; Diel, P.; et al. Ecdysteroids as non-conventional anabolic agent: Performance enhancement by ecdysterone supplementation in humans. *Arch. Toxicol.* **2019**, *93*, 1807–1816. [CrossRef]
2. Parr, M.K.; Botrè, F.; Naß, A.; Hengevoss, J.; Diel, P.; Wolber, G. Ecdysteroids: A novel class of anabolic agents? *Biol. Sport* **2015**, *32*, 169–173. [CrossRef]
3. Syrov, V.N. Comparative experimental investigation of the anabolic activity of phytoecdysteroids and steranabols. *Pharm. Chem. J.* **2000**, *34*, 193–197. [CrossRef]
4. Yusupova, U.Y.; Usmanov, D.A.; Ramazonov, N.S. Phytoecdysteroids from the Plant *Dianthus helenae*. *Chem. Nat. Compd.* **2019**, *55*, 393–394. [CrossRef]
5. Yusupova, U.Y.; Usmanov, D.A.; Ramazonov, N.S. Phytoecdysteroids from the Aerial Part of *Silene popovii*. *Chem. Nat. Compd.* **2020**, *56*, 562–563. [CrossRef]
6. Wilborn, C.D.; Taylor, L.W.; Campbell, B.I.; Kerksick, C.; Rasmussen, C.J.; Greenwood, M.; Kreider, R.B. Effects of methoxyisoflavone, ecdysterone, and sulfo-polysaccharide supplementation on training adaptations in resistance-trained males. *J. Int. Soc. Sports Nutr.* **2006**, *3*, 19–27. [CrossRef] [PubMed]
7. Sláma, K.; Koudela, K.; Tenora, J.; Maťhová, A. Insect hormones in vertebrates: Anabolic effects of 20-hydroxyecdysone in Japanese quail. *Experientia* **1996**, *52*, 702–706. [CrossRef] [PubMed]
8. Yao, T.-P.; Forman, B.M.; Jiang, Z.; Cherbas, L.; Chen, J.D.; McKeown, M.; Cherbas, P.; Evans, R.M. Functional ecdysone receptor is the product of EcR and Ultraspiracle genes. *Nature* **1993**, *366*, 476–479. [CrossRef]
9. Tomaschko, K.-H. Nongenomic effects of ecdysteroids. *Arch. Insect Biochem. Physiol.* **1999**, *41*, 89–98. [CrossRef]
10. Cherbas, L.; Yonge, C.D.; Cherbas, P.; Williams, C.M. The morphological response of Kc-H cells to ecdysteroids: Hormonal specificity. *Wilhelm Roux's Arch. Dev. Biol.* **1980**, *189*, 1–15. [CrossRef]
11. Lafont, R.; Dauphin–Villemant, C.; Warren, J.T.; Rees, H. Ecdysteroid Chemistry and Biochemistry. *Compr. Mol. Insect Sci.* **2005**, *3*, 125–195. [CrossRef]
12. Sláma, K.; Abubakirov, N.K.; Gorovits, M.B.; Baltaev, U.A.; Saatov, Z. Hormonal activity of ecdysteroids from certain asiatic plants. *Insect Biochem. Mol. Biol.* **1993**, *23*, 181–185. [CrossRef]
13. Spindler-Barth, M.; Quack, S.; Rauch, P.; Spindler, K.-D. Biological effects of muristerone A and turkesterone on the epithelial cell line from *Chironomus tentans* (Diptera: Chironomidae) and correlation with binding affinity to the ecdysteroid receptor. *Eur. J. Entomol.* **1997**, *94*, 161–166.
14. Clément, C.Y.; Bradbrook, D.A.; Lafont, R.; Dinan, L. Assessment of a microplate-based bioassay for the detection of ecdysteroid-like or antiecdysteroid activities. *Insect Biochem. Mol. Biol.* **1993**, *23*, 187–193. [CrossRef]
15. Jagiello, K.; Grzonkowska, M.; Swirog, M.; Ahmed, L.; Rasulev, B.; Avramopoulos, A.; Papadopoulos, M.G.; Leszczynski, J.; Puzyn, T. Advantages and limitations of classic and 3D QSAR approaches in nano-QSAR studies based on biological activity of fullerene derivatives. *J. Nanoparticle Res. Interdiscip. Forum Nanoscale Sci. Technol.* **2016**, *18*, 256. [CrossRef]
16. Juretic, D.; Kusic, H.; Dionysiou, D.D.; Rasulev, B.; Loncaric Bozic, A. Modeling of photooxidative degradation of aromatics in water matrix; combination of mechanistic and structural-relationship approach. *Chem. Eng. J.* **2014**, *257*, 229–241. [CrossRef]

17. Rasulev, B. Recent Developments in 3D QSAR and Molecular Docking Studies of Organic and Nanostructures. In *Handbook of Computational Chemistry*; Springer: Dordrecht, The Netherlands, 2016; pp. 1–29. [CrossRef]
18. Turabekova, M.A.; Rasulev, B.F.; Dzhakhangirov, F.N.; Salikhov, S.I. Aconitum and Delphinium alkaloids: "Drug-likeness" descriptors related to toxic mode of action. *Environ. Toxicol. Pharmacol.* **2008**, *25*, 310–320. [CrossRef]
19. Turabekova, M.A.; Rasulev, B.F.; Dzhakhangirov, F.N.; Leszczynska, D.; Leszczynski, J. Aconitum and Delphinium alkaloids of curare-like activity. *QSAR Anal. Mol. Docking Alkaloids Into AChBP. Eur. J. Med. Chem.* **2010**, *45*, 3885–3894. [CrossRef]
20. Toropova, A.P.; Toropov, A.A.; Rasulev, B.F.; Benfenati, E.; Gini, G.; Leszczynska, D.; Leszczynski, J. QSAR models for ACE-inhibitor activity of tri-peptides based on representation of the molecular structure by graph of atomic orbitals and SMILES. *Struct. Chem.* **2012**, *23*, 1873–1878. [CrossRef]
21. Toropov, A.A.; Toropova, A.P.; Rasulev, B.F.; Benfenati, E.; Gini, G.; Leszczynska, D.; Leszczynski, J. Coral: QSPR modeling of rate constants of reactions between organic aromatic pollutants and hydroxyl radical. *J. Comput. Chem.* **2012**, *33*, 1902–1906. [CrossRef] [PubMed]
22. Usmanov, D.; Rasulev, B.; Syrov, V.; Yusupova, U.; Ramazonov, N. Structure-Hepatoprotective Activity Relationship Study of Iridoids. *Int. J. Quant. Struct.-Prop. Relatsh.* **2020**, *5*, 108–118. [CrossRef]
23. Wurtz, J.M.; Guillot, B.; Fagart, J.; Moras, D.; Tietjen, K.; Schindler, M. A new model for 20-hydroxyecdysone and dibenzoylhydrazine binding: A homology modeling and docking approach. *Protein Sci. A Publ. Protein Soc.* **2000**, *9*, 1073–1084. [CrossRef] [PubMed]
24. Dinan, L. Ecdysteroid Structure-Activity Relationships. *Bioact. Nat. Prod.* **2003**, *29 Pt. J*, 3–71. [CrossRef]
25. Dinan, L.; Sarker, S.D.; Bourne, P.; Whiting, P.; Ik, V.; Rees, H.H. Phytoecdysteroids in seeds and plants of *Rhagodia baccata* (Labill.) Moq. (Chenopodiaceae). *Arch. Insect Biochem. Physiol.* **1999**, *41*, 18–23. [CrossRef]
26. Dinan, L.; Hormann, R.E.; Fujimoto, T. An extensive ecdysteroid CoMFA. *J Comput Aided Mol Des* **1999**, *13*, 185–207. [CrossRef]
27. Syrov, V.N.; Saatov, Z.; Sagdullaev, S.S.; Mamatkhanov, A.U. Study of the Structure—Anabolic Activity Relationship for Phytoecdysteroids Extracted from Some Plants of Central Asia. *Pharm. Chem. J.* **2001**, *35*, 667–671. [CrossRef]
28. Coleman, W.F.; Arumainayagam, C.R. HyperChem 5 (by Hypercube, Inc.). *J. Chem. Educ.* **1998**, *75*, 416. [CrossRef]
29. Rocha, G.B.; Freire, R.O.; Simas, A.M.; Stewart, J.J.P. RM1: A reparameterization of AM1 for H, C, N, O, P, S, F, Cl, Br, and I. *J. Comput. Chem.* **2006**, *27*, 1101–1111. [CrossRef]
30. Davis, L. *Handbook of Genetic Algorithms*; Van Nostrand Reinhold: New York, NY, USA, 1991.
31. Devillers, J. Genetic Algorithms in Computer-Aided Molecular Design. In *Genetic Algorithms in Molecular Modeling*, Academic Press: Cambridge, MA, USA, 1996; pp. 1–34. [CrossRef]
32. Gramatica, P.; Cassani, S.; Chirico, N. QSARINS-chem: Insubria datasets and new QSAR/QSPR models for environmental pollutants in QSARINS. *J. Comput. Chem.* **2014**, *35*, 1036–1044. [CrossRef]
33. Gramatica, P.; Chirico, N.; Papa, E.; Cassani, S.; Kovarich, S. QSARINS: A new software for the development, analysis, and validation of QSAR MLR models. *J. Comput. Chem.* **2013**, *34*, 2121–2132. [CrossRef]
34. Toddeschini, R.; Consonni, V.; Mauri, A.; Pavan, M. *Dragon Software for the Calculation of Molecular Descriptors, Version 6 for Windows*; Talete SRL: Milan, Italy, 2014.
35. Roy, A.B.; Basak, S.C.; Harriss, D.K.; Magnuson, V.R. NEIGHBORHOOD COMPLEXITIES AND SYMMETRY OF CHEMICAL GRAPHS AND THEIR BIOLOGICAL APPLICATIONS. In *Mathematical Modelling in Science and Technology*; Pergamon Press: Oxford, UK, 1984; pp. 745–750. [CrossRef]
36. Najafi, A.; Sobhanardakani, S.; Marjani, M. Exploring QSAR for Antimalarial Activities and Drug Distribution within Blood of a Series of 4-Aminoquinoline Drugs Using Genetic-MLR. *J. Chem.* **2013**, *2013*, 560415. [CrossRef]
37. Todeschini, R.; Lasagni, M.; Marengo, E. New molecular descriptors for 2D and 3D structures. *Theory. J. Chemom.* **1994**, *8*, 263–272. [CrossRef]
38. Todeschini, R.; Gramatica, P. 3D-modelling and Prediction by WHIM Descriptors. Part 5. Theory Development and Chemical Meaning of WHIM Descriptors. *Quant. Struct.-Act. Relatsh.* **1997**, *16*, 113–119. [CrossRef]
39. Akbar, J.; Iqbal, S.; Batool, F.; Karim, A.; Chan, K.W. Predicting retention times of naturally occurring phenolic compounds in reversed-phase liquid chromatography: A Quantitative Structure-Retention Relationship (QSRR) approach. *Int. J. Mol. Sci.* **2012**, *13*, 15387–15400. [CrossRef]
40. Voelkel, A. Structural descriptors in organic chemistry—New topological parameter based on electrotopological state of graph vertices. *Comput. Chem.* **1994**, *18*, 1–4. [CrossRef]
41. Ambre, P.; Wavhale, R.; Coutinho, E. New Horizons in Antimalarial Drug Discovery in the Last Decade by Chemoinformatic Approaches. *Comb. Chem. High Throughput Screen.* **2015**, *18*, 129–150. [CrossRef]

42. Ghose, A.K.; Crippen, G.M. Atomic physicochemical parameters for three-dimensional-structure-directed quantitative structure-activity relationships. 2. Modeling dispersive and hydrophobic interactions. *J. Chem. Inf. Comput. Sci.* **1987**, *27*, 21–35. [CrossRef]
43. Ghose, A.K.; Crippen, G.M. Atomic Physicochemical Parameters for Three-Dimensional Structure-Directed Quantitative Structure-Activity Relationships I. Partition Coefficients as a Measure of Hydrophobicity. *J. Comput. Chem.* **1986**, *7*, 565–577. [CrossRef]

computation

MDPI

Article

# Effect of Monomer Mixture Composition on $TiCl_4$-$Al(i\text{-}C_4H_9)_3$ Catalytic System Activity in Butadiene–Isoprene Copolymerization: A Theoretical Study

**Konstantin A. Tereshchenko [1,*], Rustem T. Ismagilov [1], Nikolai V. Ulitin [1], Yana L. Lyulinskaya [1] and Alexander S. Novikov [2,3,*]**

[1] Department of General Chemical Technology, Kazan National Research Technological University, 420015 Kazan, Russia; ismagilovrt@kstu.ru (R.T.I.); n.v.ulitin@mail.ru (N.V.U.); m23.lyulinskaya.y.l@inhn.ru (Y.L.L.)
[2] Department of Physical Organic Chemistry, Institute of Chemistry, Saint Petersburg State University, 199034 Saint Petersburg, Russia
[3] Scientific Center of Crystal Chemistry and Structural Analysis, Research Institute of Chemistry, Peoples' Friendship University of Russia (RUDN University), 117198 Moscow, Russia
* Correspondence: tereschenkoka@corp.knrtu.ru (K.A.T.); a.s.novikov@spbu.ru (A.S.N.)

**Abstract:** Divinylisoprene rubber, a copolymer of butadiene and isoprene, is used as raw material for rubber technical products, combining isoprene rubber's elasticity and butadiene rubber's wear resistance. These properties depend quantitatively on the copolymer composition, which depends on the kinetics of its synthesis. This work aims to theoretically describe how the monomer mixture composition in the butadiene–isoprene copolymerization affects the activity of the $TiCl_4$-$Al(i\text{-}C_4H_9)_3$ catalytic system (expressed by active sites concentration) via kinetic modeling. This enables development of a reliable kinetic model for divinylisoprene rubber synthesis, predicting reaction rate, molecular weight, and composition, applicable to reactor design and process intensification. Active sites concentrations were calculated from experimental copolymerization rates and known chain propagation constants for various monomer compositions. Kinetic equations for active sites formation were based on mass-action law and Langmuir monomolecular adsorption theory. An analytical equation relating active sites concentration to monomer composition was derived, analyzed, and optimized with experimental data. The results show that monomer composition's influence on active sites concentration is well described by a two-step kinetic model (physical adsorption followed by Ti–C bond formation), accounting for competitive adsorption: isoprene adsorbs more readily, while butadiene forms more stable active sites.

**Keywords:** adsorption; butadiene; copolymerization; heterogeneous catalysis; isoprene; mathematical analysis; Ziegler–Natta catalyst

## 1. Introduction

Butadiene and isoprene rubbers (BDR and IR) are widely used as raw materials for the production of rubber technical products [1]. Compared to each other, these rubbers have both advantages and disadvantages. The general advantages of BDR are its outstanding resilience, excellent flexibility at low temperature (better than that of IR), superior resistance to abrasion, cut growth, and flex cracking [1,2]. That is why it is used in truck tire tread composition [2]. However, its limitations are inferior processability, poor resistance to oil and gasoline, and very little resistance to heat and ozone [2]. Therefore, it is rarely used alone, but blended with various proportions of styrene butadiene rubber, natural rubber and IR [1]. IR exhibit good inherent tack, high compounded gum tensile properties, and good hot tensile properties [1].

An alternative to rubbers based on blends of BDR and IR are rubbers based on the copolymer of butadiene and isoprene (divinylisoprene rubber—DIVR) [3]. DIVR combines the properties of the corresponding homopolymers: the elasticity of IR and the wear resistance of BDR. Quantitatively, these properties also depend on the composition of DIVR. Thus, the task of optimizing the composition of DIVR for each specific application area arises. This task may seem trivial, since it is obvious that the composition of DIVR is determined by the composition of the monomer mixture. However, as shown in studies [4,5], the monomer mixture composition not only affects the composition of DIVR but also nonlinearly influences the synthesis rate of DIVR and its molecular weight characteristics. The task of predicting the synthesis patterns of DIVR is complicated by the fact that this synthesis proceeds using a heterogeneous multisite Ziegler–Natta catalytic system, and the formation history of this catalytic system affects both the number of different types of its active sites and their activity [4,5]. The rate of a heterogeneous catalytic process, such as DIVR synthesis, usually depends nonlinearly on the reaction conditions. Prediction of such processes based solely on experimental data is unreliable, as it generally relies on linear extrapolation of the observed results. A more reliable approach is based on mathematical modeling, specifically kinetic modeling of the process, since catalysis is, by definition, a kinetic phenomenon. Considering the complex nature of heterogeneous catalysis, the kinetic model should account for adsorption and desorption of reagents. Furthermore, such a kinetic model must explicitly consider the interaction of reagents with the catalytically active surface of solid particles—the active sites of catalytic systems. Therefore, within this kinetic model, the activity of the heterogeneous catalytic system is explicitly characterized by the concentration of active sites and the rate constants of reactions involving them.

Taking all of the above into account, the task of theoretically describing the influence of the monomer mixture composition in the butadiene–isoprene copolymerization (DIVR synthesis) on the activity of the catalytic system (quantitatively expressed through the concentration of its active sites) within the framework of kinetic modeling becomes highly relevant. The objective of this work is to solve this problem for the classical and industrially applied Ziegler–Natta catalytic system—$TiCl_4$-$Al(i\text{-}C_4H_9)_3$. This theoretical description will subsequently enable the development of a reliable kinetic model of DIVR synthesis, describing the synthesis rate, molecular weight characteristics, and composition of DIVR, which will allow the practical application of this model to address applied problems related to the design of DIVR synthesis reactors and the intensification of this process. This underlines the practical significance of achieving the stated goal of the work. Moreover, creating this theoretical description will advance the evaluation of active sites' concentrations in heterogeneous catalytic systems based on the rates of reactions involving that involve them. This approach differs from the currently accepted strictly experimental methods for measuring active sites concentrations, such as (1) X-ray absorption spectroscopy [6–8]; (2) infrared spectroscopy [6,7]; (3) scanning transmission electron microscopy [6,7]; (4) probe molecule spectroscopy [7,9,10]; (5) Mössbauer spectroscopy [10,11]; (6) adsorption and desorption methods [10–12]; (7) environmental scanning transmission electron microscopy with a high-angle annular dark-field [13]; and (8) titration with catalytic poisons [14].

It is impossible to achieve the objectives of this work without understanding the nature of active sites in Ziegler–Natta heterogeneous catalytic systems, the mechanism of their formation, and their performance in polymerization and copolymerization processes. Despite the industrial importance of Ziegler–Natta catalytic systems, the nature of their active sites remains a subject of debate, as their structure still cannot be directly observed [15–17]. The current understanding is primarily based on density functional theory calculations [15,16].

Ziegler–Natta catalytic systems have a multisite nature, meaning that particles within the same catalytic system may contain active sites with different structures, distinguished by their stability, chain propagation rate, and capacity for copolymerization [17]. For example, on the surface of supported catalysts such as $TiCl_4$ + $MgCl_2$ + cocatalyst (where the catalytically active $TiCl_4$ component is supported on the inert $MgCl_2$ matrix), both mononuclear active sites—octahedrally coordinated Ti(IV) sites on the $MgCl_2$ crystallites—and polynuclear clusters containing Ti(III) can exist [16]. The multisite nature of active sites directly affects polymerization kinetics and the molecular weight distribution of the polymer [17]. Sites of a single type produce polymer fractions with a narrow molecular weight distribution (described by the Flory distribution), whereas a combination of different site types together yield a polymer with a broad molecular weight distribution [17]. The activity of active sites depends on reaction conditions; the relative contribution of different types of sites to polymer formation can change with temperature [17].

The structure of the catalyst particle surface plays a major role in the formation of active sites [18]. This role can also be illustrated with supported $TiCl_4/MgCl_2$ catalysts. Surface defects and areas of the $MgCl_2$ support with low coordination numbers stabilize titanium active complexes, increasing their reactivity [18]. Such regions on the catalytic particle's surface are most likely to anchor propagating polymer chains. In its pure form, $MgCl_2$ is inactive as a catalyst support, and its particles have a low surface area [19]. The surface of $MgCl_2$ can be activated both physically and chemically by reacting $MgCl_2$ with alcohols (e.g., ethanol), but the alcohol must subsequently be removed from the reaction system, as it acts as a catalytic poison [19]. Ethanol is chemically removed from the $MgCl_2$ surface using weak Lewis acids: $TiCl_2$, triethylaluminum, triisobutylaluminum, and ethylaluminum dichloride [19]. It has been found that the concentration of ethanol in the catalytic system significantly affects the performance characteristics and properties of polyethylene [19], polypropylene [20], and the propylene/1-hexene copolymer [20].

In addition to the chemical nature of the support, steric hindrances also influence the activity and stereoselectivity of the active sites [21]. For example, realizing the propagation of an isotactic polymer chain requires sterically restricted migratory monomer insertion into the propagating polymer chain at the active site (the Cossee mechanism [22]) [21]. To achieve this, the $MgCl_2$ support must adsorb at least two adsorbate molecules on its surface on opposite sides of the active site [21].

The formation of active sites in Ziegler–Natta catalysts begins with a sequence of complexation and activation (alkylation/reduction) reactions, initiated by contact between transition metal compounds, such as titanium chlorides ($TiCl_3$ or $TiCl_4$), and aluminum alkyls. Here, $TiCl_4$ (or $TiCl_3$) acts as an electron donor, while the aluminum alkyl acts as an acceptor. The concentration of the cocatalyst directly determines the number of sites formed [16,23]. The most common cocatalyst is triethylaluminum [16]. The type of cocatalyst affects the deactivation rate of the reaction system [23]. For example, it was found that when triisobutylaluminum was used as a cocatalyst in a $TiCl_4/MgCl_2$-based catalytic system, the rate of ethylene polymerization noticeably decreased over time, whereas the use of triethylaluminum as a cocatalyst maintained a constant polymerization rate for a long period [23]. This difference was explained by the smaller molecular volume of triethylaluminum compared to triisobutylaluminum, facilitating its diffusion to the active sites of the catalytic system [23].

The combination of a cocatalyst with electron donors (Lewis bases) significantly changes both the rate of formation of active sites and their catalytic activity, as well as the properties of the resulting polymers [16]. However, the activity of the catalytic system is not constant. Even after the formation of active sites, their quantity and types continue to evolve. Some examples of such an evolution are listed below.

1. Under the influence of hydrodynamic factors (turbulent velocity pulsations in the reaction system, which cause significant shear stresses within it [24]) and chemical factors (propagation of polymer chains in the pores of catalyst particles, which wedges these particles apart [25]), the particles of the catalytic system undergo dispersion. Dispersion of the catalytic system particles during polymerization exposes previously hidden active surfaces [26,27].
2. Changes in temperature and reaction time shift the equilibrium between active sites of different types [26].
3. Introduction of comonomers accelerates activation by creating additional, more reactive sites [28].
4. Complex mechanism of active sites formation. For example, a two-step mechanism for active sites formation has been described, whereby initially a limited number of active sites are formed, and then, as the catalytic system particles disperse and their surface reorganizes, active sites of new types appear [28,29].

The functioning of active sites consists of the propagation, transfer, and termination of polymer chains [17,30]. The functioning of active sites enables their existence to be fixed; therefore, within the framework of this article, it is important to consider not only the formation of active sites but also their functioning. As a result of polymer chain propagation near active sites, polymer globules are formed [30]; these become entangled due to diffusion of their amorphous segments, forming filamentous structures [30]. At a random moment during propagation, a chain may detach from the active site and from the surface of the catalytic system particles [30]. Detached chains move away from the surface due to convective transport and diffusion, which makes it difficult to establish a relationship between the structure of the active site and the structure of the polymer chain synthesized with its participation [30]. During polymerization, each active site synthesizes a large number of polymer chains. For example, in polypropylene synthesis, each active site is capable of synthesizing approximately twenty thousand polypropylene chains per hour, each containing about $7.5 \times 10^3$ monomeric units, which corresponds to an average molecular weight of $\approx 3 \times 10^5$ g/mol [30].

The evolution of active sites, expressed by the disappearance of one type of active sites and the appearance of another type during polymerization, leads to the synthesis of polymer chains with different molecular weights and chain tacticity at various polymerization stages [31], since active sites of different types differ in stereoselectivity [31], and different copolymer chains of varying composition are synthesized at different stages of copolymerization [28]. For example, active sites of the $TiCl_4/MgCl_2$ catalytic system formed at late stages of butadiene and isoprene copolymerization due to exposure of new surfaces of the catalytic system particles have a higher rate constant for propylene chain propagation and synthesize chains of a statistical copolymer with reduced crystallinity, whereas active sites located on the initial surface of the catalytic system particles continue to synthesize copolymer chains with a higher degree of blockines [28].

Thus, the kinetics of copolymerization of monomers in the presence of Ziegler–Natta catalytic systems is determined by the number, types, and structure of active sites. The number of active sites influences the copolymerization rate, while their diversity causes heterogeneity in the molecular weight distribution of the copolymer, as well as heterogeneity in the distributions of composition and tacticity of the segments.

Kinetic modeling of the polymerization and copolymerization processes of monomers on Ziegler–Natta catalysts is based on accounting for the multisite nature of the catalytic system [17,31]. One of the key aspects of such models is the description of the interaction of reagents with active sites, including adsorption of monomer molecules on the surface of the solid particles of the catalytic system, desorption of these molecules, and coordination of monomer molecules to the active sites with subsequent migratory insertion into the polymer chain.

The construction and verification of kinetic models rely on experimental data on copolymerization rates and molecular weights, which allows determination of individual reaction rate constant values, as well as concentrations of active sites. The use of kinetic models and numerical methods for solving their equations, such as the Monte Carlo method, provides the possibility to reproduce the dynamics of the process, taking into account changes in the distribution of active sites types and their evolution over time [29]. At the same time, the development of statistical models is underway, within which the activity of catalytic systems is predicted using machine learning methods [32].

Thus, to achieve the goal of the work, the following tasks were decided (in their solution, the physicochemical nature of the formation and functioning of active sites of multisite heterogeneous Ziegler–Natta catalytic systems, described above, were taken into account).

To achieve the objective of this work, the following tasks were undertaken.

1. The concentrations of active sites ($\mu$) of the $TiCl_4$-$Al(i\text{-}C_4H_9)_3$ catalytic system during the butadiene–isoprene copolymerization were calculated at various monomer mixture compositions ($q$) based on experimental data on the copolymerization rate taken from [5]. Here, $q = [M_1]/([M_1] + [M_2])$, $[M_1]$ is the concentration of butadiene in the monomer mixture, $[M_2]$ is the concentration of isoprene in the monomer mixture, $q = 1$ corresponds to the homopolymerization of butadiene, and $q = 0$ corresponds to the homopolymerization of isoprene (here and below, [. . .]—denotes concentration) These calculated concentrations are hereafter referred to as experimental and denoted as $\mu_{\text{exp}}$.
2. Based on the Langmuir monomolecular adsorption theory [33] and the mass-action law, a kinetic model for the formation of active sites in the catalytic system was developed. As a result of the analytical solution of the system of kinetic equations, an equation was obtained which established a direct functional relationship between the concentration of active sites $\mu$ and the composition of the monomer mixture $q$. The concentration values calculated using this equation are hereafter referred to as calculated concentrations and denoted as $\mu_{calc}$.
3. An analysis of the obtained equation was performed to determine the ranges of kinetic parameters of the active sites' formation process for which the dependence of $\mu_{\text{calc}}$ on $q$ matches, in shape, the dependence of $\mu_{exp}$ on $q$.
4. Based on the results of solving the third task, specific quantitative values of the kinetic parameters of the active sites' formation process were determined within the allowable parameter ranges, for which the dependence of $\mu_{\text{calc}}$ on $q$ quantitatively coincides with the dependence of $\mu_{\text{exp}}$ on $q$.

## 2. Materials and Methods

In addressing the first task, we relied on the experimental results reported in [5]. In that study [5], by solving the inverse problem of the molecular weight distribution of the copolymer, it was established that active sites of up to four types operate during the butadiene–isoprene copolymerization. Active sites of different types are understood as catalytically active fragments of the catalytic system particle surface that possess distinct structures. Due to this structural diversity, the propagation of polymer chains at active sites of different types proceeds with varying ratios of chain propagation rate to chain termination rate. As a result, active sites of different types produce copolymer chains with varying molecular weights, leading to a broadening of the molecular weight distribution of the copolymer [34]. The number of active sites types depends on the value of $q$: at $q = 1$, all four types of active sites are active, whereas at $q < 1$, only the second and third types of active sites remain active. This suggests that even small amounts of isoprene deactivate the first and fourth types of active sites.

In [5], two methods of copolymerization were considered. In Method 1, the $TiCl_4$-$Al(i\text{-}C_4H_9)_3$ catalytic system was prepared separately and aged at 0 °C for 30 min, after which it was introduced into a 500 $cm^3$ flask containing a solution of the monomer mixture in toluene. A magnetic stirrer was used to ensure continuous agitation of the reaction system during polymerization. Toluene served as the solvent both in the preparation of the catalytic system and in the butadiene–isoprene copolymerization. Copolymerization was carried out at the same initial total monomer concentration, while the molar ratio of the monomers varied in different experiments. The copolymerization was performed under the following initial conditions: total monomer concentration $[M]$ = 1.5 mol/L; catalytic system preparation conditions—$[TiCl_4]$ = 5 mmol/L, $[Al(i\text{-}C_4H_9)_3]/[TiCl_4]$ = 1.4; polymerization temperature 25 °C.

Method 2 differed from Method 1 in that the mixing of the catalytic system with the monomer mixture solution in toluene was carried out not in the flask, but immediately before the flask in a tubular turbulent diffuser–constrictor apparatus (Figure 1). The flow velocity of the reaction mixture through the apparatus was 0.9 m/s. The resulting reaction mixture was then introduced into the flask for polymerization. In both copolymerization methods, methanol was added to the flask 60 min after the start of the process to terminate the reaction.

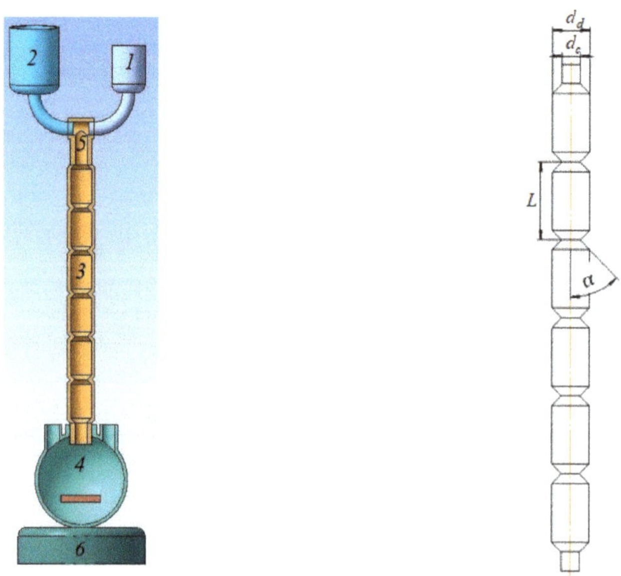


(a) (b)

**Figure 1.** Diagram of the setup for the butadiene–isoprene copolymerization: general scheme (**a**); longitudinal section of the tubular turbulent diffuser–constrictor apparatus (**b**): 1 and 2 are reagent vessels; 3 is a tubular turbulent diffuser–constrictor apparatus; 4 is a laboratory mixing reactor (500 $cm^3$); 5 is a three-way valve; 6 id stirrer; $d_d$ = 24 mm is the diffuser diameter; $d_c$ = 15 mm represents the constrictor diameter; $L$ = 48 mm is the length of the diffuser–constrictor section; and $\alpha = 45°$ is the diffuser opening angle.

In addressing the first task, theoretical results from studies [35,36] were also utilized. In [35], a kinetic model of butadiene homopolymerization involving the $TiCl_4$-$Al(i\text{-}C_4H_9)_3$ catalytic system was developed. In [36], a kinetic model of isoprene homopolymerization with the same catalytic system was developed. The classical model of chain reactivity in homo- and copolymerization is the chain-end model [37], according to which the rate constants of reactions involving active polymer chains are determined by the type of the terminal unit of these chains. Therefore, based on the terminal unit model, the rate constants of chain propagation reactions in butadiene and isoprene homopolymerization established in [35,36] were employed in this work to calculate the rates of self-propagation reactions in copolymerization (i.e., the addition of butadiene to active chains with terminal butadiene units and the addition of isoprene to active chains with terminal isoprene units). The rate constants of cross-propagation reactions were calculated based on the rate constants of self-propagation reactions and the corresponding copolymerization constants determined in [5].

## 3. Results

### *3.1. Calculation of the Concentration of Active Sites of the $TiCl_4$-$Al(i\text{-}C_4H_9)_3$ Catalytic System*

The task of calculating the concentrations of active sites of the $TiCl_4$-$Al(i\text{-}C_4H_9)_3$ catalytic system was addressed as follows. First, the experimental initial rate of copolymerization $W$ was calculated for each experiment as the product of the total monomer concentration and the initial values of the tangent of the slope angle of the copolymer yield versus time dependencies reported in [5].

The copolymerization rate $W$ was related to the concentration of active sites of the $TiCl_4$-$Al(i\text{-}C_4H_9)_3$ catalytic system through the kinetic model equations of the butadiene–isoprene copolymerization. These equations were formulated based on the mass-action law and classical kinetic schemes of coordination copolymerization [5], which include the following reactions.

1. Chain propagation:

$$R_{xy} + M_z \overset{k_{pxyz}}{\rightarrow} R_{xz}$$

2. Chain transfer to monomer:

$$R_{xy} + M_z \overset{k_{Mxyz}}{\rightarrow} P + R_{xz}$$

3. Chain transfer to cocatalyst:

$$R_{xy} + C \overset{k_{Axy}}{\rightarrow} P + R_x.$$

4. Deactivation of active sites:

$$R_{xy} \overset{k_{txy}}{\rightarrow} P.$$

5. Interconversion of active sites of different types:

$$R_{xy} \overset{k_{cxsy}}{\rightarrow} R_{sy}.$$

In the symbolic notation of the reactions, the degrees of polymerization of the chains are intentionally omitted to avoid complicating the representation.

Here, $R$ represents the active copolymer chains; $M$ represents the monomer molecules; $P$ represents the inactive copolymer chains; and $C$ is the cocatalyst molecule ($Al(i\text{-}C_4H_9)_3$); $k$ is the rate constant of the corresponding reaction; $x$ and $s$ = 1, 2, 3, 4 represent the type of active site at the active chain end; $y$ and $z$ = 1, 2 are indices reflecting the type of the chain terminal unit or the type of monomer molecule involved in the reaction: 1 corresponds to a butadiene terminal unit or butadiene molecule and 2 corresponds to an isoprene terminal unit or isoprene molecule.

The copolymerization rate $W$ is equal to the rate of change of the total monomer concentration; that is, according to the presented kinetic scheme, the copolymerization rate $W$ equals the sum of the rates of chain propagation and chain transfer to monomers. However, when calculating the copolymerization rate $W$, the chain transfer to monomers can be neglected, as it is usually several times lower than the chain propagation rate [5].

Based on the above, the equation relating the concentration of active sites to the copolymerization rate of butadiene and isoprene at $q < 1$ was obtained by solving the following system of Equations (1)–(4).

1. Equation relating the concentration of active sites to the copolymerization rate (according to the mass-action law):

$$\sum_{z=1}^{2}\sum_{y=1}^{2}\sum_{x=2}^{3} k_{pxyz}\mu_{xy}[M_z] = W, \tag{1}$$

where $\mu_{xy}$ is the concentration of active chains propagating on active sites of type $x$ with terminal unit of type $y$ (the total concentration of active sites equals the total concentration of active chains, since each active site corresponds to one active chain); $[M_z]$ is the initial concentration of monomer of type $z$.

The experimental value of the initial copolymerization rate $W$ was determined by the following equation:

$$W = [M]\left.\frac{dU}{dt}\right|_{t=0},$$

where $[M]$ = 1.5 mol/L is the total initial monomer concentration; $U$ is the experimentally measured time-dependent copolymer yield (the data for all q values were taken from [5]); and t is the copolymerization time (t = 0 indicates that the derivative was calculated at the initial segment of the $U$).

2. Next, we have an equation which establishes a direct proportionality between the experimental relative activity $S_x$ of active sites of different types x and their chain propagation rate:

$$\frac{\sum_{z=1}^{2}\sum_{y=1}^{2} k_{p3yz}\mu_{3y}[M_z]}{\sum_{z=1}^{2}\sum_{y=1}^{2} k_{p2yz}\mu_{2y}[M_z]} = \frac{S_3}{S_2}. \tag{2}$$

The relative activities $S_x$ are defined as the areas under the peaks in the activity distribution of the catalytic system according to kinetic heterogeneity (the ratio of the chain termination rate to the chain propagation rate), which was determined in study [5] by solving the inverse problem of the polymer molecular weight distribution.

3. The equations below express the equality of cross-propagation rates on active sites of each type (which essentially represent the quasi-steady-state conditions for the concentrations of active chains terminated with butadiene and isoprene units propagating on active sites of each type):

$$k_{p221}\mu_{22}[M_1] = k_{p212}\mu_{21}[M_2], \tag{3}$$

$$k_{p321}\mu_{32}[M_1] = k_{p312}\mu_{31}[M_2]. \tag{4}$$

The rate constants $k_{p211}$ and $k_{p311}$ were taken from the model presented in [35]. The rate constants $k_{p222}$ and $k_{p322}$ were taken from the model presented in [36]. The rate constants of cross-propagation reactions were calculated using the copolymerization constants $r_1 = k_{px11}/k_{px12}$, $r_2 = k_{px22}/k_{px21}$. In study [5], the calculation of copolymerization constants by the Fineman–Ross method [38] showed that $r_1 = r_2 = 1$.

In the system of Equations (1)–(4), written for each value of $q$, there are four unknowns: $\mu_{21}$, $\mu_{22}$, $\mu_{31}$, $\mu_{32}$. Since the system also contains four equations, it is closed and can be solved with respect to these unknowns.

For this purpose, the concentrations $\mu_{x1}$ were first expressed from Equations (3) and (4) as follows:

$$\mu_{x1} = \frac{k_{px21}[M_1]}{k_{px12}[M_2]}\mu_{x2}. \tag{5}$$

Equation (5) was then substituted into Equation (1), and the resulting equation was transformed accordingly:

$$\sum_{z=1}^{2}\sum_{x=2}^{3}\left(k_{px1z}\mu_{x1} + k_{px2z}\mu_{x2}\right)[M_z] = W,$$

$$\sum_{z=1}^{2}\sum_{x=2}^{3}\left(k_{px1z}\frac{k_{px21}[M_1]}{k_{px12}[M_2]}\mu_{x2} + k_{px2z}\mu_{x2}\right)[M_z] = W,$$

$$\sum_{x=2}^{3}\mu_{x2}\sum_{z=1}^{2}\left(k_{px1z}\frac{k_{px21}[M_1]}{k_{px12}[M_2]} + k_{px2z}\right)[M_z] = W. \tag{6}$$

Equation (5) was substituted into Equation (2), and the resulting equation was transformed accordingly:

$$\frac{\sum_{z=1}^{2}[M_z]\sum_{y=1}^{2}k_{p3yz}\mu_{3y}}{\sum_{z=1}^{2}[M_z]\sum_{y=1}^{2}k_{p2yz}\mu_{2y}} = \frac{S_3}{S_2},$$

$$\frac{\sum_{z=1}^{2}[M_z]\left(k_{p31z}\frac{k_{p321}[M_1]}{k_{p312}[M_2]}\mu_{32} + k_{p32z}\mu_{32}\right)}{\sum_{z=1}^{2}[M_z]\left(k_{p21z}\frac{k_{p221}[M_1]}{k_{p212}[M_2]}\mu_{22} + k_{p22z}\mu_{22}\right)} = \frac{S_3}{S_2},$$

$$\frac{\mu_{32}\sum_{z=1}^{2}[M_z]\left(k_{p31z}\frac{k_{p321}[M_1]}{k_{p312}[M_2]} + k_{p32z}\right)}{\mu_{22}\sum_{z=1}^{2}[M_z]\left(k_{p21z}\frac{k_{p221}[M_1]}{k_{p212}[M_2]} + k_{p22z}\right)} = \frac{S_3}{S_2},$$

$$\mu_{22}\sum_{z=1}^{2}[M_z]\left(k_{p21z}\frac{k_{p221}[M_1]}{k_{p212}[M_2]} + k_{p22z}\right) = \frac{S_2}{S_3}\mu_{32}\sum_{z=1}^{2}[M_z]\left(k_{p31z}\frac{k_{p321}[M_1]}{k_{p312}[M_2]} + k_{p32z}\right). \tag{7}$$

Equation (7) was substituted into Equation (6), and the resulting equation was subsequently transformed:

$$\left(1 + \frac{S_2}{S_3}\right)\mu_{32}\sum_{z=1}^{2}[M_z]\left(k_{p31z}\frac{k_{p321}[M_1]}{k_{p312}[M_2]} + k_{p32z}\right) = W,$$

$$\mu_{32} = \frac{S_3 W}{\sum_{z=1}^{2}[M_z]\left(k_{p31z}\frac{k_{p321}[M_1]}{k_{p312}[M_2]} + k_{p32z}\right)}. \tag{8}$$

The following transformation was applied here

$$1 + \frac{S_2}{S_3} = \frac{S_3 + S_2}{S_3} = \frac{1}{S_3},$$

This is because $S_3 + S_2 = 1$, according to the normalization condition.

The monomer concentrations were expressed through the composition of the monomer mixture for further transformations:

$$[M_1] = q[M], \ \ [M_2] = (1-q)[M]. \tag{9}$$

Furthermore, it was taken into account that since $r_1 = r_2 = 1$, the following equalities hold:

$$k_{pz11} = k_{pz12}, \ k_{pz22} = k_{pz21}. \tag{10}$$

Equation (8) was transformed considering Equations (9) and (10):

$$\mu_{32} = \frac{S_3 W}{\sum_{z=1}^{2}[M_z]\left(k_{p311}\frac{k_{p322}q}{k_{p311}(1-q)} + k_{p322}\right)},$$

$$\mu_{32} = \frac{S_3 W}{k_{p322}\left(\frac{q}{(1-q)}+1\right)\sum_{z=1}^{2}[M_z]},$$

$$\mu_{32} = \frac{(1-q)S_3 W}{k_{p322}[M]}. \tag{11}$$

Equation (5) was transformed considering Equations (9) and (10):

$$\mu_{x1} = \frac{k_{px22}q}{k_{px11}(1-q)}\mu_{x2}. \tag{12}$$

Equation (11) was further transformed using Equation (12):

$$\mu_{31} = \frac{q S_3 W}{k_{p311}[M]}. \tag{13}$$

The equations for calculating $\mu_{2y}$ were obtained from Equations (11) and (13), taking into account the symmetry of the problem with respect to the index $x$:

$$\mu_{21} = \frac{q S_2 W}{k_{p211}[M]}, \tag{14}$$

$$\mu_{22} = \frac{(1-q) S_2 W}{k_{p222}[M]}. \tag{15}$$

The total concentration of active sites $\mu_{exp}$ for each composition of the reaction mixture $q$ was calculated by summing Equations (11) and (13)–(15):

$$\mu_{exp} = \sum_{x=2}^{3}\left(\frac{q}{k_{px11}} + \frac{(1-q)}{k_{px22}}\right) S_x \frac{W}{[M]}. \tag{16}$$

Here, $\mu_{exp}$, $S_x$, and $W$ are quantities dependent on $q$; $k_{px11}$, $k_{px22}$, $[M]$ are quantities independent of $q$. The values of $\mu_{exp}$ calculated from Equation (16) based on experimental data from [5] for all $q < 1$ are presented in Figure 2.

To derive the equation relating the concentration of active sites to the polymerization rate of butadiene at $q = 1$, the concentration of active sites of each type $\mu_{x1}$ was expressed through the relative activity of the active sites and the polymerization rate, and then these concentrations were summed:

$$\mu_{x1} = \frac{S_x W}{k_{px11}[M]},$$

$$\mu_{exp} = \sum_{x=1}^{4}\frac{S_x}{k_{px11}}\frac{W}{[M]}. \tag{17}$$

The values of $\mu_{exp}$ calculated using Equation (17) based on the experimental data from [5] for $q = 1$ are also presented in Figure 2.

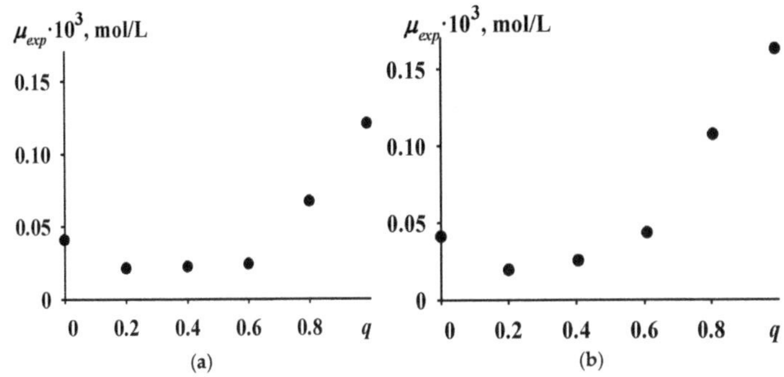


**Figure 2.** Dependence of the concentration of active sites $\mu_{exp}$ in the butadiene–isoprene copolymerization in the presence of the $TiCl_4$-$Al(i$-$C_4H_9)_3$ catalytic system on the mole fraction of butadiene in the monomer mixture, $q$; (**a**) copolymerization carried out by method 1; (**b**) copolymerization carried out by method 2.

### *3.2. Development of a Kinetic Model for the Formation of Active Sites in the $TiCl_4$-$Al(i$-$C_4H_9)_3$ Catalytic System*

Based on the Langmuir monomolecular adsorption theory [33], a kinetic model for the formation of active sites in the $TiCl_4$-$Al(i$-$C_4H_9)_3$ catalytic system was developed. The formulation of the kinetic model equations was guided by the following postulates:

1. Adsorption occurs at adsorption sites on the surface of the adsorbent. In this case, the adsorbent consists of particles of the $TiCl_4$-$Al(i$-$C_4H_9)_3$ catalytic system. The adsorbate comprises molecules of butadiene or isoprene. Adsorption is competitive, meaning that butadiene and isoprene molecules adsorb at the same adsorption sites. An active site is formed after the adsorption of a monomer molecule onto the surface of the catalytic system particles and the formation of a Ti-C bond, where C is the carbon atom of the butadiene or isoprene molecule.
2. Each adsorption site can adsorb only one adsorbate molecule.
3. The adsorption process is reversible and at equilibrium, with its rate determined by the rate of reaching equilibrium. The formation of the Ti-C bond is also assumed to be reversible.
4. Interaction between adsorbate molecules in the adsorbed state is absent.

Since the number of stages and the rate-limiting step in the formation of active sites are unknown a priori, two kinetic schemes for developing the kinetic model were considered.

Initially, it was assumed that the adsorption of monomer molecules and the formation of the Ti-C bond occur in a single stage; thus, the kinetic model was formulated based on the following kinetic scheme.

$$M_1 + A \underset{k_{-1}}{\overset{k_1}{\rightleftarrows}} R_1, \tag{18}$$

$$M_2 + A \underset{k_{-2}}{\overset{k_2}{\rightleftarrows}} R_2, \tag{19}$$

where $A$ is the adsorption site, $k$ are the rate constants of the respective stages, and $R_y$ are the active sites formed involving butadiene molecules ($y$ = 1) and isoprene molecules ($y$ = 2).

The following kinetic model of single-stage active site formation, formulated according to the mass-action law, corresponds to this scheme:

$$\frac{d[M_1]}{dt} = -k_1[M_1][A] + k_{-1}\mu_1,$$
$$\frac{d[M_2]}{dt} = -k_2[M_2][A] + k_{-2}\mu_2,$$
$$\frac{d\mu_1}{dt} = k_1[M_1][A] - k_{-1}\mu_1,$$
$$\frac{d\mu_2}{dt} = k_2[M_2][A] - k_{-2}\mu_2,$$
$$\frac{d[A]}{dt} = -k_1[M_1][A] + k_{-1}\mu_1 - k_2[M_2][A] + k_{-2}\mu_2$$

where $\mu_y$ are the concentrations of active sites formed that involve butadiene molecules ($y$ = 1) and isoprene molecules ($y$ = 2).

Considering that this system of equations does not exhibit significant nonlinearity, the reaction system is expected to approach a single stable equilibrium state. At this state, the time derivatives of the concentrations of all species are zero, and the system reduces to two equations:

$$k_1[M_1][A] - k_{-1}\mu_1 = 0, \quad (20)$$

$$k_2[M_2][A] - k_{-2}\mu_2 = 0. \quad (21)$$

The system of Equations (20) and (21) is complemented by the conservation law (since one active site forms from one adsorption site, the total concentration of adsorption sites and active sites remains constant):

$$\mu_1 + \mu_2 + [A] = [A]_0, \quad (22)$$

where $[A]_0$ is the initial concentration of adsorption sites.

As a result, a closed system of three equations with three unknowns is obtained. The concentrations of active sites were expressed from Equations (20) and (21) and substituted into Equation (22), yielding an equation that can be used to calculate the concentration of adsorption sites remaining free after the formation of active sites:

$$\mu_1 = \frac{k_1[M_1][A]}{k_{-1}}, \quad (23)$$

$$\mu_2 = \frac{k_2[M_2][A]}{k_{-2}}, \quad (24)$$

$$\frac{k_1[M_1][A]}{k_{-1}} + \frac{k_2[M_2][A]}{k_{-2}} + [A] = [A]_0,$$

$$[A] = \frac{[A]_0}{K_1[M_1] + K_2[M_2] + 1},$$

where $K_1 = k_1/k_{-1}$, $K_2 = k_2/k_{-2}$.

Substituting the obtained result into Equations (23) and (24) and summing the resulting equations, an equation for calculating the concentration of active sites was obtained:

$$\mu_{calc} = K_1[M_1][A] + K_2[M_2][A],$$

$$\mu_{calc} = \frac{K_1[M_1] + K_2[M_2]}{K_1[M_1] + K_2[M_2] + 1}[A]_0,$$

$$\mu_{calc} = \frac{K_1 q + K_2(1-q)}{K_1 q + K_2(1-q) + \frac{1}{[M]}}[A]_0. \quad (25)$$

Thus, Equation (25) shows the dependence of $\mu_{calc}$ on $q$ for a single-stage formation of active sites.

The option of active site formation in two stages was also considered.

Adsorption of monomer molecules at adsorption sites (Stage 1, physical):

$$M_1 + A \underset{k_{-f1}}{\overset{k_{f1}}{\rightleftarrows}} M_1^*, \quad (26)$$

$$M_2 + A \underset{k_{-f2}}{\overset{k_{f2}}{\rightleftarrows}} M_2^*, \quad (27)$$

Formation of the Ti-C bond (Stage 2, chemical):

$$M_1^* \underset{k_{-1}}{\overset{k_1}{\rightleftarrows}} R_1, \quad (28)$$

$$M_2^* \underset{k_{-2}}{\overset{k_2}{\rightleftarrows}} R_2, \quad (29)$$

where $M_1^*$ and $M_2^*$ are the adsorbed molecules of butadiene and isoprene, respectively.

The following kinetic model of two-stage active sites formation, formulated according to the mass-action law, corresponds to this scheme:

$$\begin{gathered}
\frac{d[A]}{dt} = -k_{f1}[A][M_1] - k_{f2}[A][M_2] + k_{-f1}[M_1^*] + k_{-f2}[M_2^*], \\
\frac{d[M_1^*]}{dt} = k_{f1}[A][M_1] - k_{-f1}[M_1^*] - k_1[M_1^*] + k_{-1}\mu_1, \\
\frac{d[M_2^*]}{dt} = k_{f2}[A][M_2] - k_{-f2}[M_2^*] - k_2[M_2^*] + k_{-2}\mu_2, \\
\frac{d\mu_1}{dt} = k_1[M_1^*] - k_{-1}\mu_1, \\
\frac{d\mu_2}{dt} = k_2[M_2^*] - k_{-2}\mu_2.
\end{gathered}$$

When the reaction system reaches equilibrium, the original system of five equations reduces to a system of four equations:

$$k_{f1}[A][M_1] - k_{-f1}[M_1^*] = 0, \quad (30)$$

$$k_{f2}[A][M_2] - k_{-f2}[M_2^*] = 0, \quad (31)$$

$$k_1[M_1^*] - k_{-1}\mu_1 = 0, \quad (32)$$

$$k_2[M_2^*] - k_{-2}\mu_2 = 0. \quad (33)$$

The system of Equations (30)–(33) is complemented by the conservation law:

$$\mu_1 + \mu_2 + [M_1^*] + [M_2^*] + [A] = [A]_0. \tag{34}$$

As a result, a closed system of five equations with five unknowns is obtained. The concentrations of adsorbed butadiene and isoprene molecules were expressed from Equations (30) and (31) and substituted into Equations (32) and (33), from which the concentrations of active sites were derived. All expressed concentrations were then substituted into Equation (34), yielding an equation for calculating the concentration of adsorption sites remaining free after the formation of active sites:

$$[M_1^*] = \frac{k_{f1}}{k_{-f1}}[A][M_1],$$

$$[M_2^*] = \frac{k_{f2}}{k_{-f2}}[A][M_2],$$

$$\mu_1 = \frac{k_1}{k_{-1}}[M_1^*] = \frac{k_1}{k_{-1}}\frac{k_{f1}}{k_{-f1}}[A][M_1], \tag{35}$$

$$\mu_2 = \frac{k_2}{k_{-2}}[M_2^*] = \frac{k_2}{k_{-2}}\frac{k_{f2}}{k_{-f2}}[A][M_2], \tag{36}$$

$$\tfrac{k_1}{k_{-1}}\tfrac{k_{f1}}{k_{-f1}}[A][M_1] + \tfrac{k_2}{k_{-2}}\tfrac{k_{f2}}{k_{-f2}}[A][M_2] + \tfrac{k_{f1}}{k_{-f1}}[A][M_1] + \tfrac{k_{f2}}{k_{-f2}}[A][M_2] + [A] = [A]_0.$$

$$[A] = \frac{[A]_0}{K_1K_{f1}[M_1] + K_2K_{f2}[M_2] + K_{f1}[M_1] + K_{f2}[M_2] + 1},$$

where $K_{f1} = k_{f1}/k_{-f1}$, $K_{f2} = k_{f2}/k_{-f2}$, $K_1 = k_1/k_{-1}$, $K_2 = k_2/k_{-2}$.

Substituting this result back into Equations (35) and (36) and summing the resulting expressions yields the equation for calculating the concentration of active sites:

$$\mu_{calc} = K_1K_{f1}[M_1][A] + K_2K_{f2}[M_2][A],$$

$$\mu_{calc} = \frac{K_1K_{f1}[M_1] + K_2K_{f2}[M_2]}{K_1K_{f1}[M_1] + K_2K_{f2}[M_2] + K_{f1}[M_1] + K_{f2}[M_2] + 1}[A]_0,$$

$$\mu_{calc} = \frac{K_1K_{f1}q + K_2K_{f2}(1-q)}{(1+K_1)K_{f1}q + (1+K_2)K_{f2}(1-q) + \frac{1}{[M]}}[A]_0. \tag{37}$$

where $[M] = [M_1] + [M_2] = 1.5$ mol/L.

Equation (37) thus shows the dependence of $\mu_{calc}$ on $q$ for the two-stage formation of active sites.

### *3.3. Determination of the Kinetic Parameter Range for the Active Sites Formation Process Based on the Shape of the Dependence of Active Sites' Concentration $\mu_{calc}$ on Monomer Mixture Composition $q$*

The experimental active sites concentration $\mu_{exp}$ versus monomer mixture composition $q$ exhibits a minimum point at $q_{min}$. This dependence is also convex downward. For the shapes of the experimental $\mu_{exp}$ and calculated $\mu_{calc}$ dependences of active site concentration on monomer mixture composition $q$ to coincide, the following conditions must be satisfied.

1. Minimum point condition:

$$\frac{d\mu_{calc}}{dq} < 0 \quad \text{before} \quad q_{min} \quad \text{and} \quad \frac{d\mu_{calc}}{dq} > 0 \ \text{after} \quad q_{min} \tag{38}$$

2. Condition for downward convexity of the dependence:

$$\frac{d^2\mu_{calc}}{dq^2} > 0. \tag{39}$$

In the case of single-stage active site formation:

$$\begin{aligned}\frac{d\mu_{calc}}{dq} &= \frac{(K_1 - K_2)\left(K_1 q + K_2(1-q) + \frac{1}{[M]}\right) - (K_1 - K_2)(K_1 q + K_2(1-q))}{\left(K_1 q + K_2(1-q) + \frac{1}{[M]}\right)^2}[A]_0 = \\ &= \frac{(K_1 - K_2)[A]_0}{[M]\left(K_1 q + K_2(1-q) + \frac{1}{[M]}\right)^2}.\end{aligned} \tag{40}$$

$$\frac{d^2\mu_{calc}}{dq^2} = \frac{d}{dq}\frac{d\mu_{calc}}{dq} = -\frac{2(K_1 - K_2)^2[A]_0}{[M]\left(K_1 q + K_2(1-q) + \frac{1}{[M]}\right)^3}. \tag{41}$$

According to Equation (40), the dependence of $\mu_{calc}$ on $q$ cannot have a minimum point because the denominator of this dependence is always positive, and the numerator is independent of $q$ (i.e., it is either strictly positive or strictly negative for all $q$). Since the region of the $\mu_{exp}$ dependence on $q$ where $\mu_{exp}$ increases is significantly larger than the region where $\mu_{exp}$ decreases (see Figure 2), it was subsequently assumed that the correct form of the $\mu_{calc}$ dependence on $q$ satisfies the condition.

$$\frac{d\mu_{exp}}{dq} > 0. \tag{42}$$

Condition (42) was transformed taking into account Equation (40):

$$\frac{(K_1 - K_2)[A]_0}{[M]\left(K_1 q + K_2(1-q) + \frac{1}{[M]}\right)^2} > 0,$$

$$K_1 > K_2. \tag{43}$$

Condition (39), taking into account Equation (41), will take the following form:

$$-\frac{2(K_1 - K_2)^2[A]_0}{[M]\left(K_1 q + K_2(1-q) + \frac{1}{[M]}\right)^3} > 0.$$

The numerator of the left side of this condition is always positive; therefore, this condition is equivalent to the following:

$$K_1 q + K_2(1-q) + \frac{1}{[M]} < 0. \tag{44}$$

It is evident that condition (44) cannot be satisfied, since each term on its left side is non-negative.

Thus, the model of active site formation in the catalytic system $TiCl_4$-$Al(i\text{-}C_4H_9)_3$, developed on the basis of a single-stage kinetic scheme for active site formation, cannot describe the experimental dependence of $\mu_{exp}$ on $q$ even qualitatively (i.e., in terms of the shape of this dependence) for any values of $K_1$ and $K_2$.

In the case of two-stage active site formation

$$\frac{d\mu_{calc}}{dq} = [A]_0 \frac{(K_1K_{f1}-K_2K_{f2})\left(\frac{1}{[M]}+(1+K_1)K_{f1}q+(1+K_2)K_{f2}(1-q)\right)}{\left(\frac{1}{[M]}+(1+K_1)K_{f1}q+(1+K_2)K_{f2}(1-q)\right)^2} -$$

$$-[A]_0 \frac{\Big((1+K_1)K_{f1}-(1+K_2)K_{f2}\Big)\Big(K_1K_{f1}q+K_2K_{f2}(1-q)\Big)}{\left(\frac{1}{[M]}+(1+K_1)K_{f1}q+(1+K_2)K_{f2}(1-q)\right)^2} =$$

$$= [A]_0 \frac{K_1K_{f1}\Big(1+K_{f2}[M]\Big)-K_2K_{f2}\Big(1+K_{f1}[M]\Big)}{[M]\left(\frac{1}{[M]}+(1+K_1)K_{f1}q+(1+K_2)K_{f2}(1-q)\right)^2}, \quad (45)$$

$$\frac{d^2\mu_{calc}}{dq^2} = \frac{d}{dq}\frac{d\mu_{calc}}{dq} = -2\Big[A]_0\Big((1+K_1)K_{f1}-(1+K_2)K_{f2}\Big)\times$$

$$\times \frac{\Big(K_1K_{f1}\Big(1+K_{f2}[M]\Big)-K_2K_{f2}\Big(1+K_{f1}[M]\Big)\Big)}{[M]\left(\frac{1}{[M]}+(1+K_1)K_{f1}q+(1+K_2)K_{f2}(1-q)\right)^3}. \quad (46)$$

The denominator in Equation (45) is always positive, and the numerator does not depend on $q$; therefore, the dependence of $\mu_{calc}$ on $q$ in the case of two-stage active site formation will also not have a minimum point. Condition (42) will be satisfied only if the numerator in Equation (45) is positive; that is, when the following condition is met:

$$K_1K_{f1}\Big(1+K_{f2}[M]\Big) > K_2K_{f2}\Big(1+K_{f1}[M]\Big),$$

$$\frac{K_1}{K_2} > \frac{K_{f2}\Big(1+K_{f1}[M]\Big)}{K_{f1}\Big(1+K_{f2}[M]\Big)}. \quad (47)$$

The denominator in Equation (46) is positive since $1/[M] > 0$, and all other terms in the denominator are at least non-negative for any value of $0 < q < 1$. Therefore, condition (39), taking into account Equation (46), is equivalent to the following condition:

$$2\Big[A]_0\Big((1+K_1)K_{f1}-(1+K_2)K_{f2}\Big)\times\Big(K_1K_{f1}\Big(1+K_{f2}[M]\Big)-K_2K_{f2}\Big(1+K_{f1}[M]\Big)\Big) < 0. \quad (48)$$

Here, the ">" sign changes to "<" because the minus sign in condition (48) was eliminated by multiplying both sides of the inequality by $-1$. Condition (48) is equivalent to the following set of two systems of inequalities:

$$\left[\begin{array}{l} \begin{cases} K_1K_{f1}\Big(1+K_{f2}[M]\Big)-K_2K_{f2}\Big(1+K_{f1}[M]\Big) > 0, & (49) \\ (1+K_1)K_{f1}-(1+K_2)K_{f2} < 0, & (50) \end{cases} \\ \begin{cases} K_1K_{f1}\Big(1+K_{f2}[M]\Big)-K_2K_{f2}\Big(1+K_{f1}[M]\Big) < 0, & (51) \\ (1+K_1)K_{f1}-(1+K_2)K_{f2} > 0. & (52) \end{cases} \end{array}\right.$$

The square bracket denotes a collection (i.e., the union of solution sets of inequalities), while the curly brace denotes a system (i.e., the intersection of solution sets of inequalities).

The solution sets of inequalities (47) and (51) do not intersect. Therefore, examining the solution set of the system of inequalities (51) and (52) is meaningless (in this region, the dependence of $\mu_{calc}$ on $q$ decreases rather than increases). In the remaining system of inequalities (49) and (50), inequality (49) is equivalent to inequality (47), while inequality (50) simplifies to the following inequality:

$$\frac{K_{f1}}{K_{f2}} < \frac{1+K_2}{1+K_1}. \tag{53}$$

Thus, the dependence of $\mu_{calc}$ on $q$, calculated using Equation (37) and derived under the assumption that active sites formation is a two-stage process, is identical in form to the dependence of $\mu_{exp}$ on $q$ when the following two conditions are simultaneously satisfied.

1. The dependence of $\mu_{calc}$ on $q$ is increasing (inequality (47)):

$$\frac{K_1}{K_2} > \frac{K_{f2}\left(1+K_{f1}[M]\right)}{K_{f1}\left(1+K_{f2}[M]\right)}.$$

2. The dependence of $\mu_{calc}$ on $q$ is convex downward (inequality (53)):

$$\frac{1+K_2}{1+K_1} > \frac{K_{f1}}{K_{f2}}.$$

Finding the general solution to the system of inequalities (47) and (53) is quite challenging. It is overly cumbersome, and this complexity obscures the physical meaning of the solution. Therefore, instead of the general solution to the system of inequalities (47) and (53), all possible asymptotic solutions were found. By an asymptotic solution of the system of inequalities (47) and (53), we mean a solution of this system obtained not over the entire set of parameter values $K_{f1} > 0$, $K_{f2} > 0$, $K_1 > 0$, $K_2 > 0$, but within certain subsets of these parameter values. For each parameter, the range of values was divided into two subsets, the physical meaning of which is easy to interpret:

1. $K_{f1}[M] >> 1$—the adsorption/desorption equilibrium of butadiene is shifted toward adsorption, i.e., butadiene is adsorbed by adsorption sites with high efficiency.
2. $K_{f1}[M] << 1$—the adsorption/desorption equilibrium of butadiene is shifted toward desorption, i.e., butadiene is adsorbed by adsorption sites with low efficiency.
3. $K_{f2}[M] >> 1$—the adsorption/desorption equilibrium of isoprene is shifted toward adsorption, i.e., isoprene is adsorbed by adsorption sites with high efficiency.
4. $K_{f2}[M] << 1$—the adsorption/desorption equilibrium of isoprene is shifted toward desorption, i.e., isoprene is adsorbed by adsorption sites with low efficiency.
5. $K_1 >> 1$—the equilibrium of formation/breaking of the bond between the Ti atom of the catalytic system and the C atom of butadiene is shifted toward bond formation, i.e., butadiene forms stable active sites.
6. $K_1 << 1$—the equilibrium of formation/breaking of the bond between the Ti atom of the catalytic system and the C atom of butadiene is shifted toward bond breaking, i.e., butadiene forms unstable active sites.
7. $K_2 >> 1$—the equilibrium of formation/breaking of the bond between the Ti atom of the catalytic system and the C atom of isoprene is shifted toward bond formation, i.e., isoprene forms stable active sites.
8. $K_2 << 1$—the equilibrium of formation/breaking of the bond between the Ti atom of the catalytic system and the C atom of isoprene is shifted toward bond breaking, i.e., isoprene forms unstable active sites.

Such boundaries of parameter subsets allow us, for each subset, to determine which terms in the sums $1 + K_{f1}[M]$, $1 + K_{f2}[M]$, $1 + K_1$, $1 + K_2$ can be neglected, thereby simplifying inequalities (47) and (53) (this transformation is hereafter referred to as asymptotic transformation).

As a result, the entire set of parameter values $K_{f1} > 0$, $K_{f2} > 0$, $K_1 > 0$, $K_2 > 0$ was divided into 16 subsets, some of which admit asymptotic solutions. The asymptotically transformed inequalities (47) and (53) for various parameter subsets are presented in Table 1.

Analysis of the asymptotically transformed inequalities (47) and (53) for all 16 subsets showed that asymptotic solutions to inequalities (47) and (53) exist only in 7 subsets.

In subset 2 ($K_{f1}[M] >> 1$, $K_{f2}[M] << 1$, $K_1 >> 1$, $K_2 >> 1$), from the inequality $K_1/K_2 > K_{f2}[M]$, it follows that $K_1 >> K_2$; from the inequality $K_2/K_1 > K_{f1}/K_{f2}$, it follows that $K_1 << K_2$. These two inequalities are mutually exclusive; therefore, there are no asymptotic solutions in subset 2.

In subset 3 ($K_{f1}[M] << 1$, $K_{f2}[M] >> 1$, $K_1 >> 1$, $K_2 >> 1$): from the inequality $K_1/K_2 > 1/\left(K_{f1}[M]\right)$ it follows that $K_1 >> K_2$; from the inequality $K_2/K_1 > K_{f1}/K_{f2}$ it follows that $K_1 << K_2$. These two inequalities are mutually exclusive; therefore, there are no asymptotic solutions in subset 3.

In subset 4 ($K_{f1}[M] << 1$, $K_{f2}[M] << 1$, $K_1 >> 1$, $K_2 >> 1$), from the inequality $K_2/K_1 > K_{f1}/K_{f2}$, it follows that $K_1/K_2 < K_{f2}/K_{f1}$, which together with the other inequality in this subset $K_1/K_2 > K_{f2}/K_{f1}$ are mutually exclusive. Therefore, there are no asymptotic solutions in subset 4.

In subset 6 ($K_{f1}[M] >> 1$, $K_{f2}[M] << 1$, $K_1 >> 1$, $K_2 << 1$), the inequality $1/K_1 > K_{f1}/K_{f2}$ is not satisfied for any parameter values in this subset. Therefore, there are no asymptotic solutions in subset 6.

**Table 1.** Asymptotically transformed inequalities (47) and (53) for various subsets of parameter values $K_{f1} > 0$, $K_{f2} > 0$, $K_1 > 0$, $K_2 > 0$.

| Boundary of the Subset (Stage 2) \ Boundary of the Subset (Stage 1) | $K_{f1}[M] >> 1$, $K_{f2}[M] >> 1$ | $K_{f1}[M] >> 1$, $K_{f2}[M] << 1$ | $K_{f1}[M] << 1$, $K_{f2}[M] >> 1$ | $K_{f1}[M] << 1$, $K_{f2}[M] << 1$ |
|---|---|---|---|---|
| $K_1 >> 1$, $K_2 >> 1$ | subset 1<br>$K_1/K_2 > 1$,<br>$K_2/K_1 > K_{f1}/K_{f2}$ | subset 2<br>$K_1/K_2 > K_{f2}[M]$,<br>$K_2/K_1 > K_{f1}/K_{f2}$ | subset 3<br>$K_1/K_2 > 1/(K_{f1}[M])$,<br>$K_2/K_1 > K_{f1}/K_{f2}$ | subset 4<br>$K_1/K_2 > K_{f2}/K_{f1}$,<br>$K_2/K_1 > K_{f1}/K_{f2}$ |
| $K_1 >> 1$, $K_2 << 1$ | subset 5<br>$K_1/K_2 > 1$,<br>$1/K_1 > K_{f1}/K_{f2}$ | subset 6<br>$K_1/K_2 > K_{f2}[M]$,<br>$1/K_1 > K_{f1}/K_{f2}$ | subset 7<br>$K_1/K_2 > 1/(K_{f1}[M])$,<br>$1/K_1 > K_{f1}/K_{f2}$ | subset 8<br>$K_1/K_2 > K_{f2}/K_{f1}$,<br>$1/K_1 > K_{f1}/K_{f2}$ |
| $K_1 << 1$, $K_2 >> 1$ | subset 9<br>$K_1/K_2 > 1$,<br>$K_2 > K_{f1}/K_{f2}$ | subset 10<br>$K_1/K_2 > K_{f2}[M]$,<br>$K_2 > K_{f1}/K_{f2}$ | subset 11<br>$K_1/K_2 > 1/(K_{f1}[M])$,<br>$K_2 > K_{f1}/K_{f2}$ | subset 12<br>$K_1/K_2 > K_{f2}/K_{f1}$,<br>$K_2 > K_{f1}/K_{f2}$ |
| $K_1 << 1$, $K_2 << 1$ | subset 13<br>$K_1/K_2 > 1$,<br>$1 > K_{f1}/K_{f2}$ | subset 14<br>$K_1/K_2 > K_{f2}[M]$,<br>$1 > K_{f1}/K_{f2}$ | subset 15<br>$K_1/K_2 > 1/(K_{f1}[M])$,<br>$1 > K_{f1}/K_{f2}$ | subset 16<br>$K_1/K_2 > K_{f2}/K_{f1}$,<br>$1 > K_{f1}/K_{f2}$ |

In subset 9 ($K_{f1}[M] >> 1$, $K_{f2}[M] >> 1$, $K_1 << 1$, $K_2 >> 1$), the inequality $K_1/K_2 > 1$ is not satisfied for any of the parameter values in this subset. Therefore, there are no asymptotic solutions in subset 9.

In subset 10 ($K_{f1}[M] >> 1$, $K_{f2}[M] << 1$, $K_1 << 1$, $K_2 >> 1$), from the inequality $K_2 > K_{f1}/K_{f2}$, it follows that $K_{f2}[M] > K_{f1}[M]/K_2$. This inequality, together with the other inequality $K_1/K_2 > K_{f2}[M]$, forms the system $K_1/K_2 > K_{f2}[M] > K_{f1}[M]/K_2$, which has no solution, since $K_{f1}[M] >> 1$, and $K_1 << 1$. Therefore, there are no asymptotic solutions in subset 10.

In subset 11 ($K_{f1}[M] << 1$, $K_{f2}[M] >> 1$, $K_1 << 1$, $K_2 >> 1$), the inequality $K_1/K_2 > 1/\left(K_{f1}[M]\right)$ is not satisfied for any parameter values in this subset. Therefore, there are no asymptotic solutions in subset 11.

In subset 12 ($K_{f1}[M] << 1$, $K_{f2}[M] << 1$, $K_1 << 1$, $K_2 >> 1$), from the inequality $K_2 > K_{f1}/K_{f2}$, it follows that $1/K_2 < K_{f2}/K_{f1}$. This inequality, together with the other inequality $K_1/K_2 > K_{f2}/K_{f1}$, forms the system $1/K_2 < K_{f2}/K_{f1} < K_1/K_2$, which has no solution since $K_1 << 1$. Therefore, there are no asymptotic solutions in subset 12.

In subset 14 ($K_{f1}[M] >> 1$, $K_{f2}[M] << 1$, $K_1 << 1$, $K_2 << 1$), the inequality $1 > K_{f1}/K_{f2}$ is not satisfied for any parameter values in this subset. Therefore, there are no asymptotic solutions in subset 14.

For all other subsets, particular asymptotic solutions of inequalities (47) and (53) were proposed (Table 2), including examples of specific parameter values $K_{f1}$, $K_{f2}$, $K_1$, $K_2$ satisfying these inequalities. Figure 3 shows the dependencies of $\mu_{calc}$ on $q$ corresponding to these particular asymptotic solutions.

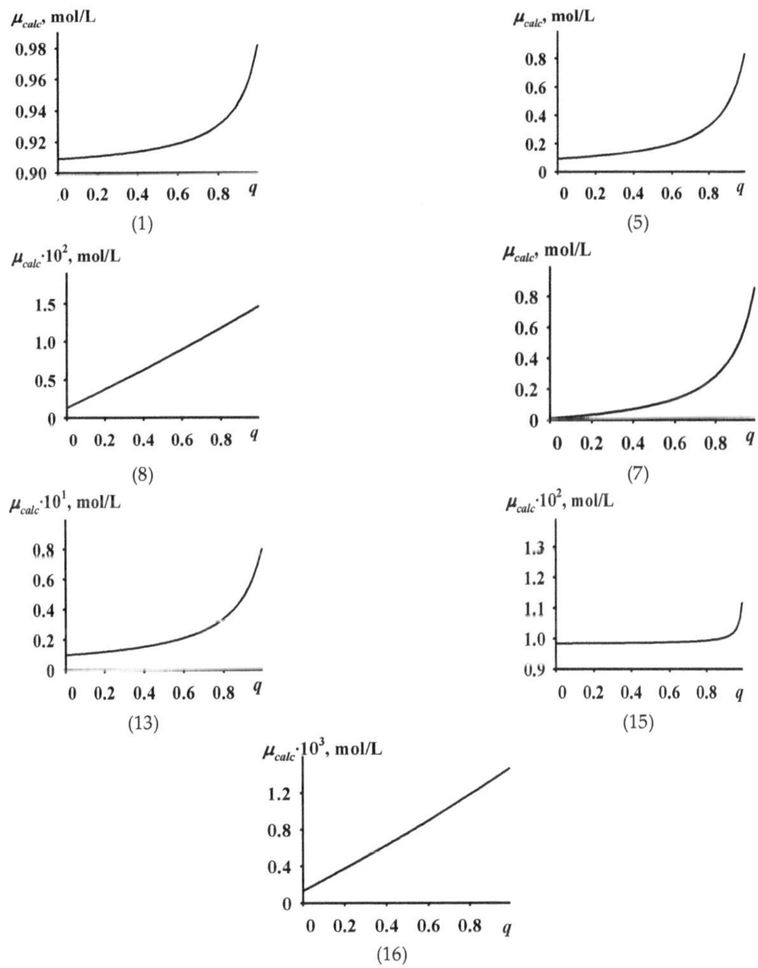


**Figure 3.** Dependencies of $\mu_{calc}$ on $q$ corresponding to particular asymptotic solutions; (numbers in parentheses indicate the subset number of parameters according to Table 1, within the boundaries of which the corresponding asymptotic solution was found). For the dependencies of $\mu_{calc}$ on $q$ in subsets (8) and (16), the values of $d^2\mu_{calc}/dq^2$ were also calculated, and these were positive for al $0 \leq q \leq 1$ (this confirms that the dependencies in (8) and (16) are convex downward).

**Table 2.** Particular asymptotic solutions of inequalities (47) and (53) for various subsets of parameter values $K_{f1} > 0$, $K_{f2} > 0$, $K_1 > 0$, $K_2 > 0$ at $[M] = 1.5$ mol/L.

| Boundaries of Parameter Subsets | $K_{f1}[M] >> 1$, $K_{f2}[M] >> 1$ | $K_{f1}[M] >> 1$, $K_{f2}[M] << 1$ | $K_{f1}[M] << 1$, $K_{f2}[M] >> 1$ | $K_{f1}[M] << 1$, $K_{f2}[M] << 1$ |
|---|---|---|---|---|
| $K_1 >> 1$, $K_2 >> 1$ | $K_{f1} = 10^1$ L/mol, $K_{f2} = 10^3$ L/mol, $K_1 = 10^2$, $K_2 = 10^1$ | No solutions | No solutions | No solutions |
| $K_1 >> 1$, $K_2 << 1$ | $K_{f1} = 10^1$ L/mol,, $K_{f2} = 10^3$ L/mol, $K_1 = 10^1$, $K_2 = 10^{-1}$ | No solutions | $K_{f1} = 10^{-2}$ L/mol, $K_{f2} = 10^2$ L/mol, $K_1 = 10^3$, $K_2 = 10^{-2}$ | $K_{f1} = 10^{-3}$ L/mol, $K_{f2} = 10^{-1}$ L/mol, $K_1 = 10^1$, $K_2 = 10^{-2}$ |
| $K_1 << 1$, $K_2 >> 1$ | No solutions | No solutions | No solutions | No solutions |
| $K_1 << 1$, $K_2 << 1$ | $K_{f1} = 10^1$ L/mol, $K_{f2} = 10^2$ L/mol, $K_1 = 10^{-1}$, $K_2 = 10^{-2}$ | No solutions | $K_{f1} = 10^{-1}$ L/mol, $K_{f2} = 10^2$ L/mol, $K_1 = 10^{-1}$, $K_2 = 10^{-2}$ | $K_{f1} = 10^{-2}$ L/mol, $K_{f2} = 10^{-1}$ L/mol,, $K_1 = 10^{-1}$, $K_2 = 10^{-3}$ |

### *3.4. Determination of Specific Quantitative Values of Kinetic Parameters of the Active Sites Formation Process, at Which the Dependence of $\mu_{calc}$ on $q$ Quantitatively Coincides with the Dependence of $\mu_{exp}$ on $q$*

The particular asymptotic solutions of inequalities (47) and (53) from Table 2, which provide qualitative agreement between the forms of the dependencies $\mu_{exp}$ on $q$ and $\mu_{calc}$ on $q$, were used as initial approximations for solving the inverse problem of finding particular asymptotic solutions of inequalities (47) and (53) that ensure quantitative coincidence of the dependencies $\mu_{exp}$ on $q$ and $\mu_{calc}$ on $q$. The inverse problem was solved using an optimization algorithm implemented in the FindMinimum operator of the Wolfram software system (Mathematica 12.0). During the solution of the inverse problem, the following function was minimized:

$$F = \left(\mu_{exp} - \mu_{calc}\right)^2 \frac{\mathrm{L}^2}{\mathrm{mol}^2} + +10^r \left( (lgK_1)^2 + (lgK_2)^2 + \left( lg\frac{K_{f1}}{\frac{\mathrm{L}}{\mathrm{mol}}} \right)^2 + \left( lg\frac{K_{f2}}{\frac{\mathrm{L}}{\mathrm{mol}}} \right)^2 \right), \quad (54)$$

where the second term is the regularization term ($r$ is the regularization coefficient). Prior to this, dependence (37) was expressed in the following form:

$$\mu_{calc} = \frac{10^{X_1}10^{X_{f1}}q + 10^{X_2}10^{X_{f2}}(1-q)}{(1+10^{X_1})10^{X_{f1}}q + (1+10^{X_2})10^{X_{f2}}(1-q) + \frac{1}{[M]}} 10^{X_0},$$

where $X_0 = \lg[A]_0$, $X_{f1} = \lg(K_{f1}/(\mathrm{L/mol}))$, $X_{f2} = \lg(K_{f2}/(\mathrm{L/mol}))$, $X_1 = \lg K_1$, $X_2 = \lg K_2$.

Thus, during the minimization of function (54), we obtained the parameters $X_0$, $X_{f1}$, $X_{f2}$, $X_1$, $X_2$. This representation of dependence (37) allowed us, firstly, to search for the minimum of function (54) within the domain of physically meaningful values $[A]_0 > 0$, $K_{f1} > 0$, $K_{f2} > 0$, $K_1 > 0$, $K_2 > 0$, and secondly, to vary not the exact values of the parameters $[A]_0$, $K_{f1}$, $K_{f2}$, $K_1$, $K_2$, but their orders of magnitude, i.e., to search for $[A]_0$, $K_{f1}$, $K_{f2}$, $K_1$, $K_2$ over very wide ranges. Since the search for $[A]_0$, $K_{f1}$, $K_{f2}$, $K_1$, $K_2$ was conducted over broad intervals, to avoid obtaining unreasonably large or small values of $X_0$, $X_{f1}$, $X_{f2}$, $X_1$, $X_2$ (e.g., $\pm 1000$), a regularization term was introduced into function (54). The purpose of the regularization term is to exclude inadequate solutions. That is, the farther the values of $X_0$, $X_{f1}$, $X_{f2}$, $X_1$, $X_2$ are from zero, the less likely these values will be accepted as a solution. Empirically, it was established that for this problem that the regularization coefficient should be taken as $r = -9$ (this value was varied in steps of 1). At lower values of $r$, the values of $X_0$, $X_{f1}$, $X_{f2}$, $X_1$, and $X_2$ obtained from minimizing function (54) were unreasonably high or low. At higher values of $r$, the contribution of the regularization term to the value of function (54) became too large, and the possibility of minimizing the first term of this function was lost. Thus, the result of minimizing function (54) is regularized, or, more simply, ordered. This result is not purely mathematical but incorporates ordering dictated by a priori chemical knowledge.

The minimization of function (54) was performed in two variants.

Variant 1. Particular asymptotic solutions of inequalities (47) and (53) from Table 2 were used as initial approximations. The initial approximation for $X_0$ varied from −4 to −2. No constraints were imposed on the values of $X_{f1}$, $X_{f2}$, $X_1$, $X_2$, i.e., the values of $X_{f1}$, $X_{f2}$, $X_1$, $X_2$ could move from one solution subset to another.

Variant 2. This variant differed from Variant 1 in that constraints were imposed on the values of $X_{f1}$, $X_{f2}$, $X_1$, $X_2$ during the minimization of function (54) to prevent the solution from leaving the subset in which the initial approximation lies.

As a result of minimizing function (54) according to Variant 1, the same minimum was found in solution subset 7 for all initial approximations. This is the global minimum (F = $4.42 \times 10^{-9}$).

By minimizing function (54) according to Variant 2, the following results were achieved:

1. No solutions were found in subsets 1, 8, 15, and 16 that provided quantitatively exact agreement between the dependencies $\mu_{exp}$ on $q$ and $\mu_{calc}$ on $q$ (specifically, none were found because they might exist if other initial approximations within these subsets were used);
2. Local minima were found in subsets 5 and 13 with values (F = $2.81 \times 10^{-8}$ and F = $1.54 \times 10^{-8}$ respectively);
3. No local minimum was found in subset 7 (!), despite the fact that the global minimum found in Variant 1 minimization lies in subset 7. This is probably due to the fact that during the optimization algorithm implementation, when searching for the global minimum, the values of $X_{f1}$, $X_{f2}$, $X_1$, $X_2$ initially located in subset 7 leave it and then re-enter it; this supports the idea that solutions in subsets 1, 8, 15, and 16 may exist but were not found with the chosen initial approximations.

Particular asymptotic solutions (values of $[A]_0$, $K_{f1}$, $K_{f2}$, $K_1$, $K_2$) that ensure quantitative coincidence of the dependencies of $\mu_{exp}$ on $q$ and $\mu_{calc}$ on $q$ are presented in Table 3. The dependencies of $\mu_{calc}$ on $q$ corresponding to these particular asymptotic solutions, which ensure quantitatively exact agreement between the dependencies of $\mu_{exp}$ on $q$ and $\mu_{calc}$ on $q$, are shown in Figure 4.

**Table 3.** Particular asymptotic solutions of inequalities (47) and (53) that ensure quantitatively exact coincidence of the dependencies $\mu_{exp}$ on $q$ and $\mu_{calc}$ on $q$ for various subsets.

| **Boundaries of Subsets of Parameter Values** | $K_{f1}[M] >> 1$, $K_{f2}[M] >> 1$ | $K_{f1}[M] >> 1$, $K_{f2}[M] << 1$ | $K_{f1}[M] << 1$, $K_{f2}[M] >> 1$ | $K_{f1}[M] << 1$, $K_{f2}[M] << 1$ |
|---|---|---|---|---|
| $K_1 >> 1$, $K_2 >> 1$ | Qualitative solution exists; no exact quantitative solution found | No solutions | No solutions | No solutions |
| $K_1 >> 1$, $K_2 << 1$ | $[A]_0 = 10^{-3.85}$ mol/L (method 1 *) $[A]_0 = 10^{-3.55}$ mol/L (method 2) $K_{f1} = 10^{1.18}$ L/mol $K_{f2} = 10^{3.16}$ L/mol, $K_1 = 10^{1.18}$, $K_2 = 10^{-1.17}$ local minimum F = $2.81 \times 10^{-8}$ | No solutions | $[A]_0 = 10^{-3.57}$ mol/L (method 1) $[A]_0 = 10^{-3.43}$ mol/L (method 2) $K_{f1} = 10^{-0.31}$ L/mol, $K_{f2} = 10^{0.91}$ L/mol, $K_1 = 10^{0.25}$, $K_2 = 10^{-1.07}$ global minimum F = $4.42 \times 10^{-9}$ | Qualitative solution exists; no exact quantitative solution found |

**Table 3.** *Cont.*

| Boundaries of Subsets of Parameter Values | $K_{f1}[M]>>1$, $K_{f2}[M]>>1$ | $K_{f1}[M]>>1$, $K_{f2}[M]<<1$ | $K_{f1}[M]<<1$, $K_{f2}[M]>>1$ | $K_{f1}[M]<<1$, $K_{f2}[M]<<1$ |
|---|---|---|---|---|
| $K_1 << 1$, $K_2 >> 1$ | No solutions | No solutions | No solutions | No solutions |
| $K_1 << 1$, $K_2 << 1$ | $[A]_0 = 10^{-2.66}$ mol/L (method 1) $[A]_0 = 10^{-2.53}$ mol/L (method 2) $K_{f1} = 10^{1.18}$ L/mol, $K_{f2} = 10^{2.16}$ L/mol, $K_1 = 10^{-1.18}$, $K_2 = 10^{-2.16}$ local minimum F = 1.54 × $10^{-8}$ | No solutions | Qualitative solution exists, no exact quantitative solution found | Qualitative solution exists, no exact quantitative solution found |

* The copolymerization achieved via method 1 and method 2 is described in the Experimental Section.

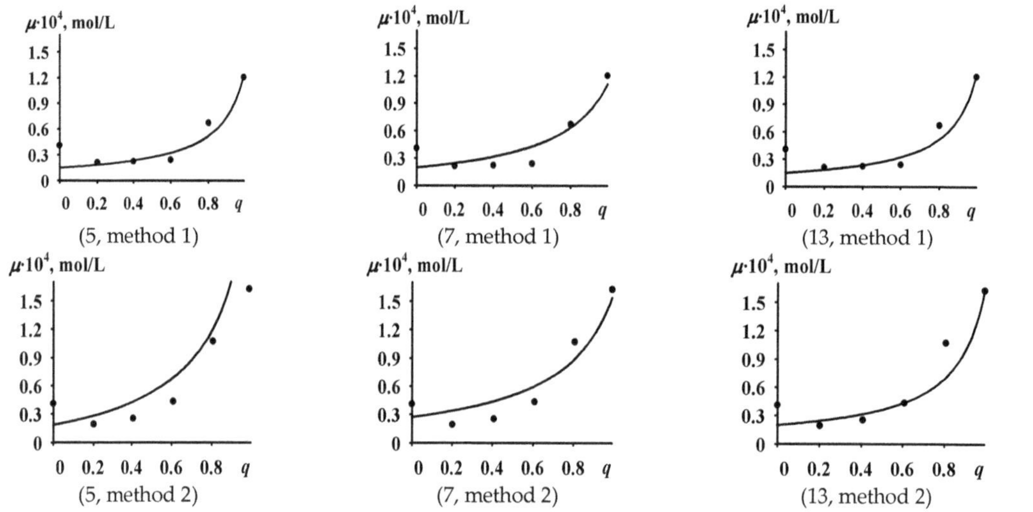


**Figure 4.** Dependencies of $\mu_{calc}$ on $q$ corresponding to particular asymptotic solutions that ensure quantitatively exact agreement between the dependencies of $\mu_{exp}$ on $q$ (points) and $\mu_{calc}$ on $q$ (lines) (the number in parentheses indicates the subset of parameters according to Table 1 within which the corresponding asymptotic solution was found, and the method of preparation of $TiCl_4$-Al(i-$C_4H_9)_3$ catalytic system).

Thus, according to the conducted analysis, it can be concluded that during the formation of active sites in the $TiCl_4$-Al(i-$C_4H_9)_3$ catalytic system, one of the following qualitative scenarios may exist:

1. Monomer molecules are easily adsorbed on the surface of the $TiCl_4$-Al(i-$C_4H_9)_3$ catalytic system particles; active sites formed by butadiene molecules are stable (i.e., the bond between the Ti atom of the catalytic system and the C atom of butadiene is stable), while active sites s formed by isoprene molecules are unstable (i.e., the bond between the Ti atom of the catalytic system and the C atom of isoprene is unstable). This description corresponds to subset 5 ($K_{f1}[M] >> 1$, $K_{f2}[M] >> 1$, $K_1 >> 1$, $K_2 << 1$).
2. Isoprene molecules are easily adsorbed, while butadiene molecules are adsorbed with difficulty; active sites formed by butadiene are stable, and active sites formed by isoprene are unstable. This description corresponds to subset 7 ($K_{f1}[M] << 1$, $K_{f2}[M] >> 1$, $K_1 >> 1$, $K_2 << 1$).

3. Monomer molecules are easily adsorbed but form unstable active sites; the stability of active sites formed by butadiene should be higher than that of active sites formed by isoprene. This description corresponds to subset 13 ($K_{f1}[M] >> 1, K_{f2}[M] >> 1$ $K_1 << 1, K_2 << 1$).

All of the solutions indicate that isoprene molecules should adsorb better on the surface of $TiCl_4$-Al(i-$C_4H_9$)$_3$ particles than butadiene molecules, while butadiene molecules should form more stable active sites than isoprene molecules.

It should also be noted that the developed two-stage model of active sites formation was unable, under any conditions, to describe the presence of a minimum point in the experimental dependence of $\mu_{exp}$ on $q$. The search for the reasons behind this phenomenon is a promising direction for further research. Among the possible causes, the following can be noted:

1. The wedging effect of active copolymer chains, which leads to dispersion of the $TiCl_4$-Al(i-$C_4H_9$)$_3$ catalytic system particles. Experimentally, it has been established that the dependence of the particle size of the $TiCl_4$-Al(i-$C_4H_9$)$_3$ catalytic system on $q$ also exhibits a minimum point [39].

2. The difference between the real adsorption process of butadiene and isoprene and the process described by the Langmuir monomolecular adsorption theory [33]. This difference may have the following causes.

2.1. The biographical nonuniformity of the surface of $TiCl_4$-Al(i-$C_4H_9$)$_3$ particles (different crystal facets have different properties, and crystals contain defects). Within the framework of the model presented in this work, this means that the equilibrium constants $K_{f1}$ and $K_{f2}$ will be functions of the concentration of adsorbed butadiene and isoprene molecules; in classical theoretical models, called adsorption isotherms, which relate the fraction of occupied adsorption sites to the pressure of the adsorbed gas, this leads to the dependence of the adsorption constant on the pressure of the adsorbed gas. In this case, adsorption is described not by the Langmuir isotherm, where the adsorption constant is constant [33], but, for example, by the Freundlich [40], Zeldovich [41], or Sips isotherms [42,43].

2.2. Induced nonuniformity of the surface of $TiCl_4$-Al(i-$C_4H_9$)$_3$ particles (the heat of adsorption depends on the number of adsorbed monomer molecules on the surface of $TiCl_4$-Al(i-$C_4H_9$)$_3$ particles, indicating interactions between adsorbed molecules [33]). To describe the induced nonuniformity, the model of active sites formation in $TiCl_4$-Al(i-$C_4H_9$)$_3$ must take into account the change in binding energy of adsorbed molecules depending on the number of adsorbed molecules due to adsorbate–adsorbate interactions. Such models include the Ising model (in which the adsorbed molecular layer corresponds to a two-dimensional lattice gas model), which considers lateral interactions between molecules in lattice sites [44]. The Ising model is closed in the Bragg–Williams approximation, which assumes that the interaction energy of nearest adsorbed molecules is estimated as if the molecules were randomly distributed among adsorption sites, i.e., this energy is estimated as the average interaction energy [45]. Adsorbate–adsorbate–adsorbent interactions are also accounted for in the Fowler–Guggenheim isotherm [46,47]. The King model also describes induced nonuniformity of particles' surfaces [33].

2.3. Adsorption is multidentate. In this case, butadiene and isoprene molecules may require different numbers of adsorption sites. More compact molecules in this respect can adsorb in the gaps between bulkier molecules. Such adsorption is described by the semi-competitive model [48].

2.4. The adsorption rate depends on the concentration of the adsorbed substance, i.e., there exist different adsorption regimes (at low concentrations, the orientation of adsorbed molecules relative to the surface of solid particles occurs in one way, while at high concentrations their orientation is different) [33].

## 4. Conclusions

The theoretical influence of the monomer mixture composition $q$ in the butadiene–isoprene copolymerization on the concentration of active sites of $TiCl_4$-$Al(i\text{-}C_4H_9)_3$ catalytic system $\mu$ has been described ($q = [M_1]/([M_1] + [M_2])$, $[M_1]$ is the concentration of butadiene in the monomer mixture and $[M_2]$ is the concentration of isoprene in the monomer mixture).

The theoretical description was developed according to the following algorithm:

1. Based on experimental values of the copolymerization rate from study [5] and known values of chain propagation rate constants [35,36] and copolymerization constants from study [5], the concentrations of active sites of the $TiCl_4$-$Al(i\text{-}C_4H_9)_3$ catalytic system were calculated at various values of $q$. The experimental dependence of $\mu$ on $q$ has the following features: 1. The minimum concentration of active sites $\mu$ corresponds to some value of $q$ in the range $q$ = 0.2–0.6, and the concentration $\mu$ predominantly increases as the butadiene concentration in the monomer mixture increases. 2. The dependence of $\mu$ on $q$ is nonlinear, with ($\frac{d^2\mu_{calc}}{dq^2} > 0$).
2. The kinetic model equations for the formation of active sites in the $TiCl_4$-$Al(i\text{-}C_4H_9)_3$ catalytic system were written. These kinetic equations were formulated based on the mass-action law and the Langmuir monomolecular adsorption theory for two variants of the kinetic scheme: one-stage and two-stage (physical stage—adsorption; chemical stage—formation of the Ti-C bond). The adsorption of butadiene and isoprene molecules on the catalytic system $TiCl_4$-$Al(i\text{-}C_4H_9)_3$ surface was considered competitive. The equation expressing the theoretical dependence of $\mu$ on $q$ was obtained by analytically solving the system of kinetic model equations under the assumption of equilibrium in all stages of the formation of active sites.
3. The obtained equation was analyzed. It was found that the kinetic model based on the one-stage kinetic scheme cannot even qualitatively describe the experimental dependence of $\mu$ on $q$ with the described features. The analogous kinetic model based on the two-stage kinetic scheme satisfactorily describes this experimental dependence (except for the existence of the minimum concentration of active sites $\mu$).
4. The domains of kinetic parameter values for active sites formation were established, at which the theoretical dependence of $\mu$ on $q$ reproduces the corresponding experimental dependence both qualitatively and quantitatively. Qualitatively, this occurs under the condition that isoprene adsorbs better than butadiene, but butadiene forms more stable active sites than isoprene. Quantitatively, this is ensured by any of the three sets of equilibrium rate constants for the stages of active sites formation found in this work.

The results of this work can be generalized to other heterogeneous catalytic systems used for binary copolymerization. Essentially, this work has developed a methodology for rapid assessment of the mechanism of active site formation in heterogeneous catalytic systems of binary copolymerization. This methodology is based on experimental data describing the relationship between the copolymerization rate $W$ and the composition $q$ of a multidimensional mixture. The shape of the dependence of $W$ on $q$ is identical to the shape of the dependence of $\mu$ on $q$. According to this methodology, three possible variants can be identified, each of which provides information about the mechanism of active site formation in the catalytic system.

Variant 1. If the dependence of $\mu$ on $q$ has no minima or maxima and is convex upward, then the simplest mechanism of active site formation in such a catalytic system is a simple one-step mechanism. Active sites may also form via a more complex mechanism; however, there is no basis for assuming a more complex mechanism of active site formation for such a catalytic system. The activity of such a catalytic system is close to maximal for most values of $q$.

Variant 2. If the dependence of $\mu$ on $q$ has no minima or maxima and is convex downward, then the simplest mechanism of active site formation in such a catalytic system is a two-step mechanism. The activity of such a catalytic system is close to minimal for most values of $q$.

In variants 1 and 2, the maximum and minimum activity of the catalytic system are observed at $q = 0$ and $q = 1$ (the maximum activity can occur at either of these two points, and the minimum activity can also occur at either of these two points).

Variant 3. If the dependence of $\mu$ on $q$ has at least one maximum or minimum point at $q \neq 0$ and $q \neq 1$, then the simplest mechanism of active site formation of such a catalytic system is more complex than a two-step mechanism.

The obtained results will allow us, in the future, to draw conclusions about the complexity of the mechanism of active sites' formation in heterogeneous catalytic systems of copolymerization based on the shape of the experimental dependence of $\mu$ on $q$ (and, correspondingly, based on the shape of the experimental dependence of $W$ on $q$).

**Author Contributions:** Conceptualization, K.A.T.; methodology, R.T.I. and K.A.T.; software, R.T.I. and K.A.T.; validation, R.T.I., K.A.T., Y.L.L., A.S.N. and N.V.U.; formal analysis, R.T.I. and K.A.T.; investigation, R.T.I. and K.A.T.; resources, N.V.U. and A.S.N.; data curation, K.A.T.; writing—original draft preparation, R.T.I. and K.A.T.; writing—review and editing, R.T.I., K.A.T., Y.L.L., A.S.N. and N.V.U.; visualization, R.T.I. and Y.L.L.; supervision, K.A.T. and N.V.U.; project administration, K.A.T. All authors have read and agreed to the published version of the manuscript.

**Funding:** This research received no external funding.

**Data Availability Statement:** The raw data supporting the conclusions of this article will be made available by the authors on request.

**Acknowledgments:** We acknowledge the valuable input from the anonymous reviewers of the manuscript, whose observations improved its quality.

**Conflicts of Interest:** The authors declare no conflicts of interest.

## References


1. Bhatia, S.; Goel, A. *Rubber Technology*; Woodhead Publishing India: New Delhi, India, 2019; p. 666.
2. Kotnees, D.; Bhomick, A. *Rubber to Rubber Adhesion*; Scrivener Publishing: Austin, TX, USA, 2021; p. 429.
3. Wang, F.; Zhang, M.; Liu, H.; Hu, Y.; Zhang, X. Randomly Coordinative Chain Transfer Copolymerization of 1,3-Butadiene and Isoprene: A Highly Atom Economic Way for Accessing Butadiene/Isoprene Rubber. *Ind. Eng. Chem. Res.* **2020**, *59*, 10754–10762. [CrossRef]
4. Taibulatov, P.A.; Mingaleev, V.Z.; Zakharov, V.P.; Ionova, I.A.; Monakov, Y.B. Kinetic Inhomogeneity of Copolymerization Sites of Butadiene and Isoprene on Titanium Catalyst. *Pol. Sci. Ser. B* **2010**, *52*, 450–458. [CrossRef]
5. Zakharov, V.P.; Ulitin, N.V.; Tereshchenko, K.A.; Zakharova, E.M. *Turbulent Technologies in the Synthesis of Polydienes Using Ziegler-Natta Catalytic Components*; Bashkir Encyclopedia: Ufa, Russia, 2018; p. 280. (In Russian)
6. Liu, L.; Meira, D.M.; Arenal, R.; Concepción, P.; Puga, A.V.; Corma, A. Determination of the Evolution of Heterogeneous Single Metal Atoms and Nanoclusters under Reaction Conditions: Which Are the Working Catalytic Sites? *ACS Catal.* **2019**, *9*, 10626–10639. [CrossRef]
7. Lu, Y.; Kuo, C.-T.; Kovarik, L.; Hoffman, A.S.; Boubnov, A.; Driscoll, D.M.; Morris, J.R.; Bare, S.R.; Karim, A.M. A Versatile Approach for Quantification of Surface Site Fractions using Reaction Kinetics: The Case of CO Oxidation on Supported Ir single Atoms and Nanoparticles. *J. Catal.* **2019**, *378*, 121–130. [CrossRef]
8. Rana, R.; Hong, J.; Hoffman, A.S.; Werghi, B.; Bare, S.R.; Kulkarni, A.R. Quantifying the Site Heterogeneities of Non-Uniform Catalysts Using QuantEXAFS. *Chem.–Meth.* **2024**, *5*, e202400020. [CrossRef]

9. DeRita, L.; Dai, S.; Lopez-Zepeda, K.; Pham, N.; Graham, G.W.; Pan, X.; Christopher, P. Catalyst Architecture for Stable Single Atom Dispersion Enables Site-Specific Spectroscopic and Reactivity Measurements of CO Adsorbed to Pt Atoms, Oxidized Pt Clusters, and Metallic Pt Clusters on $TiO_2$. *J. Am. Chem. Soc.* **2017**, *139*, 14150–14165. [CrossRef]
10. Bates, J.S.; Martinez, J.J.; Hall, M.N.; Al-Omari, A.A.; Murphy, E.; Zeng, Y.; Luo, F.; Primbs, M.; Menga, D.; Bibent, N.; et al. Chemical Kinetic Method for Active-Site Quantification in Fe-N-C Catalysts and Correlation with Molecular Probe and Spectroscopic Site-Couning Methods. *J. Am. Chem. Soc.* **2023**, *145*, 26222–26237. [CrossRef]
11. Sahraie, N.R.; Kramm, U.I.; Steinberg, J.; Zhang, Y.; Thomas, A.; Reier, T.; Paraknowitsch, J.P.; Strasser, P. Quantifying the density and utilization of active sites in non-precious metal oxygen electroreduction catalysts. *Nat. Commun.* **2015**, *6*, 8618. [CrossRef] [PubMed]
12. Jeong, B.; Abbas, H.G.; Klein, B.P.; Bae, G.; Velmurugan, A.R.; Choi, C.H.; Kim, G.; Kim, D.; Kim, K.-J.; Cha, B.J.; et al. CO Cryo-Sorption as a Surface-Sensitive Spectroscopic Probe of the Active Site Density of Single-Atom Catalysts. *Angew. Chem. Int. Ed.* **2025**, *64*, e202420673. [CrossRef]
13. Boyes, E.D.; LaGrow, A.P.; Ward, M.R.; Mitchell, R.W.; Gai, P.L. Single Atom Dynamics in Chemical Reactions. *Acc. Chem. Res.* **2020**, *53*, 390–399. [CrossRef]
14. Afrin, S.; Bollini, P. Beyond Upper Bound Estimates of Active Site Densities in Heterogeneous Catalysis: A Note on the Critical Role of Titrant Pressure. *J. Catal.* **2022**, *413*, 76–80. [CrossRef]
15. Credendino, R.; Liguori, D.; Fan, Z.; Morini, G.; Cavallo, L. Toward a Unified Model Explaining Heterogeneous Ziegler−Natta Catalysis. *ACS Catal.* **2015**, *5*, 5431–5435. [CrossRef]
16. Bahri-Laleha, N.; Hanifpour, A.; Mirmohammadi, S.A.; Poater, A.; Nekoomanesh-Haghighi, M.; Talarico, G.; Cavallo, L. Computational Modeling of Heterogeneous Ziegler-Natta Catalysts for Olefins Polymerization. *Prog. Polym. Sci.* **2018**, *84*, 89–114. [CrossRef]
17. Kissin, Y.V. Active Centers in Ziegler–Natta Catalysts: Formation Kinetics and Structure. *J. Catal.* **2012**, *292*, 188–200. [CrossRef]
18. Shetty, S. Synergistic, Reconstruction and Bonding Effects During the Adsorption of Internal Electron Donors and $TiCl_4$ on $MgCl_2$ Surface: A Periodic-DFT Investigation. *Surf. Sci.* **2016**, *653*, 55–65. [CrossRef]
19. Bazvand, R.; Bahri-Laleh, N.; Abedini, H.; Nekoomanesh, M.; Poater, A. Chemical dealcoholation of $MgCl_2{\cdot}EtOH$ Adduct by Al Compounds and Its Effect on the Performance of Ziegler–Natta Catalysts. *Appl. Organomet. Chem.* **2024**, *38*, e7300. [CrossRef]
20. Mehdizadeh, M.; Karkhaneh, F.; Nekoomanesh, M.; Sadjadi, S.; Emami, M.; Teimoury, H.; Salimi, M.; Solà, M.; Poater, A.; Bahri-Laleh, N.; et al. Influence of the Ethanol Content of Adduct on the Comonomer Incorporation of Related Ziegler–Natta Catalysts in Propylene (Co)polymerizations. *Polymers* **2023**, *15*, 4476. [CrossRef] [PubMed]
21. Vittoria, A.; Meppelder, A.; Friederichs, N.; Busico, V.; Cipullo, R. Demystifying Ziegler-Natta Catalysts: The Origin of Stereoselectivity. *ACS Catal.* **2017**, *7*, 4509–4518. [CrossRef]
22. Rahmatiyan, S.; Bahri-Laleh, N.; Hanifpour, A.; Nekoomanesh-Haghighi, M. Different Behaviors of Metallocene and Ziegler–Natta Catalysts in Ethylene/1,5-hexadiene Copolymerization. *Polym. Int.* **2018**, *68*, 94–101. [CrossRef]
23. Masoori, M.; Nekoomanesh, M.; Posada-Pérez, S.; Rashedi, R.; Bahri-Laleh, N. Exploring Cocatalyst Type Effect on the Ziegler–Natta Catalyzed Ethylene Polymerizations: Experimental and DFT Studies. *J. Polym. Res.* **2022**, *29*, 197. [CrossRef]
24. Tereshchenko, K.A.; Shiyan, D.A.; Ziganshina, A.S.; Ganiev, G.M.; Ulitin, N.V.; Zakharov, V.P. Control of Molar Mass Characteristics of Polybutadiene—A Component of Sticky Glue—By Physical Modification of the Catalytic System in Turbulent Flows. *Polym. Sci. Ser. D* **2020**, *13*, 250–257. [CrossRef]
25. Koen, W.B.; Laurens, D.B.M.; Nikolaos, N.; Yuanshuai, L.; Marcus, R.; de Peinder, P.; Bas, J.P.T.; Felix, W.; Joren, M.D.; Thomas, H.; et al. A Ziegler-type Spherical Cap Model Reveals Early Stage Ethylene Polymerization Growth versus Catalyst Fragmentation Relationships. *Nat. Commun.* **2022**, *13*, 4954. [CrossRef]
26. Wei-Ping, Z.; Ya-Ping, M.; Da-Lin, D.; Ai-Hua, H.; Hua-Feng, S.; Chen-Guang, L. Polymerization Kinetics of Propylene with the MgCl2-Supported Ziegler-Natta Catalysts—Active Centers with Different Tacticity and Fragmentation of the Catalyst. *Chin. J. Polym. Sci.* **2020**, *39*, 70–80. [CrossRef]
27. Maximilian, J.W.; Florian, M.; Bert, M.W. Visualizing the Structure, Composition and Activity of Single Catalyst Particles for Olefin Polymerization and Polyolefin Decomposition. *Angew. Chem. Int. Ed.* **2024**, *63*, e202306033. [CrossRef]
28. Khan, A.; Guo, Y.; Zhang, Z.; Ali, A.; Fu, Z.; Fan, Z. Kinetics of Short-Duration Ethylene-Propylene Copolymerization with $MgCl_2$-supported Ziegler–Natta catalyst: Differentiation of Active Centers on the External and Internal Surfaces of the Catalyst Particles. *J. Appl. Polym. Sci.* **2018**, *135*, 46030. [CrossRef]
29. Shiri, M.; Parvazinia, M.; Yousefi, A.A.; Bahri-Laleh, N.; Poater, A. A Novel Method for Dynamic Molecular Weight Distribution Determination in Organometallic Catalyzed Olefin Polymerizations. *Catalysts* **2022**, *12*, 1130. [CrossRef]
30. Kissin, Y.V.; Marin, V.P.; Nelson, P.J. Propylene Polymerization Reactions with Supported Ziegler–Natta Catalysts: Observing Polymer Material Produced by a Single Active Center. *J. Polym. Sci. Part A Polym. Chem.* **2017**, *55*, 3832–3841. [CrossRef]

31. Zhang, B.; Qian, Q.; Yang, P.; Jiang, B.; Fu, Z.; Fan, Z. Responses of a Supported Ziegler–Natta Catalyst to Comonomer Feed Ratios in Ethylene–Propylene Copolymerization: Differentiation of Active Centers with Different Catalytic Features. *Ind. Eng. Chem. Res.* **2021**, *60*, 4575–4588. [CrossRef]
32. Maity, B.; Cao, Z.; Kumawat, J.; Gupta, V.; Cavallo, L. A Multivariate Linear Regression Approach to Predict Ethene/1-Olefin Copolymerization Statistics Promoted by Group 4 Catalysts. *ACS Catal.* **2021**, *11*, 4061–4070. [CrossRef]
33. Murzin, D.; Salmi, T. Chapter 2—Catalysis. In *Catalytic Kinetics Chemistry and Engineering*, 2nd ed.; Elsevier B.V.: Amsterdam, The Netherlands, 2016; pp. 35–100. [CrossRef]
34. Monakov, Y.; Sigaeva, N.; Urazbaev, N. *Active Sites of Polymerization: Multiplicity: Stereospecific and Kinetic Heterogeneity*; Brill Academic Publishers: Leiden, The Netherlands, 2005; p. 397.
35. Tereshchenko, K.A.; Ziganshina, A.S.; Zakharov, V.P.; Ulitin, N.V. Modeling of the Physicochemical Hydrodynamics of the Synthesis of Butadiene Rubber on the $TiCl_4-Al(i\text{-}C_4H_9)_3$ Catalytic System Modified in Turbulizing Flows. *Russ. J. Phys. Chem. B* **2017**, *11*, 504–512. [CrossRef]
36. Ganiev, G.M.; Tereshchenko, K.A.; Shiyan, D.A.; Ziganshina, A.S.; Zakharov, V.P.; Ulitin, N.V. Relationship of Molecular-Mass Characteristics of Polyisoprene, Component of Vulcanized Sealant, with Particle Sizes of Catalytic System $TiCl_4$-$Al(i\text{-}C_4H_9)_3$ in Isoprene Polymerization. *Polym. Sci., Ser. D* **2021**, *14*, 392–395. [CrossRef]
37. Wu, Y.; Ding, M.; Wang, J.; Zhao, B.; Wu, Z.; Zhao, P.; Tian, D.; Ding, Y.; Hu, A. Controlled Step-Growth Polymerization. *CCS Chem.* **2020**, *2*, 64–70. [CrossRef]
38. Fazakas-Anca, I.S.; Modrea, A.; Vlase, S. Determination of Reactivity Ratios from Binary Copolymerization Using the k-Nearest Neighbor Non-Parametric Regression. *Polymers* **2021**, *13*, 3811. [CrossRef]
39. Zakharov, V.P.; Zakharova, E.M.; Nasyrov, I.S.; Zhavoronkov, D.A. Use of a Turbulent Prereactor for Affecting the Site Multiplicity of a Titanium Catalyst for (Co)polymerization of Butadiene and Isoprene. *Russ. J. Appl. Chem.* **2014**, *87*, 613–618. [CrossRef]
40. Vigdorowitsch, M.; Pchelintsev, A.; Tsygankova, L.; Tanygina, E. Freundlich Isotherm: An Adsorption Model Complete Framework. *Appl. Sci.* **2021**, *11*, 8078. [CrossRef]
41. Al-Ghouti, M.A.; Da'ana, D.A. Guidelines for the Use and Interpretation of Adsorption Isotherm Models: A Review. *J. Hazard. Mater.* **2020**, *393*, 122383. [CrossRef] [PubMed]
42. Sips, R. On the Structure of a Catalyst Surface. *J. Chem. Phys.* **1948**, *16*, 490–495. [CrossRef]
43. Sips, R. On the structure of catalyst surface. II. *J. Chem. Phys.* **1950**, *18*, 1024–1026. [CrossRef]
44. Van Tassel, P.R.; Davis, H.T.; Mccormick, A.V. New Lattice Model for Adsorption of Small molecules in Zeolite Micropores. *AIChE J.* **1994**, *40*, 925–934. [CrossRef]
45. Pazzona, F.G.; Demontis, P.; Suffritti, G.B. Thermodynamics of the One-dimensional Parallel Kawasaki Model: Exact Solution and Mean-field Approximations. *Phys. Rev. E* **2014**, *90*, 022118. [CrossRef]
46. Fowler, R.; Guggenheim, E. Stat. Thermodyn. Macmillan Inc.; Cambridge University Press: Cambridge, UK, 1956; p. 701.
47. Barbero, G.; Evangelista, L.R.; Lelidis, I. Effective Adsorption Energy and Generalization of the Frumkin-Fowler-Guggenheim isotherm. *J. Mol. Liq.* **2020**, *327*, 114795. [CrossRef]
48. Cabrera, M.I.; Grau, R.J. Methyl Oleate Isomerization and Hydrogenation over Ni/$\alpha$-$Al_2O_3$: A Kinetic Study Recognizing Differences in the Molecular Size of Hydrogen and Organic Species. *J. Mol. Catal. A Chem.* **2008**, *287*, 24–32. [CrossRef]

computation

MDPI

*Article*

# DFT-Guided Next-Generation Na-Ion Batteries Powered by Halogen-Tuned $C_{12}$ Nanorings

**Riaz Muhammad [1], Anam Gulzar [2], Naveen Kosar [2,*] and Tariq Mahmood [3,4,*]**

[1] Department of Mechanical Engineering, College of Engineering, University of Bahrain, Sakhir 32038, Bahrain; rmuhammad@uob.edu.bh
[2] Department of Chemistry, University of Management and Technology (UMT), C-11, Johar Town, Lahore 54782, Pakistan; anamgulzar410@gmail.com
[3] Department of Chemistry, College of Science, University of Bahrain, Sakhir 32038, Bahrain
[4] Department of Chemistry, COMSATS University Islamabad, Abbottabad Campus, Abbottabad 22060, Pakistan
* Correspondence: naveen.kosar@umt.edu.pk (N.K.); tmahmood@uob.edu.bh (T.M.)

**Abstract:** Recent research on the design and synthesis of new and upgraded materials for secondary batteries is growing to fulfill future energy demands around the globe. Herein, by using DFT calculations, the thermodynamic and electrochemical properties of $Na/Na^+@C_{12}$ complexes and then halogens ($X^-$ = $Br^-$, $Cl^-$, and $F^-$) as counter anions are studied for the enhancement of Na-ion battery cell voltage and overall performance. Isolated $C_{12}$ nanorings showed a lower cell voltage (−1.32 V), which was significantly increased after adsorption with halide anions as counter anions. Adsorption of halides increased the Gibbs free energy, which in turn resulted in higher cell voltage. Cell voltage increased with the increasing electronegativity of the halide anion. The Gibbs free energy of $Br^-@C_{12}$ was $-52.36$ kcal·mol$^{-1}$, corresponding to a desirable cell voltage of 2.27 V, making it suitable for use as an anode in sodium-ion batteries. The estimated cell voltage of these considered complexes ensures the effective use of these complexes in sodium-ion secondary batteries.

**Keywords:** cell voltage; Gibbs free energy; secondary battery; DFT

## 1. Introduction

Establishing sustainable renewable energy resources is one of the key goals for the twenty-first century to minimize $CO_2$ emissions [1,2]. Modern civilization must deal with the dilemma of briskly shifting towards renewable energy sources and electric automobiles, all the while grappling with the ever-growing impacts of greenhouse gas emissions. Renewable energy is used frequently, typically in the form of wind and solar power [3–10]. It demands daily electrical energy storage, for which secondary batteries seem to be a promising development in technology. One of the best storage options for renewable energy technologies is Na-ion secondary batteries because of their high energy density, broadened operational lifetime, and excellent reversible capacity [11–14]. Sodium-ion batteries face several challenges because of the rapid development of electric vehicles and smart power grids, including scarce supplies, high costs, insufficient safety, and a bottleneck in the improvement of energy density, power density, and cycle performance [15–18]. With growing demand for Na-ion batteries, issues related to the cost and availability of Na supplies are becoming more serious.

The development of sodium-ion batteries (SIBs) can be credited to various factors such as sodium's abundance, cost-effectiveness, and ease of access [19–26]. Researchers even claim that deposits of lithium will probably be depleted in the near future [27–29]. Sodium resources are globally available due to their lower cost as compared to lithium. Solid-state batteries (SIBs) are gaining considerable attention in the arena of electrical energy storage [30–32]. Because of the clear advantages of low cost and the abundance of charging devices available worldwide, as one of the most promising next-generation energy storage technologies, sodium-ion batteries (SIBs) share the same internal components and operating principles as lithium-ion batteries (LIBs) [33]. Carbon is an element that is found extensively in the atmosphere, the crust, and living organisms. It can interact with other elements in chemistry to form a wide variety of compounds. Over the past few decades, research on pure carbon molecules has gained a lot of interest [34–42]. There are a multitude of types of carbon clusters, including rings composed of single or polycyclic compounds, graphite or bowl-shaped clusters, hard carbon, closed-cage fullerenes, graphene nanotubes, etc. [43–45]. Graphite has been used as anode materials for lithium–anion batteries for decades, but they are found to be not suitable for SIB because of their thermodynamic stability. Recently, hard carbon materials have been identified as the most promising anodes for commercial sodium-ion batteries (SIBs) due to their cost-effectiveness. Dahn et al. were the first ones to report the use of hard carbon derived from glucose as an anode in SIBs. Although it showed good reversible capacity, its storage capacity remained lower than that of lithium-ion batteries (LIBs) [46]. Hu and co-workers developed a layer-by-layer solid electrolyte interphase (SEI) on hard carbon with a flexible, organic-rich outer layer and an inorganic-rich inner layer, leading to improved cycling performance and rate capability [47]. However, the limited performance of hard carbon and the still-unclear storage mechanisms have hindered the practical adoption of SIBs over LIBs [48]. Maier and co-workers introduced synthetic hollow nanosphere hard carbon anodes, which exhibited excellent rate capabilities [49]. Wan et al. recently synthesized multi-shelled hollow carbon nanospheres (MS-HCNs) as high-performance anodes for SIBs. They observed that specific capacity increased with the number of shells, with four-shell HCNs demonstrating a reversible capacity of 360 mAh $g^{-1}$ at 30 mA $g^{-1}$. However, the sloping charge–discharge profiles remained unchanged with the increase in shell number [50]. In addition to carbon-based anodes, various Sn-, Sb-, and SnSb-based anode materials have been explored. Palaniselvam et al. synthesized tin-based composites and reported excellent cycling stability over 100 cycles [51]. A two-dimensional Sb@$TiO_{2-x}$ anode demonstrated high specific capacity, good rate performance, and retained up to 95% of its capacity over multiple cycles [52].

These findings highlight that improving the electrochemical performance of anode materials often requires complex strategies—such as interface engineering, the integration of multi-dimensional nanostructures, the use of ultra-small nanoparticles, and heteroatom adsorption [53]. To address these challenges, graphene has emerged as an effective support material due to its high surface area, flexibility, and excellent conductivity [54]. For instance, Luo et al. designed a flexible, hierarchical conductive network in which Sn quantum dots (QDs) were encapsulated in 2D reduced graphene oxide (RGO) scrolls, further embedded in 1D N, S co-adsorbed carbon nanofibers (NS-CNFs). The RGO layer improved conductivity and electrolyte interaction, while the NS-CNFs prevented Sn QD aggregation. This 3D Sn/NS-CNFs@RGO composite exhibited outstanding cycling stability (373 mAh $g^{-1}$ after 5000 cycles at 1 A $g^{-1}$) and excellent rate performance (189 mAh $g^{-1}$ at 10 A $g^{-1}$) [55]. Although Sn and Sb alloy-based anodes perform well initially, they suffer from significant volume expansion during the repeated sodiation/desodiation cycles, leading to capacity decay and limiting their long-term application in SIBs [56]. Researchers have attempted to overcome this issue by designing nanostructures with large hollow interiors to accommodate volume changes and improve sodium-ion diffusion kinetics.

Small carbon nanorings have attracted increasing interest due to their regenerative activity and structural stability [57–60]. In particular, carbon nanocluster rings—composed of multiple carbon atoms in ring-like geometries—have gained attention for their unique electronic and structural properties, following Hoffmann's theoretical proposal in 1966 [61–65]. The first successful synthesis of carbon nanorings was achieved by Kawase in 2003 [66]. These nanorings, characterized by $\pi$-conjugation and high ring strain, posed significant challenges for synthesis and structural control [67]. Subsequent advancements involved using various coupling reactions with active metal catalysts, eventually enabling the controlled synthesis of carbon nanorings [68–70]. Ullah et al. researched both the electrical and thermodynamic aspects of the F-adsorbed carbyne $C_{10}$ ring to create the $C_{10}F$ complex and its potential as an anode material in alkali-ion batteries using DFT and DLPNO-CCSD(T) calculations. $Li/Li^+$ and $Na/Na^+$ produce electrochemical cell voltages of 3.12 V and 2.80 V, respectively [71]. Tayyaba Murtaza et al. theoretically examined the potency of a pristine and halogen-adsorbed Graphdiyne analogue (GDY-28) as an anode material for sodium-ion batteries (NIBs). These designs result in greater cell voltages, which vary from 0.17 V for pure GDY-28 to 0.20 V and 0.52 V for $X^-$@GDY-28 (where $X^- = F^-, Cl^-$, and $Br^-$) [72]. In another work, by using density functional theory (DFT), Parimala et al. computationally evaluated the attachment of Na and $Na^+$ ions on $Ga_{12}N_{12}$, $Ga_{12}P_{12}$, and $Ga_{12}As_{12}$ nanocages as materials used as anodes for sodium-ion rechargeable batteries (SIBs). Furthermore, in contrast with the empty nanocages of SIBs, enveloping the complexes with halogens ($F^-$, $Cl^-$, and $Br^-$) led to increased cell voltage ($V_{cell}$). Fluorine-encapsulated $Na/Ga_{12}N_{12}$ has a higher $V_{cell}$ than chlorine and bromine, based on the overall facts [73]. The scientific community has also focused on the role of the solvent (electrolyte), which plays a critical role in electrochemical studies. In computational research, solvation effects are investigated using advanced methods such as density functional theory (DFT) combined with implicit and explicit solvent models. These models have proven effective in accurately predicting electrochemical series [74]. These methods are used to explore the redox nature, Gibbs free energy of solvation, and charge transfer mechanism [75], which are helpful in understanding the estimated cell voltage of batteries in practice. Herein, by using DFT calculations, the thermodynamic and electrochemical properties of $Na/Na^+@C_{12}$ complexes and then halogens ($X^- = Br^-, Cl^-, F^-$) as counter anions in the gas phase are studied for the enhancement of Na-ion battery cell voltage and overall performance.

## 2. Computational Methodology

DFT calculations were performed by using the Gaussian 09 package [76] and the results were further visualized by using GaussView 5.0 software [77]. DFT-based approaches are more precise and frequently used for atomic property analysis and structural optimization. Among the dispersion-corrected DFT methods, the range-separated $\omega$B97XD functional is commonly employed for electronic and thermodynamic property analysis [78–82]. $\omega$B97XD, along with the 6-31 + G (d, p) people basis set, was implemented for all property analyses of the considered structures. Optimization is performed to determine the correct structure of each isolated and complex structure. Optimization was followed by frequency calculations, which confirmed that all structures designed are true minima structures on the potential energy surface with positive frequencies. Zero-point corrected energy values obtained from the frequency calculation were used for interaction energy calculations.

Interaction energy is calculated from the zero-point corrected energies by using Equation (1), as presented below:

$$E_{int} = E_{complex} - (E_{surface} + E_{analyte}) \tag{1}$$

All calculations were performed in gas phase, and the absolute voltage values are therefore qualitative estimates. Cell voltage is actually the parameter used to estimate the potential of surface usage in secondary batteries. Cell voltage was calculated by implementing the Nernst Equation (2), given as:

$$V_{cell} = -\Delta G_{cell}/Fz \tag{2}$$

where z represents the atomic charge on the sodium atom/ion, F is for Faraday constant, and $-\Delta G_{cell}$ illustrates the change in the Gibbs free energies of the complexes.

Molecular orbital behavior was analyzed by performing Frontier molecular orbital analysis. In this analysis, we obtained information about the nature of the highest occupied (HOMOs) and lowest unoccupied molecular orbitals (LUMOs). This energy gap gives insight into the reactivity and electronic stability of a complex. The complex is either more reactive and electronically less stable or less reactive and electronically more stable. The difference between these frontier orbitals is known as the HOMO and LUMO gap ($E_{H\text{-}L}$), which is calculated by using Equation (3) below:

$$E_{H\text{-}L} = E_{LUMO} - E_{HOMO} \tag{3}$$

Natural bond orbital charge analysis was also performed to determine the shifting of charge from the sodium atom/ion towards the adsorbent surface or vice versa. The total density of state spectra was generated to explore the density of electronic states, the position of the frontier molecular orbitals before and after sodium adsorption, and the nature of electronic contribution during complexation.

## 3. Results and Discussions

### 3.1. Interaction of Na/Na$^+$ with the $C_{12}$ Nanoring

First of all, the pure $C_{12}$ nanoring without symmetry constraints was optimized, and a stable geometry is shown in Figure 1. The nanoring consists of alternating double and triple bonds. The bond distance between adjacent triple and double bonds is 1.24 and 1.36 Å, respectively, which is comparable to 1.33–1.34 Å for $C_{12}$ obtained using the GA/SA technique, as highlighted in the study performed by D.P. Kosimov [83]. Four potential adsorption sites are available in the $C_{12}$ nanoring: the carbon–carbon bonds, the ring center, the top of the ring, and directly above a carbon atom. These sites are proposed based on a previous study by Ullah et al. on halide adsorption in a $C_{10}$ nanoring for alkali metal batteries [71]. Among all of these four possible adsorption sites, Na/Na$^+$ are adsorbed and optimized to obtain the most stable position. In the optimized structure of Na@$C_{12}$, the Na atom occupies the top central position on the ring with an average distance of 1.46 Å. For Na$^+$, the most suitable and stable position is the placement of Na$^+$ on one side of the carbon nanoring, with a bond distance of 2.46 Å. Interaction energies calculated for Na@$C_{12}$ and Na$^+$@$C_{12}$ are $-50.08$ kcal mol$^{-1}$ and $-18.72$ kcal mol$^{-1}$, respectively. These results are similar to the early reported data on the interaction between sodium and three-dimensional porous carbon and have higher adsorption energy [84]. The calculated values for Na@$C_{12}$ and Na$^+$@$C_{12}$ prove that atomic sodifim's interaction with $C_{12}$ is stronger than that with the sodium cation. Previous work by Kosar et al. also showed the stronger interaction of an alkali meta (lithium) atom compared to a Lithium metal cation with pure $C_{60}$ nanomaterials [85]. The HOMO and LUMO values of pure $C_{12}$ are $-8.14$ and $-2.25$ eV, respectively, along with an energy gap of 5.88 eV. The HOMO and LUMO values changed to $-6.73$ and $-1.51$, respectively, after adsorption with pure Na, and the respective energy gap was 5.21 eV. In the case of Na$^+$, the HOMO and LUMO values were $-11.12$ and $-5.35$ eV, respectively, along with the H-L energy gap of 5.76 eV. The location of

HOMO and LUMO densities on the pure $C_{12}$ and its complexes with sodium/sodium cation are equally distributed on the $C_{12}$ ring, which shows delocalization of electronic density within the nanoring. The HOMO and LUMO densities are present on $C_{12}$ in the case of sodium/sodium cation adsorption on the $C_{12}$ nanoring, which shows the shifting of electronic density from sodium towards the $C_{12}$ nanoring. The more pronounced effect is seen in the LUMO density distribution on the sodium atom-adsorbed $C_{12}$ complex, where densities are shifted towards the C-C bonds in the $C_{12}$ nanoring. These results confirmed stronger electronic density interactions in $Na@C_{12}$ than in $Na^+@C_{12}$ complexes.

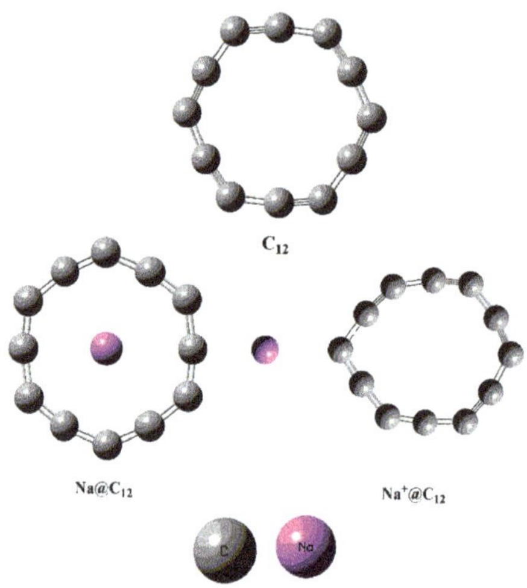


**Figure 1.** Optimized structures of the $C_{12}$ nanoring and sodium atom (Na)- and sodium cation ($Na^+$)-adsorbed $C_{12}$ complexes.

### 3.2. *Electrochemical Properties of Na/Na⁺@ Complexes C₁₂*

By assuming the $C_{12}$ nanoring as an anode for a sodium-ion battery, the following reactions occur between the anode and cathode:

Anode:

$$Na@C_{12} \leftrightarrow Na^+@C_{12} + e^- \tag{4}$$

Cathode:

$$Na^+ + e^- \leftrightarrow Na \tag{5}$$

Overall, the cell reaction is as follows:

$$Na@C_{12} + Na^+ \leftrightarrow Na + Na^+@C_{12} + \Delta G_{cell} \tag{6}$$

The overall Gibbs free energy change of the cell ($\Delta G_{cell}$) for the complete reaction occurring in a cell can be calculated using the following Equation (7):

$$\Delta G_{cell} = G(Na) + G(Na^+@C_{12}) - G(Na^+) - G(Na@C_{12}) \tag{7}$$

Here, G represents the Gibbs free energy of given complexes. The Gibbs free energy and cell voltage for $Na/Na^+$-adsorbed $C_{12}$ complexes are 30.57 kcal $mol^{-1}$ and $-1.32$ V, respectively. Another strategy was adopted to obtain the cell voltage in a favorable range. In this strategic way, the $C_{12}$ is adsorbed with the first three halide ions ($F^-$, $Cl^-$, and $Br^-$). The negative value of cell voltage depicts the destruction of the $C_{12}$ surface, which is not acceptable in practical applications, as reported in the literature [86].

### 3.3. Adsorption of the $C_{12}$ Nanoring with Halogens ($Br^-$, $Cl^-$, and $F^-$)

The $C_{12}$ nanoring adsorbed with halogens ($Br^-$, $Cl^-$, and $F^-$) by placing each halogen on four possible orientations. It was observed that for the adsorbed halogens on the $C_{12}$ nanoring, the most stable position is at one side of the carbon. After optimization, the bond distance between C and $Br^-$ is 1.93 Å in the $Br^-@C_{12}$ complex. The bond distance between C and $Cl^-$ is 1.78 Å., and in $C_{12}$ and $F^-$, the bond distance is 1.37 Å. Optimized geometries are presented in Figure 2. Adsorption of $Br^-$ with the $C_{12}$ nanoring shows stronger interaction as it is reflected through the interaction energy value of −50.32 kcal $mol^{-1}$. In the case of $Cl^-$, the interaction energy is −47.95 kcal $mol^{-1}$, and the strongest interaction is observed in the case of $F^-$ with $C_{12}$ (−84.79 kcal $mol^{-1}$). Researchers have observed strong interaction between halogens and carbon-based materials and their uses in secondary batteries, as we observed in the current study [87].

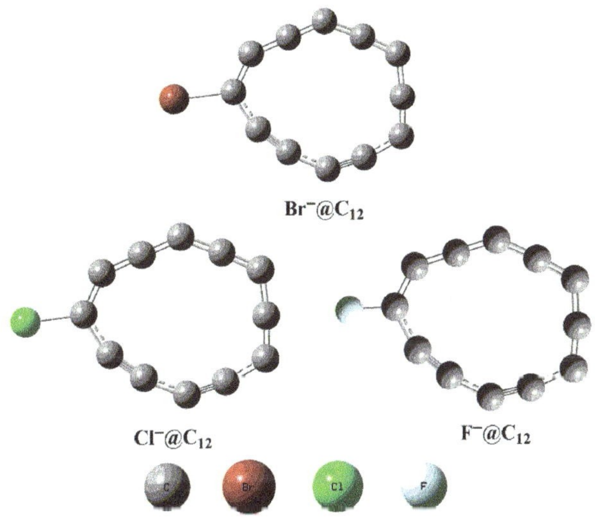


**Figure 2.** Optimized structures of halogen-adsorbed $C_{12}$ complexes.

After adsorption with bromine, the values of HOMO and LUMO change to −3.69 and 1.82 eV, respectively, with a gap of 5.52 eV. Upon adsorption of chlorine, the values of HOMO and LUMO change to −3.66 and 1.86 eV, respectively, with a gap of 5.53 eV. After adsorption with fluorine, the HOMO and LUMO energy values change to −3.54 and 2.03 eV, respectively, and have a gap of 5.58 eV, showing strong interaction between halide ions and the carbon nanoring. In halide-adsorbed complexes, the HOMO and LUMO densities are equally distributed on the $C_{12}$ nanoring. The large amount of HOMO is present on the halide ion, which shows that it is an electron-rich region and has the ability to provide density to the nanoring. This is confirmed from a smaller LUMO density localization on the halide, as well as in each of the halide-adsorbed $C_{12}$ complexes.

### 3.4. Adsorption of Na/$Na^+$ on Halides@$C_{12}$ Complexes

The presence of halide ions is supposed to enhance the interaction between $Na^+$ and the $C_{12}$ nanoring as compared to Na. The reason for the greater interaction energy of $Na^+/X^-@C_{12}$ is the electrostatic force of attraction between $Na^+$ and the $X^-@C_{12}$ nanoring.

After placing sodium in the middle of the ring adsorbed with $Br^-$, the bond distance between C and $Br^-$ is 1.92 Å, and the average distance of Na in the center of the ring is 1.20 Å (see Figure 3). In case of $Na^+$, the bond distance between C and $Br^-$ is 1.89 Å and the average distance of $Na^+$ from the center of the ring is 1.45 Å. The optimized complex of $Na^+/Cl@C_{12}$ showed that the bond distance between C and $Cl^-$ is 1.75 Å and the average distance of $Na^+$ from the center of the ring is 1.46 Å. In the case of fluorine, the bond distance between C and $F^-$ is 1.38 Å, and the average distance of Na from the center of the ring is 1.21 Å. After placing $Na^+$ in the center of the ring, the bond distance between C and $F^-$ is 1.35 Å, which is less than the former ones. The average distance of $Na^+$ from the ring in the center is 1.49 Å. In the case of the sodium cation, interaction with the halogen-adsorbed carbon nanoring is stronger, due to which the bond length is decreased as compared to interaction with the sodium atom. As reported in the literature, halide anions shifted their electronic density towards the GDY-28 surface after adsorption of the selected halide anions on the GDY-28 nanoflake. The nanoflake therefore works as a strong Lewis base, increasing the interaction between $Na^+$ and thehalides@GDY-28 nanoflake. Specifically, the electrostatic interactions between the cationic $Na^+$ and the more strongly nucleophilic $F^-$ halide anion of the halides$^-$@GDY-28 nanoflake is responsible for the significant interaction energy of the $Na^+$/halide anion@GDY-28 nanoflake. Among all halides, the strongest interaction is observed for the $Na^+/F^-$@GDY-28 nanoflake because of the higher electronegative nature of $F^-$ compared to the other two halide anions ($Cl^-$ and $Br^-$) [72]. Moreover, in the case of $Na/Na^+$ adsorbed on the halogen-adsorbed $Ga_{12}N_{12}$ surface, the sodium cation showed high values of interaction energy relative to the sodium atom [73].

Interaction energies for both $Na/Na^+$ with halides@C12 nanorings were also calculated and given in Table 1. For $Na^+$ at $Br^-@C_{12}$, the interaction energy value is −103.82 kcal mol$^{-1}$, which shows its stronger interaction with the carbon nanoring as compared to atomic Na with the $Br^-@C_{12}$ complex. For $Na^+$ at the $Cl^-$-adsorbed $C_{12}$, the interaction energy value is −103.04 kcal mol$^{-1}$, which shows its stronger interaction with the carbon nanoring as compared to Na. Lastly, Na and $Na^+$ are adsorbed on the $F^-@C_{12}$ complex where their interaction energies are −14.56 and −103.64 kcal mol$^{-1}$ for $Na/F^-@C_{12}$ and $Na^+/F^-@C_{12}$ complexes, respectively. As reported in the literature, Murtaza et al. adsorbed pure GDY_28 with halides to design a sodium-ion secondary battery, and the respective interaction energies are −14.10 and −53.62 for Na and $Na^+$ adsorbed on $Br^-@C_{12}$, −16.32 and −56.40 kcal mol$^{-1}$ for Na and $Na^+$ adsorbed on $Cl^-@C_{12}$, and −28.46 and −90.75 kcal mol$^{-1}$ for Na and $Na^+$ adsorbed on $F^-@C_{12}$, respectively [72].

**Table 1.** Bond distance Å, interaction energy $E_{int}$ (kcal mol$^{-1}$), Gibbs free energy of the cell $\Delta G_{cell}$ (kcal mol$^{-1}$), and cell voltage $V_{cell}$ (V) of pure $C_{12}$, $Na@C_{12}$, $Na^+@C_{12}$, $Br^-@C_{12}$, $Br^-/Na@C_{12}$, $Br^-/Na^+@C_{12}$, $Cl^-@C_{12}$, $Cl^-/Na@C_{12}$, $Cl^-/Na^+@C_{12}$, $F^-@C_{12}$, $F^-/Na@C_{12}$, and $F^-/Na^+@C_{12}$ complexes.

| Complexes | Bond Distance (Å) | $E_{int}$ (kcal mol$^{-1}$) | $\Delta G_{cell}$ (kcal mol$^{-1}$) | $V_{cell}$ (V) |
|---|---|---|---|---|
| Pure $C_{12}$ | 1.30 | ----- | ----- | ---- |
| $Na@C_{12}$ | C-Na = 1.46 | −50.08 | 30.57 | −1.32 |
| $Na^+@C_{12}$ | C-$Na^+$ = 2.46 | −18.72 | | |
| $Br^-@C_{12}$ | C-$Br^-$ = 1.93 | −50.32 | ----- | |

**Table 1.** *Cont.*

| Complexes | Bond Distance (Å) | $E_{int}$ (kcal mol$^{-1}$) | $\Delta G_{cell}$ (kcal mol$^{-1}$) | $V_{cell}$ (V) |
|---|---|---|---|---|
| $Br^-/Na@C_{12}$ | C-$Br^-$ = 1.92<br>C-Na = 1.20 | −51.47 | −52.36 | 2.27 |
| $Br^-/Na^+@C_{12}$ | C-$Br^-$ = 1.89<br>$Na^+$-C = 1.43 | −103.82 | | |
| $Cl^-@C_{12}$ | C-$Cl^-$ = 1.78 | −47.95 | ----- | ----- |
| $Cl^-/Na@C_{12}$ | C-$Cl^-$ = 1.78<br>Na-C = 1.20 | −50.32 | −52.56 | 2.28 |
| $Cl^-/Na^+@C_{12}$ | C-$Cl^-$ = 1.74<br>$Na^+$-C = 1.49 | −103.04 | | |
| $F^-@C_{12}$ | C-$F^-$ = 1.37 | −84.79 | | |
| $F^-/Na@C_{12}$ | C-$F^-$ = 1.38<br>Na-C = 1.21 | −14.56 | −58.31 | 2.52 |
| $F^-/Na^+@C_{12}$ | C-$F^-$ = 1.35<br>$Na^+$-C = 1.46 | −103.64 | | |

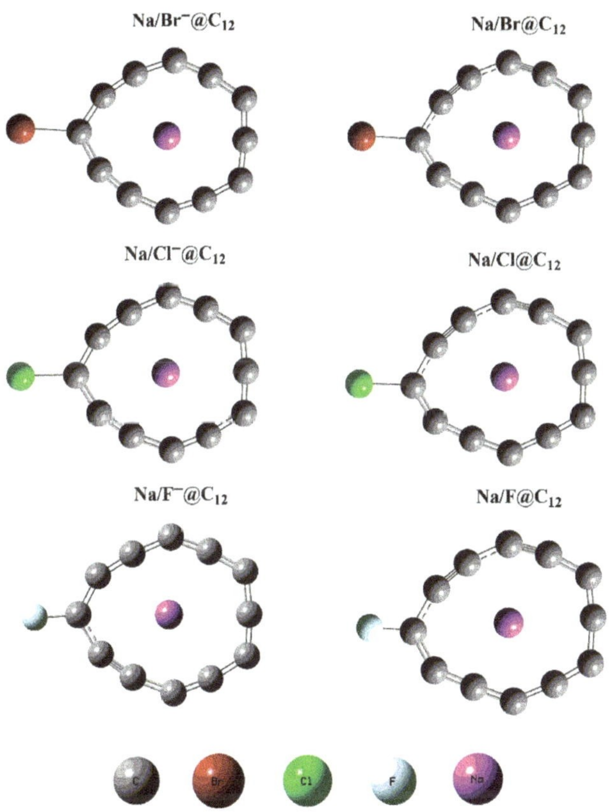


**Figure 3.** Optimized structures of Na/$Na^+$ adsorbed on halide ($Br^-$, $Cl^-$, and $F^-$)-adsorbed $C_{12}$ complexes.

By placing the Na atom in the center of the adsorbed carbon nanoring with bromine, with an obvious change in HOMO and LUMO values and in their energy, a gap is noticed. The values of HOMO, LUMO, and energy gap are −2.73, 2.14, and 4.87 eV. But the interaction between the Na cation and the halogen-adsorbed nanoring is stronger, as compared to the Na atom. As shown for Na/$Br^-$@$C_{12}$, the HOMO and LUMO and their gap values are

−7.46, −2.22, and 5.41 eV, respectively, and stabilize the complex. By placing the Na atom in the center of a carbon nanoring adsorbed with chlorine, the HOMO and LUMO energies and energy gap values are −2.67, 2.15, and 4.82 eV. But for the Na cation with $Cl^-@C_{12}$ complexes, −7.67, −2.21, and 5.46 eV are the HOMO and LUMO energies and their energy gap values, respectively. By placing the Na atom in the center of the adsorbed carbon nanoring with $F^-$, the energy values of the frontier molecular orbitals (FMOs = HOMO and LUMO) and energy gap are −2.53, 2.16, and 4.69 eV. But for Na cation@$F^-@C_{12}$, the values are −7.68, −2.12, and 5.56 eV for HOMO and LUMO energies and their energy gaps, respectively. It is clear that the sodium cation interacts more strongly with halides adsorbed on carbon nanorings and stabilizes the complexes. The reason is the shifting of electronic charge from halide anions towards the surface of the $C_{12}$ nanoring in each of the halides$^-@C_{12}$ complexes as discussed vide infra. When the Na cation is adsorbed on the halides$^-@C_{12}$ complexes, the electrostatic interactions occur between $Na^+$ and the anionic surface of halides$^-@C_{12}$. But when the sodium atom is adsorbed, there is electronic repulsion between sodium and the $C_{12}$ surface in each of the halides$^-@C_{12}$ complexes. Due to these interactions, Na cation adsorption is electronically stronger compared to the sodium atom, as reported in previous reports on halide-adsorbed carbon-based nanomaterials for sodium-ion batteries [88–90]. The localization of HOMO and LUMO is presented in Figure 4, which clearly shows the localization of HOMO on the halide and $C_{12}$ nanoring in sodium cation-adsorbed halides$^-@C_{12}$ complexes. A small amount of LUMO is also seen on the halide and $C_{12}$ nanoring, which illustrates the shifting of charge from the halide to the ring and then from the ring towards the sodium cation. On the other side, HOMO is found on C-C bonds in the $C_{12}$ nanoring in atomic sodium-adsorbed halides$^-@C_{12}$ complexes. A sufficient amount of LUMO is also seen on the top of the sodium atom, which illustrates the shifting of charge from the halide to the ring and also from the sodium atom towards the $C_{12}$ nanoring, which results in electronic repulsion, as discussed vide supra.

In secondary batteries, the major goal is to increase cell voltage. The required cell voltage is obtained if there is strong interaction between the sodium cation and the halide-adsorbed nanomaterials because stronger interaction results in higher interaction energies and Gibbs free energies, which results in achieving the required cell voltage. In the current work, an increase in interaction energy favors the increase in the Gibbs free energy of the cell ($\Delta G_{cell}$) for the designed complexes. Gibbs free energy increased due to the strong interaction between $Na/Na^+$ and halide ($Br^-$, $Cl^-$, and $F^-$) @$C_{12}$ complexes. This increase in Gibbs free energy produces a larger cell potential and increases the cell voltage of the $C_{12}$ nanoring. The chemical reaction of the $C_{12}$ nanoring with the sodium atom/cation is endothermic in nature, but the reaction becomes exothermic after introducing halide ions into the $C_{12}$ nanoring. The Gibbs free energies of bromide-adsorbed $C_{12}$, chloride-adsorbed $C_{12}$, and fluoride-adsorbed $C_{12}$ complexes for complexation with sodium atom/cations are −52.36, −52.56, and −58.31 kcal $mol^{-1}$, respectively. A higher Gibbs free energy corresponds to an increase in the cell voltage of these complexes. The calculated cell voltages for $Br^-$, $Cl^-$, and $F^-$-adsorbed $C_{12}$ nanorings in the gas phase are 2.27 V, 2.28 V, and 2.52 V, respectively, for potential use in sodium-ion batteries. These values are significantly higher than the cell voltage of the unadsorbed $C_{12}$ nanoring, which is –1.32 V. The Gibbs free energy of the pure $C_{12}$ nanoring is calculated as 30.57 kcal $mol^{-1}$.

The positive Gibbs free energy makes the $C_{12}$ nanoring unfavorable for the generation of the required cell voltage, which is also clear from its calculated cell voltage (−1.32 V). Among all complexes, the desired cell voltage is obtained for the $Br^-@C_{12}$ complex. In a previous report by Murtaza et al., the required cell voltage of the halide-adsorbed porous carbon nanosheet is the desired cell voltage [72], which justifies our result. The reason for the better cell voltage of the bromide-adsorbed $C_{12}$ nanoring is the strong interaction between the sodium atom and cation with the $Br^{-}@C_{12}$ nanoring, as discussed vide supra.

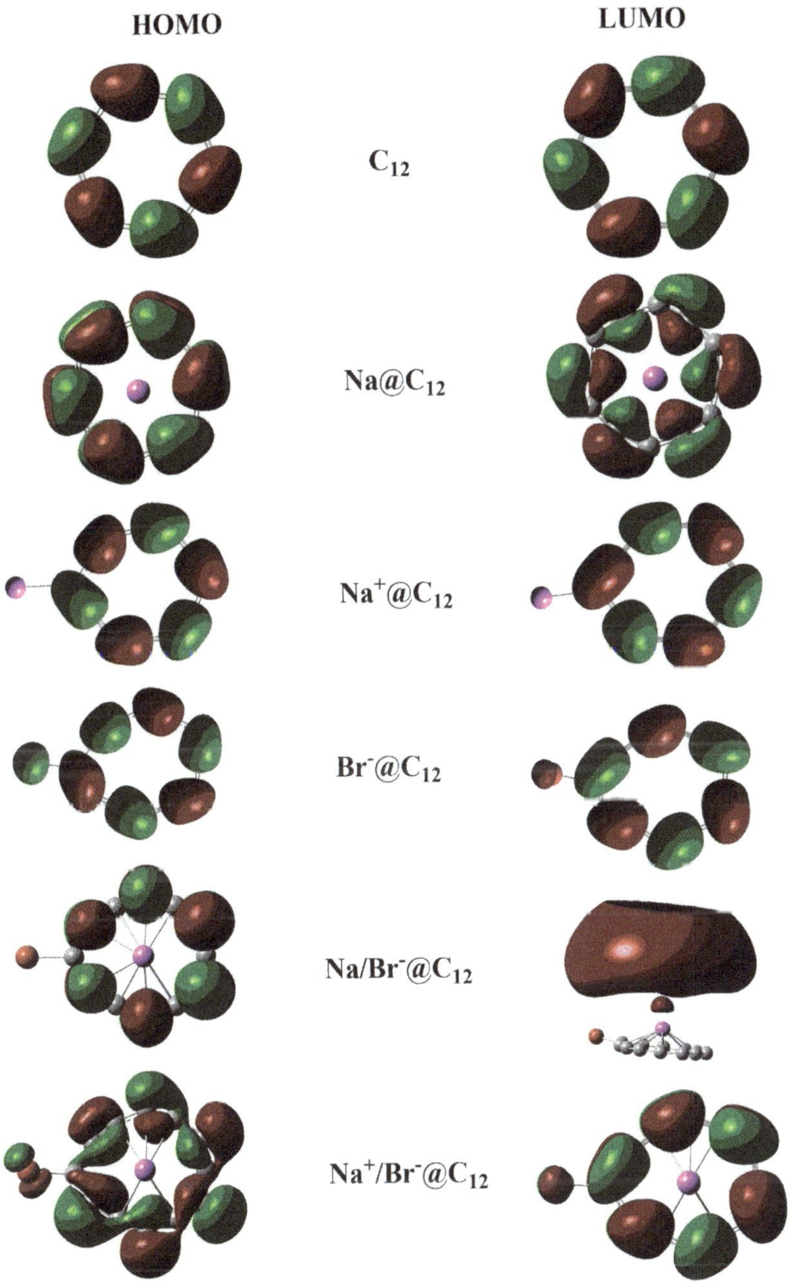


**Figure 4.** Frontier molecular orbitals such as HOMO and LUMO of pure $C_{12}$, $Na@C_{12}$, $Na^{+}@C_{12}$, $Na/Br^{-}@C_{12}$, and $Na^{+}/Br^{-}@C_{12}$.

### 3.5. NBO Charge Analysis

Natural bond orbital (NBO) charge analysis was performed using the same method (ωB97XD/6-31 + G (d, p)). From the NBO results reported in Table 2, the overall charge on the $C_{12}$ nanoring is 0.00 | e | and the surface is neutral. After Na adsorption with $C_{12}$, the charge on sodium is 0.96 | e |, and the surface charge changes to −0.96 | e |, showing that charge is transferred from Na to the carbon surface. When the $C_{12}$ ring is adsorbed with $Na^+$, the charge on the cation is 0.97 | e |, and the surface charge is at a positive value of 0.02 | e |, showing the fact that charge has been transferred from the carbon surface towards the cation. Upon adsorption of halogens ($Br^-$, $Cl^-$, and $F^-$) on the carbon surface, an obvious change in carbon surface charge is observed due to the transfer of charge from halide ions towards the surface, as halogens are electronegative in nature and are anions, so they have a tendency to donate electrons to the surface. Values of charges obtained through NBO analysis show that after adsorption of $Br^-$ on the $C_{12}$ nanoring, charge on the halide ion is −0.01 | e |, and charge on the surface changes from 0.00 | e | to −0.98 | e |. This indicates that charge is transferred from the halide ion towards the carbon surface. Upon adsorption of Na with the $Br^-$-adsorbed carbon nanoring, charge on Na is 0.95 | e |, on $Br^-$, it is 0.01 | e |, and the surface charge is −1.96 | e |. This shows greater charge transfer from the halide towards the carbon surface. When $Na^+$ is adsorbed, charge on the halide changes to 0.10 | e |, on $Na^+$, it is 0.96 | e |, and charge on the carbon surface is −1.06 | e |. When $Cl^-$ is adsorbed on the carbon nanoring, charge on $Cl^-$ is −0.07 | e |, and the surface charge is −0.92 | e |. This indicates that the charge is transferred from $Cl^-$ towards the carbon surface. Upon adsorption of Na with this complex, charge on $Cl^-$ changes from −0.07 | e | to −0.05 | e |, and the surface charge becomes −1.89 | e |. Likewise, in the case of $Cl^-/Na^+@C_{12}$, the surface charge changes to −0.98 | e |, and charge on $Cl^-$ is 0.02 | e |, indicating that charge is transferred towards the sodium cation. In the case of fluorine adsorption with the pure carbon nanoring, the charge on $F^-$ is −0.37 | e | and on the carbon surface, it is −0.62 | e |, showing that from $F^-$, the charge is transferred towards the nanoring's surface. Upon adsorbing Na, charge on Na is 0.95 | e |, charge on $F^-$ changes from −0.37 | e | to −0.39 | e |, and charge on the carbon surface is −1.56 | e | In the case of $Na^+$, charge on $F^-$ is −0.33 | e |, on $Na^+$, it is 0.96 | e |, and charge on the surface is −0.62 | e |. It is clear from the above analysis that charge is transferred from Na and halogens towards the carbon surface.

**Table 2.** HOMO–LUMO energies, energy gap ($E_{H\text{-}L}$ gap), NBO charges on the pure $C_{12}$ surface ($NBO_s$), NBO charges on the pure sodium metal/cation ($NBO_m$), and NBO charges on each halide ion ($NBO_x$) in pure $C_{12}$, $Na@C_{12}$, $Na^+@C_{12}$, $Br^-@C_{12}$, $Br^-/Na@C_{12}$, $Br^-/Na^+@C_{12}$, $Cl^-@C_{12}$, $Cl^-/Na@C_{12}$, $Cl^-/Na^+@C_{12}$, $F^-@C_{12}$, $F^-/Na@C_{12}$, and $F^-/Na^+@C_{12}$ complexes.

| Complexes | $E_H$ eV | $E_L$ eV | $E_{H\text{-}L}$ | $NBO_s$ \| e \| | $NBO_m$ \| e \| | $NBO_x$ \| e \| |
|---|---|---|---|---|---|---|
| Pure $C_{12}$ | −8.14 | −2.25 | 5.88 | 0.00 | ----- | ----- |
| $Na@C_{12}$ | −6.73 | −1.51 | 5.21 | −0.96 | 0.96 | ----- |
| $Na^+@C_{12}$ | −11.12 | −5.35 | 5.76 | 0.02 | 0.97 | ----- |
| $Br^-@C_{12}$ | −3.69 | 1.82 | 5.52 | −0.98 | ----- | −0.01 |
| $Br^-/Na@C_{12}$ | −2.73 | 2.14 | 4.87 | −1.96 | 0.95 | 0.01 |
| $Br^-/Na^+@C_{12}$ | −7.64 | −2.22 | 5.41 | −1.06 | 0.96 | 0.10 |
| $Cl^-@C_{12}$ | −3.66 | 1.86 | 5.53 | −0.92 | ----- | −0.07 |
| $Cl^-/Na@C_{12}$ | −2.67 | 2.15 | 4.82 | −1.89 | 0.95 | −0.05 |
| $Cl^-/Na^+@C_{12}$ | −7.67 | −2.21 | 5.46 | −0.98 | 0.96 | 0.02 |
| $F^-@C_{12}$ | −3.54 | 2.03 | 5.58 | −0.62 | ----- | −0.37 |
| $F^-/Na@C_{12}$ | −2.53 | 2.16 | 4.69 | −1.56 | 0.95 | −0.39 |
| $F^-/Na^+@C_{12}$ | −7.68 | −2.12 | 5.56 | −0.62 | 0.96 | −0.33 |

### 3.6. Partial Density of State (PDOS) and Total Density of State (TDOS) Analysis

TDOS analysis is used to study density of states, which provides information about the values of energy states in occupied and unoccupied orbitals in pure form ($C_{12}$ nanoring) and adsorbed complexes. TDOS gives information about the complexes, and PDOS gives additional information about the involvement of individual species ($C_{12}$ nanoring, sodium atom/cation, and halide ions ($X^-$ = $Br^-$, $Cl^-$, $F^-$) in each of the complexes. Graphical representations of TDOS and PDOS spectra are given in Figure 5. From Figure 5, energy gaps in the case of pure $C_{12}$ and after adsorption with Na/$Na^+$ are quite visible, as discussed in the FMO analysis. Adsorption with Na shows a significant difference in the shifting of energy states, hence proving stronger interaction with the pure $C_{12}$ nanoring as compared to $Na^+$. The PDOS peak of Na shows more involvement in HOMO than the sodium cation. The overlapping of the peaks is shown in both, but more overlapping is seen in sodium, which justifies the FMO results. The graphs show that TDOS peaks are quite intense for the Na@$C_{12}$ complex and depict their high electrostatic interactions.

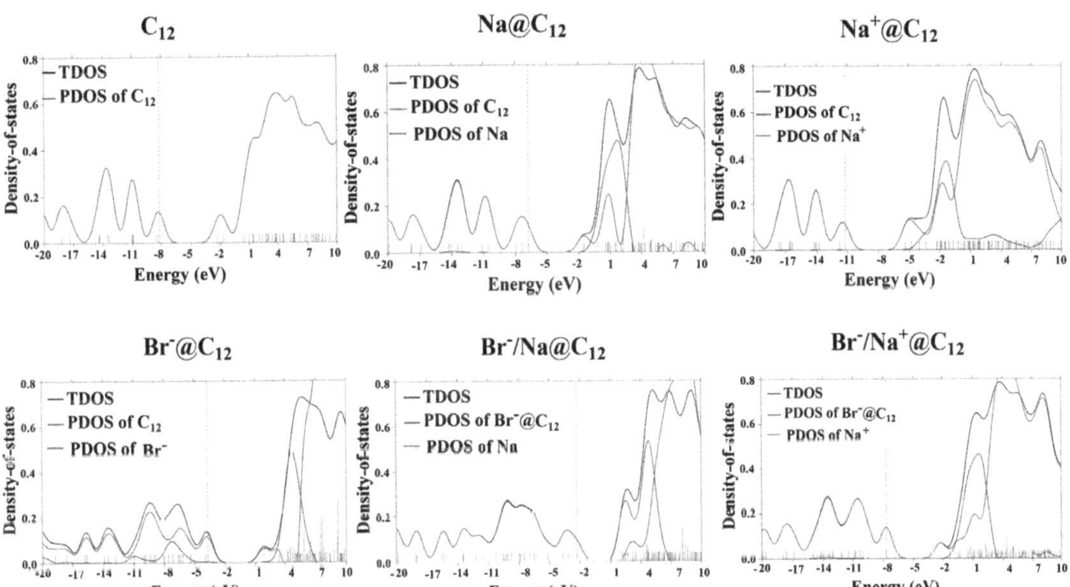


**Figure 5.** Partial density of states (PDOS) and total density of states (TDOS) of the pure Na/$Na^+$-adsorbed $C_{12}$ nanoring and the Na/$Na^+$-adsorbed $Br^-$@$C_{12}$ complex.

We noticed that halides have prominent involvement in the HOMOs of all of the halide-adsorbed $C_{12}$ complexes. The reason may be the formation of new orbitals due to shifting of electronic density from halides to the $C_{12}$ nanoring. By adsorbing Na and $Na^+$ on halide-adsorbed $C_{12}$ complexes, there is a significant change in energy states for the sodium cation as it interacts more strongly with the halide-adsorbed $C_{12}$ complexes as compared to the sodium atom. In the above case, the $Na^+$-adsorbed halogen-adsorbed carbon nanoring shows more intense peaks due to strong electrostatic interaction with the halide-adsorbed $C_{12}$ nanoring. The overlapping of the peaks also depicts the stronger interactions between the sodium cation and the halide-adsorbed $C_{12}$ complexes. The spectra of DOS analysis support the FMO results.

## 4. Conclusions

The electrochemical properties of a $C_{12}$ nanoring are explored by using the DFT method to assess its potential application as an anode material in Na-ion batteries. For this purpose, the thermodynamic stability of Na@$C_{12}$ and $Na^+$@$C_{12}$ was analyzed, whereby sodium forms more stable complexes than the sodium cation. The $E_{int.}$ of sodium atom is −50.08 and that of the sodium cation is −18.72 kcal $mol^{-1}$ with $C_{12}$. The small change in Gibbs free energy and cell voltage of −1.32 V is not acceptable for the practical use of the sodium-adsorbed $C_{12}$ nanoring. Using another strategy, counter halide anion ($F^-$, $Cl^-$, and $Br^-$) adsorption on the $C_{12}$ nanoring is investigated in this study to examine the cell voltage. Adsorption of Na/$Na^+$ on the halogen-adsorbed ($X^-$ = $Br^-$, $Cl^-$, $F^-$) $C_{12}$ significantly enhances the change in Gibbs free energy value, which ultimately increases their cell voltage. The strong interaction of $Na^+$ is seen with halide-adsorbed $C_{12}$ complexes in comparison with the Na atom. These interactions result in increasing interaction energies, Gibbs free energies, and, ultimately, increasing cell voltage. The cell voltage increases as the electronegativity of halide ions increases. In the gas phase, $Br^-$@$C_{12}$ exhibits a Gibbs free energy of -52.36 kcal·$mol^{-1}$, corresponding to a cell voltage of 2.27 V. Overall, these calculations were performed in the gas phase without the implementation of an electrolyte, and we conclude that these are qualitative estimations.

**Author Contributions:** Conceptualization, A.G. and N.K.; methodology, A.G. and R.M.; validation, T.M., R.M., and N.K.; formal analysis, N.K. and A.G.; investigation and resources, T.M. and N.K.; data curation, T.M.; writing—original draft, R.M. and T.M. All authors have read and agreed to the published version of the manuscript.

**Funding:** HEC Pakistan (20-16279/NRPU/HEC/2021-2020).

**Institutional Review Board Statement:** Not applicable.

**Informed Consent Statement:** Not applicable.

**Data Availability Statement:** Data will be made available by the corresponding author upon request.

**Acknowledgments:** Naveen Kosar acknowledges the Higher Education Commission of Pakistan for awarding HEC-NRPU project (20-16279/NRPU/HEC/2021-2020). The authors also acknowledge COMSATS University Islamabad, Abbottabad Campus, and the University of Management and Technology, Lahore, for their financial and technical support.

**Conflicts of Interest:** The authors declare no conflicts of interest.

## References

1. Shao, Z.; Haile, S.M. A High-Performance Cathode for the next Generation of Solid-Oxide Fuel Cells. *Mater. Sustain. Energy A Collect. Peer-Rev. Res. Rev. Artic. Nat. Publ. Gr.* **2010**, *3*, 255–258. [CrossRef]
2. Cheng, F.; Chen, J. Lithium-Air Batteries: Something from Nothing. *Nat. Chem.* **2012**, *4*, 962–963. [CrossRef] [PubMed]
3. Schon, T.B.; McAllister, B.T.; Li, P.-F.; Seferos, D.S. The Rise of Organic Electrode Materials for Energy Storage. *Chem. Soc. Rev.* **2016**, *45*, 6345–6404. [CrossRef] [PubMed]
4. Bashir, S.; Hanumandla, P.; Huang, H.-Y.; Liu, J.L. Nanostructured Materials for Advanced Energy Conversion and Storage Devices: Safety Implications at End-of-Life Disposal. In *Nanostructured Materials for Next-Generation Energy Storage and Conversion*; Springer: Berlin/Heidelberg, Germany, 2018; Volume 4, pp. 517–542. ISBN 9783662563649.
5. Liang, Y.; Tao, Z.; Chen, J. Organic Electrode Materials for Rechargeable Lithium Batteries. *Adv. Energy Mater.* **2012**, *2*, 742–769. [CrossRef]
6. Song, Z.; Zhou, H. Towards Sustainable and Versatile Energy Storage Devices: An Overview of Organic Electrode Materials. *Energy Environ. Sci.* **2013**, *6*, 2280. [CrossRef]
7. Morita, Y.; Nishida, S.; Murata, T.; Moriguchi, M.; Ueda, A.; Satoh, M.; Arifuku, K.; Sato, K.; Takui, T. Organic Tailored Batteries Materials Using Stable Open-Shell Molecules with Degenerate Frontier Orbitals. *Nat. Mater.* **2011**, *10*, 947–951. [CrossRef]
8. Wu, H.; Shevlin, S.A.; Meng, Q.; Guo, W.; Meng, Y.; Lu, K.; Wei, Z.; Guo, Z. Flexible and Binder-Free Organic Cathode for High-Performance Lithium-Ion Batteries. *Adv. Mater.* **2014**, *26*, 3338–3343. [CrossRef]

9. Nishide, H.; Oyaizu, K. Toward Flexible Batteries. *Science (80-)* **2008**, *319*, 737–738. [CrossRef]
10. Williams, D.L.; Byrne, J.J.; Driscoll, J.S. A High Energy Density Lithium/Dichloroisocyanuric Acid Battery System. *J. Electrochem. Soc.* **1969**, *116*, 2. [CrossRef]
11. Rudola, A.; Rennie, A.J.R.; Heap, R.; Meysami, S.S.; Lowbridge, A.; Mazzali, F.; Sayers, R.; Wright, C.J.; Barker, J. Commercialisation of High Energy Density Sodium-Ion Batteries: Faradion's Journey and Outlook. *J. Mater. Chem. A* **2021**, *9*, 8279–8302. [CrossRef]
12. Chen, R.; Luo, R.; Huang, Y.; Wu, F.; Li, L. Advanced High Energy Density Secondary Batteries with Multi-Electron Reaction Materials. *Adv. Sci.* **2016**, *3*, 1600051. [CrossRef]
13. Chen, C.-Y.; Kiko, T.; Hosokawa, T.; Matsumoto, K.; Nohira, T.; Hagiwara, R. Ionic Liquid Electrolytes with High Sodium Ion Fraction for High-Rate and Long-Life Sodium Secondary Batteries. *J. Power Sources* **2016**, *332*, 51–59. [CrossRef]
14. Xie, F.; Niu, Y.; Zhang, Q.; Guo, Z.; Hu, Z.; Zhou, Q.; Xu, Z.; Li, Y.; Yan, R.; Lu, Y.; et al. Screening Heteroatom Configurations for Reversible Sloping Capacity Promises High-Power Na-Ion Batteries. *Angew. Chem. Int. Ed.* **2022**, *61*, e202116394. [CrossRef] [PubMed]
15. Nagmani; Pahari, D.; Verma, P.; Puravankara, S. Are Na-Ion Batteries Nearing the Energy Storage Tipping Point?—Current Status of Non-Aqueous, Aqueous, and Solid-Sate Na-Ion Battery Technologies for Sustainable Energy Storage. *J. Energy Storage* **2022**, *56*, 105961. [CrossRef]
16. Jian, Z.; Raju, V.; Li, Z.; Xing, Z.; Hu, Y.; Ji, X. A High-Power Symmetric Na-Ion Pseudocapacitor. *Adv. Funct. Mater.* **2015**, *25*, 5778–5785. [CrossRef]
17. Nithya, C.; Gopukumar, S. Sodium Ion Batteries: A Newer Electrochemical Storage. *WIREs Energy Environ.* **2015**, *4*, 253–278. [CrossRef]
18. Larcher, D.; Tarascon, J.-M. Towards Greener and More Sustainable Batteries for Electrical Energy Storage. *Nat. Chem.* **2015**, *7*, 19–29. [CrossRef]
19. Delmas, C. Sodium and Sodium-Ion Batteries: 50 Years of Research. *Adv. Energy Mater.* **2018**, *8*, 1703137. [CrossRef]
20. Zhang, Y.; Liu, W.; Wang, T.; Du, Y.; Cui, Y.; Liu, S.; Wang, H.; Liu, S.; Chen, M.; Zhou, J. Space-Confined Fabrication of MoS 2 @Carbon Tubes with Semienclosed Architecture Achieving Superior Cycling Capability for Sodium Ion Storage. *Adv. Mater. Interfaces* **2020**, *7*, 2000953. [CrossRef]
21. Park, J.; Lee, M.; Feng, D.; Huang, Z.; Hinckley, A.C.; Yakovenko, A.; Zou, X.; Cui, Y.; Bao, Z. Stabilization of Hexaaminobenzene in a 2D Conductive Metal–Organic Framework for High Power Sodium Storage. *J. Am. Chem. Soc.* **2018**, *140*, 10315–10323. [CrossRef]
22. Fang, G.; Wu, Z.; Zhou, J.; Zhu, C.; Cao, X.; Lin, T.; Chen, Y.; Wang, C.; Pan, A.; Liang, S. Observation of Pseudocapacitive Effect and Fast Ion Diffusion in Bimetallic Sulfides as an Advanced Sodium-Ion Battery Anode. *Adv. Energy Mater.* **2018**, *8*, 1703155. [CrossRef]
23. Chen, Y.; Li, X.; Park, K.; Lu, W.; Wang, C.; Xue, W.; Yang, F.; Zhou, J.; Suo, L.; Lin, T.; et al. Nitrogen-Doped Carbon for Sodium-Ion Battery Anode by Self-Etching and Graphitization of Bimetallic MOF-Based Composite. *Chem* **2017**, *3*, 152–163. [CrossRef]
24. Ding, J.; Wang, H.; Li, Z.; Kohandehghan, A.; Cui, K.; Xu, Z.; Zahiri, B.; Tan, X.; Lotfabad, E.M.; Olsen, B.C.; et al. Carbon Nanosheet Frameworks Derived from Peat Moss as High Performance Sodium Ion Battery Anodes. *ACS Nano* **2013**, *7*, 11004–11015. [CrossRef] [PubMed]
25. Li, L.; Zheng, Y.; Zhang, S.; Yang, J.; Shao, Z.; Guo, Z. Recent Progress on Sodium Ion Batteries: Potential High-Performance Anodes. *Energy Environ. Sci.* **2018**, *11*, 2310–2340. [CrossRef]
26. Fatima, H.; Zhong, Y.; Wu, H.; Shao, Z. Recent Advances in Functional Oxides for High Energy Density Sodium-Ion Batteries. *Mater. Rep. Energy* **2021**, *1*, 100022. [CrossRef]
27. Muñoz-Márquez, M.Á.; Saurel, D.; Gómez-Cámer, J.L.; Casas-Cabanas, M.; Castillo-Martínez, E.; Rojo, T. Na-Ion Batteries for Large Scale Applications: A Review on Anode Materials and Solid Electrolyte Interphase Formation. *Adv. Energy Mater.* **2017**, *7*, 1700463. [CrossRef]
28. Park, J.Y.; Kim, S.J.; Chang, J.H.; Seo, H.K.; Lee, J.Y.; Yuk, J.M. Atomic Visualization of a Non-Equilibrium Sodiation Pathway in Copper Sulfide. *Nat. Commun.* **2018**, *9*, 922. [CrossRef]
29. Olsson, E.; Chai, G.; Dove, M.; Cai, Q. Adsorption and Migration of Alkali Metals (Li, Na, and K) on Pristine and Defective Graphene Surfaces. *Nanoscale* **2019**, *11*, 5274–5284. [CrossRef]
30. Kulish, V.V.; Malyi, O.I.; Persson, C.; Wu, P. Phosphorene as an Anode Material for Na-Ion Batteries: A First-Principles Study. *Phys. Chem. Chem. Phys.* **2015**, *17*, 13921–13928. [CrossRef]
31. Liu, Q.; Wu, F.; Mu, D.; Wu, B. A Theoretical Study on Na + Solvation in Carbonate Ester and Ether Solvents for Sodium-Ion Batteries. *Phys. Chem. Chem. Phys.* **2020**, *22*, 2164–2175. [CrossRef]
32. Jin, T.; Li, H.; Zhu, K.; Wang, P.-F.; Liu, P.; Jiao, L. Polyanion-Type Cathode Materials for Sodium-Ion Batteries. *Chem. Soc. Rev.* **2020**, *49*, 2342–2377. [CrossRef] [PubMed]

33. Hwang, J.-Y.; Myung, S.-T.; Sun, Y.-K. Sodium-Ion Batteries: Present and Future. *Chem. Soc. Rev.* **2017**, *46*, 3529–3614. [CrossRef] [PubMed]
34. Weltner, W., Jr.; Van Zee, R.J. Carbon Molecules, Ions and Clusters. *Chem. Rev.* **1989**, *89*, 1713–1747. [CrossRef]
35. Raghavachari, K.; Whiteside, R.A.; Pople, J.A. Structures of Small Carbon Clusters: Cyclic Ground State of C6. *J. Chem. Phys.* **1986**, *85*, 6623–6628. [CrossRef]
36. Raghavachari, K.; Binkley, J.S. Structure, Stability, and Fragmentation of Small Carbon Clusters. *J. Chem. Phys.* **1987**, *87*, 2191–2197. [CrossRef]
37. Lifshitz, C. Carbon Clusters. *Int. J. Mass Spectrom.* **2000**, *200*, 423–442. [CrossRef]
38. Saha, K.; Chandrasekaran, V.; Heber, O.; Iron, M.A.; Rappaport, M.L.; Zajfman, D. Ultraslow Isomerization in Photoexcited Gas-Phase Carbon Cluster -10. *Nat. Commun.* **2018**, *9*, 912. [CrossRef]
39. Zhao, W.; Cao, A.; Tian, J.; Gan, L. Structural Connectivity and Formation Mechanism of Monometallic Cluster Fullerenes YCN@C n (n = 68–84). *Int. J. Quantum Chem.* **2018**, *118*, e25647. [CrossRef]
40. Jäntschi, L.; Bolboacă, S.D. Conformational Study of C 24 Cyclic Polyyne Clusters. *Int. J. Quantum Chem.* **2018**, *118*, e25614. [CrossRef]
41. Sheng, X.; Song, X.; Ngwenya, C.A.; Li, J.; Zhao, H. Study of Carbon Suboxide-Containing Clusters: A Potential Sink for Cumulene. *Comput. Theor. Chem.* **2018**, *1142*, 78–82. [CrossRef]
42. Moreno-Armenta, M.G.; Pearce, H.R.; Winter, P.; Cooksy, A.L. Computational Search for Metastable High-Spin C5Hn (n = 4, 5, 6) Species. *Comput. Theor. Chem.* **2018**, *1140*, 1–6. [CrossRef]
43. Feygelson, T.I.; Tadjer, M.J.; Hobart, K.D.; Anderson, T.J.; Pate, B.B. Reduced-Stress Nanocrystalline Diamond Films for Heat Spreading in Electronic Devices. In *Thermal Management of Gallium Nitride Electronics*; Elsevier: Amsterdam, The Netherlands, 2022; pp. 275–294.
44. Van Orden, A.; Saykally, R.J. Small Carbon Clusters: Spectroscopy, Structure, and Energetics. *Chem. Rev.* **1998**, *98*, 2313–2357. [CrossRef] [PubMed]
45. Kroto, H.W. The Spectra of Interstellar Molecules. *Int. Rev. Phys. Chem.* **1981**, *1*, 309–376. [CrossRef]
46. Stevens, D.A.; Dahn, J.R. High Capacity Anode Materials for Rechargeable Sodium-Ion Batteries. *J. Electrochem. Soc.* **2000**, *147*, 1271. [CrossRef]
47. Ma, M.; Cai, H.; Xu, C.; Huang, R.; Wang, S.; Pan, H.; Hu, Y. Engineering Solid Electrolyte Interface at Nano-Scale for High-Performance Hard Carbon in Sodium-Ion Batteries. *Adv. Funct. Mater.* **2021**, *31*, 2100278. [CrossRef]
48. Xie, F.; Xu, Z.; Guo, Z.; Titirici, M.-M. Hard Carbons for Sodium-Ion Batteries and Beyond. *Prog. Energy* **2020**, *2*, 042002. [CrossRef]
49. Tang, K.; Fu, L.; White, R.J.; Yu, L.; Titirici, M.; Antonietti, M.; Maier, J. Hollow Carbon Nanospheres with Superior Rate Capability for Sodium-Based Batteries. *Adv. Energy Mater.* **2012**, *2*, 873–877. [CrossRef]
50. Bin, D.; Li, Y.; Sun, Y.; Duan, S.; Lu, Y.; Ma, J.; Cao, A.; Hu, Y.; Wan, L. Structural Engineering of Multishelled Hollow Carbon Nanostructures for High-Performance Na-Ion Battery Anode. *Adv. Energy Mater.* **2018**, *8*, 1800855. [CrossRef]
51. Palaniselvam, T.; Goktas, M.; Anothumakkool, B.; Sun, Y.; Schmuch, R.; Zhao, L.; Han, B.; Winter, M.; Adelhelm, P. Sodium Storage and Electrode Dynamics of Tin–Carbon Composite Electrodes from Bulk Precursors for Sodium-Ion Batteries. *Adv. Funct. Mater.* **2019**, *29*, 1900790. [CrossRef]
52. Li, P.; Guo, X.; Wang, S.; Zang, R.; Li, X.; Man, Z.; Li, P.; Liu, S.; Wu, Y.; Wang, G. Two-Dimensional Sb@TiO 2−x Nanoplates as a High-Performance Anode Material for Sodium-Ion Batteries. *J. Mater. Chem. A* **2019**, *7*, 2553–2559. [CrossRef]
53. Jing, W.T.; Yang, C.C.; Jiang, Q. Recent Progress on Metallic Sn- and Sb-Based Anodes for Sodium-Ion Batteries. *J. Mater. Chem. A* **2020**, *8*, 2913–2933. [CrossRef]
54. Wallace, G.G.; Higgins, M.J.; Moulton, S.E.; Wang, C. Nanobionics: The Impact of Nanotechnology on Implantable Medical Bionic Devices. *Nanoscale* **2012**, *4*, 4327. [CrossRef]
55. Luo, L.; Song, J.; Song, L.; Zhang, H.; Bi, Y.; Liu, L.; Yin, L.; Wang, F.; Wang, G. Flexible Conductive Anodes Based on 3D Hierarchical Sn/NS-CNFs@rGO Network for Sodium-Ion Batteries. *Nano-Micro Lett.* **2019**, *11*, 63. [CrossRef] [PubMed]
56. Li, X.; Ni, J.; Savilov, S.V.; Li, L. Materials Based on Antimony and Bismuth for Sodium Storage. *Chem. A Eur. J.* **2018**, *24*, 13719–13727. [CrossRef]
57. Bell, M.B.; Feldman, P.A.; Kwok, S.; Matthews, H.E. Detection of HC11N in IRC + 10°216. *Nature* **1982**, *295*, 389–391. [CrossRef]
58. Bernath, P.F.; Hinkle, K.H.; Keady, J.J. Detection of C 5 in the Circumstellar Shell of IRC+10216. *Science (80-)* **1989**, *244*, 562–564. [CrossRef] [PubMed]
59. Čermák, I.; Förderer, M.; Čermáková, I.; Kalhofer, S.; Stopka-Ebeler, H.; Monninger, G.; Krätschmer, W. Laser-Induced Emission Spectroscopy of Matrix-Isolated Carbon Molecules: Experimental Setup and New Results on C3. *J. Chem. Phys.* **1998**, *108*, 10129–10142. [CrossRef]
60. McElvany, S.W.; Ross, M.M.; Goroff, N.S., Diederich, F. Cyclocarbon Coalescence: Mechanisms for Tailor-Made Fullerene Formation. *Science (80-)* **1993**, *259*, 1594–1596. [CrossRef]
61. Arulmozhiraja, S.; Ohno, T. CCSD Calculations on C14, C18, and C22 Carbon Clusters. *J. Chem. Phys.* **2008**, *128*, 114301. [CrossRef]

62. Neiss, C.; Trushin, E.; Görling, A. The Nature of One-Dimensional Carbon: Polyynic versus Cumulenic. *ChemPhysChem* **2014**, *15*, 2497–2502. [CrossRef]
63. Pavliček, N.; Gawel, P.; Kohn, D.R.; Majzik, Z.; Xiong, Y.; Meyer, G.; Anderson, H.L.; Gross, L. Polyyne Formation via Skeletal Rearrangement Induced by Atomic Manipulation. *Nat. Chem.* **2018**, *10*, 853–858. [CrossRef] [PubMed]
64. Hoffmann, R. Extended Hückel Theory—V. *Tetrahedron* **1966**, *22*, 521–538. [CrossRef]
65. Narita, N.; Nagai, S.; Suzuki, S.; Nakao, K. Optimized Geometries and Electronic Structures of Graphyne and Its Family. *Phys. Rev. B* **1998**, *58*, 11009–11014. [CrossRef]
66. Georgakilas, V.; Perman, J.A.; Tucek, J.; Zboril, R. Broad Family of Carbon Nanoallotropes: Classification, Chemistry, and Applications of Fullerenes, Carbon Dots, Nanotubes, Graphene, Nanodiamonds, and Combined Superstructures. *Chem. Rev.* **2015**, *115*, 4744–4822. [CrossRef]
67. Li, Y.; Kono, H.; Maekawa, T.; Segawa, Y.; Yagi, A.; Itami, K. Chemical Synthesis of Carbon Nanorings and Nanobelts. *Acc. Mater. Res.* **2021**, *2*, 681–691. [CrossRef]
68. Yamago, S.; Watanabe, Y.; Iwamoto, T. Synthesis of [8]Cycloparaphenylene from a Square-Shaped Tetranuclear Platinum Complex. *Angew. Chem. Int. Ed.* **2010**, *49*, 757–759. [CrossRef]
69. Segawa, Y.; Miyamoto, S.; Omachi, H.; Matsuura, S.; Šenel, P.; Sasamori, T.; Tokitoh, N.; Itami, K. Concise Synthesis and Crystal Structure of [12]Cycloparaphenylene. *Angew. Chem. Int. Ed.* **2011**, *50*, 3244–3248. [CrossRef]
70. Friederich, R.; Nieger, M.; Vögtle, F. Auf Dem Weg Zu Makrocyclischen Para -Phenylenen. *Chem. Ber.* **1993**, *126*, 1723–1732. [CrossRef]
71. Ullah, F.; Ayub, K.; Gilani, M.A.; Imran, M.; Mahmood, T. C10F as a Potential Anode Material for Alkali-Ion Batteries; a Quantum Chemical Approach. *Comput. Theor. Chem.* **2021**, *1206*, 113470. [CrossRef]
72. Murtaza, T.; Kosar, N.; Amjad Gilani, M.; Ayub, K.; Hussain Shah, K.; Mahmood, T. DFT Studies on Electrochemical Properties of Halide Ions Doped GDY-28 Nanoflake for Na-Ion Battery Applications. *Mater. Sci. Semicond. Process.* **2022**, *145*, 106651. [CrossRef]
73. Duraisamy, P.D.; Paul, S.P.M.; Gopalan, P.; Paranthaman, S.; Angamuthu, A. A DFT Study of Halogen (F−, Cl−, and Br−) Encapsulated Ga12X12 (X = N, P, and As) Nanocages for Sodium-Ion Batteries. *J. Inorg. Organomet. Polym. Mater.* **2022**, *32*, 4173–4185. [CrossRef]
74. Chapman, N.; Borodin, O.; Yoon, T.; Nguyen, C.C.; Lucht, B.L. Spectroscopic and Density Functional Theory Characterization of Common Lithium Salt Solvates in Carbonate Electrolytes for Lithium Batteries. *J. Phys. Chem. C* **2017**, *121*, 2135–2148. [CrossRef]
75. Dziedzic, J.; Bhandari, A.; Anton, L.; Peng, C.; Womack, J.C.; Famili, M.; Kramer, D.; Skylaris, C.-K. Practical Approach to Large-Scale Electronic Structure Calculations in Electrolyte Solutions via Continuum-Embedded Linear-Scaling Density Functional Theory. *J. Phys. Chem. C* **2020**, *124*, 7860–7872. [CrossRef]
76. Frisch, M.J.; Trucks, G.W.; Schlegel, H.B.; Scuseria, G.E.; Robb, M.A.; Cheeseman, J.R.; Scalmani, G.; Barone, V.; Mennucci, B.; Petersson, G.A.; et al. *Gaussian 09 (D01)*; Gaussian, Inc.: Wallingford, CT, USA, 2010.
77. Dennington, R.R.; Keith, T.; Millam, J. *GaussView, version 5*; Semichem Inc.: Shawnee Mission, KS, USA, 2009.
78. Kosar, N.; Mahmood, T.; Hafeez, F.; Ayub, K. Detailed Mechanistic Study of Radical Mediated Chemoselective Phosphination of Aryl Halide. *ChemistrySelect* **2018**, *3*, 11302–11308. [CrossRef]
79. Kosar, N.; Shehzadi, K.; Ayub, K.; Mahmood, T. Theoretical Study on Novel Superalkali Doped Graphdiyne Complexes: Unique Approach for the Enhancement of Electronic and Nonlinear Optical Response. *J. Mol. Graph. Model.* **2020**, *97*, 107573. [CrossRef]
80. Kosar, N.; Mahmood, T.; Ayub, K. Role of Dispersion Corrected Hybrid GGA Class in Accurately Calculating the Bond Dissociation Energy of Carbon Halogen Bond: A Benchmark Study. *J. Mol. Struct.* **2017**, *1150*, 447–458. [CrossRef]
81. Ullah, F.; Kosar, N.; Arshad, M.N.; Gilani, M.A.; Ayub, K.; Mahmood, T. Design of Novel Superalkali Doped Silicon Carbide Nanocages with Giant Nonlinear Optical Response. *Opt. Laser Technol.* **2020**, *122*, 105855. [CrossRef]
82. Kosar, N.; Shehzadi, K.; Ayub, K.; Mahmood, T. Nonlinear Optical Response of Sodium Based Superalkalis Decorated Graphdiyne Surface: A DFT Study. *Optik* **2020**, *218*, 165033. [CrossRef]
83. Kosimov, D.P.; Dzhurakhalov, A.A.; Peeters, F.M. Carbon Clusters: From Ring Structures to Nanographene. *Phys. Rev. B Condens. Matter Mater. Phys.* **2010**, *81*, 1–13. [CrossRef]
84. Younis, U.; Qayyum, F.; Muhammad, I.; Yaseen, M.; Sun, Q. A Stable Three-Dimensional Porous Carbon as a High-Performance Anode Material for Lithium, Sodium, and Potassium Ion Batteries. *Adv. Theory Simul.* **2022**, *5*, 2200230. [CrossRef]
85. Kosar, N.; Asgar, M.; Mahmood, T.; Ayub, K.; Sajid, H.; Albaqami, M.D.; Gilani, M.A. Electrochemical Properties of Lithium Metal Doped C60 Fullerene for Battery Applications. *Mater. Sci. Semicond. Process.* **2024**, *175*, 108256. [CrossRef]
86. Xu, W.; Zhu, J.; Zhang, J.; Tian, M.; Cai, J.; Wu, H.; Wei, G.; Chen, T.; Wei, X.; Dai, H. Investigation of Lithium-Ion Battery Degradation by Corrected Differential Voltage Analysis Based on Reference Electrode. *Appl. Energy* **2025**, *389*, 125735. [CrossRef]
87. Zhang, K.; Jin, Z. Halogen-Enabled Rechargeable Batteries: Current Advances and Future Perspectives. *Energy Storage Mater.* **2022**, *45*, 332–369. [CrossRef]

88. Ma, S.; Yan, W.; Dong, Y.; Su, Y.; Ma, L.; Li, Y.; Fang, Y.; Wang, B.; Wu, S.; Liu, C.; et al. Recent Advances in Carbon-Based Anodes for High-Performance Sodium-Ion Batteries: Mechanism, Modification and Characterizations. *Mater. Today* **2024**, *75*, 334–358. [CrossRef]
89. Zhao, Y.; Wang, L.P.; Sougrati, M.T.; Feng, Z.; Leconte, Y.; Fisher, A.; Srinivasan, M.; Xu, Z. A Review on Design Strategies for Carbon Based Metal Oxides and Sulfides Nanocomposites for High Performance Li and Na Ion Battery Anodes. *Adv. Energy Mater.* **2017**, *7*, 1601424. [CrossRef]
90. Zhu, M.; Yang, Y.; Ma, Y. Salt-Assisted Synthesis of Advanced Carbon-Based Materials for Energy-Related Applications. *Green Chem.* **2023**, *25*, 10263–10303. [CrossRef]

*computation*

MDPI

*Article*

# First-Principles Insights into Mo and Chalcogen Dopant Positions in Anatase, $TiO_2$

**W. A. Chapa Pamodani Wanniarachchi [1,2,*], Ponniah Vajeeston [3], Talal Rahman [1] and Dhayalan Velauthapillai [1,*]**

[1] Faculty of Engineering, Western Norway University of Applied Sciences, 5020 Bergen, Norway; talal.rahman@hvl.no

[2] Clean Energy Research Laboratory (CERL), Department of Physics, University of Jaffna, Jaffna 40000, Sri Lanka

[3] Department of Chemistry, Center for Materials Science and Nanotechnology, University of Oslo, P.O. Box 1033, Blindern, NO-0315 Oslo, Norway; vajeeston.ponniah@kjemi.uio.no

* Correspondence: chapa@univ.jfn.ac.lk (W.A.C.P.W.); dhayalan.velauthapillai@hvl.no (D.V.)

**Abstract:** This study employs density functional theory (DFT) to investigate the electronic and optical properties of molybdenum (Mo) and chalcogen (S, Se, Te) co-doped anatase $TiO_2$. Two co-doping configurations were examined: Model 1, where the dopants are adjacent, and Model 2, where the dopants are farther apart. The incorporation of Mo into anatase $TiO_2$ resulted in a significant bandgap reduction, lowering it from 3.22 eV (pure $TiO_2$) to range of 2.52–0.68 eV, depending on the specific doping model. The introduction of Mo-4d states below the conduction band led to a shift in the Fermi level from the top of the valence band to the bottom of the conduction band, confirming the n-type doping characteristics of Mo in $TiO_2$. Chalcogen doping introduced isolated electronic states from Te-5*p*, S-3*p*, and Se-4*p* located above the valence band maximum, further reducing the bandgap. Among the examined configurations, Mo–S co-doping in Model 1 exhibited most optimal structural stability structure with the fewer impurity states, enhancing photocatalytic efficiency by reducing charge recombination. With the exception of Mo–Te co-doping, all co-doped systems demonstrated strong oxidation power under visible light, making Mo-S and Mo-Se co-doped $TiO_2$ promising candidates for oxidation-driven photocatalysis. However, their limited reduction ability suggests they may be less suitable for water-splitting applications. The study also revealed that dopant positioning significantly influences charge transfer and optoelectronic properties. Model 1 favored localized electron density and weaker magnetization, while Model 2 exhibited delocalized charge density and stronger magnetization. These findings underscore the critical role of dopant arrangement in optimizing $TiO_2$-based photocatalysts for solar energy applications.

**Keywords:** DFT; co-doped; bandgap; photocatalysis

## 1. Introduction

Titanium dioxide ($TiO_2$) is widely recognized for its photocatalytic capabilities, which are harnessed in applications such as water splitting, pollutant degradation, and solar energy conversion [1]. $TiO_2$ has a wide bandgap of about 3.2 eV for anatase, which limits its ability to absorb visible light [2]. Most solar energy is in the visible range (approximately 400–700 nm), so $TiO_2$'s efficiency at utilizing sunlight is inherently limited by its bandgap. Through the doping of foreign atoms, the bandgap of $TiO_2$ can be optimized, leading to enhanced absorption of solar energy in the visible spectrum. Numerous experimental and theoretical studies have investigated this approach in depth [3–6]. Molybdenum (Mo) doping in $TiO_2$ can effectively shift the absorption edge toward the visible light region because the size of the Mo cation is comparable to that of the Ti cation. This can result in a stable doped system [7]. Ohno et al. developed S-doped $TiO_2$ photocatalysts by substituting sulfur ($S^{4+}$) in place of certain titanium atoms within the lattice structure. These modified photocatalysts exhibit enhanced visible light absorption at wavelengths beyond 500 nm and demonstrate high photocatalytic activity. S-doped $TiO_2$ powder shows potential for various applications, including the oxidation of 2-propanol in aqueous solution, degradation of methylene blue, and partial oxidation of adamantane when exposed to wavelengths above 440 nm [8]. A few studies have shown that S-doped anatase enhances visible light absorption [9–11].

The experimental study investigated the effects of S, Se, and Te doping on the anatase-to-rutile phase transition and microbial disinfection properties of chalcogen-doped $TiO_2$ at high calcination temperatures. $TiO_2$ samples doped with 2 mol% S, Se, or Te were synthesized using a sol–gel method. The substitutional incorporation of chalcogens into the $TiO_2$ lattice improved visible light absorption. It was concluded that Te-doped $TiO_2$ displayed similar bactericidal efficiency to control anatase under visible light, indicating that Te maintains $TiO_2$'s photocatalytic activity even at temperatures up to 750 °C [12]. Titanium dioxide samples doped with varying amounts of $Se^{4+}$ and $Te^{4+}$ ions were synthesized via homogeneous hydrolysis using amorphous Se and Te. The $Se^{4+}$- and $Te^{4+}$-doped titania samples with the highest photocatalytic activity under UV and visible light were identified as $TiSe_3$ (11.5 wt% Se) and $TiTe_3$ (8.0 wt% Te), respectively. This demonstrates that incorporating Se and Te into the anatase lattice positively influences photocatalytic activity in the visible light range [13]. Another study investigated the Se (IV)-doped $TiO_2$ system using both experimental methods and density functional theory (DFT) to assess its optoelectronic and photocatalytic properties. Se-doped $TiO_2$ demonstrated photocatalytic activity when exposed to direct sunlight, with its bandgap extending from 420 to 650 nm. The 3*p* orbitals of Se contribute to the formation of additional electronic states within the bandgap, which reduces the wide bandgap of pristine anatase and enhances its photocatalytic activity [14]. It was found that substituting anions such as S, Se, and Te is more effective than cation doping, with the redshift becoming more pronounced as the atomic number of the chalcogen element increases [15]. Doping $TiO_2$ by replacing O sites with chalcogen atoms has become a prominent research focus due to the unique electronic and optical properties of chalcogens. It is also of interest to explore Mo co-doping within the chalcogen element series, as this is a novel approach that has never been reported before.

As demonstrated in previous experimental studies, doping $TiO_2$ with metal atoms such as molybdenum (Mo) and chalcogen elements like sulfur (S), selenium (Se), and tellurium (Te) can enhance its photocatalytic properties. In this work, we investigated the material characteristics of anatase $TiO_2$ when co-doped with Mo and chalcogen atoms. Specifically, we studied the optoelectronic properties of anatase $TiO_2$ doped with Mo at titanium sites and S, Se, or Te at oxygen sites, and we further explored how the spatial arrangement of dopants when the doped atoms are in the adjacent position or at a distant position in the anatase $TiO_2$ structure affects these ground state properties. The electronic structure was calculated using the GGA+U method, while the HSE hybrid functional was employed for accurate optical property predictions. We examined the structural, electronic, and optical characteristics and compared them with the existing mono-doped chalcogen models. Additionally, formation energies were analyzed under oxygen-rich and titanium-rich conditions to assess the thermodynamic stability of the dopants within the anatase lattice. The photocatalytic potential of the doped systems was evaluated by analyzing their band edge positions relative to the normal hydrogen electrode (NHE) for water splitting

## 2. Computational Methodology

The projector-augmented wave (PAW) pseudopotentials [16] were used for all the DFT calculations in the VASP code [17]. Initially, geometry optimization was performed for both the pure and doped models in the GGA method, which was parametrized at the Perdew–Burke–Ernzerhof (PBE) level [18] with the Monkhorst–Pack k-point mesh [19] of 4 × 4 × 4. Here, we used the plane wave basis set with a cutoff energy of 560 eV for our calculations [1]. For the electronic property calculations, the spin-polarized density of states (DOS) of the doped structures were computed on the Monkhorst–Pack k-point grid on 7 × 7 × 5 along the x, y, and z directions of high symmetry in the first Brillouin zone [1]. The DFT+U approach, as seen in Equation (1), incorporates an on-site correction to account for intra-atomic electron–electron interactions [20,21], which helps improve the description of systems with localized d and f electrons, often resulting in more accurate bandgap predictions than standard GGA.

$$E_{DFT+U} = E_{DFT} + \sum\nolimits_{\sigma} \frac{U-J}{2} \mathrm{Tr}[\mathrm{n}_{\sigma}(1-\mathrm{n}_{\sigma})] \quad (1)$$

Here, $n_\sigma$ is the occupation matrix for spin σ, and Tr is the trace operator. The spherically averaged Hubbard parameter U quantifies the energy increase associated with adding an extra electron to the system. The parameter J represents (1 eV) as the screened exchange energy. In this case, the effective on-site Coulomb interactions were set to U = 7.0 eV for Ti 3*d* and U = 5.38 eV for transition metal (TM) d electrons in the GGA+U approach. To determine the U value for pure anatase $TiO_2$, we computed the bandgap values by varying U from 0 to 8 eV and found that U = 7 eV gives a value closest to the experimental bandgap of 3.22 eV, as shown in Figure 1. The U value for Mo was taken from the Materials Project [22].

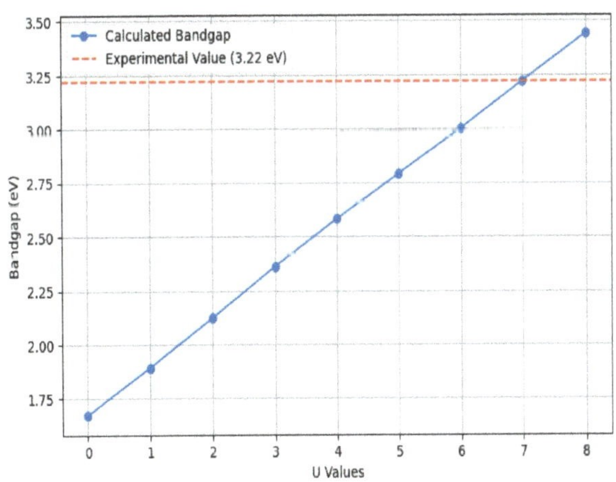


**Figure 1.** The calculated bandgap for anatase, $TiO_2$ as a function DFT + U value change.

Simulating a system that has strong electron correlation and a need to correct the electronic structure, especially in transition metal oxides or correlated materials, GGA+U could be more effective, but it may not offer the same accuracy for optical properties as HSE06. Thus, optical property calculations were performed in the screened hybrid functional called (Heyd–Scuseria–Ernzerhof) HSE06 [23]. VESTA is a three-dimensional visualization program that was used to visualize the equilibrium crystal lattices [24].

The doped system consists of a 2 × 2 × 1 supercell containing a total of 48 atoms, which provides a realistic environment for introducing dopants at low concentrations while minimizing artificial interactions between periodic images of atoms [1]. The supercell was generated using the Phonopy code to ensure proper structural setup for the simulations [25]. S, Se, and Te doping in the anatase $TiO_2$ supercell was performed by replacing a single O atom with S, Se, or Te at its regular lattice site, while Mo-doped $TiO_2$ was obtained by replacing the Ti site with the Mo atom simultaneously. Here, $Mo^{4+}$ substitutes $Ti^{4+}$, and the valence band remains fully occupied, with no free carriers (electrons or holes). The concentration of each dopant element in this supercell is approximately 2.08%.

Two different models were constructed for the co-doping system to investigate the impact of dopant locations on the electronic and optical properties of these six configurations. In the first model (hereafter referred to as Model 1), S, Se, Te, and Mo were doped adjacently by replacing O and Ti atoms at a distance of 1.9576 Å. In the second model (hereafter referred to as Model 2), S, Se, Te, and Mo were placed at a distance of 4.3099 Å. Both doped models were geometrically optimized, and their electronic and optical properties were subsequently evaluated. The configurations of these models are illustrated in Figure 2. Energy versus volume data for these doped structures concluded that Model 1 exhibits a lower ground state energy than Model 2, indicating that Model 1 is more stable across all doped structures. The S-doped configuration of Model 1 has the most stable structure among the Se- and Te-doped compounds. Consequently, the adjacent positioning of the Mo and S dopants results in the most optimal structural stability relative to the other models, as seen in Figures S1–S4. In adjacent co-doping, the introduced cation and anion can form a strong bond via direct charge transfer, which generally results in the system achieving the lowest total energy [26].

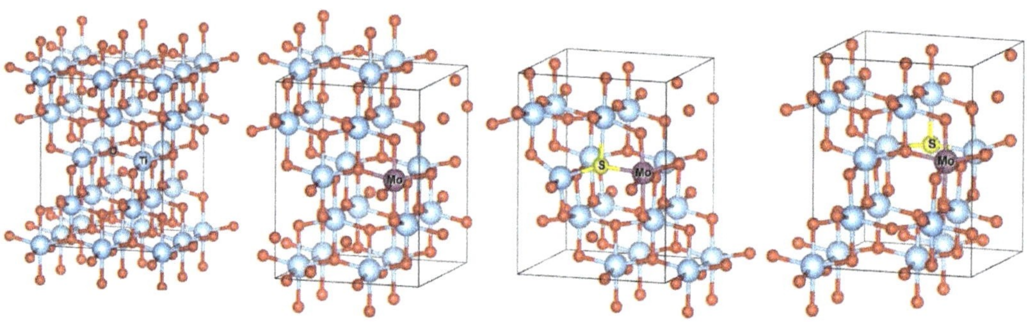


(a) (b) (c) (d)

**Figure 2.** (**a**) $TiO_2$ supercell; (**b**) Mo-doped supercell; (**c**) co-doped Model 1; (**d**) co-doped Model 2. In these models, red, blue, yellow, and violet represent oxygen, titanium, S (or Se, Te), and molybdenum atoms, respectively.

## 3. Results and Discussion

*Structural Optimization*

The geometrical optimization of pure anatase $TiO_2$, as well as mono-doped and co-doped models, was performed using the PBE functional. The equilibrium lattice parameters for anatase $TiO_2$ are a = 3.8179 Å and c = 9.7473 Å [1], which align well with the experimental values of a = 3.78512 Å and c = 9.51185 Å [27]. Upon doping of the heavy metal Mo, the cell volume increased four times, to 570.71 $Å^3$ compared with the pristine anatase structure, 142.08 $Å^3$ [1]. Furthermore, the cell volume increased slightly upon the co-doping with the chalcogen elements. The largest cell volume was found for the Mo/Te co-doped $TiO_2$ models, which is 5% larger compared with the Mo-doped $TiO_2$ structure model, as seen in Figure 3.

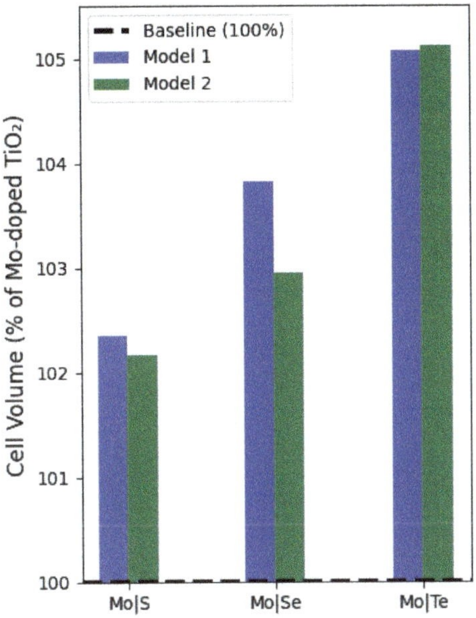


**Figure 3.** Calculated cell volume % relative to the Mo-doped $TiO_2$.

Here, Model 1 has a lower ground state energy but still results in a higher cell volume compared with Model 2, except for the Te-doped structure. A system that is energetically favorable (lower ground state energy) might undergo structural distortions such as increased lattice expansion as a result of stronger dopant interactions. In Table 1, we have listed calculated bond lengths for both pure and doped structures. The variations among them can be attributed to differences in atomic size and electronegativity. For instance, the Mo–S bond length is generally longer than the Ti–O bond due to the larger atomic radius of sulfur compared with oxygen. Additionally, the ionic radius increases in the order $S < Se < Te$, and the associated bond lengths increase accordingly.

**Table 1.** Bond lengths of pure and doped models.

| System Bonds | Pure $TiO_2$ | Mo and S Co-Doped $TiO_2$ | | Mo and Se Co-Doped $TiO_2$ | | Mo and Te Co-Doped $TiO_2$ | |
|---|---|---|---|---|---|---|---|
| | | **Model 1** | **Model 2** | **Model 1** | **Model 2** | **Model 1** | **Model 2** |
| Ti-O | 1.9564 Å | 1.9517 Å | 1.9430 Å | 1.9512 Å | 1.9452 Å | 1.9856 Å | 1.9641 Å |
| Mo-S | | 2.2351 Å | 4.3079 Å | | | | |
| Mo-Se | | | | 2.3487 Å | 4.2974 Å | | |
| Mo-Te | | | | | | 2.5487 Å | 4.2794 Å |
| Mo-O | | 1.9581 Å | 1.9291 Å | 1.9609 Å | 1.9324 Å | 1.9723 Å | 1.9525 Å |
| Ti-S | | 2.2373 Å | 2.2009 Å | | | | |
| Ti-Se | | | | 2.3431 Å | 2.3036 Å | | |
| Ti-Te | | | | | | 2.6342 Å | 2.5039Å |

## 4. Formation Energy

The formation energies for co-doped anatase models were calculated and analyzed under both oxygen-rich and titanium-rich conditions. The formation energy is given by Equation (2),

$$E^f[X^q] = E_{tot}[X^q] - E_{tot}[Ti_{16}O_{32}] - \mu_{TM} + \mu_{Ti} - \mu_{NM} + \mu_O \quad (2)$$

where $E_{tot}[Ti_{16}O_{32}]$ represents the total energy of the pure titanium dioxide supercell, $\mu_{TM}$ and $\mu_{Ti}$ represent the chemical potentials of the transition metal and titanium atom, respectively, and $\mu_{NM}$ and $\mu_O$ are used to represent the chemical potentials of the nonmetal and oxygen atoms, respectively.

The formation energy as in Equation (3) of $TiO_2$-based photocatalysts depends on the growth conditions and varies between Ti-rich (TRC) and O-rich (ORC) chemical environments. Here, $\mu_{TiO_2}$ was computed by normalizing the energy value of the pure supercell.

$$\mu_{TiO_2} = \mu_{Ti} + 2\mu_O \quad (3)$$

Under the oxygen-rich growth conditions, the chemical potential of oxygen is the one calculated from the ground state energy of $O_2$, $\mu_O = \mu_{O_2}/2$. Then, $\mu_{Ti}$ is obtained using Equation (3). Conversely, under the titanium-rich conditions, $\mu_{Ti}$ is the energy of one titanium atom in bulk titanium, and $\mu_O$ is then computed.

The chemical potentials for the chalcogen elements S, Se, and Te are determined with Equation (4):

$$\mu_X = \mu_{XO_2} - 2\mu_O \quad (4)$$

Here, $\mu_X$ was calculated by Equations (3) and (4) through $\mu_O$. The chemical potentials ($\mu_X$), where X represents S, Se, and Te, were calculated under ORC, TRC, and in their respective bulk phases. Among these, the chemical potentials under O-rich conditions were found to be stable, and therefore, they were used for further calculations. The formation energies of the dopant elements are calculated using Equation (1) within the GGA approximation and are presented in a heatmap in Figure 4 to convey the precise values. The computed values for $E_{tot}$ $[Ti_{16}O_{32}]$, $\mu_O$, $\mu_{Ti}$, and $\mu_{Mo}$ are −423.89, −4.94, −16.64 eV, and −10.95 eV, respectively [1].

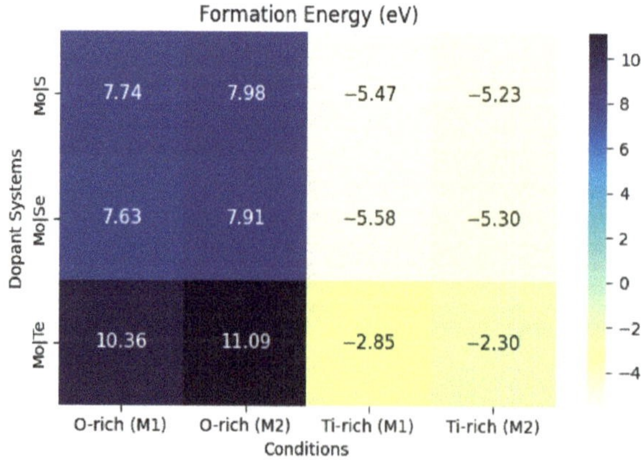


**Figure 4.** The formation energy values, eV, depicted in the heatmap highlight the thermodynamic stability of different co-doped $TiO_2$ systems under ORC and TRC. Lower formation energies (lighter colors) indicate greater stability, while higher values (darker colors) suggest less favorable configurations.

Overall, the results in Figure 4 show that ORC obtained higher positive formation energy values, as under TRC it has negative formation energy values. Under ORC, the formation energy ($E_f$) values follow almost this order: Mo/Se doping < Mo/S doping < Mo/Te doping. These positive formation energies can be attributed to the significant electronic and structural disruptions caused by the dopants within the $TiO_2$ lattice, which adversely affect the overall stability of the system. Specifically, the incorporation of Mo/Te induces substantial distortion in the $TiO_2$ lattice, and additional energy is required to overcome unfavorable lattice interactions. As a result, higher formation energies are observed. These materials may still be synthesized under specific conditions (e.g., high temperatures or particular partial pressures of gases) that provide the necessary energy for their formation. However, the high formation energy values indicate that while these configurations are theoretically possible, they may not be easily achievable or stable in typical synthesis environments. On the other hand, under TRC conditions, all the formation energies are negative, indicating that the material has a thermodynamically spontaneous tendency to form.

The impact of dopants on the stability of the host material can be understood through Bader charge analysis. As shown in Figure 5, in Section 7 dopants that exhibit more negative Bader charges tend to withdraw more electron density from their surroundings. This strong electron-withdrawing behavior may disrupt the local electronic environment and bonding structure within the host lattice. As a result, such dopants can destabilize the system, which is reflected in their higher formation energies. There are limited previous results available for comparing the formation energies of doped models. However, the co-doped models with other dopants (such as Cr/B and Co/B) exhibit higher positive formation energies rather than lower or negative values [4]. This indicates that the co-doped models have higher formation energies, which are positive rather than negative, suggesting that additional effort is required to form these systems. Furthermore, the high formation energies suggest that these materials may be prone to decomposing back into their constituent phases or transforming into more stable forms under standard conditions. This indicates that the materials may not be practical for certain applications due to the significant energy required to maintain their structures.

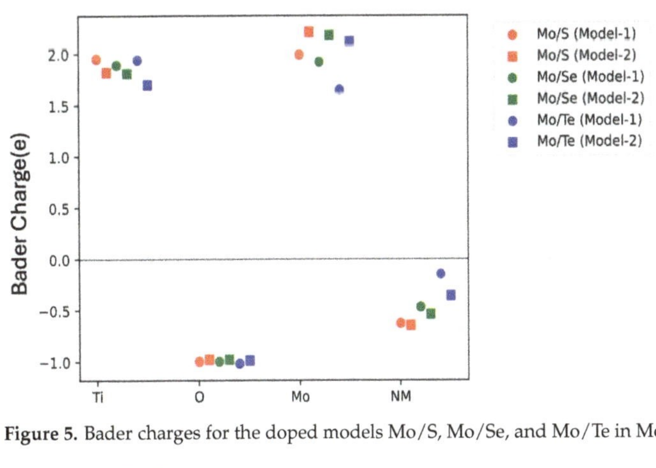


**Figure 5.** Bader charges for the doped models Mo/S, Mo/Se, and Mo/Te in Model 1 and Model 2.

## 5. Electronic Properties

The GGA + U calculation was introduced to obtain values closer to the experimental bandgaps. The pure anatase bandgap value was computed as 3.22 eV, which is almost equal to the experimentally found bandgap value of 3.23 eV [28]. The energy values of the bands are shifted by subtracting the Fermi level from all energy values, effectively setting the Fermi level to 0 in the plot. The band structure in Figure 6a along the high-symmetry directions of the Brillouin zone (BZ) and the density of states (DOS) for the valence band (VB) and conduction band (CB) of a perfect $TiO_2$ crystal are shown in Figure 7. According to Figure 7, the VB and CB are composed of contributions from both the Ti-3$d$ and O-2$p$ orbitals. Figure 8 illustrates the decomposition of the $TiO_2$ DOS, where the Ti-3$d$ orbital is split into two components: the $t_{2g}$ and $e_g$ states.

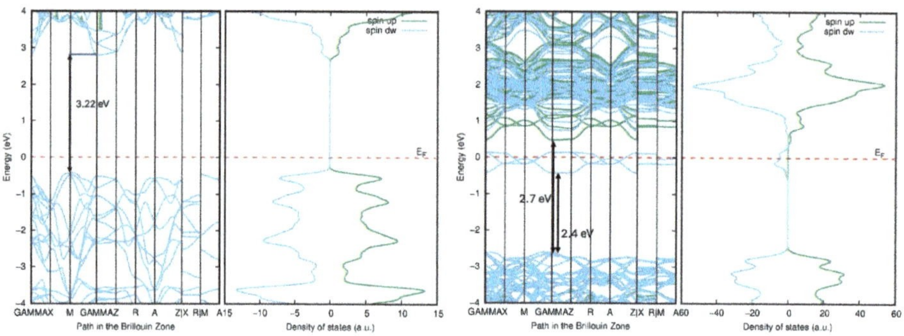


(a) (b)

**Figure 6.** Electronic structure of the (**a**) Pure anatase $TiO_2$ and (**b**) Mo-doped anatase $TiO_2$.

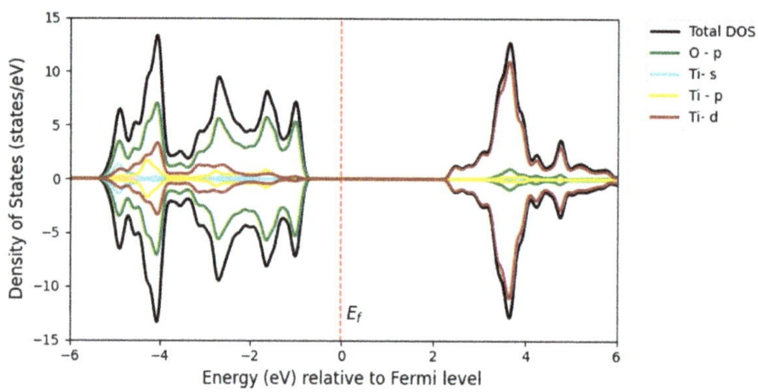


**Figure 7.** Calculated total and site-projected density of states for pure anatase, $TiO_2$.

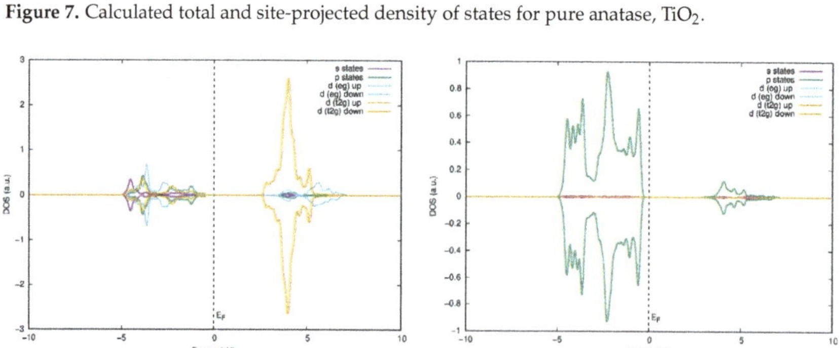


(a) (b)

**Figure 8.** Decomposition of the $TiO_2$ DOS (**a**) for Ti atom and (**b**) Oxygen atom.

In the anatase $TiO_2$ lattice, each titanium (Ti) atom is coordinated with six oxygen (O) atoms in an octahedral arrangement as depicted in Figure 2a. The bonding between the Ti *d*-orbitals and O *p*-orbitals can be explained using molecular orbital theory (Figure 9). The Ti $e_g$ orbitals, with lobes pointing directly toward the oxygen atoms, form strong $\sigma$ bonds with the O *p* orbitals. These highly directional $\sigma$ bonds play a crucial role in stabilizing the metal–ligand interactions within the lattice. According to Figure 8, VBs are primarily composed of O *p* and Ti $e_g$ states, whereas the CB consists of Ti $t_{2g}$ states. The Ti $e_g$ orbitals, which include the $d_z{}^2$ and $d_x{}^2{}_{-y}{}^2$ orbitals, play a significant role in the CB. In contrast, the Ti $t_{2g}$ orbitals, comprising the $d_{xy}$, $d_{xz}$, and $d_{yz}$ orbitals, contribute largely to the CB. The energy bands of pure $TiO_2$ within the groups of bands where the bands are between 0 and −5 eV originate mainly from oxygen 2*p* orbitals, and the bands above the Fermi energy are dominated by contributions from titanium 3*d* orbitals. The bonding nature of the conduction and valence bands arises from the hybridization and interaction of these orbitals between the Ti and O atoms, which directly influence the material's electronic and optical properties.

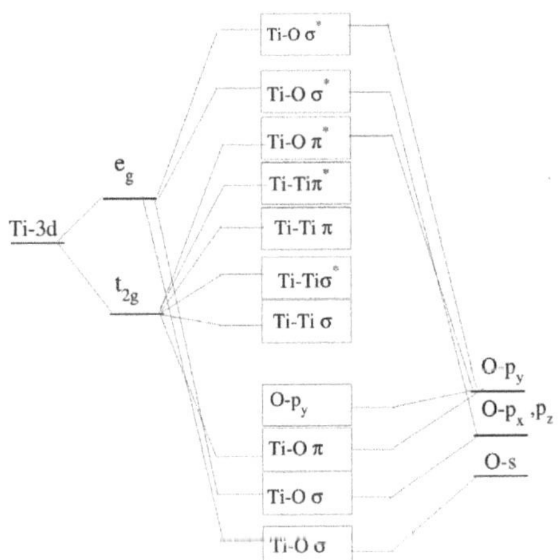


**Figure 9.** The molecular orbital diagram of pure $TiO_2$ proposed by Soratin and Schwarz (* represents the $\pi$ bonding) [29].

When examining the bonding nature of the conduction band and valence band between the atoms, Soratin and Schwarz provide a detailed description of the molecular orbital diagram [29], where the lower conduction band (CB) consists of the sigma bonding and antibonding interactions of the Ti $t_{2g}$-Ti $t_{2g}$ states. In the middle of the CB, the remaining Ti $t_{2g}$ states participate in pi bonding and antibonding with Ti $t_{2g}$-Ti $t_{2g}$ interactions, as well as antibonding interactions between Ti $t_{2g}$ and O $p_y$ orbitals. The upper CB consists of sigma antibonding interactions between O $p_y$ and Ti $e_g$ states. The valence band (VB) is divided into two regions: the lower-energy region is composed of sigma bonding interactions involving Ti $e_g$ and O s, $p_x$, and $p_z$ orbitals, while the upper region of the VB is primarily made up of O $p_y$ orbitals and pi-bonding interactions between Ti $t_{2g}$ and O $p_y$.

In molybdenum-doped $TiO_2$, molybdenum, which has more valence electrons than titanium, creates defect states within the bandgap, leading to the formation of intermediate bands (IBs). These intermediate states arise from Mo-4*d* states and are localized at the conduction band, as shown in Figure 10. According to Figure 6b, the impurity states act as shallow donor states at the Fermi level (indicated by the red dashed line), exhibiting half-metallic ferromagnetic behavior, metallic in the spin-down channel but semiconducting in the spin-up channel in the band diagram. In the Mo-doped model, the bandgap was reduced by 2.7 eV compared with the pure compound of 3.22 eV, and the reduction was about 0.52 eV. These states extend into the conduction band, contributing to the reduction in the bandgap in pristine $TiO_2$. This bandgap reduction occurs due to the hybridization of Mo-4*d* and Ti-3*d* states. Soussi et al. analyzed the electronic structure of $TiO_2$ with varying concentrations of Mo doping. Their findings revealed that, in all cases, the Fermi level shifted into the conduction band, indicating n-type metallic doping behavior [30]. This reduction in the bandgap is able to shift the absorption edge to the visible light region, which is good for the optical absorption efficiency. Thus, it could enhance photocatalytic efficiency. Experimentally proved, Mo-doped $TiO_2$ nano powders were synthesized, significantly enhancing light absorption, even in the visible light range, and the photocatalytic activity of the synthesized $TiO_2$ nano powders was improved by Mo doping [31].

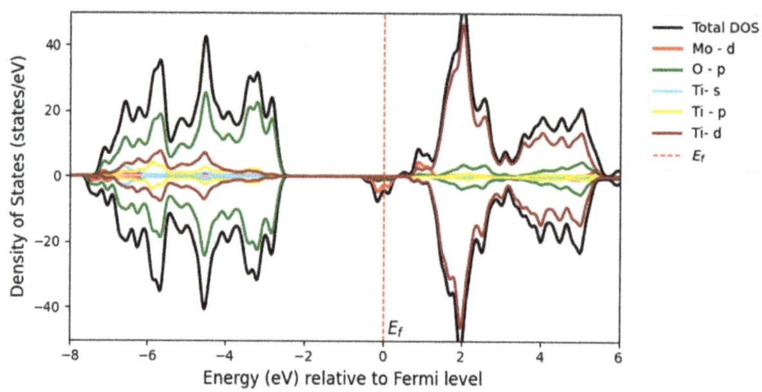


**Figure 10.** Calculated total and site-projected density of states for Mo-doped $TiO_2$.

The incorporation of the chalcogen atom as a secondary dopant into Mo-doped $TiO_2$ further shifts the absorption edge of $TiO_2$ into the visible spectrum and even toward longer wavelengths. The redshift of the bandgap transition occurs further in the visible light region after doping with S, Se, and Te along with Mo. Additionally, the Fermi level shifts to the bottom of the conduction band minimum, indicating the absence of metallic nature. The bandgap of the Mo/S-doped system for Model 1 is 2.52 eV in Figure 11a, and Model 2 shows the narrower bandgap of 2.26 eV in Figure 11b. However, its interaction with Mo-*d* may be stronger in Model 2, influencing the electronic properties.

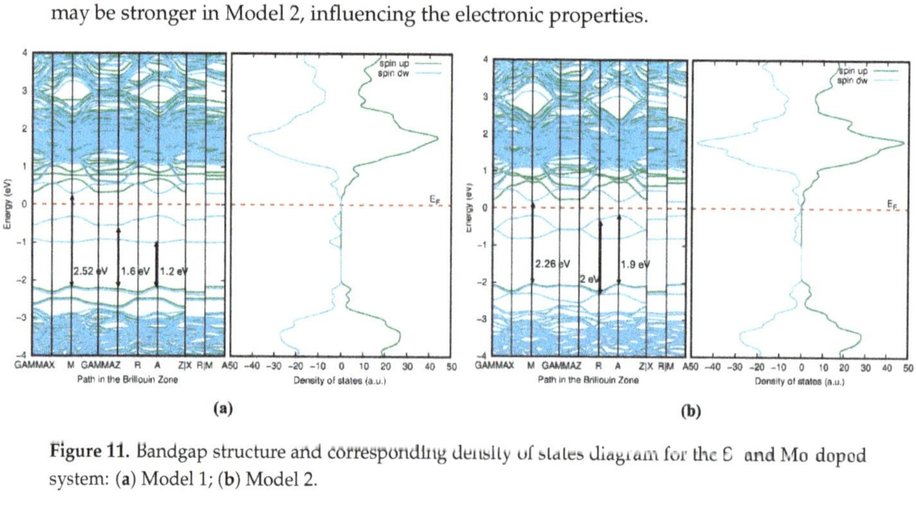


(a) (b)

**Figure 11.** Bandgap structure and corresponding density of states diagram for the S and Mo doped system: (**a**) Model 1; (**b**) Model 2.

The S substitution at the oxygen site introduces S-$p$ states located at the edge of the valence band maximum, forming a tail of the valence band (blue) with a minor contribution, as seen in Figures 12 and 13. This contributes to a further bandgap reduction compared with the mono-doped Mo model by hybridizing S-3$p$ states with O-2$p$ states, making it capable of absorbing visible light. The literature shows that doping with S can lower the bandgap and cause a redshift in the absorption spectra of $TiO_2$ as sulfur concentration increases. This effect is attributed to the presence of impurity states of S-3$p$ at the valence band maximum, which aligns with our findings [32]. Experimentally, it has been proven that sulfur doping shifts the absorption edge of $TiO_2$ to a lower energy region within the wavelength range of 650 nm [33].

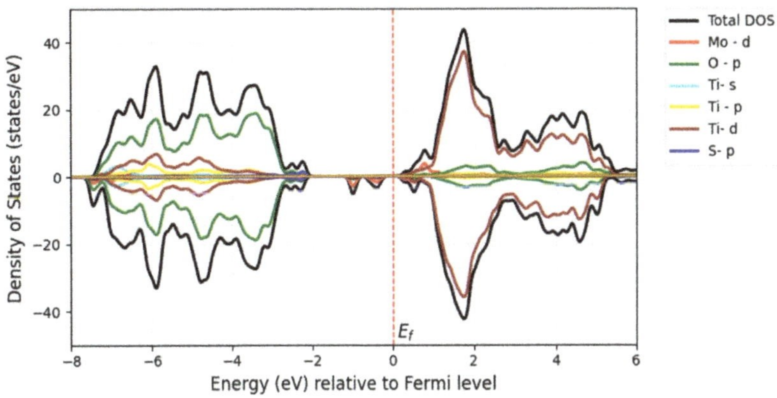


**Figure 12.** Calculated total and site-projected density of states for Mo/S-doped $TiO_2$ in Model 1.

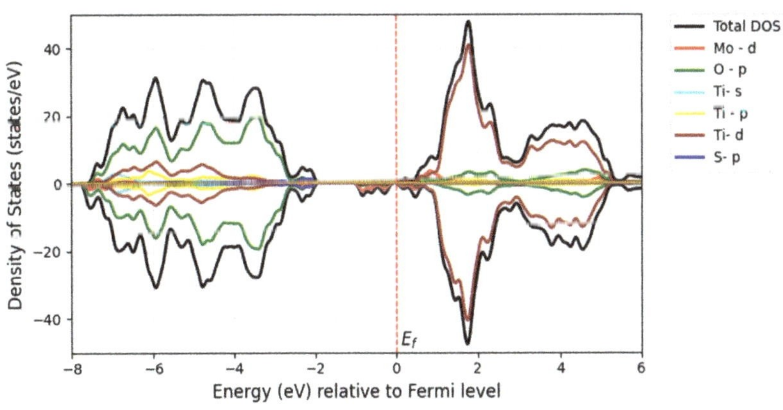


**Figure 13.** Calculated total and site-projected density of states for Mo/S-doped $TiO_2$ in Model 2.

Overall, our findings for the doped Mo, S/$TiO_2$ system show that the decrease in the bandgap of pure $TiO_2$ is related to the hybridization between the 3$p$ S states and the 3$d$ Ti and 4$d$ Mo orbitals, which leads to the formation of new states within the bandgap.

When Mo and Se are doped adjacently in $TiO_2$, their close proximity leads to strong interactions between the dopants and the $TiO_2$ lattice. The $d$-orbitals of Mo and the $p$-orbitals of Se strongly hybridize with the Ti-3$d$ and O-2$p$ orbitals of $TiO_2$. This hybridization creates new states in the band structures (Figure 14), particularly near the Fermi level. The strong interaction introduces mid-gap states (defect states) within the bandgap of $TiO_2$, which can act as trapping centers for electrons or holes, thereby altering the material's optical and electronic properties. The new states near the Fermi level increase the density of the free charge carriers, enhancing the material's electrical conductivity. Model 1 (adjacent doping), shown in Figure 14a, exhibits a bandgap of 2 eV with deeper mid-gap states due to strong dopant interactions. In contrast, Model 2 (far apart doping), which represents the electron distribution in the density of states (Figure 14b), shows a bandgap of 2.2 eV with shallower mid-gap states due to weaker dopant interactions. These mid-gap states arise from the Mo-4*d* and Se-4*p* states in both models, as observed in the corresponding DOS figures of Figures 15 and 16.

In Model 1, the band structure in Figure 14a displays flatter bands near the Fermi level, suggesting localized states due to strong dopant interactions. Additional bands or split bands may appear due to hybridization between Mo, Se, and $TiO_2$ orbitals. According to Model 2, the DOS plot in Figure 16 may exhibit broader peaks closer to the band edges, corresponding to shallow defect states resulting from weaker dopant interactions. The valence band and conduction band edges are closer together, indicating a smaller bandgap. The band structure in Figure 14b shows more dispersed bands, indicating delocalized states caused by weaker dopant interactions. The bands may appear smoother, with fewer split bands or additional states.

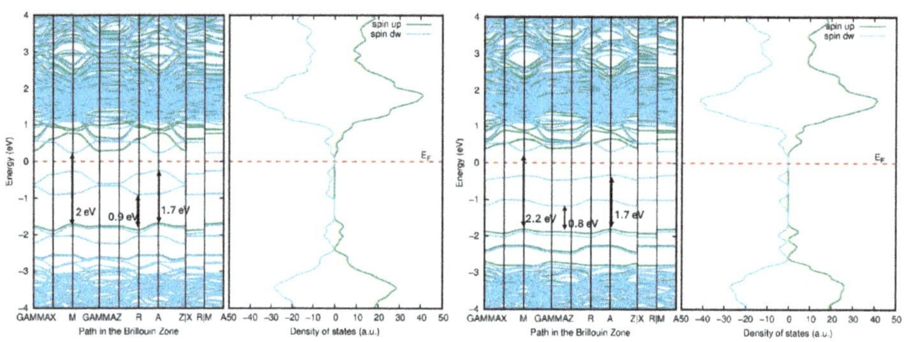


(**a**) (**b**)

**Figure 14.** Bandgap structure and corresponding density of states diagram for the Se- and Mo-doped system: (**a**) Model 1; (**b**) Model 2.

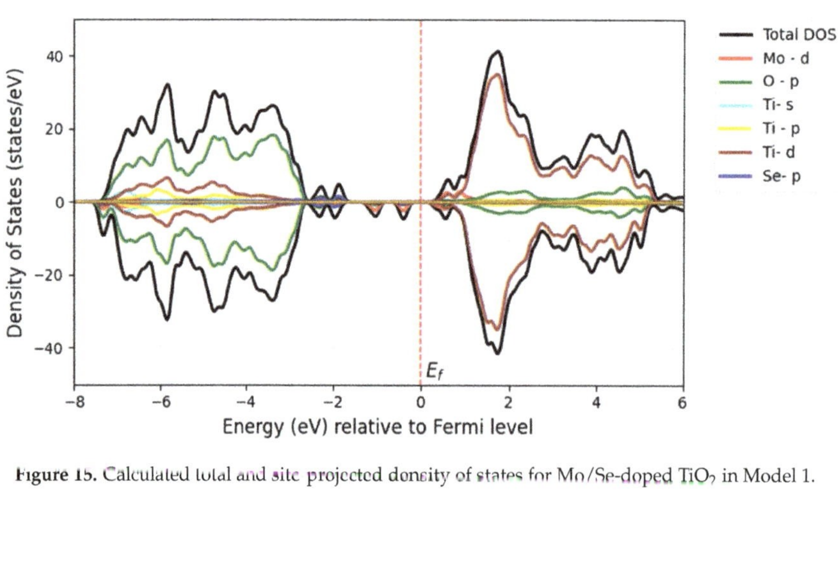


**Figure 15.** Calculated total and site projected density of states for Mo/Se-doped $TiO_2$ in Model 1.

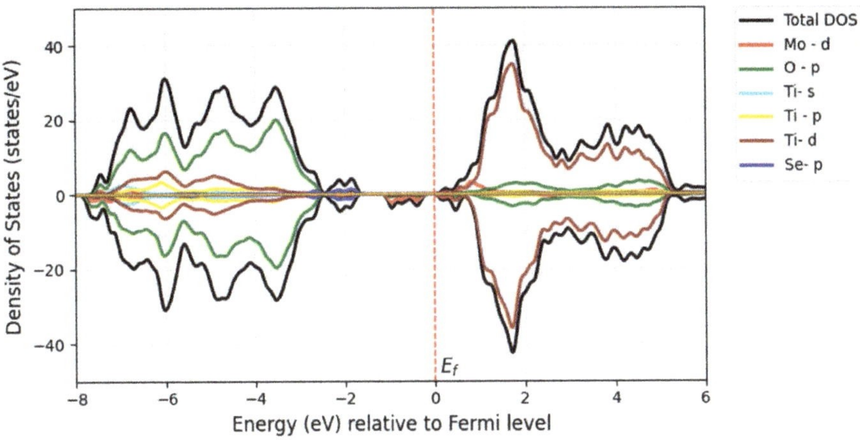


**Figure 16.** Calculated total and site-projected density of states for Mo/Se-doped $TiO_2$ in Model 2.

The significant reduction or near-closure of the bandgap in Mo- and Te-doped structures fundamentally alters the electronic properties of $TiO_2$. Instead of behaving as a wide-bandgap semiconductor, the material becomes semi-metallic or highly conductive. This transformation may enhance its performance in applications requiring high electrical conductivity, such as electrocatalysis or sensing devices, but could compromise its effectiveness in photocatalytic processes, where a sizable bandgap is critical for efficient charge carrier separation.

The strong hybridization between Mo-4*d*, Te-5*p*, and Ti-3*d* orbitals in Model 1, Figure 17 leads to significant bandgap reduction and enhanced visible light absorption. However, the adjacent positioning of dopants may also introduce localized defect states (Figure 18a) that could act as recombination centers for electron–hole pairs. The DOS plot is more symmetric and shows broader peaks, indicating a more uniform distribution of electronic states. The sharp peaks shown in Figures 17 and 19 in the valence band are dominated by O 2*p* and Te-5*p* states. The introduction of Mo-4*d* and Te-5*p* states creates defect states within the bandgap of $TiO_2$, effectively reducing the bandgap. This is crucial for enhancing the material's photocatalytic activity under visible light. The mid-gap states from Te-5*p* orbitals are located just above the valence band, while the Mo-4*d* states are near the conduction band. In Model 2, Figures 18b and 19, the Mo-4*d* orbitals contribute to the DOS, particularly near the conduction band. However, the peaks are broader and less sharp compared with Model 1, indicating weaker interactions due to the spatial separation of dopants. The Te-5*p* and Mo-4*d* orbitals introduce broader mid-gap states above the valence band maximum, as seen in Figure 19. These states are more delocalized and lie closer to both the conduction and valence bands.

Overall, these findings highlight how Mo doping in combination with S, Se, and Te can create beneficial electronic states that improve the material's ability to harness light energy for photocatalytic applications. The strong hybridization among the 5*p* orbitals of Te, 3*p* orbitals of S, and 4*p* orbitals of Se, along with the 3*d* orbitals of Ti and 4*d* orbitals of Mo, produces intermediate peaks within the bandgap of the doped models. Zheng et al. reported that anionic doping with heavy chalcogen elements such as Te and Se significantly reduces the bandgap of $TiO_2$, extending its absorption into the visible light spectrum [15]. Previous studies on mono-doping with S, Se, and Te align with our findings on bandgap reduction and localized electronic states in co-doped systems, as demonstrated by both DFT calculations and experimental results [34,35]. Due to the reduction in bandgap energy, the material can absorb visible light. However, partially occupied impurity states appear above the VBM and below the CBM, which can act as traps for excited electrons. This leads to faster electron–hole recombination, thereby limiting the efficiency of the compound in the visible light region. These intermediate states, except for those in the sulfur-doped models, are located near the VBM and function as shallow acceptor levels, primarily consisting of Se-4*p* and Te-5*p* orbitals. These states have the ability to capture photoexcited holes, which help to reduce the recombination rate of electron–hole pairs. Additionally, the presence of electron vacancies near the valence band can generate an anodic photocurrent, indicating a higher likelihood for electrons to be excited into the intermediate states. In these states, lower photon energy is sufficient to promote electrons into the conduction band. These results suggest that the degree of bandgap narrowing depends on the distance between the doped Mo atom and the chalcogen atom. Model 2, where the dopants are farther apart, exhibits a more significant bandgap reduction compared with Model 1, where the dopants are adjacent.

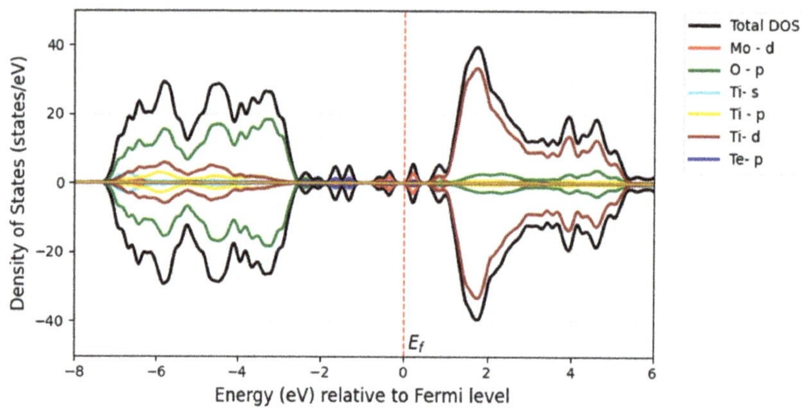


**Figure 17.** Calculated total and site-projected density of states for Mo/Te-doped $TiO_2$ in Model 1.

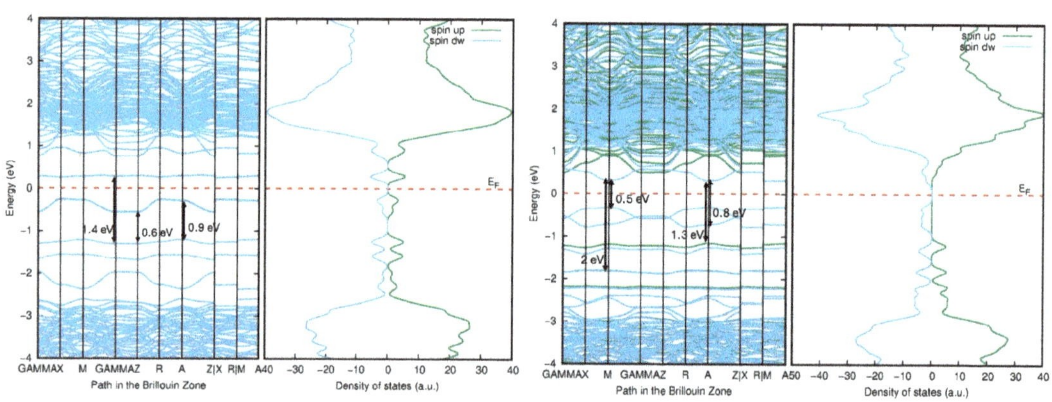


**(a)** **(b)**

**Figure 18.** Bandgap structure and corresponding density of states diagram for the Te- and Mo-doped system: (**a**) Model 1; (**b**) Model 2.

The electronic structures of the three co-doped models are nearly identical; however, the Mo and S co-doped structures exhibit fewer impurity states compared with the Se and Te co-doped structures. This reduction in impurity states may enhance the efficiency of the S-doped models by decreasing the recombination rate compared with the other doped models. The MoS-1 model exhibited a reduced bandgap of 2.52 eV and demonstrated optical absorption in Figure 20 comparable to the other models. It was concluded that the adjacent positioning of the dopants in the MoS-1 model is the most optimal structure, compared with the other co-doped configurations.

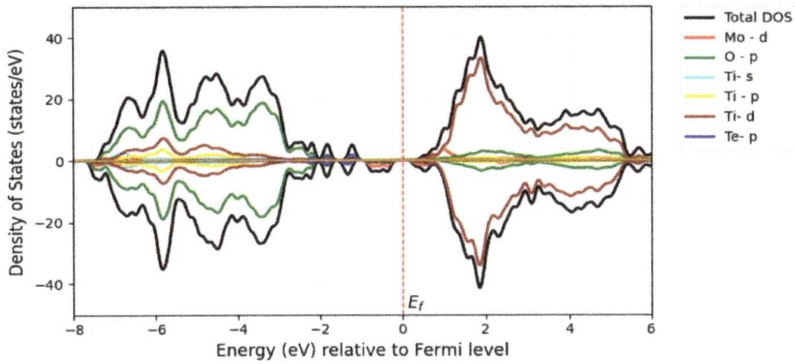


**Figure 19.** Calculated total and site-projected density of states for Mo/Te-doped $TiO_2$ in Model 2.

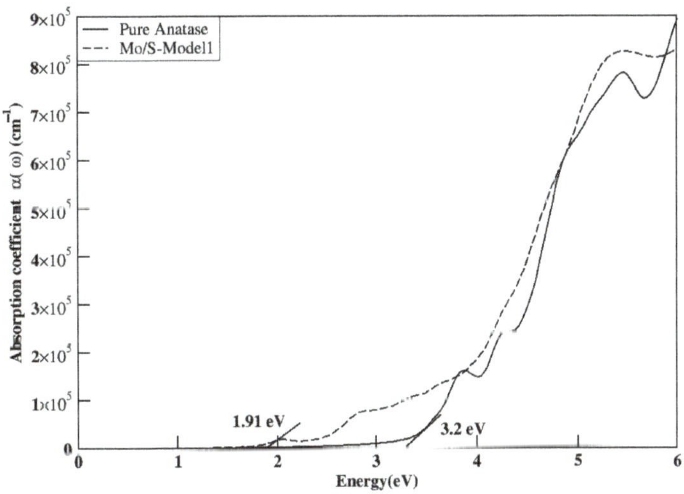


**Figure 20.** Computed absorption spectra for the pure and Mo-doped S, Model 1 anatase-doped structures.

*Photocatalytic Properties*

The CBM and VBM potentials of the co-doped systems in both Model 1 and Model 2 can be determined as shown in Figure 21 (Table 2) relative to the water reduction potential of $H^+/H_2$ (0 eV against the normal hydrogen electrode, NHE) and the water oxidation potential of $O_2/H_2O$ (1.23 eV). These calculations follow the formula established by Butler and Ginley [36]. We determined the CBM and VBM potentials for both the pure and co-doped systems by applying the relevant Equations (5)–(9).

$$E_{CB} = X + E_o - \tfrac{1}{2}E_g \quad E_{VB} = E_g + E_{CB}, \tag{5}$$

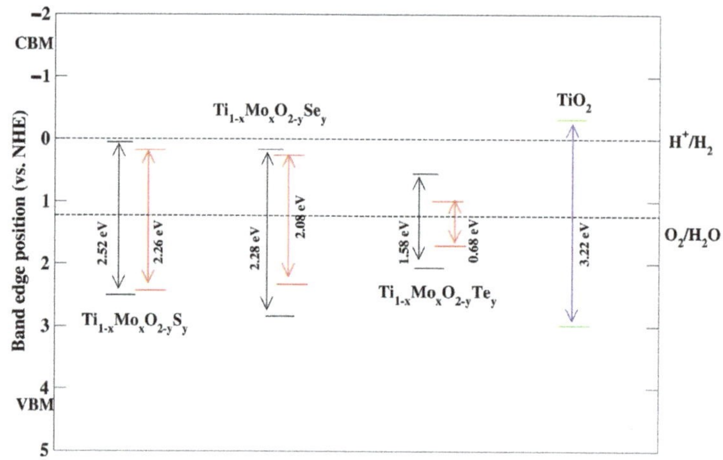


**Figure 21.** The VBM and CBM positions for the co-doped anatase models were determined in relation to the water redox level. The horizontal dotted lines indicate the energy levels of the redox potentials for $H^+/H_2$ (0 eV vs. NHE) and $O_2/H_2O$ (1.23 eV). The black and red colors represent Model 1 and Model 2, respectively.

**Table 2.** Band edge positions of co-doped models and pure $TiO_2$.

| Band Edges (eV) | Mo/S ($X_S$ = 5.807) | | Mo/Se ($X_{Se}$ = 5.805) | | Mo/Te ($X_{Te}$ = 5.802) | | Pure $TiO_2$ |
|---|---|---|---|---|---|---|---|
| | Model 1 | Model 2 | Model 1 | Model 2 | Model 1 | Model 2 | |
| CBM | 0.05 | 0.18 | 0.16 | 0.27 | 0.51 | 0.96 | −0.3 |
| VBM | 2.57 | 2.44 | 2.45 | 2.34 | 2.09 | 1.64 | 2.92 |

Here, $E_0$ =−4.5 eV is the scale factor that bridges the absolute vacuum scale with the reference redox level of the normal hydrogen electrode (NHE), $E_g$ signifies the bandgap energy, while $X$ denotes the absolute electronegativity of the system, calculated using the following formulas:

For pure $TiO_2$:

$$X_{TiO_2} = \left(X_{Ti}X_O^2\right)^{\frac{1}{3}} \tag{6}$$

For Mo-doped S:

$$X_{Ti_{1-x}Mo_xO_{2-y}S_y} = \left(X_{Ti}^{1-x}X_{Mo}^{x}X_O^{2-y}X_S^{y}\right)^{\frac{1}{3}} \tag{7}$$

For Mo-doped Se:

$$X_{Ti_{1-x}Mo_xO_{2-y}Se_y} = \left(X_{Ti}^{1-x}X_{Mo}^{x}X_O^{2-y}X_{Se}^{y}\right)^{\frac{1}{3}} \tag{8}$$

For Mo-doped Te:

$$X_{Ti_{1-x}Mo_xO_{2-y}Te_y} = \left(X_{Ti}^{1-x}X_{Mo}^{x}X_O^{2-y}X_{Te}^{y}\right)^{\frac{1}{3}} \tag{9}$$

where (x = 0.0208, y = 0.0208) and $X_{Ti}$, $X_O$, $X_{Mo}$, $X_S$, $X_{Se}$, and $X_{Te}$ are the absolute electronegativities of Ti, O, Mo, S, Se, and Te atoms, respectively, and their corresponding values are 3.45, 7.54, 3.9, 6.22, 5.89, and 5.49 eV [37].

All the co-doped systems except the Mo and Te co-doped models show stronger oxidation power as much as pure $TiO_2$ does compound under visible light irradiation. Mo and Te co-doped models have better oxidation abilities in the infrared region. However, they show a lower ability of oxidation power than the pure anatase. Our findings suggest that the Mo/S and Mo/Se co-doped anatase systems possess significant oxidation power, making them suitable candidates for applications in oxidative photocatalysis under visible light. However, their limited reduction ability indicates that they may be less effective for photocatalytic applications that require both oxidation and reduction capabilities such as overall water splitting. In this case, these co-doped systems are effective for oxidation-driven photocatalytic applications, such as the degradation of organic pollutants or water oxidation reactions, where oxidative power is critical.

## 6. Optical Calculations

HSE06 optical calculations were performed to obtain more accurate values, though only for the S-doped models due to time constraints, as shown in Figures 20 and 22. Because of its wide bandgap, pure anatase cannot absorb photon energy in the visible region and is responsive only to UV light. In contrast, the optical absorption spectrum of Mo-doped $TiO_2$ indicates visible light absorption, as shown in Figure 22. The electron excitations involve transitions from O-2*p* states to Mo-4*d* states, aligning with recent theoretical calculations [38,39].

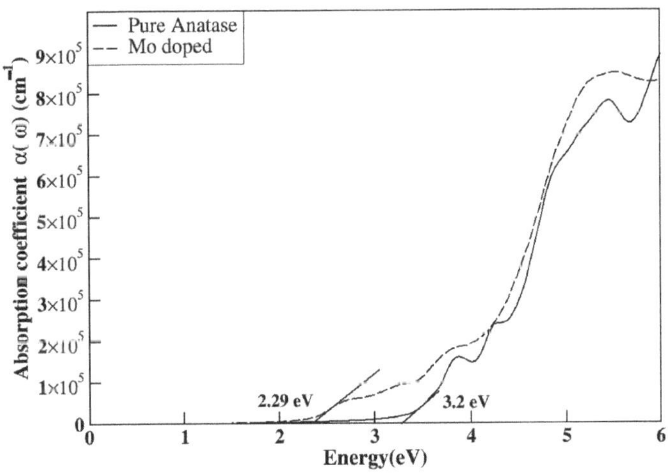


**Figure 22.** Computed absorption coefficient for the Mo-doped anatase $TiO_2$ in HSE06 approximation [1].

Absorption spectrums show that the co-doping affects the shifting of the absorption edge to the visible region and enhances the absorption peak in both the visible and UV regions other than the mono-doped Mo anatase structure. This could happen because of the impurity states present between the bandgaps of the undoped $TiO_2$. Regarding the different locations of doped Mo and S relative to one another, the Model 2 structure in Figure 23 shows the enhancement of the absorption of both UV and visible light region compared with the Model 1 structure in Figure 20. The electrons are initially excited from the O-2*p* state and transferred through the S-3*p* and Mo-4*d* states to the conduction band of Ti-3*d*. Electronic property calculations reveal that impurity states are located within the bandgaps of co-doped anatase $TiO_2$ structures, resulting in a shift of the absorbance spectrum toward the visible light region and an increased absorbance of $10^5$ $cm^{-1}$. The introduction of Mo and S into anatase $TiO_2$ shifts the absorption edge of pure $TiO_2$ from 3.2 eV to 1.91 eV and 1.5 eV for Model 1 and Model 2, respectively. The Tauc method is used to determine the absorption edge and estimate the optical band gap for direct electronic transitions [40]. The absorption edge shift is more significant in the co-doped $TiO_2$ in both the models than in $TiO_2$ doped solely with Mo. A similar observation was made for the Mo and N co-doped model, which shows a greater shift in the absorption edge compared with $TiO_2$ mono-doped with Mo or N [38].

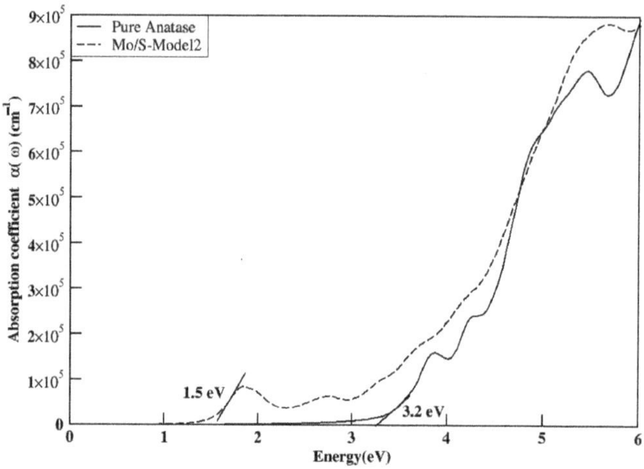


**Figure 23.** Computed absorption spectra for the pure and Mo-doped S, Model 2 anatase-doped structures.

## 7. Bader Charge Analysis

The Bader charge (BC) analysis was performed for all Mo- and chalcogen-doped structures, and the corresponding charge distribution plots are shown in Figure 24. Introducing foreign atoms into the $TiO_2$ lattice can result in charge imbalance. The charge density difference, $\Delta_{\rho\ \mathrm{Chargedifference}}$, was calculated using a self-consistent approach by subtracting the electron densities of the doped system, $\rho_{\mathrm{Dopedmodel}}$, which includes the Mo- and chalcogen-doped models, from the pure $TiO_2$, $\rho_{\mathrm{pure}}$, and the dopants, $\rho_{\mathrm{Dopants}}$, as expressed by Equation (10):

$$\Delta_{\rho\ \mathrm{Chargedifference}} = \rho_{\mathrm{Dopedmodel}} - \rho_{\mathrm{pure}} - \rho_{\mathrm{Dopants}} \quad (10)$$

According to the Bader charges in Figure 5, the Mo atoms in Model 2 have significantly higher positive charges (2.12–2.21). The dopants being farther apart might result in a different kind of charge interaction, where the dopants are more evenly distributed throughout the structure. This could allow Mo to donate more electrons compared with when the dopants are close, resulting in a stronger positive charge on Mo. The increased charge on Mo in Model 2 suggests that Mo might interact differently with the surrounding atoms when the dopants are more spread out. The nonmetallic dopants in Model 2 exhibit slightly more negative Bader charges (−0.65, −0.54, −0.36) compared with Model 1 (see Table S1). This suggests that when the dopants are positioned farther apart, they may attract more electron density, potentially increasing their influence on local charge redistribution in the system. The Mo dopant and the neighboring titanium atoms donate electrons, whereas the adjacent oxygen atoms and chalcogen nonmetals tend to attract electrons, as depicted in Figure 24. This is consistent with the BC analysis, which is illustrated in Figure 5.

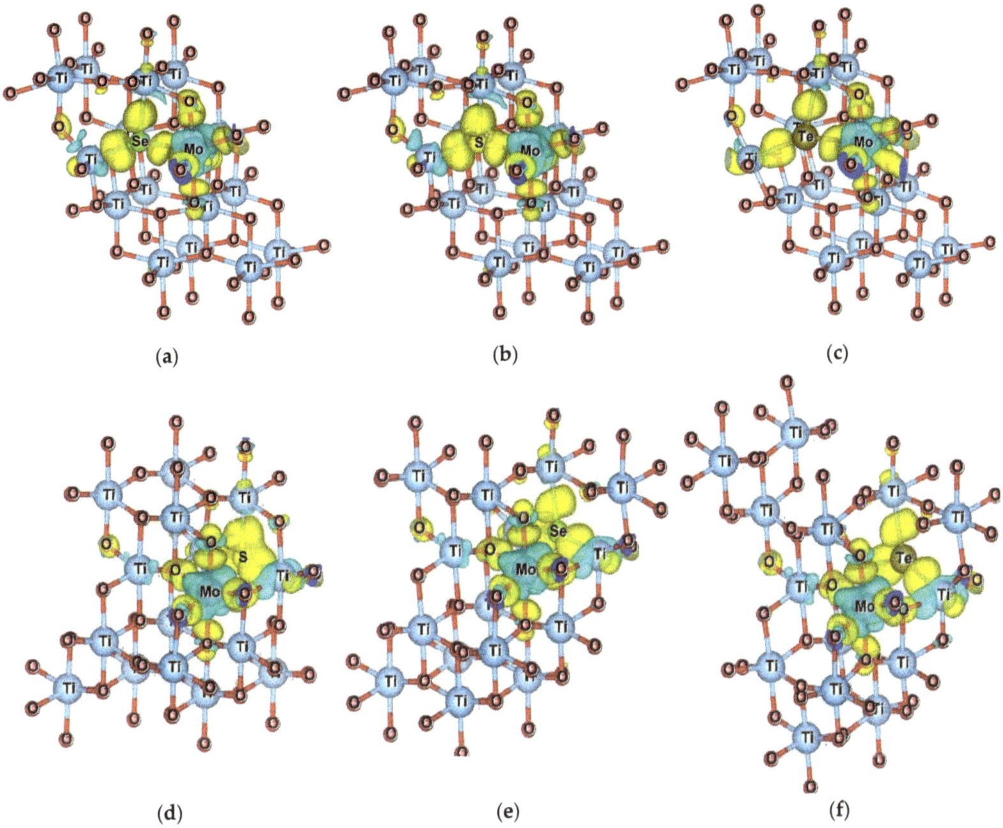


**Figure 24.** Charge density difference of Mo-doped chalcogen anatase $TiO_2$. Figures (**a**,**d**) represent Mo-doped S for Model 1 and Model 2; (**b**,**e**) correspond to Mo-doped Se for Model 1 and Model 2; (**c**,**f**) show Mo-doped Te for Model 1 and Model 2. Yellow and cyan colors represent charge accumulation and depletion, respectively.

In summary, in Model 1 (adjacent dopants), Ti atoms are slightly more positively charged, likely due to stronger interactions with the nearby dopants. In Model 2 (doped atoms far apart), Ti atoms are less positively charged because the interactions with the dopants are weaker. Mo atoms are more positively charged in Model 2 (where the dopants are far apart), suggesting that this configuration leads to stronger electron donation by Mo. This increased donation in Model 2 may influence the material's optoelectronic properties, as reflected in the absorption spectrum shown in Figure 22. In Model 1, the closer positioning of dopants leads to more localized charge transfer to Mo, resulting in slightly lower charges. Oxygen charges are very similar between the two models, with only a minor decrease in Model 2. This suggests that the positioning of dopants has a minimal effect on the oxygen charge distribution. In Model 2, the nonmetallic dopants exhibit slightly more negative Bader charges, suggesting that when the dopants are positioned farther apart, they may attract more electron density from the surrounding lattice. In contrast, in Model 1, the closer proximity of Mo and the nonmetal may lead to stronger Mo–NM interactions, resulting in a more balanced charge distribution. The position of the dopants significantly influences the charge transfer behavior and could affect the material's electronic properties such as its optoelectronic behavior, which is crucial for applications in clean-energy materials.

## 8. Spin Density

For the Te-doped Model 1, the net magnetization is zero, suggesting the system may have antiparallel spin polarization, where spin-up and spin-down regions cancel each other out, as shown in the density of states in Figure 17. Even though localized spin density exists, the antiparallel alignment results in zero net magnetization. As a result, the overall spin density could be symmetric or negligible, leading to zero magnetization. Tellurium (Te) is a non-magnetic element, which may not contribute to spin polarization, unlike Mo. According to the Figure 25, in Model 2, the net magnetic moment is −1.98 μB, similar to the Se/Mo system, indicating that the delocalization effect allows Mo to retain its spin contribution. The observed trends in the chart confirm that dopant positioning significantly affects spin polarization.

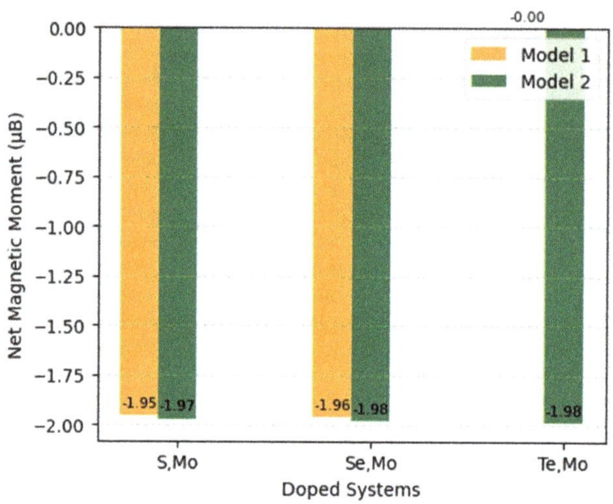


**Figure 25.** Bar chart of net magnetic moment for the doped models Mo/S, Mo/Se, and Mo/Te in Model 1 and Model 2.

These results highlight a fundamental trade-off in dopant configuration design. Model 1, where dopants are positioned closely, offers better structural stability, lower ground-state energy, and reduced lattice distortion, which helps minimize defect states and charge recombination. This makes Model 1 more favorable for stable photocatalytic applications. In contrast, Model 2, with dopants placed farther apart, shows greater reductions in bandgap and stronger optical absorption in the visible range, along with enhanced magnetization. However, this comes at the cost of increased lattice strain and reduced stability. Thus, while Model 1 excels in structural and electronic cleanliness, Model 2 is better suited for enhanced optoelectronic and magnetic performance. This trade-off suggests that there is no universally optimal doping configuration. The selection between Model 1 and Model 2 should be based on the specific property requirements of the intended application, such as photocatalysis, photovoltaics, or spintronics, as well as on the feasibility of synthesizing the desired configuration experimentally.

## 9. Conclusions

This paper presents a calculation and analysis of the electronic and optical properties of anatase $TiO_2$ doped with Mo and S, Se, or Te in two different configurations using density functional theory.

- When Mo and the chalcogen atoms are placed in adjacent positions (Model 1), the system may exhibit a lower ground-state energy due to more stable interactions between the dopants, such as bonding, charge transfer, or lattice strain compensation, which reduce the overall energy.
- Model 2 has higher energy because the dopants are farther apart, leading to less interaction and possibly a less stable electronic structure, but the volume remains smaller due to less distortion.
- The degree of bandgap reduction depends on the distance between the doped Mo and chalcogen atoms, with Model 2 showing a greater reduction. The MoS-1 model, with adjacent dopants, exhibited fewer impurity states and the most optimal structural stability, potentially enhancing photocatalytic efficiency by reducing recombination.
- Except for Mo/Te co-doped models, all co-doped systems show stronger oxidation power under visible light, similar to pure $TiO_2$. Mo/S and Mo/Se co-doped anatase are effective for oxidation-driven photocatalytic applications but have limited reduction ability, making them less suitable for water splitting.
- The thermodynamic stability of co-doped $TiO_2$ systems is reflected in their formation energies, with Ti-rich environments being the most favorable for practical applications. This insight can guide further research to enhance material performance.
- Co-doping $TiO_2$ with Mo and S shifts the absorption edge into the visible region and enhances light absorption, with Mo/S–Model 2 showing a more significant shift from 3.2 eV (pure $TiO_2$) to 1.5 eV.

**Supplementary Materials:** The following supporting information can be downloaded at: https://www.mdpi.com/article/10.3390/computation13070170/s1, Figure S1: Structural Optimization of Mo and S doped models; Figure S2: Structural Optimization of Mo and Se doped models; Figure S3: Structural Optimization of Mo and Te doped models; Figure S4: Structural Optimization of the doped structures under the Model-1 category. Table S1: Bader charges for doped systems (Model 1 and Model 2).

**Author Contributions:** Conceptualization, W.A.C.P.W.; Methodology, W.A.C.P.W. and P.V.; Software, W.A.C.P.W.; Validation, W.A.C.P.W.; Formal analysis, W.A.C.P.W. and D.V.; Investigation, W.A.C.P.W.; Writing—original draft, W.A.C.P.W.; Writing—review & editing, W.A.C.P.W., P.V., T.R. and D.V.; Visualization, W.A.C.P.W.; Supervision, P.V., T.R. and D.V.; Project administration, D.V., Funding acquisition, D.V. All authors have read and agreed to the published version of the manuscript.

**Funding:** This research received no external funding.

**Data Availability Statement:** All data included in this article along with the Supplementary Document.

**Acknowledgments:** The authors extend their gratitude to the Research Council of Norway for the allocation of computational resources (project number NN2867k) at the Norwegian supercomputing facility. This research was supported by Grant No. NORPART2021/10095: Higher Education and Research Collaboration on Nanomaterials for Clean Energy Technologies 2.0 (HRNCET 2.0).

**Conflicts of Interest:** The authors declare no conflict of interest.

## References

1. Wanniarachchi, W.A.C.P.; Arunasalam, T.; Ravirajan, P.; Velauthapillai, D.; Vajeeston, P. Hybrid Functional Study on Electronic and Optical Properties of the Dopants in Anatase $TiO_2$. *ACS Omega* **2023**, *8*, 42275–42289. [CrossRef] [PubMed]
2. Jiang, L.; Zhou, S.; Yang, J.; Wang, H.; Yu, H.; Chen, H.; Zhao, Y.; Yuan, X.; Chu, W.; Li, H. Near-Infrared Light Responsive $TiO_2$ for Efficient Solar Energy Utilization. *Adv. Funct. Mater.* **2021**, *32*, 2108977. [CrossRef]
3. Zaleska, A. Doped-$TiO_2$: A review Doped-$TiO_2$: A Review. *Recent Patents Eng.* **2008**, *2*, 157–164. [CrossRef]
4. Ibrahim, H.H.; Mohamed, A.A.; Ibrahim, I.A.M. Electronic sand optical properties of mono and co-doped anatase $TiO_2$: First principles calculations. *Mater. Chem. Phys.* **2020**, *252*, 123285. [CrossRef]

5. Pan, J.; Li, C.; Zhao, Y.; Liu, R.; Gong, Y.; Niu, L.; Liu, X.; Chi, B. Electronic properties of $TiO_2$ doped with Sc, Y, La, Zr, Hf, V, Nb and Ta. *Chem. Phys. Lett.* **2015**, *628*, 43–48. [CrossRef]
6. Umebayashi, T.; Yamaki, T.; Itoh, H.; Asai, K. Analysis of electronic structures of 3d transition metal-doped $TiO_2$ based on band calculations. *J. Phys. Chem. Solids* **2002**, *63*, 1909–1920. [CrossRef]
7. Devi, L.G.; Murthy, B.N.; Kumar, S.G. Photocatalytic activity of V5+, Mo6+ and Th4+ doped polycrystalline $TiO_2$ for the degradation of chlorpyrifos under UV/solar light. *J. Mol. Catal. A Chem.* **2009**, *308*, 174–181. [CrossRef]
8. Ohno, T.; Akiyoshi, M.; Umebayashi, T.; Asai, K.; Mitsui, T.; Matsumura, M. Preparation of S-doped $TiO_2$ photocatalysts and their photocatalytic activities under visible light. *Appl. Catal. A Gen.* **2004**, *265*, 115–121. [CrossRef]
9. Eslami, A.; Amini, M.M.; Yazdanbakhsh, A.R.; Mohseni-Bandpei, A.; Safari, A.A.; Asadi, A. N,S co-doped $TiO_2$ nanoparticles and nanosheets in simulated solar light for photocatalytic degradation of non-steroidal anti-inflammatory drugs in water: A comparative study. *J. Chem. Technol. Biotechnol.* **2016**, *91*, 2693–2704. [CrossRef]
10. Bu, X.; Wang, Y.; Li, J.; Zhang, C. Improving the visible light photocatalytic activity of $TiO_2$ by combining sulfur doping and rectorite carrier. *J. Alloys Compd.* **2015**, *628*, 20–26. [CrossRef]
11. El-Sheikh, S.M.; Zhang, G.; El-Hosainy, H.M.; Ismail, A.A.; O'SHea, K.E.; Falaras, P.; Kontos, A.G.; Dionysiou, D.D. High performance sulfur, nitrogen and carbon doped mesoporous anatase–brookite $TiO_2$ photocatalyst for the removal of microcystin-LR under visible light irradiation. *J. Hazard. Mater.* **2014**, *280*, 723–733. [CrossRef] [PubMed]
12. Mathew, S.; Ganguly, P.; Kumaravel, V.; Harrison, J.; Hinder, S.J.; Bartlett, J.; Pillai, S.C. Effect of chalcogens (S, Se, and Te) on the anatase phase stability and photocatalytic antimicrobial activity of $TiO_2$. *Mater. Today Proc.* **2020**, *33*, 2458–2464. [CrossRef]
13. Štengl, V.; Bakardjieva, S.; Bludská, J. Se and Te-modified titania for photocatalytic applications. *J. Mater. Sci.* **2011**, *46*, 3523–3536. [CrossRef]
14. Gurkan, Y.Y.; Kasapbasi, E.; Cinar, Z. Enhanced solar photocatalytic activity of $TiO_2$ by selenium(IV) ion-doping: Characterization and DFT modeling of the surface. *Chem. Eng. J.* **2013**, *214*, 34–44. [CrossRef]
15. Zheng, J.W.; Bhattcahrayya, A.; Wu, P.; Chen, Z.; Highfield, J.; Dong, Z.; Xu, R. The origin of visible light absorption in chalcogen element (S, Se, and Te)-doped anatase $TiO_2$ photoatalysts. *J. Phys. Chem. C* **2010**, *114*, 7063–7069. [CrossRef]
16. Blöchl, P.E. Projector augmented-wave method. *Phys. Rev. B* **1994**, *50*, 17953–17979. [CrossRef]
17. Kertesz, M.; Kresse, G. Performance of the Vienna ab iniTiO simulation package (VASP). *J. Mol. Struct.* **2003**, *624*, 37.
18. Perdew, J.P.; Burke, K.; Ernzerhof, M. Generalized Gradient approximation Made Simple. *Phys. Rev. Lett.* **1996**, *77*, 3865. [CrossRef]
19. Monkhorst, H.J.; Pack, J.D. Special points for Brillouin-zone integrations. *Phys. Rev. B* **1976**, *13*, 5188–5192. [CrossRef]
20. Meng, Q.; Wang, T.; Liu, E.; Ma, X.; Ge, Q.; Gong, J. Understanding electronic and optical properties of anatase $TiO_2$ photocatalysts co-doped with nitrogen and transition metals. *Phys. Chem. Chem. Phys.* **2013**, *15*, 9549–9561. [CrossRef]
21. Shishkin, M.; Sato, H. DFT+ U in Dudarev's formulation with corrected interactions between the electrons with opposite spins: The form of Hamiltonian, calculation of forces, and bandgap adjustments. *J. Chem. Phys.* **2019**, *151*, 024102. [CrossRef] [PubMed]
22. Jain, A.; Ong, S.P.; Hautier, G.; Chen, W.; Richards, W.D.; Dacek, S.; Cholia, S.; Gunter, D.; Skinner, D.; Ceder, G.; et al. The Materials Project: A materials genome approach to accelerating materials innovation. *APL Mater.* **2013**, *1*, 011002. [CrossRef]
23. Heyd, J.; Scuseria, G.E. Efficient hybrid density functional calculations in solids: Assessment of the Heyd-Scuseria-Ernzerhof screened coulomb hybrid functional articles you may be interested in. *J. Chem. Phys.* **2004**, *121*, 1187. [CrossRef]
24. Momma, K.; Izumi, F. VESTA 3 for three-dimensional visualization of crystal, volumetric and morphology data. *J. Appl. Crystallogr.* **2011**, *44*, 1272–1276. [CrossRef]
25. Togo, A. First-principles phonon calculations with phonopy and phono3py. *J. Phys. Soc. Jpn.* **2023**, *92*, 012001. [CrossRef]
26. Zhu, H.X.; Liu, J.M. First principles calculations of electronic and optical properties of Mo and C co-doped anatase $TiO_2$. *Appl. Phys. A Mater. Sci. Process* **2014**, *117*, 831–839. [CrossRef]
27. Arlt, T.; Bermejo, M.; Blanco, M.A.; Gerward, L.; Jiang, J.Z.; Olsen, J.S.; Recio, J.M. High-pressure polymorphs of anatase. *Phys. Rev. B Condens. Matter Mater. Phys.* **2000**, *61*, 14414–14419. [CrossRef]
28. Al-Oubidy, E.A.; Kadhim, F.J. Photocatalytic activity of anatase titanium dioxide nanostructures prepared by reactive magnetron sputtering technique. *Opt. Quantum Electron.* **2019**, *51*, 23. [CrossRef]
29. Sorantin, P.I.; Schwarz, K. Chemical bonding in rutile-type compounds. *Inorg. Chem.* **1992**, *31*, 567–576. [CrossRef]
30. Soussi, A.; Hssi, A.A.; Boulkaddat, L.; Boujnah, M.; Abouabassi, K.; Haounati, R.; Asbayou, A.; Elfanaoui, A.; Markazi, R.; Ihlal, A.; et al. First principle study of electronic, optical and electrical properties of Mo doped $TiO_2$. *Comput. Condens. Matter* **2021**, *29*, e00606. [CrossRef]
31. Wang, S.; Bai, L.N.; Sun, H.M.; Jiang, Q.; Lian, J.S. Structure and photocatalytic property of Mo-doped $TiO_2$ nanoparticles. *Powder Technol.* **2013**, *244*, 9–15. [CrossRef]
32. Tian, F.H.; Liu, C.B. DFT description on electronic structure and optical absorption properties of anionic S-doped anatase $TiO_2$. *J. Phys. Chem. B* **2006**, *110*, 17866–17871. [CrossRef] [PubMed]

33. Liu, R.; Zhou, X.; Yang, F.; Yu, Y. Combination study of DFT calculation and experiment for photocatalytic properties of S-doped anatase $TiO_2$. *Appl. Surf. Sci.* **2014**, *319*, 50–59. [CrossRef]
34. Erikat, I.; Alkhabbas, M.; Hamad, B.; Alahmad, W. The Chalcogen (S, Se, and Te) Doping Effects on the Structural and Electronic Properties of Anatase (101) $TiO_2$ Thin Surface Layers: DFT Study. *Int. J. Photoenergy* **2024**, *2024*, 3489162. [CrossRef]
35. Xie, W.; Li, R.; Xu, Q. Enhanced photocatalytic activity of Se-doped $TiO_2$ under visible light irradiation. *Sci. Rep.* **2018**, *8*, 8752. [CrossRef] [PubMed]
36. Wang, G.Z.; Chen, H.; Luo, X.K.; Yuan, H.K.; Kuang, A.L. Bandgap engineering of $SrTiO_3/NaTaO_3$ heterojunction for visible light photocatalysis. *Int. J. Quantum Chem.* **2017**, *117*, e25424. [CrossRef]
37. Pearson, R.G. Absolute electronegativity and hardness: Application to inorganic chemistry. *Inorg. Chem.* **1988**, *27*, 734–740. [CrossRef]
38. Khan, M.; Xu, J.; Chen, N.; Cao, W. First principle calculations of the electronic and optical properties of pure and (Mo, N) co-doped anatase $TiO_2$. *J. Alloys Compd.* **2012**, *513*, 539–545. [CrossRef]
39. Yu, X.; Li, C.; Ling, Y.; Tang, T.A.; Wu, Q.; Kong, J. First principles calculations of electronic and optical properties of Mo-doped rutile $TiO_2$. *J. Alloys Compd.* **2010**, *507*, 33–37. [CrossRef]
40. Makuła, P.; Pacia, M.; Macyk, W. How To Correctly Determine the Band Gap Energy of Modified Semiconductor Photocatalysts Based on UV-Vis Spectra. *J. Phys. Chem. Lett.* **2018**, *9*, 6814–6817. [CrossRef]

computation

MDPI

Article

# CrystalShift: A Versatile Command-Line Tool for Crystallographic Structural Data Analysis, Modification, and Format Conversion Prior to Solid-State DFT Calculations of Organic Crystals

**Ilona A. Isupova [1,2,3] and Denis A. Rychkov [1,3,*]**

1 Laboratory of Mechanochemistry, Institute of Solid State Chemistry and Mechanochemistry, Kutateladze 18, Novosibirsk 630090, Russia; i.isupova@g.nsu.ru
2 Faculty of Natural Sciences, Novosibirsk State University, Pirogova 1, Novosibirsk 630090, Russia
3 SRF "SKIF", Boreskov Institute of Catalysis, Koltsovo 630559, Russia
* Correspondence: rychkov.dennis@gmail.com

**Abstract:** *CrystalShift* is an open-source computational tool tailored for the analysis, transformation, and conversion of crystallographic data, with a particular emphasis on organic crystal structures. It offers a comprehensive suite of features valuable for the computational study of solids: format conversion, crystallographic basis transformation, atomic coordinate editing, and molecular layer analysis. These options are especially valuable for studying the mechanical properties of molecular crystals with potential applications in organic materials science. Written in the C programming language, *CrystalShift* offers computational efficiency and compatibility with widely used crystallographic formats such as CIF, POSCAR, and XYZ. It provides a command-line interface, enabling seamless integration into research workflows while addressing specific challenges in crystallography, such as handling non-standard file formats and robust error correction. *CrystalShift* may be applied for both in-depth study of particular crystal structure origins and the high-throughput conversion of crystallographic datasets prior to DFT calculations with periodic boundary conditions using *VASP* code.

**Keywords:** crystal structure converter; crystallographic basis change; coordinates editor; molecular layers; organic crystals; molecular crystals; bending crystals; plastic crystals

## 1. Introduction

Crystallographic data analysis and processing is a substantial step in materials science, solid-state physics, and computational chemistry. It helps to obtain various data on the nature of the crystal structure: its stability, mechanical properties depending on applied pressure, temperature changes, etc. [1–7]. In some cases, it is important to perform numerical experiments using computational tools to overcome experimental challenges, save time, and achieve reproducibility [8–10].

The visualization and analysis of crystal structure can be performed using multiple software packages, such as CCDC Mercury [11,12], VESTA [13], Chemcraft [14], and VMD [15]. Some of these packages (e.g., CCDC Mercury [12] and ToposPro [16]) provide internal modules and implemented algorithms for advanced crystallographic and topological analysis, as well as basic molecular mechanics calculations. Others, such as VESTA, are more aimed at crystal structure editing using mainly a graphical user interface (GUI) but lack valuable crystal structure analysis tools. Nevertheless, most of the above-mentioned software packages generate mainly crystallographic files, which cannot be used directly by most computational programs (except the peculiar CrystalExplorer21 [17] and OCC [18]). Thus, several scripts and other tools have been published to overcome chemical file formatting issues, which are different for various computational programs. Among others, OpenBabel [19] and Cif2Cell [20] seem to be the most widespread in the community but have to maintain up-to-date input file formats for different programs, which may result in some inconsistencies. There are also services that are designed for specific tasks, such as mechanical properties calculation and different modulus evaluation—some aim to prepare and simplify routine prior to calculations (e.g., DeformCell [21], VASPKIT [22]), while others aim to analyze obtained data (EoSFit7 [23,24], ELATE [25], etc.). Obviously, there are numerous less popular scripts for the particular conversion of files to exact formats (e.g., cif2vasp and vasp2cif [26]), which usually generate input and output files for DFT calculations. Other complex tools, such as pymatgen (a robust, open-source Python library for materials analysis) [27] and ASE (a set of tools and Python modules for setting up, manipulating, running, visualizing, and analyzing atomistic simulations) [28] may be used for comprehensive computational tasks, including not only file format conversion but also data manipulation and results analysis. Nevertheless, both tools require Python knowledge and have a relatively high entry barrier and steep learning curve, which does not encourage their use by computational chemists for simple workflows or very specific tasks.

On the one hand, some software provides a GUI, which helps to inspect crystal structures visually and provides an in-depth analysis of a particular system, but usually limits the possibility of a high-throughput workflow in terms of further DFT calculations. On the other hand, command-line programs are limited in terms of crystal structure analysis and may be sensitive to installed libraries and operating systems, primarily on the supercomputer. An attempt to provide a seamless workflow for calculating the mechanical properties of "bending" crystals results in the usage of multiple programs, as shown in Scheme 1 below:

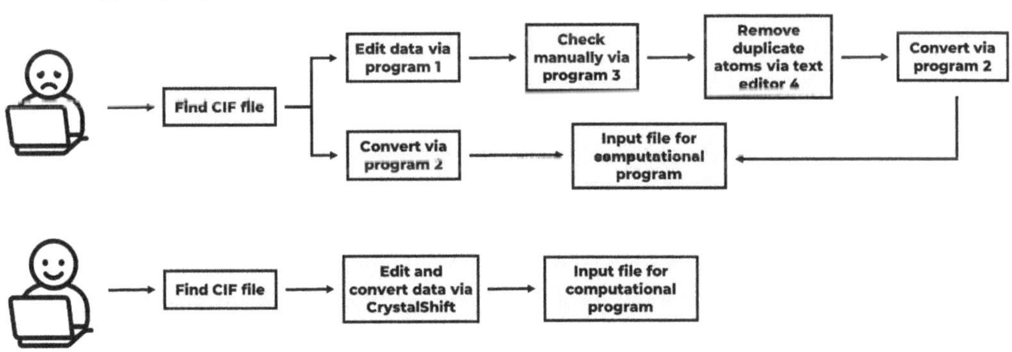


**Scheme 1.** A use case describing a computational chemist's experience in preparing input files, before and after the introduction of *CrystalShift*.

Thus, despite the availability of these tools, there remains a need for versatile, high-performance software that integrates advanced crystallographic editing, molecular layer analysis, and efficient format conversion. *CrystalShift* was developed to address this gap, combining robust command-line functionalities with algorithms tailored for detailed structural analysis. It does not require knowledge of any programming language and may be easily used in various workflows on supercomputers using ordinary Bash scripts. Notably, it includes a molecular layer analysis module that identifies clusters of atoms (molecules), detects crystallographic disorders, and calculates interlayer distances using DBSCAN [29] and KD-Tree [30] algorithms, which is valuable for organic systems. Understanding the geometry of molecular layers and their influence on material characteristics is crucial for crystallographic and topological analysis for advancing materials sciences, especially for bending crystals [31]. While electronic structure ultimately governs a material's behavior, geometric patterns such as interlayer distances, symmetry, and cluster distributions offer predictive insights into a structure's properties.

## 2. Software

### *2.1. Software Design and Architecture*

*CrystalShift* is a command-line tool written in the C programming language, designed for the efficient processing of crystallographic data. It consists of two subroutines: "crystalshift" and "crystalshift_layers". The "crystalshift" subroutine is designed for converting formats, crystallographic basis and unit cell change, supercell generation, and atomic coordinate editing directly for CIF files from CSD and can be easily adopted for high-throughput workflow. The "crystalshift_layers" subroutine is designed for molecular layer analysis, which is usually needed for specific in-depth modification of the crystal structure prior to solid-state calculations (Scheme 2).

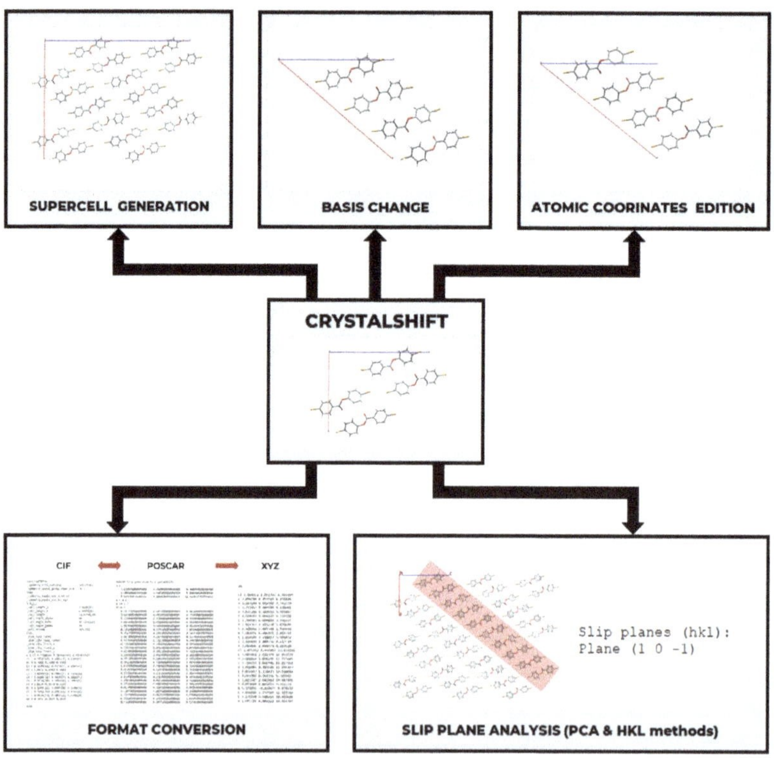


**Scheme 2.** Visualization of the main functionality of the *CrystalShift* software, including both "crystalshift" and "crystalshift_layers" subroutines.

Key modules of "crystalshift" and "crystalshift_layers" subroutines include several source and header files (Scheme 3). The modular structure of the *CrystalShift* program allows users to isolate and refine specific components of the software without disrupting the entire system. This flexibility is essential, as it allows developers, or even users themselves, to incorporate new algorithms or data processing methods effortlessly (if needed), thereby enhancing the program's capabilities and versatility. However, this does not hinder the user experience, as all modules are compiled using a single command or Makefile invocation. For installation instructions and access to the program's code, please refer to the project page on GitHub (https://github.com/shes73/CrystalShift) (accessed on 29 May 2025).

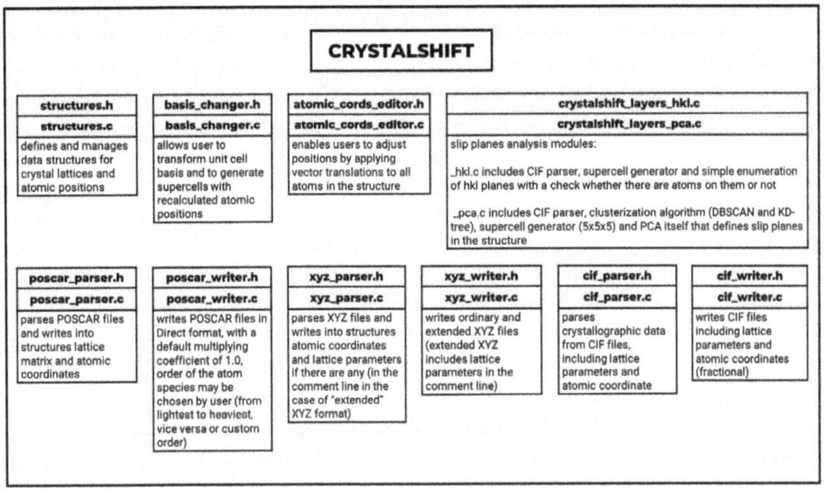


**Scheme 3.** Description of all source and header files of the program for both the "crystalshift" and "crystalshift_layers" modules.

### 2.2. Input and Output Formats (Converter)

*CrystalShift* (currently) supports three widely used crystallographic file formats:

- CIF (Crystallographic Information File) is the most widely used format for crystallographic data. CIF files are parsed to extract lattice parameters, atomic coordinates, and additional data. Experimental error data and non-crystallographic information are stripped for clarity during editing. When writing CIF files, *CrystalShift* simplifies structures by assuming a triclinic lattice with space group P1, avoiding complications from symmetry operations.
- The POSCAR file format is specific to the Vienna Ab initio Simulation Package (VASP) [32–35], which is widely used for computational materials science. It represents lattice parameters in the form of a matrix and atomic coordinates. This format is extensively used in Density Functional Theory (DFT) calculations and other atomistic simulations. The output from *CrystalShift* POSCAR files is written in fractional (direct) coordinates, with support for reordering atomic species based on user-defined criteria (e.g., from lightest to heaviest element, otherwise, or user-defined order).
- The XYZ file format is a simple, human-readable format, used primarily for calculations and visualizations of single molecules. It lists the number of atoms and atomic coordinates only. In the extended version of XYZ, there are additionally added lattice parameters in the comment line. This format is very useful for further calculations using other computational software (ORCA [36], Gaussian [37], etc.).

### 2.3. Basis Change and Supercell Generation

The basis change module includes the creation of supercells since they differ only in the addition of new atoms. When changing the basis, only the vectors and angles of the crystal lattice change, and the number of atoms remains the same. It is worth noting the limitation in the work of the module for creating supercells—*CrystalShift* can add new atoms only if the new vector components are integers. *CrystalShift* handles symmetry operations from the CIF file with a separate command, while this module adds atoms solely based on the principle of translation. Thus, if only a unit cell is provided, it is mandatory to convert it to the primitive cell using the appropriate *CrystalShift* option and then use basis change or supercell generation.

### 2.4. Molecular Layer Analysis

The molecular layer analysis subroutine "crystalshift_layers" of *CrystalShift* is designed to identify and characterize molecular layers within crystal lattices, with a focus on applications in material science, particularly for studying flexible organic crystals. The subroutine employs a combination of advanced algorithms and computational techniques to deliver accurate and insightful results. Two approaches were evaluated for identifying sliding planes during the development of the "crystalshift_layers" module—including the PCA algorithm [38–40] and the HKL algorithm (Scheme 4).

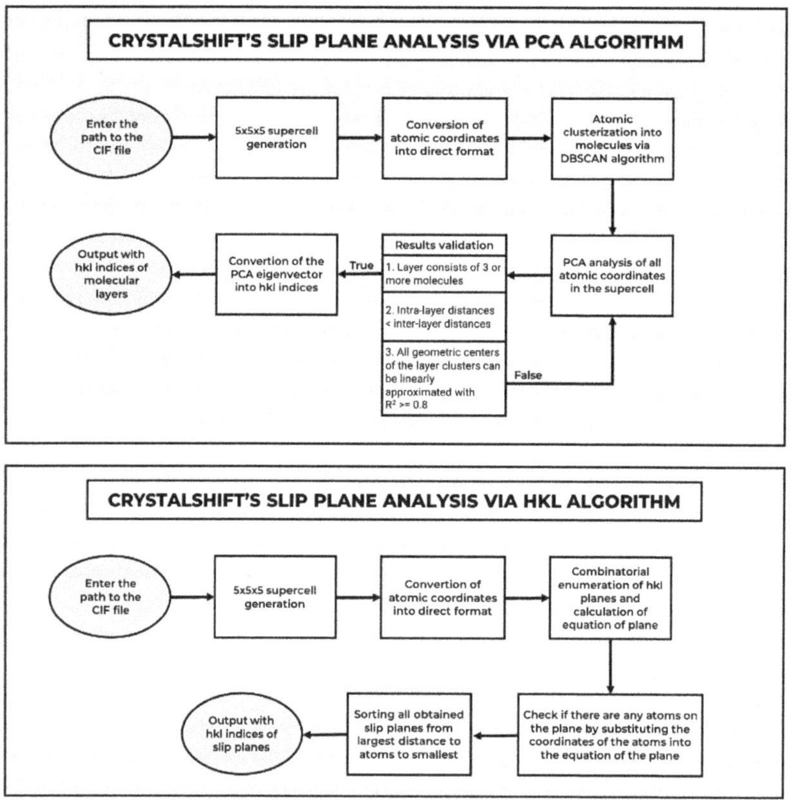


**Scheme 4.** Molecular layer analysis workflow of the "crystalshift_layers" subroutine.

In the case of PCA, the analysis begins with identifying molecular clusters within the crystal lattice using the Density-Based Spatial Clustering of Applications with Noise (DBSCAN) algorithm [29]. DBSCAN is particularly effective for this purpose, as it groups atoms based on their proximity while treating isolated or "noise" atoms as potential lattice disorders. This ensures a robust differentiation between meaningful molecular clusters and extraneous atomic noise.

To optimize spatial queries, such as finding neighboring atoms and clusters, the module leverages a KD-Tree data structure [30]. This significantly enhances computational efficiency, particularly for large datasets with complex geometries.

All obtained data after parsing are used to calculate the eigenvalues and vectors of the covariance matrix via Principal Component Analysis (PCA).

PCA is a widely used statistical method in data analysis and machine learning. Its primary goal is to reduce the dimensionality of a dataset while retaining as much variability (information) as possible. The first principal component captures the direction of the highest variance in the data, the second principal component captures the next highest variance (orthogonal to the first), and so on. PCA involves calculating the eigenvalues and eigenvectors of the covariance matrix of the data. The eigenvectors determine the directions of the principal components, while the eigenvalues indicate the amount of variance captured by each component [38–40]. When applied to atomic coordinates, the eigenvector corresponding to the highest variance is expected to align with the molecular layer direction in the crystal lattice.

However, several limitations were identified when PCA was used:

- Molecular layers should be "sufficiently" spaced apart.
- Errors may occur if the molecules are large and bulky. At best, the direction may be slightly incorrect, and at worst, an erroneous result may be obtained.
- PCA analyzes the spatial distribution of atoms rather than explicitly identifying unoccupied surfaces. Consequently, the obtained Miller indices (hkl) may be suboptimal for further analysis.

If the principal axis identified in the first iteration does not meet the criteria above, the program attempts the next (orthogonal) principal axis.

As an alternative approach, a systematic enumeration of all possible Miller index combinations was implemented, ranging from −7 to +7 for each index (h, k, l). The algorithm iterates through each combination, formulates the corresponding plane equation, and evaluates whether atomic positions align with the plane within a predefined threshold.

This approach also has some disadvantages:

- To correctly check large Miller indices, it is necessary to construct supercells.
- The algorithm is unable to identify molecular layers if they correspond to multiple distinct sets of low Miller indices. For instance, if molecular layers are located on the (200) and (300) planes, the method cannot determine an appropriate index combination to define an intermediate plane between them.

For an enhanced user experience, it is advisable to employ these approaches in conjunction to avoid overlooking potential slip planes. While this tool does not guarantee absolute precision, it serves as an excellent supplementary tool.

The molecular layer analysis module is particularly valuable for studying flexible organic crystals, where layered structures are often key to their mechanical properties, such as plasticity or elasticity. By identifying layers, assessing interlayer distances, and detecting lattice disorders, the tool provides researchers with a deeper understanding of how molecular geometry influences material behavior.

### 2.5. Programming Requirements

*CrystalShift* is distributed as open-source software, allowing researchers to compile and run the program on various operating systems. The compilation process requires only a standard C compiler, and the Makefile included in the repository simplifies the build process.

By maintaining a minimal dependency footprint while offering advanced analytical capabilities, *CrystalShift* ensures accessibility and usability across diverse research environments. This careful balance of simplicity and sophistication underpins its versatility as a tool for crystallographic data manipulation and analysis prior to DFT calculations.

All *CrystalShift* modules, including basis transformations, atomic coordinate editing, format conversion, and molecular layer searching, rely solely on standard C libraries, ensuring broad compatibility, ease of deployment, and usage.

## 3. Results

The principal idea of *CrystalShift* is to help computational chemists process CIF-to-VASP input POSCAR files, with the possibility of additional in-depth modification and analysis without using multiple software tools or programming knowledge.

In order to help process multiple crystallographic data used for specific scientific aims, benchmarking, dataset construction, and other possible tasks, we provide feasible tests for converting file formats, estimating calculation speed, possible inaccuracies and mistakes during various procedures, possible misuse by inexperienced users, and formulating current limitations and future improvements. An example of *CrystalShift* use for a change in the basis, atomic coordinate shift, and conversion to POSCAR from a CIF file is provided in the Worked Example section and on the GitHub project page.

### 3.1. Feature Validation and Testing

*CrystalShift* was tested across its core functionalities to validate accuracy, compatibility, and computational efficiency. Validation included the following:

- A semi-automated inspection of the correctness of the output file structure, as well as of the obtained results after editing the crystallographic data, starting with calculations in VASP (controlling possible errors during input file reading).
- A comparison with results from existing tools (e.g., Open Babel, cif2cell, pymatgen, ASE).
- The testing of converters was carried out automatically using Bash scripts. The conversion of CIF $\rightarrow$ POSCAR $\rightarrow$ CIF and CIF $\rightarrow$ XYZ $\rightarrow$ CIF was carried out. Due to the fact that atoms are recorded in groups classified by elements in POSCAR files, an additional program was written for sorting and obtaining statistics by comparing coordinates in the original CIF file with those in the CIF file obtained after conversion. In this way, 1000 structures, randomly selected from the CSD, were analyzed and showed a 100% success rate. Speed tests were conducted on 100 random structures from the CSD.
- The testing of the layer analysis module was carried out manually, by comparing visually observed molecular layers, slip planes calculated via CCDC Mercury, and results calculated by *CrystalShift*.

One can find all the results obtained during feature validation and testing on the project's GitHub page.

### 3.2. Error Handling

In the structures, all data (e.g., lengths of lattice vectors, volume, atomic coordinates, etc.) is stored in double float format. The range of doubles is $1.7 \times 10^{-308}$ to $1.7 \times 10^{308}$. Hence, when a file is converted from the CIF format to POSCAR, no coordinate transformations occur. All experimental measurement errors from CIF files are removed for correct recording into structures and, accordingly, are lost during conversion.

When the basis or recording is changed in the XYZ format (which implies conversion into the Cartesian basis), minor discrepancies may occur in the calculation. To calculate new lattice parameters and angles, a scalar product is used, but to recalculate coordinates, an inverse matrix must be used. The inverse matrix is calculated using the Gauss–Jordan method, and then it is reduced to an upper-triangular form using the Gauss method, which entails some inaccuracy due to the iterative approach. Nevertheless, possible inaccuracies are less than experimental uncertainties in SCXRD experimental data and, thus, do not influence further calculations.

Additionally, *CrystalShift* autonomously detects irregularities in lattice parameters and atomic coordinates, such as duplicate atoms or inconsistencies in atomic groupings. When such anomalies are identified, the program provides warnings to the user, highlighting potential issues. Along with the warnings, *CrystalShift* suggests corrective actions to address these irregularities, ensuring data integrity and reliable analysis. This proactive feature minimizes the risk of errors in downstream operations while maintaining user control over data adjustments.

### 3.3. User Warnings

*CrystalShift* includes several user-focused warnings and safeguards to enhance reliability and prevent unintended errors during use. The program automatically identifies and removes duplicate atoms in the structure if needed, alerting users to potential issues in their input data.

Users are also strongly advised to carefully review both input and output files to ensure accuracy, as this is a crucial step for any crystallographic or computational tool. In the event of an error, *CrystalShift* provides clear and detailed explanations of possible issues, helping users to diagnose and correct them prior to further DFT calculations.

These measures contribute to a robust and user-friendly experience, minimizing disruptions and ensuring reliable operation.

### 3.4. Limitations and Areas for Improvement

*CrystalShift*, while robust in its core functionalities, has certain limitations that present opportunities for enhancement. The reliance on a command-line interface may pose challenges for users who are less familiar with non graphical tools, potentially limiting accessibility.

The current version of the program writes POSCAR files in direct coordinates, which restricts compatibility with workflows that require the Cartesian format. Implementing this feature is planned for upcoming updates.

While molecular layer analysis offers valuable insights, expanding the range of geometric analyses to include features like bond length distributions, angular analysis, and void space quantification would significantly enhance its utility and broaden its applicability across diverse research domains.

### 3.5. Worked Example

To reveal the practical use of *CrystalShift*, a 4-bromophenyl 4-bromobenzoate structure was selected. Crystals of 4-bromophenyl 4-bromobenzoate demonstrate phenomenal plasticity under mechanical stress, which is explained by the layered structure and significant anisotropy in the crystal structure [41–43]. Thus, the calculation of mechanical properties and their correlation with crystal structure seems to provide valuable information for better understanding the nature of the "bending crystals" phenomenon [44–46].

A CIF file of 4-bromophenyl 4-bromobenzoate (VEWSIC) was downloaded from CSD and submitted to *CrystalShift*. "Crystalshift_layers" suggested the (1 0 −1) slip plane as the most favorable. Visual inspection in CCDC Mercury software confirmed this choice (Figure 1).

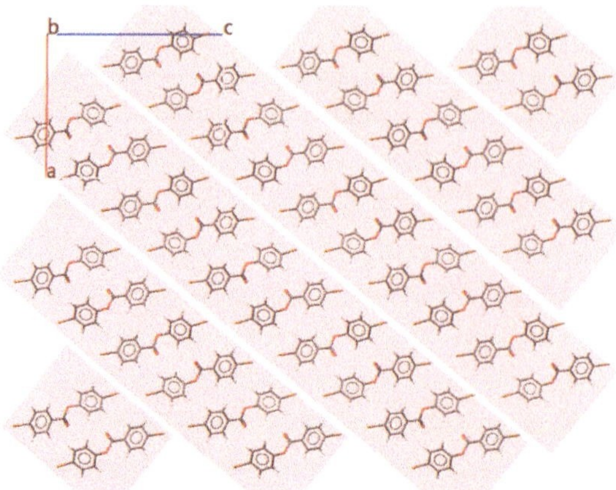

**Figure 1.** Crystal structure of 4-bromophenyl 4-bromobenzoate with highlighted layers according to Reddy's model [47,48].

The straightforward calculation of second-order derivatives, taking into account multiple computational parameters, elucidates the mechanical characteristics along crystallographic axes. Nevertheless, the 4-bromophenyl 4-bromobenzoate crystal structure is constructed of "diagonal" layers, which are not aligned with the a, b, or c crystallographic axis. This peculiarity limits the convenience of the obtained data interpretation. It becomes obvious that a basis change may help to obtain mechanical properties and correlate them to the crystal structure in a straightforward and convenient manner.

To address the task of identifying quantitative criteria for determining the unique mechanical properties of organic crystals, extensive data manipulation is required. The following steps outline the process of editing a file using the example of 4-bromophenyl 4-bromobenzoate within a practical workflow. Thus, the "crystalshift" subroutine was used to change the basis and prepare the input file for DFT calculations in the VASP package (Figure 2).

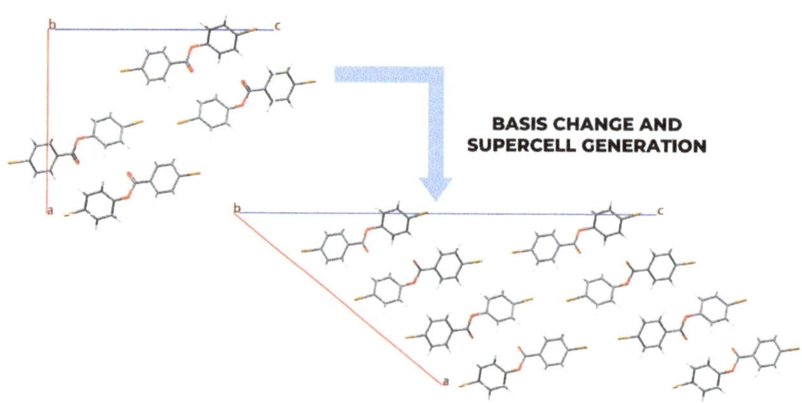


**Figure 2.** Crystal structure of 4-bromophenyl 4-bromobenzoate with two different crystallographic bases prepared for further DFT calculations.

To verify the accuracy of the aforementioned procedures in *CrystalShift*, DFT calculations of lattice energies were performed using the PBE functional [49], a plane-wave basis set with a kinetic energy cutoff of 800 eV and projector augmented wave (PAW) atomic pseudopotentials [50,51], using the D3BJ dispersion correction scheme [52]. Monkhorst–Pack k-point meshes [53] of 2 × 5 × 1 and 1 × 6 × 1 were used for the initial and modified structures. The normalized energy for the lattice after the basis change (×2 supercell) differed by only 0.02 kJ/mol, with a minimal 0.049 RMSD for the atoms in the initial and changed cells (Figure 3).

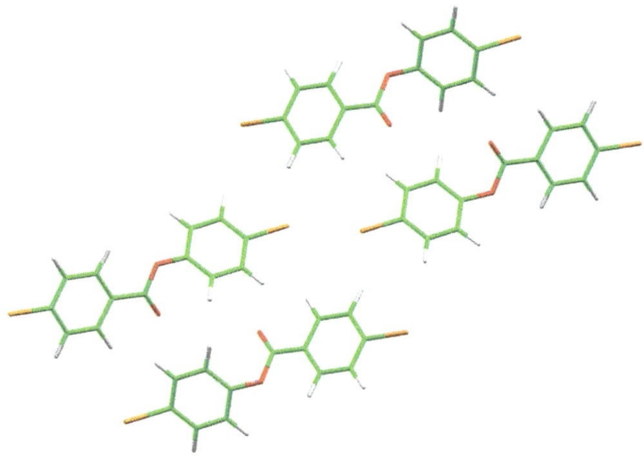

**Figure 3.** Initial and modified structure overlay, showing minimal change in atomic coordinates after basis change using *CrystalShift*.

Finally, the calculated mechanical properties (using a finite-difference approach [54]) indicate the presence of anisotropy along the z-axis, which coincides with the c crystallographic axis in the structure after the basis change (Figure 4). The obtained results correspond to the detected molecular layers in the structure. This fully coincides with Reddy's model, describing bending crystals as layered structures with strong interactions within the layers and weak interactions in nearly perpendicular directions [48]. Moreover, the obtained results support previous data on the calculated mechanical properties of the plastic form of 4-bromophenyl 4-bromobenzoate [42,43].

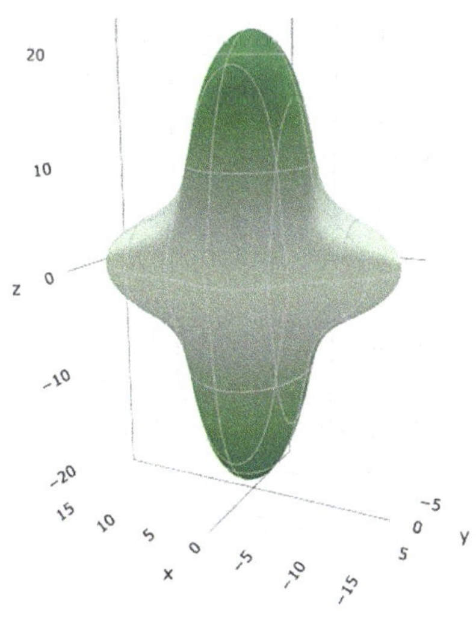


**Figure 4.** Young's modulus of 4-bromophentyl 4-bromobenzoate (VEWSIC) after basis change (obtained via ELATE online tool for analysis of elastic tensors).

This example of bending 4-bromophenyl 4-bromobenzoate crystals shows how *CrystalShift* may help with research preparation and data interpretation more simply and intuitively in comparison to the current workflow.

## 4. Discussion

The development and implementation of *CrystalShift* addresses several longstanding challenges in crystallographic data processing, positioning it as a valuable alternative and supplement to existing tools. While programs like Open Babel, Mercury, Chemcraft, VESTA, cif2cell, pymatgen, ASE, etc. offer distinct advantages, *CrystalShift* fills critical gaps in functionality and versatility, particularly for computational workflows involving molecular crystals. It is written in the C programming language, has minimal dependency requirements, is compatible across multiple computing environments, and does not require programming knowledge from the user.

The molecular layer analysis module of *CrystalShift* represents a significant advancement over existing tools. By employing DBSCAN and KD-Tree algorithms, this module not only identifies molecular clusters and detects lattice disorders but also calculates interlayer distances and structural patterns. This functionality is particularly valuable for studying bending organic crystals, where understanding geometric layering is essential for predicting mechanical flexibility, thermal stability, and other material properties.

Despite its strengths, *CrystalShift* does have certain limitations. For example, while the current version supports CIF, POSCAR, and XYZ file formats, additional format compatibility (.mol, .pdb, etc.) could further expand its utility. Future developments could also enhance features such as more comprehensive molecular distribution analysis, ensuring *CrystalShift* remains competitive in the rapidly evolving field of crystallography.

## 5. Conclusions

*CrystalShift* is a command-line tool that can be easily used by computational chemists in order to process and modify original crystallographic data for VASP calculations. It has minimal dependencies and can be installed on almost any supercomputer or workstation.

It contains a basic file converter that can be effectively used for high-throughput VASP calculations of selected structures from the CSD. It is also useful for the in-depth study of molecular crystals and their properties, offering intuitive crystallographic basis change and supercell generation options, as well as a layer analysis module. The latter is of significant importance for bending crystals, which exhibit plastic or elastic behavior.

*CrystalShift* helps researchers study organic crystals by addressing key technical and practical challenges in crystallographic and computational workflows.

**Author Contributions:** Conceptualization, D.A.R. and I.A.I.; methodology, I.A.I.; software, I.A.I.; validation, I.A.I.; formal analysis, I.A.I.; investigation, D.A.R. and I.A.I.; resources, D.A.R.; data curation, I.A.I.; writing—original draft preparation, D.A.R. and I.A.I.; writing—review and editing, D.A.R. and I.A.I.; visualization, I.A.I.; supervision, D.A.R.; project administration, D.A.R.; funding acquisition, D.A.R. All authors have read and agreed to the published version of the manuscript.

**Funding:** This work was supported by the RSF (Russian Science Foundation) project 23-73-10142 (https://rscf.ru/en/project/23-73-10142/) (accessed on 25 April 2025).

**Data Availability Statement:** The data are available on the GitHub page of the project (https://github.com/shes73/CrystalShift) (accessed on 29 May 2025) and upon reasonable request.

**Acknowledgments:** The Siberian Branch of the Russian Academy of Sciences (SB RAS) Siberian Supercomputer Center is gratefully acknowledged for providing the supercomputer facilities (http://www.sscc.icmmg.nsc.ru) (accessed on 25 April 2025). The authors also acknowledge the Supercomputing Center of the Novosibirsk State University (http://nusc.nsu.ru) (accessed on 25 April 2025) for providing computational resources.

**Conflicts of Interest:** The authors declare no conflicts of interest. The funders had no role in the design of this study; in the collection, analysis, or interpretation of the data; in the writing of the manuscript; or in the decision to publish the results.

## References

1. Bryant, M.J.; Maloney, A.G.P.; Sykes, R.A. Predicting Mechanical Properties of Crystalline Materials through Topological Analysis. *CrystEngComm* **2018**, *20*, 2698–2704. [CrossRef]
2. Mondal, S.; Reddy, C.M.; Saha, S. Crystal Property Engineering Using Molecular-Supramolecular Equivalence: Mechanical Property Alteration in Hydrogen Bonded Systems. *Chem. Sci.* **2024**, *15*, 3578–3587. [CrossRef] [PubMed]
3. Wahlberg, N.; Ciochoń, P.; Petriček, V.; Madsen, A.Ø. Polymorph Stability Prediction: On the Importance of Accurate Structures: A Case Study of Pyrazinamide. *Cryst. Growth Des.* **2014**, *14*, 381–388. [CrossRef]
4. Gavezzotti, A. Crystal Formation and Stability: Physical Principles and Molecular Simulation. *Cryst. Res. Technol.* **2013**, *48*, 793–810. [CrossRef]
5. Korabel'nikov, D.V.; Zhuravlev, Y.N. Semi-Empirical and Ab Initio Calculations for Crystals under Pressure at Fixed Temperatures: The Case of Guanidinium Perchlorate. *RSC Adv.* **2020**, *10*, 42204–42211. [CrossRef]
6. Rychkov, D.A.; Hunter, S.; Kovalskii, V.Y.; Lomzov, A.A.; Pulham, C.R.; Boldyreva, E.V. Towards an Understanding of Crystallization from Solution. DFT Studies of Multi-Component Serotonin Crystals. *Comput. Theor. Chem.* **2016**, *1088*, 52–61. [CrossRef]
7. Smirnova, V.Y.; Iurchenkova, A.A.; Rychkov, D.A. Computational Investigation of the Stability of Di-p-Tolyl Disulfide "Hidden" and "Conventional" Polymorphs at High Pressures. *Crystals* **2022**, *12*, 1157. [CrossRef]
8. Mazurek, A.H.; Szeleszczuk, Ł.; Pisklak, D.M. Periodic DFT Calculations—Review of Applications in the Pharmaceutical Sciences. *Pharmaceutics* **2020**, *12*, 415. [CrossRef]
9. Bučar, D.-K.; Lancaster, R.W.; Bernstein, J. Disappearing Polymorphs Revisited. *Angew. Chemie Int. Ed.* **2015**, *54*, 6972–6993. [CrossRef]
10. Togo, A.; Tanaka, I. First Principles Phonon Calculations in Materials Science. *Scr. Mater.* **2015**, *108*, 1–5. [CrossRef]
11. Macrae, C.F.; Edgington, P.R.; McCabe, P.; Pidcock, E.; Shields, G.P.; Taylor, R.; Towler, M.; van de Streek, J. Mercury: Visualization and Analysis of Crystal Structures. *J. Appl. Crystallogr.* **2006**, *39*, 453–457. [CrossRef]
12. Macrae, C.F.; Sovago, I.; Cottrell, S.J.; Galek, P.T.A.; McCabe, P.; Pidcock, E.; Platings, M.; Shields, G.P.; Stevens, J.S.; Towler, M.; et al. Mercury 4.0: From Visualization to Analysis, Design and Prediction. *J. Appl. Crystallogr.* **2020**, *53*, 226–235. [CrossRef] [PubMed]
13. Momma, K.; Izumi, F. VESTA: A Three-Dimensional Visualization System for Electronic and Structural Analysis. *J. Appl. Crystallogr.* **2008**, *41*, 653–658. [CrossRef]
14. Available online: http://www.chemcraftprog.com (accessed on 29 April 2025).
15. Humphrey, W.; Dalke, A.; Schulten, K. VMD: Visual Molecular Dynamics. *J. Mol. Graph.* **1996**, *14*, 33–38. [CrossRef]
16. Blatov, V.A.; Shevchenko, A.P.; Proserpio, D.M. Applied Topological Analysis of Crystal Structures with the Program Package ToposPro. *Cryst. Growth Des.* **2014**, *14*, 3576–3586. [CrossRef]
17. Spackman, P.R.; Turner, M.J.; McKinnon, J.J.; Wolff, S.K.; Grimwood, D.J.; Jayatilaka, D.; Spackman, M.A. CrystalExplorer: A Program for Hirshfeld Surface Analysis, Visualization and Quantitative Analysis of Molecular Crystals. *J. Appl. Crystallogr.* **2021**, *54*, 1006–1011. [CrossRef]
18. OCC. Available online: https://github.com/peterspackman/occ (accessed on 29 April 2025).
19. O'Boyle, N.M.; Banck, M.; James, C.A.; Morley, C.; Vandermeersch, T.; Hutchison, G.R. Open Babel: An Open Chemical Toolbox. *J. Cheminform.* **2011**, *3*, 33. [CrossRef]
20. Björkman, T. CIF2Cell: Generating Geometries for Electronic Structure Programs. *Comput. Phys. Commun.* **2011**, *182*, 1183–1186. [CrossRef]
21. Dubok, A.S.; Rychkov, D.A. Deformcell: A Python Script to Simplify and Fasten Mechanical Properties Calculations of Molecular Crystals in VASP Package for Research and Teaching Purposes. *J. Struct. Chem.* **2024**, *65*, 1784–1793. [CrossRef]
22. Wang, V.; Xu, N.; Liu, J.-C.; Tang, G.; Geng, W.-T. VASPKIT: A User-Friendly Interface Facilitating High-Throughput Computing and Analysis Using VASP Code. *Comput. Phys. Commun.* **2021**, *267*, 108033. [CrossRef]

23. Angel, R.J.; Alvaro, M.; Gonzalez-Platas, J. EosFit7c and a Fortran Module (Library) for Equation of State Calculations. *Z. Für Krist.-Cryst. Mater.* **2014**, *229*, 405–419. [CrossRef]
24. Gonzalez-Platas, J.; Alvaro, M.; Nestola, F.; Angel, R. EosFit7-GUI: A New Graphical User Interface for Equation of State Calculations, Analyses and Teaching. *J. Appl. Crystallogr.* **2016**, *49*, 1377–1382. [CrossRef]
25. Gaillac, R.; Pullumbi, P.; Coudert, F.-X. ELATE: An Open-Source Online Application for Analysis and Visualization of Elastic Tensors. *J. Phys. Condens. Matter* **2016**, *28*, 275201. [CrossRef] [PubMed]
26. Vasp2cif Cif2vasp. Available online: https://www.nsc.liu.se/~pla/vasptools/ (accessed on 29 April 2025).
27. Jain, A.; Hautier, G.; Moore, C.J.; Ping Ong, S.; Fischer, C.C.; Mueller, T.; Persson, K.A.; Ceder, G. A High-Throughput Infrastructure for Density Functional Theory Calculations. *Comput. Mater. Sci.* **2011**, *50*, 2295–2310. [CrossRef]
28. Hjorth Larsen, A.; Jørgen Mortensen, J.; Blomqvist, J.; Castelli, I.E.; Christensen, R.; Dułak, M.; Friis, J.; Groves, M.N.; Hammer, B.; Hargus, C.; et al. The Atomic Simulation Environment—A Python Library for Working with Atoms. *J. Phys. Condens. Matter* **2017**, *29*, 273002. [CrossRef]
29. Ester, M.; Kriegel, H.P.; Sander, J.; Xu, X. A Density-Based Algorithm for Discovering Clusters A Density-Based Algorithm for Discovering Clusters in Large Spatial Databases with Noise. In Proceedings of the 2nd International Conference on Knowledge Discovery and Data Mining, Portland, Oregon, 2–4 August 1996.
30. Bentley, J.L. Multidimensional Binary Search Trees Used for Associative Searching. *Commun. ACM* **1975**, *18*, 509–517. [CrossRef]
31. Krishna, G.R.; Devarapalli, R.; Lal, G.; Reddy, C.M. Mechanically Flexible Organic Crystals Achieved by Introducing Weak Interactions in Structure: Supramolecular Shape Synthons. *J. Am. Chem. Soc.* **2016**, *138*, 13561–13567. [CrossRef]
32. Kresse, G.; Hafner, J. Ab Initio Molecular Dynamics for Liquid Metals. *Phys. Rev. B* **1993**, *47*, 558–561. [CrossRef]
33. Kresse, G.; Hafner, J. Ab Initio Molecular-Dynamics Simulation of the Liquid-Metal–Amorphous-Semiconductor Transition in Germanium. *Phys. Rev. B* **1994**, *49*, 14251–14269. [CrossRef]
34. Kresse, G.; Furthmüller, J. Efficient Iterative Schemes for Ab Initio Total-Energy Calculations Using a Plane-Wave Basis Set. *Phys. Rev. B* **1996**, *54*, 11169–11186. [CrossRef]
35. Kresse, G.; Furthmüller, J. Efficiency of Ab-Initio Total Energy Calculations for Metals and Semiconductors Using a Plane-Wave Basis Set. *Comput. Mater. Sci.* **1996**, *6*, 15–50. [CrossRef]
36. Neese, F. The ORCA Program System. *Wiley Interdiscip. Rev. Comput. Mol. Sci.* **2012**, *2*, 73–78. [CrossRef]
37. Frisch, M.J.; Trucks, G.W.; Schlegel, H.B.; Scuseria, G.E.; Robb, M.A.; Cheeseman, J.R.; Scalmani, G.; Barone, V.; Mennucci, B.; Petersson, G.A.; et al. *Gaussian 09, Revision D.01*; Gaussian, Inc.: Wallingford, CT, USA, 2009.
38. Pearson, K. LIII. On Lines and Planes of Closest Fit to Systems of Points in Space. *Lond. Edinb. Dublin Philos. Mag. J. Sci.* **1901**, *2*, 559–572. [CrossRef]
39. Hotelling, H. Analysis of a Complex of Statistical Variables into Principal Components. *J. Educ. Psychol.* **1933**, *24*, 417–441. [CrossRef]
40. Jolliffe, I.T.; Cadima, J. Principal Component Analysis: A Review and Recent Developments. *Philos. Trans. R. Soc. A Math. Phys. Eng. Sci.* **2016**, *374*, 20150202. [CrossRef]
41. Saha, S.; Desiraju, G.R. Trimorphs of 4-Bromophenyl 4-Bromobenzoate. Elastic, Brittle, Plastic. *Chem. Commun.* **2018**, *54*, 6348–6351. [CrossRef] [PubMed]
42. Masunov, A.E.; Wiratmo, M.; Dyakov, A.A.; Matveychuk, Y.V.; Bartashevich, E.V. Virtual Tensile Test for Brittle, Plastic, and Elastic Polymorphs of 4-Bromophenyl 4-Bromobenzoate. *Cryst. Growth Des.* **2020**, *20*, 6093–6100. [CrossRef]
43. Masunov, A.E.; Wiratmo, M.; Dyakov, A.A.; Matveychuk, Y.V.; Bartashevich, E.V. Prediction of Crystal Structures and Mechanical Properties for Brittle, Plastic, and Elastic Polymorphs of 4-Bromophenyl 4-Bromobenzoate. *Cryst. Growth Des.* **2022**, *22*, 4546–4558. [CrossRef]
44. Paikar, A.; Podder, D.; Chowdhury, S.R.; Sasmal, S.; Haldar, D. Bromine-Bromine Interactions Enhanced Plasticity for the Bending of a Single Crystal without Affecting Fluorescent Properties. *CrystEngComm* **2019**, *21*, 589–593. [CrossRef]
45. Chen, K.; Wang, J.; Wu, W.; Shan, H.; Zhao, H.; Wang, N.; Wang, T.; Huang, X.; Hao, H. Multi-Flexible Organic Crystal Responding to Different Mechanical Forces for Flexible Optical Waveguides. *Dye. Pigment.* **2023**, *219*, 111536. [CrossRef]
46. Wang, C.; Sun, C.C. Computational Techniques for Predicting Mechanical Properties of Organic Crystals: A Systematic Evaluation. *Mol. Pharm.* **2019**, *16*, 1732–1741. [CrossRef] [PubMed]
47. Reddy, C.M.; Gundakaram, R.C.; Basavoju, S.; Kirchner, M.T.; Padmanabhan, K.A.; Desiraju, G.R. Structural Basis for Bending of Organic Crystals. *Chem. Commun.* **2005**, *1*, 3945. [CrossRef]
48. Reddy, C.M.; Padmanabhan, K.A.; Desiraju, G.R. Structure−Property Correlations in Bending and Brittle Organic Crystals. *Cryst. Growth Des.* **2006**, *6*, 2720–2731. [CrossRef]
49. Perdew, J.P.; Burke, K.; Ernzerhof, M. Generalized Gradient Approximation Made Simple. *Phys. Rev. Lett.* **1996**, *77*, 3865–3868. [CrossRef]
50. Blöchl, P.E. Projector Augmented-Wave Method. *Phys. Rev. B* **1994**, *50*, 17953–17979. [CrossRef] [PubMed]

51. Kresse, G.; Joubert, D. From Ultrasoft Pseudopotentials to the Projector Augmented-Wave Method. *Phys. Rev. B* **1999**, *59*, 1758–1775. [CrossRef]
52. Grimme, S.; Ehrlich, S.; Goerigk, L. Effect of the Damping Function in Dispersion Corrected Density Functional Theory. *J. Comput. Chem.* **2011**, *32*, 1456–1465. [CrossRef] [PubMed]
53. Monkhorst, H.J.; Pack, J.D. Special Points for Brillouin-Zone Integrations. *Phys. Rev. B* **1976**, *13*, 5188–5192. [CrossRef]
54. Dubok, A.S.; Rychkov, D.A. What Is More Important When Calculating the Thermodynamic Properties of Organic Crystals, Density Functional, Supercell, or Energy Second-Order Derivative Method Choice? *Crystals* **2025**, *15*, 274. [CrossRef]

computation

MDPI

*Review*

# Mathematical Optimization in Machine Learning for Computational Chemistry

**Ana Zekić**

Department of Mathematical Sciences, Faculty of Technology and Metallurgy, University of Belgrade, 11000 Belgrade, Serbia; azekovic@tmf.bg.ac.rs

**Abstract:** Machine learning (ML) is transforming computational chemistry by accelerating molecular simulations, property prediction, and inverse design. Central to this transformation is mathematical optimization, which underpins nearly every stage of model development, from training neural networks and tuning hyperparameters to navigating chemical space for molecular discovery. This review presents a structured overview of optimization techniques used in ML for computational chemistry, including gradient-based methods (e.g., SGD and Adam), probabilistic approaches (e.g., Monte Carlo sampling and Bayesian optimization), and spectral methods. We classify optimization targets into model parameter optimization, hyperparameter selection, and molecular optimization and analyze their application across supervised, unsupervised, and reinforcement learning frameworks. Additionally, we examine key challenges such as data scarcity, limited generalization, and computational cost, outlining how mathematical strategies like active learning, meta-learning, and hybrid physics-informed models can address these issues. By bridging optimization methodology with domain-specific challenges, this review highlights how tailored optimization strategies enhance the accuracy, efficiency, and scalability of ML models in computational chemistry.

**Keywords:** mathematical optimization; machine learning in chemistry; computational chemistry; Bayesian optimization

## 1. Introduction

Machine learning (ML) has become a cornerstone of computational chemistry, enabling the prediction of molecular properties, materials discovery, and reaction modeling with unprecedented speed and accuracy. However, the performance of ML models critically depends on mathematical optimization techniques.

Optimization plays a central role at multiple levels of the ML pipeline. It is used to minimize loss functions, fine-tune hyperparameters, select data points in active learning, and ensure stable training of deep architectures such as graph neural networks (GNNs). These tasks are especially important in chemistry, where datasets are often high-dimensional, noisy, and computationally expensive to generate.

In this review, we examine how mathematical optimization supports diverse ML tasks in computational chemistry. Rather than limiting the discussion to a single application domain, we illustrate optimization's versatility across a range of representative challenges, from general property prediction to quantum-level modeling tasks such as learning interatomic potentials. This approach enables us to highlight both methodological depth and domain-specific relevance.

We review core optimization methods widely used in chemical ML workflows, including gradient-based algorithms like stochastic gradient descent (SGD) and Adam, global optimization methods like Bayesian optimization and Monte Carlo techniques, and spectral methods applied in graph-based models. Each method is discussed in terms of its mathematical foundation, implementation strategy, and relevance to applications such as quantum chemistry, molecular design, and supervised or unsupervised learning.

Throughout this review, we use the term optimization in a broad sense, encompassing (1) model parameter learning, (2) hyperparameter tuning, and (3) search over molecular or latent input space. Each of these targets presents distinct challenges and is addressed using different mathematical approaches, which we clarify throughout the following sections.

Finally, we highlight ongoing challenges, such as data scarcity, transferability, and computational trade-offs, and explore how optimization frameworks can help address these limitations. Our goal is to provide both a conceptual and practical guide for researchers applying optimization in chemical machine learning.

## 2. Optimization Methods in Machine Learning for Chemistry

Machine learning models rely on an objective function known as the loss function, which quantifies the error between the model's predictions and the true values. The goal of mathematical optimization in machine learning is to minimize the loss function by iteratively adjusting the model parameters. Different optimization techniques are applied to efficiently navigate the parameter space and improve machine learning models. In the context of computational chemistry, these techniques ensure convergence, enhance accuracy, and reduce computational costs. Below, we discuss key optimization methods employed in machine learning for chemical applications.

### 2.1. Optimization Targets and Learning Settings

In the context of machine learning applied to chemistry, the term "optimization" can refer to several distinct processes, each targeting a different component of the modeling pipeline. These include the following:

- Model parameter optimization: This refers to the adjustment of internal model weights during training to minimize a predefined loss function. Common methods include stochastic gradient descent (SGD), Adam, and other gradient-based optimizers. This process is central to supervised learning tasks such as molecular property prediction or spectroscopic signal modeling.
- Hyperparameter optimization: Hyperparameters, such as the learning rate, number of layers, and regularization coefficients, are not learned during training and must be selected externally. Methods such as grid search, random search, and Bayesian optimization are commonly used to identify optimal hyperparameter configurations that maximize model performance on validation sets.
- Molecular optimization: In generative tasks or molecular design, the optimization target is not the model itself but rather the molecular input or its latent representation. The goal is to discover new chemical structures that maximize or minimize desired properties, such as solubility or reactivity. This type of molecular optimization is typically approached via Bayesian optimization, reinforcement learning, or differentiable surrogate models.

Although these forms of optimization share algorithmic foundations, they differ significantly in their objectives, evaluation criteria, and constraints. Throughout this review, we highlight how mathematical optimization contributes to each of these settings.

In addition to the optimization targets, chemical machine learning tasks also differ in learning settings. In supervised learning, models are trained using labeled data, such as molecular structures paired with known properties (e.g., energy, solubility, and toxicity). This setting is dominant in property prediction tasks. In contrast, unsupervised learning focuses on extracting patterns from unlabeled data, often used for clustering molecular fingerprints or learning low-dimensional latent representations. Reinforcement learning, though less common, is increasingly applied in molecular optimization and generative design, where the model interacts with an environment (e.g., chemical space) and is rewarded for producing molecules with desired properties.

Optimization strategies in machine learning differ not only in algorithmic formulation but also in search behavior and scope. Some methods are designed for local optimization, refining solutions by following local gradients toward nearby minima. Others are formulated for global optimization, aiming to search more broadly and escape local traps by evaluating diverse regions of the solution space.

These behaviors map onto the concepts of exploitation, leveraging known high-performing regions of the search space, and exploration, which prioritizes information gain from uncertain or underexplored regions. The balance between these two objectives is central to designing effective optimization routines, particularly in chemical applications where objective functions may be multi-modal, non-convex, or expensive to evaluate.

### 2.2. Stochastic Gradient Descent (SGD)

Stochastic gradient descent (SGD) is a foundational optimization algorithm widely used in training machine learning models, particularly deep neural networks. It belongs to the family of first-order methods and operates by iteratively updating model parameters in the direction that minimizes a given loss function. Unlike full-batch gradient descent, which computes the gradient using the entire dataset, SGD estimates the gradient using a single randomly selected sample or a small mini-batch. This approach introduces stochasticity into the learning process and reduces the computational cost per iteration [1].

To better understand its mechanics and relevance to chemical learning tasks, we next present the mathematical formulation of SGD and its key variants. The update rule for SGD is provided by the following:

$$\boldsymbol{\theta}_{t+1} = \boldsymbol{\theta}_t - \eta \nabla L(\boldsymbol{\theta}_t; \boldsymbol{x}_i, y_i). \quad (1)$$

We use bold symbols (e.g., $\boldsymbol{\theta}_t$, $\boldsymbol{x}_i$) to denote vectors and regular font for scalar quantities. Here, $\boldsymbol{\theta}_t$ represents the model parameters at iteration $t$, $\eta$ is the learning rate, and $\nabla L(\boldsymbol{\theta}_t; \boldsymbol{x}_i, y_i)$ is the gradient of the loss function with respect to the model parameters, computed using input $\boldsymbol{x}_i$ and the true label $y_i$. In the context of chemical machine learning, $\boldsymbol{x}_i$ could represent molecular descriptors or graph embeddings, while $y_i$ could be a quantum chemical property such as dipole moment, energy gap, or solvation energy.

While SGD is fundamentally a local optimization method, relying on gradient information at each step, its stochasticity introduces small-scale exploration, which can help the model avoid sharp local minima without providing true global search capabilities [1]. However, it also introduces noise, which may destabilize convergence if not properly controlled.

To improve performance, several enhanced variants of SGD have been proposed:

- Momentum-based SGD incorporates an exponentially weighted average of past gradients to smooth updates and accelerate convergence, particularly in ravine-shaped loss landscapes.
- Nesterov accelerated gradient (NAG) improves upon classical momentum by computing the gradient not at the current position but at the anticipated future position of the parameters. This often leads to faster convergence in practice [2].
- Mini-batch SGD uses batches of 16–256 samples to strike a balance between noisy single-sample updates and slow full-batch updates.

These variants mitigate the effects of noisy gradients and help stabilize training, especially in deep architectures used in quantum chemistry or molecular design tasks.

A representative application in chemical machine learning is the work of Rupp et al. [3], who trained neural networks using mini-batch SGD to predict molecular atomization energies in the QM7 dataset based on Coulomb matrix descriptors. This approach demonstrated that SGD could efficiently scale to chemically diverse datasets while maintaining predictive accuracy.

While these techniques improve the basic behavior of SGD, its performance still depends heavily on the choice of hyperparameters, such as the learning rate and batch size.

This sensitivity has motivated the development of optimizers such as RMSprop [4], which adapt the learning rate using exponentially decaying averages of squared gradients. By adjusting the step size dynamically, these methods improve convergence in noisy or curved loss landscapes often encountered in chemical datasets.

The limitations of both SGD and RMSprop have led to further developments, such as the Adam optimizer, which combines ideas from both momentum and adaptive learning rates. This method will be discussed in the following section.

### 2.3. Adam Optimizer

Adam (adaptive moment estimation) is an extension of SGD incorporating adaptive learning rates for better convergence. It combines the benefits of momentum-based acceleration and adaptive learning rates to improve convergence. Introduced by Kingma and Ba [5], Adam dynamically adjusts learning rates based on first and second moment estimates of the gradients, making it robust to noisy updates and effective across a wide range of machine learning applications. These two estimates are denoted by $\boldsymbol{m}_t$ and $\boldsymbol{v}_t$, respectively, and are used to scale the update step for each parameter individually.

The Adam update rule is provided by the following:

$$\boldsymbol{\theta}_{t+1} = \boldsymbol{\theta}_t - \eta \frac{\hat{\boldsymbol{m}}_t}{\sqrt{\hat{\boldsymbol{v}}_t} + \epsilon}, \tag{2}$$

where

- $\hat{\boldsymbol{m}}_t = \frac{\boldsymbol{m}_t}{1-\beta_1^t}, \quad \hat{\boldsymbol{v}}_t = \frac{\boldsymbol{v}_t}{1-\beta_2^t}$ are bias-corrected estimates;
- $\beta_1$ and $\beta_2$ are hyperparameters controlling the decay rates of the moment estimates (commonly set to 0.9 and 0.999, respectively);
- $\epsilon$ is a small constant added to avoid division by zero;
- $\eta$ is the learning rate.

The model takes into account previous steps, which helps achieve faster and more stable convergence. The first moment helps reduce oscillations, allowing the optimization process to move more consistently toward the global minimum rather than varying unpredictably in different directions. Despite this improved stability, it is important to note that Adam remains a local optimization method. Its adaptive update mechanism enables smoother convergence within the local loss landscape, but it does not perform global search or incorporate mechanisms for broader exploration, unlike methods such as Bayesian optimization.

One important class of problems in computational chemistry involves learning quantum-level properties from data, including total energies, electron densities, and molecular potential energy surfaces. These quantities, typically derived from first-principles methods like density functional theory (DFT), are computationally intensive to calculate, motivating the use of machine learning models trained to approximate them.

Schütt et al. (2017) [6] developed a neural network-based approach for approximating DFT calculations and predicting electronic structure properties. Their model was trained using the Adam optimizer on molecular datasets to learn relationships between electron density distributions, total energies, and molecular potential energy surfaces. In particular, their approach approximates wavefunctions and potential energy surfaces, enabling efficient predictions of electronic properties. Their study evaluates the capability of machine learning models to reproduce DFT-derived quantities while analyzing the trade-off between computational cost and predictive accuracy.

Later, Wu et al. (2018) [7] introduced MoleculeNet, a benchmarking platform designed to evaluate machine learning models for predicting molecular and biophysical properties. They applied graph neural networks (GNNs) trained with the Adam optimizer to predict chemical properties such as dipole moments, polarizability, atomic partial charges, and reaction energies. Their results demonstrated that GNNs when optimized appropriately, can effectively capture molecular representations and achieve high accuracy across diverse chemical datasets.

The Adam optimizer combines the benefits of SGD with momentum and RMSprop, making it popular for training deep learning models. It is more suitable than SGD for problems with sparse gradients and noisy datasets by adapting the learning rate for each parameter. Additionally, it requires less hyperparameter tuning compared to standard gradient descent methods. However, Adam may lead to suboptimal convergence in some cases, as its adaptive updates can result in overly aggressive parameter changes that prevent the model from settling into a good local minimum. To mitigate these issues, several variants of Adam have been proposed. AMSGrad [8] introduces a more stable second-moment estimate to avoid rapid oscillations. AdaBelief [9] modifies the update rule to adapt based on the difference between predicted and actual gradients, improving generalization. Other methods like QHM (quasi-hyperbolic momentum) balance fast learning with better convergence stability [10]. While SGD is often preferred for large-scale datasets due to its simplicity and strong theoretical guarantees, Adam is particularly useful in computational chemistry applications where optimization landscapes are complex and adaptive learning rates improve the stability of training quantum and molecular models.

In addition to widely used first-order optimizers such as SGD and Adam, several quasi-Newton methods based on second-order approximations are gaining traction in scientific machine learning, particularly in physics-informed neural networks (PINNs). Among them, L-BFGS (limited-memory Broyden–Fletcher–Goldfarb–Shanno) provides a memory-efficient approximation of the inverse Hessian matrix, improving convergence near optimality without incurring the full cost of second-order derivatives. It is frequently used in PINNs for fine-tuning, often in tandem with Adam, which handles the early stages of training. This hybrid strategy improves both training stability and final model accuracy [11].

A more recent development is the self-scaled Broyden (SSBroyden) method, a symmetric quasi-Newton algorithm that uses rescaled gradient information to achieve faster convergence and greater numerical stability. It has shown promising results in physics-informed training regimes, often outperforming traditional L-BFGS in terms of convergence speed and robustness.

These quasi-Newton methods enrich the optimization toolkit in computational chemistry ML, particularly for problems with stiff gradients, complex physical constraints, or highly non-linear loss surfaces, conditions under which purely gradient-based optimizers like Adam may converge slowly or become unstable. Recent comparative studies of optimizer performance in physics-informed and scientific ML models have highlighted several concrete limitations of Adam. Notably, its reliance on historical gradient magnitudes to scale updates can lead to poor alignment between the update direction and the true gradient, especially in regions of high curvature or stiff dynamics. This misalignment often results in oscillatory behavior, instability, or premature convergence to suboptimal solutions [12]. In contrast, quasi-Newton approaches such as L-BFGS and SSBroyden incorporate curvature information more effectively, enabling faster and more reliable convergence in such challenging settings.

In the following section, we describe the backpropagation algorithm, which serves as the computational backbone for gradient calculation in optimizers such as Adam and SGD.

### 2.4. Backpropagation Algorithm

The backpropagation algorithm originally introduced in [13] is an essential component of training deep neural networks, providing a way to compute gradients required for local optimization. It is primarily used in conjunction with gradient-based optimization techniques, such as SGD and its variants. Backpropagation enables neural networks to adjust their parameters by propagating errors from the output layer back through the network, ensuring that updates are performed efficiently across multiple layers.

Backpropagation operates by computing the gradient of the loss function $L(\boldsymbol{\theta}; x_i, y_i)$ with respect to the model parameters $\boldsymbol{\theta}$ using the chain rule. The process consists of two main steps:

- Forward Pass: Computes the output of the neural network by applying a series of weighted transformations and activation functions to the input $x_i$.
- Backward Pass (Backpropagation Step): Computes the gradient of the loss function by propagating the error signal backward through the network using the chain rule.

The backpropagation update rule is provided by the following:

$$\boldsymbol{\theta}_{t+1} = \boldsymbol{\theta}_t - \eta \nabla_\theta L(\boldsymbol{\theta}_t; x_i, y_i), \tag{3}$$

where $\nabla_\theta L(\boldsymbol{\theta}_t; x_i, y_i)$ represents the gradient of the loss function with respect to the model parameters $\boldsymbol{\theta}$, computed using the chain rule in a multi-layer neural network. Unlike standard optimization methods, backpropagation propagates the gradient backward through each layer of the network, allowing all parameters to be updated efficiently.

The gradient computation follows the general rule below:

$$\nabla_\theta L(\boldsymbol{\theta}; x_i, y_i) = \frac{\partial L(\boldsymbol{\theta}; x_i, y_i)}{\partial \boldsymbol{\theta}}. \tag{4}$$

Backpropagation itself does not perform optimization but provides the gradients needed for optimizers like SGD or Adam. The loss gradient is first computed at the output layer and then propagated backward through the hidden layers using the chain rule. This ensures that each parameter update accounts for its contribution to the total loss. This ability to efficiently compute gradients supports a wide range of learning tasks in chemical modeling. One notable application is in quantum chemistry, where backpropagation has been used to learn representations of complex physical quantities, such as energy functionals and electron density distributions.

Deep learning models trained with backpropagation have also been applied to quantum chemistry tasks that involve approximating complex energy terms, such as exchange-correlation functionals in DFT. These applications highlight how optimization enables learning of quantum-level structure–property relationships.

Snyder et al. (2012) [14] employed backpropagation in training neural networks to approximate exchange-correlation functionals in DFT, using gradient-based optimization to iteratively refine model parameters. They applied SGD to minimize the loss function, allowing the neural network to approximate exchange-correlation functionals from training data and apply them accurately to new molecular systems not included in the training set. This is a typical supervised learning setting, where the model learns from input–output pairs (e.g., molecular configurations and known DFT-calculated energies), and backpropagation is used to update the model based on prediction errors.

As discussed in previous sections, GNNs have also been applied to molecular property prediction, as demonstrated in [7]. Here, backpropagation was essential for optimizing the network weights to improve predictive accuracy for molecular descriptors. Furthermore, deep learning models trained using backpropagation have been successfully applied to refine wavefunction-based methods and accelerate energy evaluations, as described in [6].

While backpropagation provides an efficient mechanism for computing gradients in differentiable models, other chemical learning tasks require optimization strategies that do not rely on gradient information, such as Monte Carlo methods, which we explore in the following section.

### 2.5. Monte Carlo Optimization

Monte Carlo optimization methods are used in computational chemistry and machine learning to optimize complex, high-dimensional functions. These methods rely on stochastic sampling to explore the parameter space and find optimal solutions, making them particularly useful when gradient-based techniques struggle due to non-differentiability or highly non-convex function.

The Metropolis Monte Carlo (MMC) algorithm is a stochastic optimization method used to sample from a probability distribution by iteratively updating model parameters. Originally introduced by Metropolis et al. (1953) [15], this algorithm was designed to simulate the equilibrium properties of statistical mechanical systems by generating representative configurations according to the Boltzmann distribution.

The general acceptance criterion for an update from $\boldsymbol{\theta}_t$ to $\boldsymbol{\theta}_{t+1}$ is determined by the following probability:

$$P_{\text{accept}} = \min\left(1, e^{-\frac{L(\boldsymbol{\theta}_{t+1};x_i,y_i)-L(\boldsymbol{\theta}_t;x_i,y_i)}{T}}\right), \tag{5}$$

where $T$ is a control parameter. By tuning the control parameter $T$, the MMC algorithm can balance exploration and exploitation, allowing occasional uphill moves and reducing the likelihood of premature convergence to local minima. For this reason, Monte Carlo methods are generally regarded as global optimization techniques. This global behavior makes them complementary to local techniques such as gradient descent.

Self-learning hybrid Monte Carlo (SLHMC), introduced by Nagai et al. (2019) [16], integrates machine learning with Monte Carlo sampling to enhance the efficiency of DFT-based simulations. The algorithm employs an artificial neural network (ANN) to approximate the potential energy surface of a molecular system, generating proposed configurations that are then validated using the Metropolis acceptance criterion. This approach has been applied in quantum chemistry to improve the sampling of molecular conformations and accelerate simulations of reaction mechanisms, reducing the computational cost of first-principles calculations while maintaining high accuracy. These Monte Carlo-based methods operate without requiring labeled data and are, therefore, naturally suited for unsupervised learning tasks, particularly in sampling and exploration of molecular conformational spaces.

More recently, Karandashev et al. (2023) [17] introduced an evolutionary Monte Carlo algorithm, MOSAiCS, designed for molecular optimization in chemical space. This method applies Monte Carlo sampling to explore molecular configurations that optimize properties, such as solvation energy and dipole moment while preserving key energetic characteristics. By leveraging Monte Carlo-based search strategies, MOSAiCS enables efficient molecular design by iteratively refining candidate structures based on their predicted electronic properties. This approach highlights the versatility of Monte Carlo algorithms in machine learning-driven molecular optimization and their potential for accelerating the discovery of novel functional materials.

### 2.6. Bayesian Optimization

Bayesian optimization (BO) is a probabilistic optimization technique that models the loss function as a Gaussian process (GP) and selects new evaluation points based on an acquisition function. In machine learning, BO is commonly used for hyperparameter tuning, where the goal is to identify settings such as learning rate, number of layers, or regularization strength that yield the best model performance on a validation set. Unlike model training, which adjusts internal weights via gradients, hyperparameter optimization operates externally and does not involve gradient-based updates. This makes BO especially valuable in chemistry-related tasks where each model evaluation (e.g., with quantum-level accuracy) can be computationally expensive [18]. The acquisition function quantifies the utility of evaluating the loss function at a given point, guiding the search toward promising regions of the parameter space.

The core idea of Bayesian Optimization is to continuously update our probabilistic model of the loss function (posterior distribution) as we gather new data and use this improved model to select the next points for evaluation. Given a prior belief over $L(\boldsymbol{\theta}; x_i, y_i)$, the posterior mean $\mu(\boldsymbol{\theta})$ and variance $\sigma^2(\boldsymbol{\theta})$ are updated at each step. The next candidate, $\boldsymbol{\theta}_{t+1}$, is chosen by maximizing an acquisition function $a(\boldsymbol{\theta})$. The expected improvement (EI) acquisition function selects the next evaluation point by estimating the expected amount by which the new function value $L(\boldsymbol{\theta})$ will improve upon the current best observed value $L_{min}$:

$$a(\boldsymbol{\theta}) = \mathbb{E}[\max(0, L_{\min} - L(\boldsymbol{\theta}; x_i, y_i))]. \tag{6}$$

Similar to the role of the control parameter $T$ in MMC, BO controls the trade-off between exploration and exploitation through the choice of the acquisition function. Unlike MMC, which allows probabilistic acceptance of suboptimal solutions, BO actively models uncertainty to guide the search towards promising regions in the parameter space. Its ability to explore the entire search space through uncertainty modeling makes it a powerful strategy for identifying globally optimal solutions.

This makes BO especially valuable for chemical tasks that involve expensive simulations or multi-modal design spaces, where efficient global search is essential.

In their 2017 study, Hernández-Lobato et al. [19] explored the application of BO to enhance the accuracy of surrogate models in electronic structure calculations. The authors focused on predicting exchange-correlation functionals within DFT. By employing BO, they optimized the hyperparameters of machine learning models to improve the prediction of these functionals. This approach led to a reduction in computational cost.

Beyond hyperparameter tuning, Bayesian optimization has been applied to a very different type of problem in chemistry: optimizing molecular structures themselves by searching over latent spaces to maximize the desired chemical properties.

A 2018 study by Gómez-Bombarelli et al. [20] introduced a novel approach for converting discrete molecular representations into a multidimensional continuous space. Traditional molecular representations, such as SMILES notation, are inherently discrete and not well-suited for smooth optimization. By mapping molecules into a continuous latent space, optimization algorithms, including BO, can operate more efficiently. In this context, optimization refers not to the model itself but to the input space, which is often a latent vector or molecular representation, with the goal of finding structures that maximize desired chemical properties such as solubility, selectivity, or electronic stability. This form of optimization is widely used in inverse molecular design, where models are trained to suggest new candidate molecules with optimal predicted properties. To achieve this, the authors trained a deep neural network to construct an encoder, a decoder, and a property predictor. The encoder transforms discrete molecular representations into continuous real-valued vectors while the decoder reconstructs these vectors back into valid molecular structures. The model was trained to predict molecular properties such as quantum energy levels and solubility, enabling the generation of new molecules with tailored characteristics.

Bayesian optimization is most commonly used in supervised learning settings, where the objective function is learned from known input–output relationships. In contrast, reinforcement learning offers an alternative optimization framework particularly suited to sequential decision problems such as molecule generation. In this setting, the model explores chemical space by learning from reward signals that reflect property constraints or design goals. For example, Olivecrona et al. [21] trained a recurrent neural network with reinforcement learning to generate valid SMILES strings optimized for drug-likeness scores. Their work illustrates how reward-guided training can steer molecular generation toward chemically desirable outputs.

Case Study: Multi-task Bayesian optimization for C–H Activation in Drug Development

A concrete and well-documented example of how machine learning can accelerate real-world chemical discovery comes from the work of Taylor et al. [22], who applied multi-task Bayesian optimization (MTBO) to the yield optimization of pharmaceutical intermediates involving C–H activation reactions. This study exemplifies the end-to-end integration of machine learning, historical chemical data, and experimental automation to efficiently identify optimal reaction conditions, including catalyst selection, within a drug discovery context.

**Problem Formulation**: The authors focused on the optimization of reaction conditions for six distinct C–H functionalization reactions, representative of real challenges encountered in medicinal chemistry. Traditional methods would approach each new reaction from scratch, often requiring 20 to 30 experimental iterations to reach optimal yields. To improve efficiency, Taylor et al. reformulated the problem as a Bayesian optimization task, leveraging prior data from 23 previously optimized reactions.

Each reaction was characterized by a set of experimental parameters, including the following:

- Type of catalyst or catalyst precursor;
- Solvent;
- Base;
- Temperature;
- Residence time in a flow reactor.

These were treated as categorical and continuous variables to be optimized simultaneously.

**Model Design and Training**: To guide this optimization, the authors trained a multi-task GP surrogate model. The multi-task component allowed the model to generalize across chemically related reactions by sharing statistical strength from prior tasks (i.e., reactions). This means that instead of starting from a blank slate, the model was initialized with historical knowledge, giving it an informed prior over the expected reaction outcomes.

The objective function (reaction yield) was treated probabilistically. The GP predicted both the mean yield and variance for each combination of experimental parameters. An EI acquisition function was then used to iteratively propose new experiments that balance exploration (uncertain areas) and exploitation (promising areas).

**Experimental Execution**: The optimization loop was implemented on an autonomous flow-based reactor platform. For each target reaction, the system began with a small number of randomly selected combinations of experimental parameters (typically 3–5). These combinations were tested in real reactions, and the observed yields were fed back into the model.

The surrogate model then updated its predictions based on the new data and proposed the next batch of experimental conditions by optimizing the EI acquisition function.

This iterative loop continued until convergence was reached, usually defined as no significant improvement in yield across successive rounds.

**Results and Impact**: The results demonstrated a dramatic reduction in experimental effort:

- For each new reaction, the optimal yield was typically reached in 6–8 experiments, compared to 20+ in conventional practice.
- The system also demonstrated strong transfer learning capabilities, performing better on reactions that were chemically related to those in the historical dataset.
- Cost savings were realized through reduced use of reagents and instrument time, and optimization times were cut by more than half in most cases.

Moreover, the MTBO model correctly identified unusual or non-intuitive reaction conditions that outperformed human intuition, highlighting the added value of model-driven discovery.

**Conclusion**: This case study demonstrates how multi-task Bayesian optimization can solve a real and recurring problem in catalyst and condition selection for C–H activation. By integrating machine learning with historical data and automated experimentation, researchers achieved highly efficient, data-driven optimization with significant practical benefits [22].

While Bayesian optimization focuses on global search in continuous parameter spaces, many chemical problems also require structured representations of molecules, such as graphs, motivating the use of graph-based optimization methods explored in the next section.

### 2.7. *Optimization in Graph-Based Models*

Graph-based models [23], particularly graph neural networks (GNNs), have gained significant attention in machine learning applications for chemistry, where molecular structures and electronic properties can be naturally represented as graphs. Optimization techniques play a crucial role in improving the performance and efficiency of GNNs by enhancing stability, reducing computational complexity, and ensuring smooth propagation of information across the graph structure.

Two key optimization approaches in graph-based models are graph Laplacian optimization, which leverages the graph Laplacian matrix to enforce smoothness and improve generalization, and spectral methods, which utilize eigendecomposition and graph Fourier transforms to reduce computational overhead and enhance learning efficiency. These methods are particularly useful in tasks such as charge density prediction, molecular property estimation, and quantum chemistry simulations. These will be discussed in the following subsections.

#### 2.7.1. Graph Laplacian Optimization

Graph Laplacian optimization is used in graph-based machine learning models, particularly in GNNs, where it improves stability and generalization by encouraging neighboring nodes to share similar feature representations. This is achieved by incorporating the graph

Laplacian matrix [24], which acts as a regularization mechanism to smooth node features and control information propagation.

The graph Laplacian matrix is defined as follows:

$$\mathcal{L} = D - A, \tag{7}$$

where $A$ is the adjacency matrix of the graph, encoding connections between nodes, and $D$ is the diagonal degree matrix, representing the number of connections for each node. The Laplacian matrix plays a key role in controlling how information spreads across the network, ensuring that connected nodes influence each other's feature representations.

In GNNs, regularization using the graph Laplacian ensures that neighboring nodes maintain similar feature values, reducing overfitting and improving generalization [25]. The node feature matrix $X$ represents the numerical attributes of each node, such as atomic properties in molecular graphs. The smoothness constraint imposed by the Laplacian is expressed as follows:

$$\mathcal{L}_{\text{smooth}} = \text{Tr}(X^T \mathcal{L} X), \tag{8}$$

where $\text{Tr}(\cdot)$ denotes the trace of a matrix. This penalty function minimizes differences between connected nodes, leading to more stable and coherent learned representations.

Graph Laplacian optimization is a pivotal technique in computational chemistry, particularly when employing GNNs to model complex molecular structures. In tasks such as charge density prediction, it's essential to ensure smooth transitions of electronic properties across bonded atoms for accurate modeling. Regularization through the Laplacian matrix enhances the numerical stability of GNNs in electronic structure problems. These applications illustrate how chemical problems involving spatial or topological structure, such as force field parameterization, naturally motivate the use of Laplacian-based regularization.

Recent work has extended graph optimization techniques to the prediction of physical interaction parameters in force fields, connecting learned graph structures with classical molecular mechanics. While graph Laplacian optimization operates on structured representations, the parameter tuning involved is typically local, adjusting force-field or interaction parameters based on local loss feedback, which is a typical feature of local optimization. However, the graph topology itself often reflects global molecular structure, indirectly guiding the model toward more globally coherent solutions, thereby introducing a topology-driven form of global optimization.

In their study, Thürlemann et al. (2022) [26] proposed a novel approach to parameterize force fields (FFs) by integrating machine learning with gradient-descent optimization while maintaining a physics-based functional form. They employed graph neural networks (GNNs) to predict FF parameters from potential energy surfaces, focusing on intramolecular interactions. Their method enables the GNN to learn and predict parameters such as bond lengths, angles, and dihedral angles, which are crucial for accurately modeling molecular geometries and dynamics. This approach enabled flexible, data-driven simulations by removing the need for manually defined functional forms. To encourage physically meaningful parameter variation, their method also leverages smoothness penalties, such as Laplacian-based regularization, which promote coherence across the molecular graph topology. This application represents a form of molecular optimization where model-driven learning is used to fine-tune physical parameters that define molecular structure and behavior.

These findings motivate further exploration of spectral techniques, which analyze graph structure through eigenvalue decomposition to enhance model performance, a topic we discuss in the following section.

### 2.7.2. Spectral Methods

Spectral methods are a class of optimization techniques that utilize the eigenvalues and eigenvectors of matrices associated with graphs to improve the efficiency and accuracy of machine learning models. These methods are particularly useful in GNNs, where they enable a more efficient representation of graph structures and facilitate computationally efficient learning. Unlike Laplacian regularization, which promotes local smoothness across neighboring nodes, spectral methods capture global structural patterns by analyzing the overall connectivity encoded in the Laplacian graph.

A key concept in spectral methods is the spectral decomposition of the graph Laplacian $\mathcal{L}$, defined as follows:

$$\mathcal{L} = U\Lambda U^T, \tag{9}$$

where $U$ is the matrix of eigenvectors, and $\Lambda$ is the diagonal matrix containing the corresponding eigenvalues. This decomposition provides a basis for spectral analysis of graph structures and allows for transformations such as spectral filtering.

The spectral decomposition enables the definition of the graph Fourier transform (GFT), which maps signals on a graph into the spectral domain:

$$\hat{X} = U^T X. \tag{10}$$

Here, $X$ represents the node feature matrix, and $\hat{X}$ denotes the transformed representation in the spectral domain. This transformation is fundamental for spectral filtering, where specific frequency components can be enhanced or suppressed to optimize learning. This type of filtering is particularly useful in molecular graphs for reducing noise, highlighting relevant structural patterns, and improving generalization in downstream tasks.

Spectral methods are particularly effective in tasks that require dimensionality reduction or structural clustering, such as visualizing large chemical libraries or uncovering latent molecular features. Spectral clustering has been applied to group molecules based on structural similarity [27], while Laplacian Eigenmaps preserve local relationships among molecular descriptors. Reutlinger et al. used this approach to improve the visualization of chemical libraries [28], and Gill et al. applied unsupervised learning with spectral embeddings to support emergent property prediction from SMILES representations [29].

Although spectral methods are not optimization algorithms in the traditional sense, they enable global structural analysis by capturing the overall topology of molecular graphs. This facilitates the exploration of chemical space and supports downstream optimization tasks by improving latent representations and clustering structure. Unsupervised learning methods such as spectral clustering and dimensionality reduction are particularly valuable in chemical ML when labeled data are scarce. These methods help uncover latent structures in molecular datasets, organize chemical space, and facilitate the pre-training of models that are later fine-tuned in supervised tasks.

Extending beyond unsupervised learning, spectral methods have been integrated into ML frameworks for quantum chemistry, where they support both molecular property prediction and quantum interaction modeling. Their integration into GNNs has shown notable improvements in predicting electronic structure and chemical reactivity by leveraging the spectral properties of molecular graph Laplacians [30]. These approaches include message-passing neural networks [31], spectral graph convolutions, and models tailored to learning quantum chemical interactions, all contributing to more accurate and efficient molecular simulations.

Notable examples include SchNet, DimeNet, and PaiNN [32–34], with the latter belonging to the class of E(3)-equivariant models specifically designed to preserve rotational and reflection symmetries in molecular systems. Such equivariant architectures enable more accurate predictions of tensorial properties, such as dipole moments, vibrational modes, and molecular spectra [35].

These advancements demonstrate how spectral techniques bridge the gap between structural representation and quantum-level prediction, making them a powerful complement to other optimization strategies in chemical machine learning.

### 2.8. Summary of Optimization Strategies and Their Applications

The previous subsections discussed various mathematical optimization techniques used in machine learning for computational chemistry. These methods differ in their roles within the learning process, their scope (local vs. global), and the learning paradigms they support. The table 1 provides an integrative overview, categorizing each method by its optimization target, associated learning setting and search scope.

**Table 1.** Summary of optimization strategies and their applications in chemical ML.

| Optimization Method | Optimization Target(s) | Learning Setting(s) | Search Scope |
|---|---|---|---|
| Stochastic Gradient Descent (SGD) | Model parameter optimization | Supervised learning | Local optimization |
| Adam | Model parameter optimization | Supervised learning | Local optimization |
| Backpropagation | Gradient computation (for model training) | Supervised learning | Supports local optimization (via optimizers) |
| Monte Carlo (MMC, SLHMC) | Molecular optimization | Reinforcement learning, Unsupervised | Global optimization |
| Bayesian Optimization | Hyperparameter, Molecular optimization | Supervised, Reinforcement | Global optimization |
| Graph-based Models | Molecular optimisation | Supervised, Unsupervised | Local (parameter tuning) and global (topology-driven) |

As shown in the table, each optimization method plays a distinct role depending on the stage of the learning pipeline and the specific demands of chemical modeling tasks. While these methods are powerful enablers of accurate and scalable ML, their effectiveness is often constrained by real-world challenges such as limited data availability, model transferability, and computational cost. These limitations are addressed in the following section.

## 3. Challenges in Machine Learning for Computational Chemistry

### 3.1. Data Scarcity and Quality

Machine learning models for density functional theory and molecular mechanics heavily rely on high-quality datasets. However, obtaining sufficient labeled data is often computationally expensive and limited by the accuracy of quantum chemical calculations [36,37]. The lack of sufficient data presents several key challenges:

Overfitting: Small datasets lead to overfitting, where models memorize training data instead of learning generalizable patterns. This is particularly problematic in computational chemistry, where molecular diversity is high, but the cost of generating labeled examples severely limits dataset size. As a result, models may capture noise or dataset-specific artifacts, performing well on seen molecules but failing to generalize to new chemical structures. This undermines the predictive reliability in downstream tasks such as drug discovery, molecular screening, or reaction modeling.

Computational Cost: High-fidelity quantum chemical calculations, such as coupled cluster or DFT-based simulations, demand substantial computational resources, sometimes requiring hours or days per molecule. This bottleneck restricts not only dataset size but also the diversity and complexity of chemical systems that can be explored. As a result, optimization workflows that depend on repeated model evaluations, such as hyperparameter tuning or active molecule selection, become prohibitively expensive.

Data Bias: Limited datasets often undersample specific regions of chemical space, leading to biased models that overfit common scaffolds or molecular features. Such bias reduces model robustness and hampers generalization across compound classes, physical conditions, or functional groups. This is particularly concerning in applications like materials discovery or catalyst design, where extrapolation is essential. For instance, in molecular property prediction tasks, even a modest bias in training data, such as the overrepresentation of small molecules, has been shown to reduce predictive accuracy by up to 15–20% when tested on larger, more complex compounds [38].

These challenges significantly impact the development of robust machine learning models in computational chemistry, limiting both the predictive accuracy and the effectiveness of optimization strategies. Addressing them requires carefully designed mathematical methods, which are discussed in the following sections.

Mathematical Models for Improving Data Quality

To address challenges associated with data scarcity and quality in computational chemistry, various mathematical techniques have been developed.

Regularization Techniques: Regularization methods, such as L2 regularization (ridge regression), add a penalty for large coefficients in the model, leading to simpler and more generalizable solutions. In the context of neural networks used for chemical property prediction, regularization reduces model variance and discourages overfitting to noisy or small datasets. This is particularly valuable when training on sparse quantum chemical datasets, where small perturbations in data could lead to unstable or biased models. The application of L2 regularization has been shown to improve the generalization ability of chemical models by promoting smoother parameter updates and preventing overfitting [39,40].

Data Augmentation in Chemical Space: Generating synthetic molecular data using generative models, such as variational autoencoders (VAEs [41]) or graph neural networks (GNNs), increases the diversity and volume of available data. These models sample from a learned latent space to create novel yet chemically valid structures, effectively enriching the training distribution. For example, the materials graph network (MEGNet) model has demonstrated improved performance in predicting molecular properties by leveraging graph-based representations to augment training data [42]. Augmentation not only mitigates data scarcity but also helps models learn more robust features, reducing their sensitivity to dataset-specific biases.

Active Learning: This strategy enables models to identify and select the most informative molecules for annotation, optimizing resource utilization and improving training efficiency. Instead of randomly choosing training samples, active learning prioritizes the most uncertain data points, where the model exhibits the highest prediction uncertainty. By focusing on examples where the model struggles the most, such as molecules with conflicting property predictions or high entropy in the output distribution, active learning significantly accelerates learning while reducing the number of required annotated samples. Implementing this approach in chemistry has led to notable improvements in model accuracy, particularly in molecular property prediction and reaction optimization [43,44]. This trade-off between exploiting known regions of chemical space and exploring uncertain ones parallels strategies found in global optimization algorithms.

Bayesian Optimization for Data Selection: Utilizing Bayesian optimization to identify the most valuable data points enables minimization of computational costs. Wu, Walsh, and Ganose demonstrated how Bayesian optimization can navigate parameter spaces by iteratively selecting experiments to balance exploration with exploitation [45]. This approach has been shown to accelerate the discovery of optimal molecules and materials while reducing the number of required experiments or calculations.

By integrating these mathematical strategies, machine learning models in computational chemistry can achieve higher accuracy and better generalization, even when faced with limited or low-quality data.

### 3.2. *Transferability and Generalization*

Machine learning models trained on a specific set of molecular systems often struggle to generalize to new, unseen chemical environments due to variations in molecular representation, data distribution, and quantum mechanical effects [46]. The ability to transfer knowledge from one dataset to another is a crucial requirement for developing robust models. Generalization ensures that models can make accurate predictions across diverse chemical domains, but several key challenges hinder this capability:

Limited Extrapolation Capabilities: Neural networks often fail to make accurate predictions for out-of-distribution molecules, particularly those with significantly different atomic compositions or electronic properties compared to the training set [47]. This is because most models are inherently designed to interpolate within the training domain rather than extrapolate beyond it. As a result, when confronted with molecules that exhibit novel bonding patterns, unusual charge distributions, or rare functional groups, these models tend to produce unreliable outputs. The inability to extrapolate limits the practical application of ML in scenarios such as the discovery of new materials or drugs, where generalization to unexplored chemical space is essential.

Molecular Representation Bias: The choice of molecular descriptors and embeddings (e.g., graph-based representations and SMILES encoding) heavily influences how well a model generalizes [48]. Different representations emphasize different chemical features; for instance, some may better capture local bonding environments, while others are more effective at preserving global topology. A model trained on one representation may not effectively interpret or generalize to molecules encoded differently, introducing a form of structural bias. Moreover, some representations may obscure key quantum or spatial information, which further reduces model transferability across tasks or datasets.

Long-Range Interactions and Quantum Effects: Machine learning models frequently struggle to capture long-range electron correlation and nonlocal quantum effects, which are essential for accurately predicting chemical reactivity, excited-state dynamics, and intermolecular interactions [49]. Many models rely on local information or limited neighborhood aggregation, which may omit subtle but significant quantum phenomena such as polarization or dispersion forces. These limitations are especially problematic in larger or more flexible molecular systems, where the interplay of distant atomic interactions significantly influences energy landscapes and reactivity profiles.

Domain Shift in Experimental vs. Simulated Data: Many ML models in chemistry are trained on simulated datasets, such as DFT-calculated properties, while real-world applications often require extrapolation to experimental data. This discrepancy, known as domain shift, can cause significant performance degradation when models transition from theoretical calculations to experimental validation [50]. Experimental datasets may include noise, measurement error, or artifacts not present in clean simulation data, which introduces a mismatch in data distributions. Consequently, models may appear highly accurate in silico but fail to replicate their performance when tested under real experimental conditions.

Taken together, these limitations underscore a fundamental obstacle in the development of reliable chemical machine learning models: the inability to consistently generalize beyond the training domain. To mitigate these challenges, the following section surveys established mathematical approaches aimed at enhancing generalization across heterogeneous chemical spaces and data regimes.

Mathematical Strategies for Improving Generalization

To enhance the generalizability of machine learning models in chemistry, researchers have explored various mathematical approaches. These strategies address the underlying causes of poor transferability, such as distribution shifts, representation limitations, and the lack of physical constraints.

Bayesian Optimization: This method is employed to identify optimal hyperparameters and neural architecture configurations in a principled, data-efficient manner. By modeling the uncertainty in the objective function, Bayesian optimization enables efficient exploration of hyperparameter space, which contributes to improved robustness across diverse chemical datasets and molecular structures [45].

Adversarial Training and Domain Adaptation: These techniques introduce deliberate perturbations to molecular inputs during training, forcing the model to generalize better under slight variations. Adversarial examples simulate domain shift scenarios, while domain adaptation methods explicitly align the feature distributions between source (training) and target (test) domains. Together, they enhance resilience to out-of-distribution chemical data and improve real-world applicability [51,52].

Meta-Learning and Few-Shot Learning: These approaches are designed to enable rapid adaptation to new chemical tasks or molecular families using only a small number of labeled examples. By learning to generalize from limited data, such models are particularly useful in low-resource domains where collecting new quantum chemical data is expensive or impractical. Meta-learning frameworks help models internalize inductive biases that are transferable across related chemical tasks [53].

Hybrid ML–Physics Models: Combining machine learning with physics-based constraints improves extrapolation to molecules beyond the training set. These hybrid models enhance predictive reliability by incorporating domain knowledge, such as symmetry, conservation laws, or electronic structure principles, helping ensure that outputs remain physically meaningful even in out-of-distribution scenarios [54].

However, integrating physical constraints into ML architectures is far from trivial and presents several implementation challenges. One major difficulty lies in encoding domain-specific physical laws, such as energy conservation, permutation invariance, or force fields, into differentiable neural network structures. This often requires extending existing equivariant neural network architectures to ensure they respect additional symmetry constraints specific to the task (e.g., energy conservation or force matching), crafting problem-specific loss functions, or incorporating symbolic terms to preserve quantum mechanical priors. These approaches demand extensive domain expertise, complicate model implementation, and hinder transferability to other chemical systems with different physical characteristics [55]. Furthermore, enforcing these constraints strictly (e.g., through hard architectural rules) can make optimization more brittle and sensitive to initialization, while softer regularization-based approaches may compromise physical fidelity in favor of smoother convergence [56]. These trade-offs between accuracy, generalizability, and tractability are still an active area of research in physics-informed ML, particularly in applications involving quantum chemistry and molecular dynamics.

### 3.3. *Computational Cost vs. Accuracy Trade-Offs*

One of the key challenges in ML-driven computational chemistry is balancing high predictive accuracy with affordable computational cost. Many high-fidelity quantum chemistry calculations, such as coupled cluster (CCSD(T)) and DFT, require substantial computational resources, often scaling poorly with system size. As a result, large-scale applications, such as molecular screening or material discovery, become impractical [57].

The integration of machine learning models aims to alleviate this burden, yet the models themselves must be carefully designed and trained to avoid excessive computational overhead. Deep neural networks, while powerful, may involve millions of parameters and require extensive training data and resources, especially when tailored to quantum-level accuracy. Furthermore, increasing model complexity does not always yield proportionally better performance and may even lead to diminishing returns.

This creates a fundamental trade-off: achieving high chemical accuracy often comes at the cost of computational scalability. Understanding and navigating this trade-off is essential for the practical deployment of ML in chemistry. It involves careful choices in model architecture, training protocols, and data selection, which are topics addressed in the following section.

#### Optimization Strategies for Cost-Accuracy Trade-Offs

To address the challenge of balancing computational cost and accuracy in machine learning for computational chemistry, researchers have developed several optimization strategies that make model training and inference more efficient without significantly sacrificing performance:

Grid search vs. Bayesian optimization: Selecting appropriate hyperparameters, such as learning rate, batch size, or network depth, is crucial for controlling both model complexity and resource usage. While traditional grid search exhaustively evaluates combinations of parameters, this approach quickly becomes infeasible in high-dimensional spaces. In contrast, Bayesian optimization models the performance landscape and intelligently selects the most promising configurations to evaluate next. This reduces the number of costly evaluations required to find high-performing configurations and is particularly advantageous when each model training cycle is computationally expensive [58].

While Bayesian optimization has proven advantageous over grid search in many low- to moderate-dimensional tasks, its performance deteriorates in high-dimensional hyperparameter spaces, a common setting in deep learning for computational chemistry. Although BO is valued for its sample efficiency, it suffers from exponentially increased search complexity and poor surrogate model fidelity as dimensionality grows. For instance, simulations have shown that when the dimensionality increases from 2D to 3D, the number of evaluations required to converge to an optimal solution can increase by several hundred iterations, even in synthetic settings for materials synthesis [59]. This combinatorial explosion is primarily due to the difficulty of accurately modeling acquisition functions in high-dimensional regimes, which tend to become nearly flat with few distinguishable optima, hindering effective exploration [60]. As a result, BO may converge to suboptimal hyperparameters or require prohibitively expensive evaluations, especially when each function call involves time-consuming simulations or quantum chemistry calculations.

Adaptive learning rate techniques: Gradient based optimizers like Adam, RMSprop, and AdaGrad adaptively adjust the learning rate during training by incorporating information about gradient magnitude and variance over time. These methods accelerate convergence, prevent oscillations in flat regions of the loss surface, and reduce the number of iterations needed for model training [5]. In computational chemistry, where each training iteration might involve large molecular datasets or simulation-derived features, reducing redundant updates contributes significantly to cost efficiency.

Active learning: Beyond improving data quality, active learning offers a powerful mechanism to reduce the number of expensive quantum chemistry calculations. By querying only the most informative or uncertain samples, typically those with high prediction uncertainty, active learning frameworks concentrate resources on cases where model improvement is most needed. In reaction screening tasks, this approach has been shown to reduce the number of DFT evaluations by up to 70% without compromising predictive performance [61]. Similar efficiency gains have been observed in other domains, such as potential energy surface estimation and reaction outcome prediction, where active learning significantly reduces dataset size while preserving target accuracy [44].

While active learning has proven effective in reducing annotation costs by strategically selecting informative samples, it introduces nontrivial practical overheads. After each acquisition step, the model must be retrained from scratch or incrementally updated, which becomes increasingly expensive for deep learning models or ensembles. In computational chemistry, this cost is compounded by the fact that labeling often requires quantum mechanical simulations or DFT calculations, which are time-consuming and resource-intensive. Another significant challenge is the design and selection of acquisition functions. Common strategies such as uncertainty sampling or expected model change may not effectively capture the diversity and complexity of chemical space. If the acquisition function over-focuses on uncertain but chemically redundant regions or conversely ignores rare but important motifs, the result can be suboptimal coverage and wasted computational effort. Tuning these acquisition functions to reflect both predictive uncertainty and chemical diversity remains an open and application-specific problem [62].

Low-Fidelity Approximations with Correction Models: Instead of relying solely on computationally intensive first-principle methods like CCSD(T) or DFT, researchers increasingly adopt multi-fidelity approaches that combine low-cost approximations with learned correction functions. For instance, semi-empirical methods or low-tier DFT can be used to generate large datasets at low cost, and models such as Δ-learning or transfer-learning are trained to learn systematic corrections that map these outputs to high-fidelity results [63]. This enables scalable exploration of chemical space while preserving the accuracy of high-level quantum mechanical methods.

Together, these strategies exemplify how mathematical and algorithmic optimization can directly impact the scalability and feasibility of machine learning in chemistry. By intelligently allocating computational resources and leveraging principled approximations, researchers can extend the applicability of ML models to larger, more diverse molecular systems without prohibitive cost.

Generative modeling frameworks: Generative models, such as variational autoencoders, generative adversarial networks, and diffusion-based architectures, have shown great potential for automated molecular design. However, their integration into practical computational chemistry pipelines is hampered by several technical and domain-specific challenges. First, generated molecules often fall outside the domain of chemical validity, producing invalid SMILES strings, unstable molecular graphs, or compounds that violate basic valence rules. Second, even when chemically valid, many generated candidates are synthetically infeasible, lacking accessible reaction pathways or requiring costly multistep synthesis [64]. Third, the objectives optimized during generation, such as latent space similarity or predicted property scores, may not align with experimentally meaningful endpoints, leading to unrealistic or non-functional molecules [65]. Finally, evaluating each generated structure for target properties (e.g., binding affinity and HOMO-LUMO gap) typically requires computationally intensive post hoc validation, often involving quantum mechanical methods like DFT [66]. These bottlenecks make it difficult to scale generative approaches or incorporate them directly into iterative design–test cycles in chemistry workflows.

## 4. Future Directions

Ongoing advances in quantum computing, machine-learned potentials, and large-scale pretraining signal transformative possibilities for optimization in computational chemistry. The future development of these technologies promises to address many of the challenges outlined in this review, including generalization, data scarcity, and computational cost.

Quantum-Classical Hybrid Optimization: Quantum algorithms have already demonstrated potential in simulating molecular systems, yet their integration with classical ML workflows remains at an early stage. Future research may focus on hybrid quantum–classical optimization approaches, where quantum subroutines (e.g., variational quantum eigensolvers or quantum annealing) are embedded into classical ML pipelines. Such methods could enable scalable optimization in high-dimensional chemical spaces, improve sampling, and accelerate hyperparameter tuning for complex models [67].

Machine-Learned Potentials and Transferable Force Fields: Another promising direction is the development of machine-learned interatomic potentials to improve molecular simulations. Current ML-driven FFs are limited by training data and accuracy trade-offs, making it essential to explore transferable and self-improving potential models. Further development of ML-based energy functions could improve the accuracy and efficiency of molecular simulations, enabling faster exploration of chemical space while reducing the reliance on costly quantum chemistry calculations [68].

Optimization for Molecular Discovery and Catalysis: Optimization strategies will continue to play a central role in inverse design tasks. Bayesian optimization, combined with graph-based and spectral methods, offers promising avenues for accelerating ligand design, reaction prediction, and catalyst discovery. The integration of ML with enhanced sampling techniques, such as metadynamics, may further improve the exploration of reaction pathways and rare event dynamics [69].

Interpretability and Explainable Models: To foster greater trust and adoption of ML in scientific domains, models must become more interpretable. Explainability techniques, such as saliency maps, gradient-based attribution (e.g., Grad-CAM), and attention visualization, can help identify the molecular features most responsible for a model's predictions, particularly in tasks like molecular property prediction or drug-likeness evaluation.

Foundation Models and Transfer Learning: Finally, the emergence of large pre-trained chemical foundation models (e.g., ChemBERTa and OC20) opens the door to flexible, data-efficient modeling across tasks. These models, trained on extensive chemical corpora, enable fine-tuning in low-data regimes and enhance cross-domain generalization. Future work may focus on combining foundation models with optimization pipelines to build modular and adaptable frameworks for chemical discovery [70,71].

Together, these future directions suggest a path toward more integrated, scalable, and interpretable frameworks for chemical machine learning. As optimization methods evolve, their potential synergy with quantum computing, foundation models, and physical constraints may play a pivotal role in shaping the next generation of predictive tools in computational chemistry.

Despite these promising directions, several critical challenges remain unresolved in the field of optimization for chemical machine learning. Key issues include improving generalization across chemical space in the presence of biased or sparse data, incorporating physical constraints into ML architectures without introducing excessive complexity, and designing active learning strategies that are both efficient and practical to implement. Furthermore, optimization algorithms such as Bayesian optimization continue to face scalability barriers in high-dimensional parameter spaces.

We believe that addressing these challenges will require tighter integration between theoretical model development and experimental validation, as well as hybrid approaches that combine domain knowledge with data-driven flexibility. In particular, establishing benchmark datasets and reproducible evaluation frameworks will be essential for comparing methods and driving progress in the field.

## 5. Conclusions

Mathematical optimization plays a critical role in enhancing machine learning models for computational chemistry, enabling more accurate, efficient, and scalable predictions of molecular properties. This review explored key optimization techniques, including stochastic gradient descent, Bayesian optimization, Monte Carlo methods, and spectral approaches, emphasizing their impact on improving ML performance in chemistry applications.

Despite significant progress, challenges such as data scarcity, model generalization, and computational cost remain central issues. Advanced mathematical techniques, including active learning, meta-learning, and hybrid quantum–classical methods, are emerging as promising solutions to overcome these limitations. Additionally, the integration of machine learning with traditional computational chemistry approaches holds great potential for accelerating chemical discovery.

By framing optimization along three principal targets (model training, hyperparameter tuning, and molecular design) this review provides a unified perspective that connects general ML methodology with chemistry-specific needs, such as quantum property prediction and force field development. As optimization techniques evolve, aligning methods with their appropriate targets will be critical to building more robust, transferable, and interpretable chemical ML models. Achieving this will require sustained collaboration across machine learning, quantum chemistry, and materials science, bringing us closer to practical, scalable applications in drug discovery, catalyst design, and materials engineering.

**Funding:** This research was supported by the Ministry of Science, Technological Development, and Innovation of the Republic of Serbia (Contract No. 451-03-136/2025-03/200135).

**Acknowledgments:** The author gratefully acknowledges Bojana Nedić Vasiljević for her valuable insights and conceptual input that helped shape the direction of this work. Warm thanks are also extended to Zoran Hadžibabić for thoughtful stylistic suggestions on an earlier draft, as well as for his kind support and encouragement throughout the writing process. Finally, the author is grateful to the referee for their careful reading and insightful comments, which significantly improved the quality of the paper.

**Conflicts of Interest:** The author declares no conflict of interest.

## References

1. Bottou, L. Large-Scale Machine Learning with Stochastic Gradient Descent. In Proceedings of the COMPSTAT'2010, Paris, France, 22–27 August 2010. [CrossRef]
2. Sutskever, I.; Martens, J.; Dahl, G.; Hinton, G. On the importance of initialization and momentum in deep learning. In Proceedings of the 30th International Conference on Machine Learning, Atlanta, GA, USA, 17–19 June 2013; Volume 28, pp. 1139–1147. Available online: https://proceedings.mlr.press/v28/sutskever13.html (accessed on 9 July 2025).
3. Rupp, M.; Tkatchenko, A.; Müller, K.-R.; von Lilienfeld, O.A. Fast and Accurate Modeling of Molecular Atomization Energies with Machine Learning. *Phys. Rev. Lett.* **2012**, *108*, 058301. [CrossRef] [PubMed]
4. Ruder, S. An overview of gradient descent optimization algorithms. *arXiv* **2016**, arXiv:1609.04747. [CrossRef]

5. Kingma, D.P.; Ba, J. Adam: A Method for Stochastic Optimization. In Proceedings of the 3rd International Conference for Learning Representations, San Diego, CA, USA, 7–9 May 2015. [CrossRef]
6. Schütt, K.T.; Arbabzadah, F.; Chmiela, S.; Müller, K.R.; Tkatchenko, A. Quantum-Chemical Insights from Deep Tensor Neural Networks. *Nat. Commun.* **2017**, *8*, 13890. [CrossRef] [PubMed]
7. Wu, Z.; Ramsundar, B.; Feinberg, E.N.; Gomes, J.; Geniesse, C.; Pappu, A.S.; Leswing, K.; Pande, V. MoleculeNet: A Benchmark for Molecular Machine Learning. *Chem. Sci.* **2018**, *9*, 513–530. [CrossRef]
8. Reddi, S.J.; Kale, S.; Kumar, S. On the Convergence of Adam and Beyond. *arXiv* **2019**, arXiv:1904.09237. [CrossRef]
9. Zhuang, J.; Tang, T.; Ding, Y.; Wang, S.; Liu, Z.; Castro, C.D.; Dvornek, N.; Papademetris, X.; Duncan, J.S. AdaBelief Optimizer: Adapting Stepsizes by the Belief in Observed Gradients. *arXiv* **2020**, arXiv:2010.07468. [CrossRef]
10. Ma, N.Q.; Yarats, D.; Kapturowski, S. Quasi-Hyperbolic Momentum and Adam for Deep Learning. *arXiv* **2018**, arXiv:1810.06801. [CrossRef]
11. Kollmannsberger, S.; D'Angella, D.; Jokeit, M.; Herrmann, L. *Deep Learning in Computational Mechanics*; Springer: Cham, Switzerland, 2021. [CrossRef]
12. Kiyani, E.; Shukla, K.; Urbán, J.F.; Darbon, J.; Karniadakis, G.E. Which Optimizer Works Best for Physics-Informed Neural Networks and Kolmogorov-Arnold Networks? *arXiv* **2025**, arXiv:2501.16371. https://arxiv.org/abs/2501.16371.
13. Rumelhart, D.E.; Hinton, G.E.; Williams, R.J. Learning representations by back-propagating errors. *Nature* **1986**, *323*, 533–536. [CrossRef]
14. Snyder, J.C.; Rupp, M.; Hansen, K.; Müller, K.R.; Burke, K. Finding Density Functionals with Machine Learning. *Phys. Rev. Lett.* **2012**, *108*, 253002. [CrossRef]
15. Metropolis, N.; Rosenbluth, A.W.; Rosenbluth, M.N.; Teller, A.H.; Teller, E. Equation of State Calculations by Fast Computing Machines. *J. Chem. Phys.* **1953**, *21*, 1087–1092. [CrossRef]
16. Nagai, Y.; Okumura, M.; Kobayashi, K.; Shiga, M. Self-learning hybrid Monte Carlo: A first-principles approach. *Phys. Rev. B* **2020**, *102*, 041124. [CrossRef]
17. Karandashev, K.; Weinreich, J.; Heinen, S.; Arismendi Arrieta, D.J.; von Rudorff, G.F.; Hermansson, K.; von Lilienfeld, O.A. Evolutionary Monte Carlo of QM Properties in Chemical Space: Electrolyte Design. *J. Chem. Theory Comput.* **2023**, *19*, 8861–8870. [CrossRef] [PubMed]
18. Shahriari, B.; Swersky, K.; Wang, Z.; Adams, R.P.; De Freitas, N. Taking the human out of the loop: A review of Bayesian optimization. *Proc. IEEE* **2016**, *104*, 148–175. [CrossRef]
19. Hernández-Lobato, J.M.; Requeima, J.; Pyzer-Knapp, E.O.; Aspuru-Guzik, A. Parallel and Distributed Thompson Sampling for Large-scale Accelerated Exploration of Chemical Space. In Proceedings of the 34th International Conference on Machine Learning, Sydney, Australia, 6–11 August 2017; Volume 70, pp. 1470–1479. Available online: https://arxiv.org/abs/1706.01825 (accessed on 9 July 2025).
20. Gómez-Bombarelli, R. Automatic Chemical Design Using a Data-Driven Continuous Representation of Molecules. *ACS Cent. Sci.* **2018**, *4*, 268–276. [CrossRef]
21. Olivecrona, M.; Blaschke, T.; Engkvist, O.; Chen, H. Molecular de-novo design through deep reinforcement learning. *J. Cheminform.* **2017**, *9*, 48. [CrossRef]
22. Wigh, D.; Jeraal, M.; Johnson, C.; Taylor, C.; Felton, K.; Chessari, G.; Lapkin, A.; Grainger, R. Accelerated Chemical Reaction Optimization Using Multi-Task Learning. *ACS Cent. Sci.* **2023**, *9*, 957–968. [CrossRef]
23. Kipf, T.N.; Welling, M. Semi-Supervised Classification with Graph Convolutional Networks. *arXiv* **2017**, arXiv:1609.02907. [CrossRef]
24. Chung, F.R.K. *Spectral Graph Theory*; CBMS Regional Conference Series in Mathematics; American Mathematical Society: Providence, RI, USA, 1997. Available online: https://bookstore.ams.org/cbms-92 (accessed on 9 July 2025).
25. Zhou, D.; Bousquet, O.; Lal, T.N.; Weston, J.; Schölkopf, B. Learning with Local and Global Consistency. In Proceedings of the 17th International Conference on Neural Information Processing Systems, Whistler, BC, Canada, 9–11 December 2004; Advances in Neural Information Processing Systems.
26. Thürlemann, M.; Böselt, L.; Riniker, S. Regularized by Physics: Graph Neural Network Parametrized Differentiable Force Field Models. *J. Chem. Theory Comput.* **2022**, *18*, 7569–7582. [CrossRef]
27. Ningombam, S.S.; Larson, E.J.L.; Indira, G.; Madhavan, B.L.; Khatri, P. Aerosol classification by application of machine learning spectral clustering algorithm. *Atmos. Pollut. Res.* **2024**, *15*, 102026. [CrossRef]
28. Reutlinger, M.; Schneider, G. Nonlinear dimensionality reduction and mapping of compound libraries for drug discovery. *J. Mol. Graph. Model.* **2012**, *34*, 108–117. [CrossRef] [PubMed]
29. Gill, J.; Chakraborty, R.; Gubba, R.; Liu, A.; Jain, S.; Iyer, C.; Khwaja, O.; Kumar, S. Unsupervised Learning of Molecular Embeddings for Enhanced Clustering and Emergent Properties for Chemical Compounds. *arXiv* **2023**, arXiv:2310.18367. [CrossRef]
30. Yu, S.; Dong, H.; Wang, P.; Wu, C.; Guo, Y. Generative Creativity: Adversarial Learning for Bionic Design. *arXiv* **2018**, arXiv:1805.07615. [CrossRef]

31. Gilmer, J.; Schoenholz, S.S.; Riley, P.F.; Vinyals, O.; Dahl, G.E. Neural Message Passing for Quantum Chemistry. *arXiv* **2017**, arXiv:1704.01212. [CrossRef]
32. Gasteiger, J.; Groß, J.; Günnemann, S. Directional Message Passing for Molecular Graphs. *arXiv* **2020**, arXiv:2003.03123. [CrossRef]
33. Schütt, K.T.; Kindermans, P.-J.; Sauceda, H.E.; Chmiela, S.; Tkatchenko, A.; Müller, K.-R. SchNet—A continuous-filter convolutional neural network for modeling quantum interactions. *J. Chem. Phys.* **2018**, *148*, 241722. Available online: https://proceedings.neurips.cc/paper_files/paper/2017/file/303ed4c69846ab36c2904d3ba8573050-Paper.pdf (accessed on 9 July 2025). [CrossRef]
34. Schütt, K.T.; Unke, O.T.; Gastegger, M. Equivariant message passing for the prediction of tensorial properties and molecular spectra. *arXiv* **2021**, arXiv:2102.03150. Available online: https://arxiv.org/abs/2102.03150 (accessed on 9 July 2025).
35. Batzner, S.; Musaelian, A.; Sun, L.; Geiger, M.; Mailoa, J.P.; Kornbluth, M.; Molinari, N.; Smidt, T.E.; Kozinsky, B. E(3)-equivariant graph neural networks for data-efficient and accurate interatomic potentials. *Nat. Commun.* **2022**, *13*, 2453. [CrossRef]
36. Huang, B.; von Rudorff, G.F.; von Lilienfeld, O.A. The central role of density functional theory in the AI age. *Science* **2023**, *81*, 170–175. [CrossRef]
37. Nandy, A.; Duan, C.; Kulik, H.J. Audacity of huge: Overcoming challenges of data scarcity and data quality for machine learning in computational materials discovery. *arXiv* **2021**, arXiv:2111.01905. [CrossRef]
38. Liu, Y.-Y.; Kashima, H. Chemical property prediction under experimental biases. *Sci. Rep.* **2022**, *12*, 8206. [CrossRef]
39. Demir-Kavuk, O.; Kamada, M.; Akutsu, T.; Knapp, E.W. Prediction using step-wise L1, L2 regularization and feature selection for small data sets with large number of features. *BMC Bioinform.* **2011**, *12*, 412. [CrossRef]
40. Lo Y.C.; Rensi, S.E.; Torng, W.; Altman, R.B. Machine learning in chemoinformatics and drug discovery. *Drug Discov. Today* **2018**, *23*, 1538–1546. [CrossRef] [PubMed]
41. Ochiai, T.; Inukai, T.; Akiyama, M.; Furui, K.; Ohue, M.; Matsumori, N.; Inuki, S.; Uesugi, M.; Sunazuka, T.; Kikuchi, K.; et al. Variational autoencoder-based chemical latent space for large molecular structures with 3D complexity. *Commun. Chem.* **2023**, *6*, 249. [CrossRef] [PubMed]
42. Chen, C.; Ye, W.; Zuo, Y.; Zheng, C.; Ong, S.P. Graph Networks as a Universal Machine Learning Framework for Molecules and Crystals. *Chem. Mater.* **2019**, *31*, 3564–3572. [CrossRef]
43. van Tilborg, D.; Grisoni, F. Traversing chemical space with active deep learning for low-data drug discovery. *Nat. Comput. Sci.* **2024**, *4*, 786–796. [CrossRef]
44. Khalak, Y.; Tresadern, G.; Hahn, D.F.; de Groot, B.L.; Gapsys, V. Chemical Space Exploration with Active Learning and Alchemical Free Energies. *J. Chem. Theory Comput.* **2022**, *18*, 6259–6270. [CrossRef]
45. Wu, Y.; Walsh, A.; Ganose, A.M. Race to the bottom: Bayesian optimisation for chemical problems. *Digit. Discov.* **2024**, *3*, 1086–1100. [CrossRef]
46. Bartók, A.P.; De, S.; Poelking, C.; Bernstein, N.; Kermode, J.R.; Csányi, G.; Ceriotti, M. Machine learning unifies the modeling of materials and molecules. *Sci. Adv.* **2017**, *3*. [CrossRef]
47. Tossou, P.; Wognum, C.; Craig, M.; Mary, H.; Noutahi, E. Real-World Molecular Out-of-Distribution: Specification and Investigation. *J. Chem. Inf. Model.* **2024**, *64*, 697–711. [CrossRef]
48. Wigh, D.S.; Goodman, J.M.; Lapkin, A.A. A review of molecular representation in the age of machine learning. *WIREs Comput. Mol. Sci.* **2022**, *12*, e1603. [CrossRef]
49. McDonagh, J.L.; Silva, A.F.; Vincent, M.A.; Popelier, P.L.A. Machine Learning of Dynamic Electron Correlation Energies from Topological Atoms. *J. Chem. Theory Comput.* **2018**, *14*, 216–224. [CrossRef] [PubMed]
50. Han, H.; Choi, S. Transfer Learning from Simulation to Experimental Data: NMR Chemical Shift Predictions. *J. Phys. Chem. Lett.* **2021**, *12*, 3662–3668. [CrossRef] [PubMed]
51. Gani, Y.; Ustinova, E.; Ajakan, H.; Germain, P.; Larochelle, H.; Laviolette, F.; March, M.; Lempitsky, V. Domain-Adversarial Training of Neural Networks. *arXiv* **2015**, arXiv:1505.07818. [CrossRef]
52. Xie, L.; He, S.; Zhang, Z.; Lin, K.; Bo, X.; Yang, S.; Feng, B.; Wan, K.; Yang, K.; Yang, J.; et al. Domain-adversarial multi-task framework for novel therapeutic property prediction of compounds. *Bioinformatics* **2020**, *36*, 2848–2855. [CrossRef]
53. Qian, X.; Ju, B.; Shen, P.; Yang, K.; Li, L.; Liu, Q. Meta Learning with Attention Based FP-GNNs for Few-Shot Molecular Property Prediction. *ACS Omega* **2024**, *9*, 23940–23948. [CrossRef]
54. Keith, J.A.; Vassilev-Galindo, V.; Cheng, B.; Chmiela, S.; Gastegger, M.; Müller, K.-R.; Tkatchenko, A. Combining Machine Learning and Computational Chemistry for Predictive Insights Into Chemical Systems. *Chem. Rev.* **2021**, *121*, 9816–9872. [CrossRef]
55. Wang, X.; Zhang, M. Graph Neural Network with Local Frame for Molecular Potential Energy Surface. In Proceedings of the First Learning on Graphs Conference, Virtual Event, 9–12 December 2022; Volume 198, pp. 19:1–19:30. Available online: https://proceedings.mlr.press/v198/wang22d.html (accessed on 9 July 2025).
56. Karniadakis, G.E.; Kevrekidis, I.G.; Lu, L.; Perdikaris, P.; Wang, S.; Yang, L. Physics-informed machine learning. *Nat. Rev. Phys.* **2021**, *3*, 422–440. [CrossRef]

57. Bogojeski, M.; Vogt-Maranto, L.; Tuckerman, M.E.; Müller, K.-R.; Burke, K. Quantum chemical accuracy from density functional approximations via machine learning. *Nat. Commun.* **2020**, *11*, 5223. [CrossRef]
58. Snoek, J.; Larochelle, H.; Adams, R.P. Practical Bayesian Optimization of Machine Learning Algorithms. *arXiv* **2012**, arXiv:1206.2944. [CrossRef]
59. Hickman, R.J.; Aldeghi, M.; Häse, F.; Aspuru-Guzik, A. Bayesian optimization with known experimental and design constraints for chemistry applications. *Digit. Discov.* **2022**, *1*, 732–744. [CrossRef]
60. Jin, Y.; Kumar, P.V. Bayesian optimisation for efficient material discovery: A mini review. *Nanoscale* **2023**, *15*, 10975–10984. [CrossRef] [PubMed]
61. Eyke, N.S.; Green, W.H.; Jensen, K.F. Iterative Experimental Design Based on Active Machine Learning Reduces the Experimental Burden Associated with Reaction Screening. *React. Chem. Eng.* **2020**, *5*, 1963–1972. [CrossRef]
62. Kulichenko, M.; Barros, K.; Lubbers, N.; Li, Y.W.; Messerly, R.A.; Tretiak, S.; Smith, J.S.; Nebgen, B. Uncertainty-driven dynamics for active learning of interatomic potentials. *Nat. Comput. Sci.* **2023**, *3*, 148–157. [CrossRef]
63. Ko, T.W.; Ong, S.P. Data-efficient construction of high-fidelity graph deep learning interatomic potentials. *npj Comput. Mater.* **2025**, *11*, 65. [CrossRef]
64. Polykovskiy, D.; Zhebrak, A.; Sanchez-Lengeling, B.; Golovanov, S.; Tatanov, O.; Belyaev, S.; Kurbanov, R.; Artamonov, A.; Aladinskiy, V.; Veselov, M.; et al. Molecular Sets (MOSES): A Benchmarking Platform for Molecular Generation Models. *Nat. Mach. Intell.* **2020**, *2*, 554–562. [CrossRef]
65. Bilodeau, C.; Jin, W.; Barzilay, R.; Jaakkola, T.; Jensen, K. Generative models for molecular discovery: Recent advances and challenges. *Wiley Interdiscip. Rev. Comput. Mol. Sci.* **2022**, *12*, e1608. [CrossRef]
66. Blanchard, A.E.; Zhang, P.; Bhowmik, D.; Mehta, K.; Gounley, J.; Reeve, S.T.; Irle, S.; Pasini, M.L. Computational Workflow for Accelerated Molecular Design Using Quantum Chemical Simulations and Deep Learning Models. *Commun. Comput. Inf. Sci.* **2023**. [CrossRef]
67. Fiedler, L.; Hoffmann, N.; Mohammed, P.; Popoola, G.A.; Yovell, T.; Oles, V.; Ellis, J.A.; Rajamanickam, S.; Cangi, A. Training-free hyperparameter optimization of neural networks for electronic structures in matter. *arXiv* **2022**, arXiv:2202.09186. [CrossRef]
68. Sivaraman, G.; Krishnamoorthy, A.N.; Baur, M.; Holm, C.; Stan, M.; Csányi, G.; Benmore, C.; Vázquez-Mayagoitia, Á. Machine-learned interatomic potentials by active learning: amorphous and liquid hafnium dioxide. *npj Comput. Mater.* **2020**, *6*, 104. [CrossRef]
69. Abrams, C.; Bussi, G. Enhanced Sampling in Molecular Dynamics Using Metadynamics, Replica-Exchange, and Temperature-Acceleration. *arXiv* **2014**, arXiv:1401.0387. [CrossRef]
70. Ahmad, W.; Simon, E.; Chithrananda, S.; Grand, G.; Ramsundar, B. ChemBERTa-2: Towards Chemical Foundation Models. *arXiv* **2022**, arXiv:2209.01712. [CrossRef].
71. Chanussot, L.; Das, A.; Goyal, S.; Lavril, T.; Shuaibi, M.; Riviere, M.; Tran, K.; Heras-Domingo, J.; Ho, C.; Hu, W.; et al. Open Catalyst 2020 (OC20) Dataset and Community Challenges. *ACS Catal.* **2021**, *11*, 6059–6072. [CrossRef]

MDPI AG
Grosspeteranlage 5
4052 Basel
Switzerland
Tel.: +41 61 683 77 34

*Computation* Editorial Office
E-mail: computation@mdpi.com
www.mdpi.com/journal/computation

www.ingramcontent.com/pod-product-compliance
Lightning Source LLC
Chambersburg PA
CBHW061500210926
51850CB00008B/1769